The words of Jesus
as recorded
in the
Gospel of Matthew

Published by Crossbridge Books
Worcester
www.crossbridgeeducational.com
© Crossbridge Books 2024

ISBN 978 1 916945 04 3

British Library Cataloguing in Publication Data
A catalogue record for this book is available from the British Library

Scripture taken from the New King James Version®. Copyright © 1982 by
Thomas Nelson. Used by permission. All rights reserved.

*All proceeds from the sale of this book will be used to further the mission of
Crossbridge Books to publish Christian literature.*

Also published by Crossbridge Books:

By Trevor Dearing:
TOTAL HEALING
GOD AND HEALING OF THE MIND
MEDITATE AND BE MADE WHOLE THROUGH JESUS CHRIST
THE GOD OF MIRACLES
IT'S TRUE
ALWAYS HERE FOR YOU
DIVINE HEALING, DELIVERANCE, AND THE KINGDOM OF GOD
WALKING WITH GOD
THE LIVING WORD – The Psalms in Everyday Life
THE LIVING WORD II – A Treasury of Devotions
THE LIVING WORD III – God's Life-Transforming Promises
THE GREATEST PHYSICIAN ON EARTH

By Andrew Hill:
TAKE ANOTHER STEP

By Michael Arthern:
MOUNTAINS ON THE MOON

By Leslene Peat-Brown:
ORDINARY PEOPLE, EXTRAORDINARY STORIES

The words of Jesus as recorded in the Gospel of Matthew

by

Dr R M Price-Mohr

FOREWORD

These Bible study notes are a look at the words of Jesus as they are recorded in the Gospel of Matthew.

When Jesus Himself referred to Scriptures, He could not possibly have meant what we term the New Testament since it had not yet been written! Therefore, all the studies in this book refer only to Old Testament Scripture, and I have endeavoured to find references that accord with Jesus' own statement that He came not to destroy the Law or the Prophets, but to fulfil them (Matthew 5:17).

Jesus' words are presented each time initially as a transliteration from the Greek. As a bilingual myself, I have been used since infancy to understand languages with different word order, waiting patiently until the end of a sentence to fully understand its meaning. Often a literal translation, though clunky and harder to grasp, reveals subtle meanings that would otherwise be lost, so I make no apology for its use. I have also retained what have been referred to as 'archaisms'. In modern English, we have lost the ability to indicate that we are addressing someone who is close in an informal manner compared to addressing someone formally. Other languages.have retained this, for example 'tu and vous' in French or 'Du and Sie' in German. In former times You was a formal mode of address and Thou informal, this distinction renders, for example, The Lord's Prayer more intimate in its informal address to the Heavenly Father.

CONTENTS

INTRODUCTION

When I began this project, more than four years ago, my aim was to explore all that Jesus said, as recorded in Matthew's Gospel, in the context of the Old Testament. The passages vary in length, but each study passage has hopefully kept its intended cohesion. Inevitably some of the Old Testament Scriptures are repeated, but where possible I have aimed to seek out those that seem to me to be a source of Jesus' words.

These study notes are intended to be a starting point from which I hope the reader will be inspired to seek for further insight from the New Testament and consider how Jesus' words impact on our lives and the lives of the Church today.

As you read through and ponder these offerings, consider this question: Was Jesus speaking about things that were new and radical or was He reaffirming what had already been spoken of in the law and the prophets?

"For we did not follow cleverly devised myths when we made known to you the power and coming of our Lord Jesus Christ, but we were eyewitnesses of His majesty. For when He received honour and glory from God the Father and the voice was borne to Him by the Majestic Glory "This is my Son, my beloved, with whom I am well pleased," we heard this voice borne from Heaven, for we were with Him on the holy mountain. And we have the prophetic word made surer. You will do well to take heed to this as to a lamp shining in a dark place, until the day dawns and the morning star rises in your hearts. First of all, you must understand that no prophecy of scripture is a matter of one's own interpretation, because no prophecy ever came by the impulse of man, but men moved by the Holy Spirit from God." (2 Peter 1:16-21)

MATTHEW CHAPTER THREE

Matthew 3:15

The first recorded words of Jesus are found in the third chapter of Matthew's gospel at verse 15. The occasion is His baptism in the River Jordan at the hands of John the Baptist. John remonstrated with Jesus, suggesting that instead he, John, should be baptised by Jesus. Jesus replied saying,

> "Permit this now for thus it is fitting for us to fulfil all righteousness."

Hundreds of years before, Isaiah had made a prophecy about John coming in advance of Jesus to 'prepare the way'. Isaiah is believed by some to have lived between 730 and 680 BC. In Isaiah chapter 40 verse 3 you can find one of the most well-known passages from the Old Testament:

> "A voice cries in the wilderness 'prepare the way of the Lord, make straight in the desert a highway for our God. Every valley shall be lifted up, and every mountain and hill be made low; the uneven ground shall become level, and the rough places a plain."

So why are Jesus' first recorded words about fulfilling righteousness? And what does that mean? What does the word righteousness mean to you? Is it being pious? Maybe doing good or being a good person? Someone who has good morals? Someone who tries to live a good life? Perhaps to you it means someone who is ethical, honest, and fair?

The origins of the word righteous, according to Chambers Etymological dictionary, in old English meant lawful, true, genuine, just, good, fair, proper, fitting and straight. In Latin it meant straight and in Greek it meant upright. In Psalm 32 verse 11 we read:

> "Be glad in the Lord, and rejoice, O righteous, and shout for joy, all you upright in heart!"

Here the psalmist is equating righteousness with being upright. In Psalm 37 verse 17 we read:

> "For the arms of the wicked shall be broken; but the Lord upholds the righteous."

Here the psalmist is contrasting righteousness with wickedness; in other words, righteousness is the opposite of wickedness. In Psalm 18 verse 21, we read:

"For I have kept the ways of the Lord and have not wickedly departed from my God."

Here the psalmist is describing what wickedness is. Wickedness is departing from God; not following God's ways. Suppose you are about to go on a journey, and you carefully write down the directions or put the post code into the satnav. If you stray from the route and get lost people are more likely to think you daft than wicked. But if you stray from the route in life and get lost, what are the chances that you will find yourself among people that we would consider wicked and that your lifestyle would indeed be wicked?

It may be that by making this first statement, Jesus was starting as He meant to go on; He was going to follow the path that God, His Father had set before Him. He was taking the first step along the straight road that leads to God's intended destination.

MATTHEW CHAPTER FOUR

Matthew 4:4

The second occasion that Jesus' spoken words are recorded, in Chapter 4, is during His temptation in the wilderness. The tempter, knowing that He has not eaten for forty days and nights, tried to persuade Jesus to change stones into loaves of bread. Jesus replied saying,

> "It has been written, 'Not on bread only shall man live, but on every word proceeding through the mouth of God'."

Jesus himself would have been very familiar with this passage from the Torah, the early Old Testament books for teaching and instruction. This verse is found in Deuteronomy Chapter 8:1-3. The readers of Matthew's Gospel would also have been familiar with this passage:

> "All the commandments which I command you this day you shall be careful to do, that you may live and multiply, and go in and possess the land which the Lord swore to give to your fathers. And you shall remember all the way which the Lord your God has led you these forty years in the wilderness, that he might humble you, testing you to know what was in your heart, whether you would keep his commandments or not. And he humbled you and let you hunger and fed you with manna, which you did not know, nor did your fathers know; that he might make you know that man does not live by bread alone, but that man lives by everything that proceeds out of the mouth of the Lord."

It seems clear that mankind is to live a life of faith, depending on God. Bread, or food, is a mere detail in that life. There are obvious parallels between the forty days that Jesus spent in the wilderness and the forty years that the Jews spent also in the wilderness. God wanted to prove what was in His people's heart – whether or not they would keep His commandments. Christ's test is also of obedience and entire trust in God, who alone is the giver of every good gift.

Here Jesus refers to Scripture, and simply cites its assertions and at the same time shows the high authority of Scripture itself. He makes Scripture the rule of His conduct and demonstrates to us how to oppose temptation, by making use of the word of God. The tempter takes advantage of our circumstances, tempting us to complain or even be dishonest in order to satisfy our physical needs. We are often at our most vulnerable to temptation when we feel we have just done something well. Then we are vulnerable to pride and self-conceit or to the persuasion that what we are being tempted to do seems good. Like Jesus, we should enquire of Scripture if a thing is good and right according to God's teaching and instruction, rather than trusting our own feelings or wishes. In the book 'The Heavenly Man', Brother Yun describes how he was imprisoned in China in 1984 as a Christian pastor. He fasted for much longer than 40 days but was kept alive by 'everything proceeding out of the mouth of the Lord'. Although he had no Bible, he was able to remember and hold on to promises in scripture such as the promise of Jesus in Luke's Gospel 6:22-23:

> "Blessed are you when men hate you, and when they exclude you and revile you, and cast out your name as evil, on account of the Son of Man. Rejoice in that day, and leap for joy, for behold, your reward is great in heaven; for so their fathers did to the prophets."

Brother Yun's book is a truly remarkable modern account of how God's sustaining power is so much more than physical food.

Matthew 4:7

In Matthew's gospel, Jesus begins by making clear that He is setting out on the straight road. He then makes it clear that Scripture will be the rule of His conduct. He then goes on to demonstrate His trust in God that requires no proof. In verses 5 - 6 we read about the second temptation:

> 'Then the devil took him to the holy city, and set him on a pinnacle of the temple and said to him: "If you are the Son of God, throw yourself down; for it is written 'He will give his angels charge of you' and 'On their hands they will bear you up, lest you strike your foot against a stone'."

This is a quote from one of the Psalms, number 91. For those who trust in the Lord, this psalm promises His protection. Here are verses 7 – 13:

> "Because you have made the Lord your refuge, the Most High your habitation, no evil shall befall you, no scourge come near your tent. For he will give his angels charge of you to guard you in all your ways. On their hands they will bear you up, lest you dash your foot against a stone. You will tread on the lion and the adder, the young lion and the serpent you will trample under foot."

So once again Jesus answers the tempter, saying,

> "It has been written: You shall not tempt the Lord your God."

Here Jesus is again using Scripture as the rule of His conduct, referring back to Deuteronomy chapter 6, verses 16 and 17 that read:

> "You shall not put the Lord your God to the test, as you tested him at Massah. You shall diligently keep the commandments of the Lord your God, and his testimonies, and his statutes, which he has commanded you."

The writer in Deuteronomy is himself referring back to Exodus chapter 17, verse 7, when the Israelites demanded proof from Moses that the Lord would provide for them. Moses called the place where this occurred Massah which means proof, because the people "put the Lord to the proof" by asking "Is the Lord among us or not?" The testing described here and in other parts of the Old Testament (Exodus 15:25; Numbers 14:22) is more about doubt, about seeking proof that God cares rather than testing his abilities (the Hebrew word – nisahu - can be translated as tempt, over-tempt, test or prove).

In today's society, as with the Jews at the time of Jesus, we are always looking for proof or evidence. Is Jesus saying this is wrong? After all, the apostle Thomas sought proof from Jesus himself. The way this passage is typically translated into English gives the impression that God can be tempted. This is not the case. Neither can He be tested as to His nature. If we instead think of it as saying 'you shall not try to get proof of God' we will be closer to the real meaning. Jesus is saying that we should have total trust in God; a trust that neither needs nor seeks proof.

Matthew 4:10

The final temptation of Jesus in the wilderness that we read about in Matthew's Gospel is written in verses 8 to 9:

> 'Again the devil took him to a very high mountain, and showed him all the kingdoms of the world and the glory of them; and he said to him "All these I will give you, if you will fall down and worship me".

The tempter will insinuate his lies under cover of the truth in order to deceive us. He offers Jesus a quick and painless route to a kingdom. He offers the worldly throne of David instead of a spiritual kingdom. The temptation is to turn away from the path of self-denial and the cross, and instead establish a worldly kingdom. This temptation was plausible; Jesus is the King of the Jews, and as the Messiah, had come to take possession of His people. He was poor and unarmed and without followers or armies. Satan offered to put Him in possession of a kingdom at once, without any difficulty, if He would trust to him rather than to God; to acknowledge dependence on him rather than God. Satan seemed not to be asking too much, if he gave these things to Jesus, that Jesus should express gratitude for it – so plausible are his temptations and so artful are his allurements.

In Genesis 14:21, the king of Sodom offered Abraham the spoils of war, but he refused, saying,

> "I have sworn to the Lord God Most High, maker of heaven and earth, that I would not take a thread or a sandal-thong or anything else that is yours lest you should say 'I have made Abraham rich'."

Abraham had sworn to depend only on the Lord. Jesus once again uses Scripture as the rule of His conduct. Referring back to the Ten Commandments in Exodus 20, and chapter 6 of Deuteronomy, He replies:

> "Go, Satan; for it has been written: The Lord the God of thee shalt thou worship and him only shalt thou serve".

In Deuteronomy 6:13 it says in the Hebrew:

> "You shall fear only the Lord your God; and you shall worship Him and swear by His name."

In Exodus 20:3 it says in the Hebrew literally:

12

"Not shall you have to yourselves gods other before the face of me."

This is usually translated as "Thou shalt not have other gods before me." Here the word 'before' means in my face or in my sight. Clearly this means that God wants no other gods to be worshipped in addition to Him – He alone is to be worshipped.

How often in its history has the church taken the easy route to establish its 'kingdom'? The result has been corruption, decline in numbers, and a lukewarm theology at risk, according to Revelation 3:15-19, of being 'spat out'.

> "I know your works: you are neither cold nor hot. Would that you were cold or hot! So, because you are lukewarm, and neither cold nor hot, I will spew you out of my mouth. For you say, I am rich, I have prospered, and I need nothing; not knowing that you are wretched, pitiable, poor, blind, and naked. Therefore, I counsel you to buy gold from me, gold refined by fire that you may be rich and white garments to clothe you and to keep the shame of your nakedness from being seen, and salve to anoint your eyes that you may see. Those whom I love, I reprove and chasten; so be zealous and repent."

Jesus' words remind us that we are to worship and depend only on the Lord God.

Matthew 4:17

After the temptations in the wilderness, we read in Matthew's Gospel that Jesus hears of John the Baptist's arrest and goes to Galilee where He begins to preach (or proclaim). The first proclamation that Jesus is recorded to have given was the call to repentance and the announcement of the coming Kingdom. Jesus continues John's call to repentance in preparation for the coming Kingdom, saying,

"Repent ye, for has drawn near the kingdom of the heavens."

Jesus endorses John's call for repentance as the primary and urgent need for the people. Repentance must come first before true life in Christ's Kingdom can begin. Jesus came to establish His Kingdom in the hearts of people, but repentance is a necessary preparation for that inner Kingdom. This applies not just to individuals, but to the church as the whole body of believers. So, what does the word repentance mean to you? Repentance is not just saying sorry. I have heard it described as changing direction, or change of mind, or turning away from sin or selfishness. Perhaps you think of it as becoming aware of your sin, a sorrow for or confession of your sin. Perhaps you think of it as the utter forsaking of sin, or a commitment to being good or to Christian values.

There are some references to people repenting in Old Testament Scripture that Jesus would have been familiar with, and I think perhaps the most helpful is the example of Job in chapter 42, verses 1-6.

'Then Job answered the Lord: "I know that thou canst do all things, and that no purpose of thine can be thwarted. Who is this that hides counsel without knowledge? Therefore, I have uttered what I did not understand, things too wonderful for me which I did not know. Hear, and I will speak, I will question you, and you declare to me. I had heard of thee by the hearing of the ear, but now my eye sees thee, therefore I despise myself, and repent in dust and ashes".'

The bitter experience of Job should lead us to the utmost carefulness in all our conduct, even our thoughts. Job repents 'in dust and ashes'. These were a symbol of mourning amongst the ancient Hebrews. For example, in Ezekiel chapter 27:30-3:

'They cast dust on their heads and wallow in ashes; they make themselves bald for you, and gird themselves with sackcloth, and they weep over you in bitterness of soul, with bitter mourning.'

Dust (or earth) most probably represented ancient burial rites as it would today. Burial in earth was practiced at least as far back as the ancient Babylonians. This suggests an element of burial in repentance, the burial of sin and selfishness. Ashes were also used for ceremonial purification, described in Numbers chapter 19:9:

> 'And a man who is clean shall gather up the ashes of the heifer, and deposit them outside the camp in a clean place, and they shall be kept for the congregations of the people of Israel for the water for impurity, for the removal of sin.'

Repentance then can be thought of as a two-fold process - the burial of sin and the purification from, or removal of, sin. Jesus is pointing to Scripture as the rule for our conduct. Only after repentance can we enter into His wonderful Kingdom.

Matthew 4:19

Jesus calls us first to repentance and then to discipleship. He asks us to come after, or follow, Him and promises that if we do, He will make us 'fishers of men'. Matthew chapter 4:18-19 continues:

> 'As he walked by the Sea of Galilee, he saw two brothers, Simon who is called Peter and Andrew his brother, casting a net into the sea; for they were fishermen. And he said to them "Come after me, and I will make you fishers of men."

So, what does it mean - to follow Him? What does it mean to you? How far are you prepared to follow Him? Does it mean going to church regularly, or having a daily Bible study time, or keeping to a regular prayer time, or volunteering at the local charity shop? What does discipleship mean to you? Is it more Bible study, going to Bible College, or even becoming ordained as a minister?

The Biblical idea of discipleship, or of being a follower, meant imitating both the life and teaching of the master; it was an apprenticeship whereby the disciple would become a living copy of the master. As an apprentice to a good teacher, you learn not just the skills of the job, but about the person. Jesus' disciples will have learned how He talked, how He joked, how He prayed, how He talked and behaved towards others, and how He loved others. To follow Jesus fully we must imitate His whole life as well as adhere to His teaching.

Simon (Peter) and Andrew were fisherman so it seems natural that Jesus would have used fishing as an analogy with them to illustrate the work of making disciples of others. Fishing was the every-day work for these men. Should making disciples of others also be every-day work for us? Jesus promised them that they would be fishers still but for a more noble employment; the net they were to spread and cast was the Gospel. The sea into which the net was to be cast was first Judea and then the whole world. The fish they were to catch were the souls of men and women, both Jews and Gentiles. Fishermen need to know and understand the locality where they fish, they need to know how to find and catch them with patience. For many fishermen there is even the need to face hazards and learn perseverance.

But was there more to it? Jesus would have been familiar with the prophets Ezekiel, Habakkuk, and Jeremiah who all spoke about fish and fishing. Perhaps He had Ezekiel chapter 47:10 in mind:

"Fishermen will stand beside the sea from Engedi to Eneglaim it will be a place for the spreading of nets; its fish will be of very many kinds like the fish of the Great Sea."

Comparing men to fish in the sea is an apt metaphor. The world, like the sea, is unsettled, tumultuous and filled with dangers as well as beauty. Jesus' disciples, like fishermen, need to spend time in preparation, mending nets, casting their nets abroad, pulling their nets in. Jesus may also have had in mind the words of the prophet Jeremiah in chapter 16:16,

"Behold, I am going to send for many fishermen," declares the Lord, "and they will fish for them..."

Jesus calls us to discipleship, to imitate His life, and to spread the net of the Gospel in order to share that life with others.

MATTHEW CHAPTER FIVE

Matthew 5:3

Following the call to discipleship, the next recorded words of Jesus are known as the beatitudes, part of the Sermon on the Mount. The word beatitude comes from the Latin word 'beatitudinem' and means state of blessedness – or being supremely happy. The first of these blessings is in chapter 5:3; Jesus says:

> "Blessed are the poor in spirit for them is the kingdom of the heavens."

Having looked at the meaning of the word 'blessed', we could restate Jesus' words as 'supremely happy are the poor in spirit'. In order to understand what Jesus is saying here, we need to understand what is meant by 'poor in spirit'. The meaning of the Greek word has multiple connotations including being reduced to being a beggar, but also to fall down from a height or to be prostrate before something. We could think of this as meaning that a 'poor' person is one who is deeply sensible of their own spiritual poverty and wretchedness. We could restate what Jesus is saying as 'supremely happy are those who are aware of their own spiritual poverty.' Jesus would have been very familiar with this passage from Isaiah chapter 57:14-15:

> 'And it shall be said, "Build up, build up, prepare the way, remove every obstacle from my people's way." For thus says the high and lofty One who inhabits eternity, whose name is Holy: "I dwell in the high and holy place, and also with him who is of a contrite and humble spirit, to revive the heart of the contrite."

To be poor in spirit is to have a humble opinion of ourselves; to be aware that we are sinners; to be willing to be saved only by God's grace and mercy; to bear what He asks us to carry, and to pray daily for His grace. In Psalm 25:8-10 we read:

> 'Good and upright is the Lord; therefore He instructs sinners in the way. He leads the humble in what is right, and teaches the humble His way. All the paths of the Lord are steadfast love and faithfulness, for those who keep his covenant and His testimonies.'

And in Psalm 34:18

> 'The Lord is near to the broken hearted, and saves the crushed in spirit.'

And again in Psalm 149:4

'For the Lord takes pleasure in his people; He adorns the humble with victory.'

Jesus would also have been familiar with these words from Isaiah 66:3

'All these things my hand has made, and so all these things are mine says the Lord. But this is the man to whom I will look, he that is humble and contrite in spirit, and trembles at my word.

But Jesus doesn't leave it there; He goes on to promise the reward of entering the Kingdom of Heaven. These well-known words from Isaiah 40:28-31 remind us of this promise.

'Have you not known? Have you not heard? The Lord is the everlasting God, the Creator of the ends of the earth. He does not faint or grow weary, His understanding is unsearchable. He gives power to the faint, and to him who has no might He increases strength. Even youths shall faint and be weary, and young men shall fall exhausted; but they who wait for the Lord shall renew their strength, they shall mount up with wings like eagles, they shall run and not be weary, they shall walk and not faint.'

Matthew 5:4

The second of the blessings, or Beatitudes, recorded in Matthew's Gospel is in chapter 5 verse 4; Jesus says:

'Blessed are the mourning ones for they shall be comforted."

In today's society, we associate the word 'mourning' with bereavement, but the word in this context does not necessarily mean bereaved, but grieving. Given that this blessing follows immediately after the acknowledgement of our spiritual poverty (being 'poor in spirit') it seems clear that the blessing is for those who then mourn or grieve over that same spiritual poverty. Christ came to preach repentance; to induce people to mourn over their sins and to forsake them. The Sermon on the Mount was early on in Jesus' ministry and He and those listening to Him would have been familiar with the words in the prophet Isaiah chapter 61 verses 1-3, that clearly refer to Jesus and would have reminded the disciples that only the Gospel can give true comfort to those in affliction,

'The Spirit of the Lord God is upon me, because the Lord has anointed me to bring good tidings to the afflicted, he has sent me to bind up the broken hearted, to proclaim liberty to the captives, and the opening of the prison to those who are bound; to proclaim the year of the Lord's favour and the day of vengeance of our God; to comfort all who mourn; to grant to those who mourn in Zion – to give them a garland instead of ashes, the oil of gladness instead of mourning, the mantle of praise instead of a faint spirit; that they might be called oaks of righteousness, the planting of the Lord, that he may be glorified.'

It is worth pointing out here that the original meaning of the word vengeance included to 'lay claim to' or 'set free'; it is not the same as retribution. Jesus reiterates the promise in Scripture that those who mourn for their spiritual poverty will be comforted, as it says in Isaiah chapter 60:20:

'Your sun shall no more go down, nor your moon withdraw itself; for the Lord will be your everlasting light, and your days of mourning shall be ended.'

So Jesus calls us to mourn for our sin; the sin of our nature - indwelling sin, that is always working in us, and is a continual grief of mind to us; the unbelief of our hearts that grieves the Spirit, and dishonours the Gospel of Christ; and to mourn also for the sins of others, for the sins of the world. But always there is the promise of comfort. Here are the words of Jeremiah in chapter 31:13-14:

> 'I will turn their mourning into joy; I will comfort them and give them gladness for sorrow. I will feast the soul of the priests with abundance, and my people shall be satisfied with my goodness, says the Lord.'

And in Psalm 126: 6 we read:

> 'May those who sow in tears reap with shouts of joy; he that goes forth weeping, bearing the seed for sowing, shall come home with shouts of joy, bringing his sheaves with him'.

Matthew 5:5

The third of the blessings, or Beatitudes, is in Chapter 5 verse 5; Jesus says:

'Blessed are the meek for they shall inherit the earth.'

The contemporary definition of the word 'meek' includes being quiet, gentle, easily imposed on and submissive. But the modern interpretation of this word is somewhat different from the original Greek use. The classical Greek word used to translate meekness was that used for a horse that had been tamed or bridled. There are similar references in James 1:26 and 3:8 to taming or bridling, in this case the tongue. Meekness is not the same as humility. Humility refers to our behaviour towards others, whereas meekness refers to our behaviour towards our own selves, meaning restraining our own ego, being teachable, patient under suffering, long suffering, and willing to follow the teaching of the Gospel. Jesus was quoting almost directly from Psalm 37:11.

"But the meek shall possess the land, and delight themselves in abundant prosperity."

The original word used was also related to 'friend' in terms of gentleness; quiet friendly composure that does not become embittered or angry. It was not passive submission, but an active and deliberate acceptance. It is an active submission to authority, a willingness to be obedient. Jesus knows our hearts, our weaknesses, and our strengths; He is reminding us to be meekly obedient to our Master and promises that this will reap rewards. Isaiah's prophecy about Jesus in Chapter 11: 3-5 would have been familiar to His listeners:

"He shall not judge by what his eyes see, or decide by what his ears hear; but with righteousness he shall judge the poor, and decide with equity for the meek of the earth; and he shall smite the earth with the rod of his mouth, and with the breath of his lips he shall slay the wicked. Righteousness shall be the girdle of his waist, and faithfulness the girdle of his loins."

Sometimes it is easier to understand a thing when you can describe what it is not. Meekness is not meanness, or a surrender of our rights, nor is it cowardice. It is the opposite of sudden anger, of malice, of long-harboured enmity. Christ was the very model of meekness; it was one of His characteristics. No man endured more wrong, or endured it more patiently than He. He did not demand His rights, position or privilege, or trample down the rights of others to secure His own. As we read in Isaiah 29:19:

> "The meek shall obtain fresh joy in the Lord, and the poor among men shall exult in the Holy One of Israel."

So who will inherit the earth? Verses 3 - 9 of Psalm 37 that Jesus Himself referred to gives us some clues:

> 'Trust in the Lord and do good; so you will dwell in the land and enjoy security. Take delight in the Lord, and he will give you the desires of your heart. Commit your way to the Lord; trust in him, and he will act. He will bring forth your vindication as the light and your right as the noonday. Be still before the Lord and wait patiently for him; fret not yourself over him who prospers in his way, over the man who carries out evil devices. Refrain from anger, and forsake wrath. Fret not yourself; it tends only to evil. For the wicked shall be cut off; but those who wait for the Lord shall possess the land.'

It will not be the person who commits unlawful deeds, who is angry, who is violent, who resorts to evil, or who breaks the law. Rather it will be those who submit themselves to the Lord, who petition the lord, those who are not envious, those who wait for the Lord, those who yield readily to God. Jesus wasn't suggesting that the meek would inherit property or land, but that they would possess special blessings and be received into His glorious Kingdom.

Matthew 5:6

The fourth blessing, or Beatitude, is in chapter 5:6; Jesus says:

> 'Blessed are the hungering and thirsting ones after righteousness, for they shall be satisfied.'

The meaning of the word righteous was discussed earlier when looking at chapter 3:15; it is a word that means being upright and following the path that Jesus has set before us. Jesus is talking about those who seek to be upright, obedient, and follow God's way. Once again, He may have been referring to the prophet Isaiah who says in chapter 32:17,

> 'And the effect of righteousness will be peace and the result of righteousness quietness and trust forever.'

And in chapter 1:19,

> 'If you are willing and obedient, you shall eat the good of the land.'

And in chapter 41:17,

> 'When the poor and needy seek water, and there is none, and their tongue is parched with thirst, I the Lord will answer them, I the God of Israel will not forsake them.'

Just as the body has a natural appetite for food and water, so also our soul seeks nourishment. When our body needs nourishment it creates a hunger or thirst; a desire for what we need. As Christians, our souls need to awaken to our need for spiritual nourishment, for righteousness or holiness. This comes from our own discovery of the righteousness of Christ through the Gospel and by the Holy Spirit. The blessing then is for those who desire righteousness. This is beautifully portrayed by the Psalmist who says in Psalm 42:1-2,

> 'As a hart longs for flowing streams, so longs my soul for thee, O God. My soul thirsts for God, for the living God.'

And in Psalm 63:1,

> 'O God, thou art my God, I seek thee, my soul thirsts for thee; my flesh faints for thee, as in a dry and weary land where no water is.'

Bodily hunger and thirst are constant and daily desires that are not satisfied by a single event, a single meal or drink. In the same way, our desire for righteousness must be sought daily and cannot be found at a single moment, but should occupy our whole lifespan. Unlike bodily hunger and thirst, the desire for righteousness can be truly and fully satisfied. Moreover, as with the other Beatitudes, Jesus makes us a promise; as it says in Proverbs 10:3,

'The Lord does not let the righteous go hungry'

And in 10:16,

'The wage of the righteous leads to life.'

And in 10:28,

'The hope of the righteous ends in gladness.'

The promise is that those who seek righteousness will be satisfied; will be well fed, since God's desire is that we become righteous or holy. For those that seek it, they will be filled and satisfied with righteousness and with all other good things in consequence - with joy and peace. The Greek word 'chortazó' literally means to feed, fatten, fill and satisfy. Jesus is promising that the desire to be righteous, or holy, will be gratified by God. As it says in Psalm 17:15:

'As for me, I shall behold thy face in righteousness; when I awake, I shall be satisfied with beholding thy form.'

Matthew 5:7

The fifth blessing, or Beatitude, is in chapter 5 verse 7; Jesus says:

> 'Blessed are the merciful, for they shall obtain mercy.'

The English word mercy comes from the Latin word, meaning favour, pity, or more specifically in this context, the heavenly reward earned by those who show kindness to the helpless from whom no earthly reward can be expected. The merciful are those who seek to show mercy to others in order to glorify God, in obedience to His commands, and out of love for their neighbour. Being merciful is a quality of God that He requires of His people; compassion and love, not just feelings or emotions. God does not ask us to 'feel sorry' for people, to sing songs about how sad things might be for some people, or pray vague prayers that things will be better, whilst we *do* nothing. This is clearly expressed by the prophet Amos in chapter 5:21-24:

> 'I hate, I despise your feasts, and I take no delight in your solemn assemblies. Even though you offer me your burnt offerings and cereal offerings, I will not accept them, and the peace offerings of your fatted beasts I will not look upon. Take away from me the noise of your songs; to the melody of your harps I will not listen. But let justice roll down like water, and righteousness like an ever-flowing stream.'

As Christians, we receive God's mercy and this follows repentance and a desire for His righteousness. This righteousness includes living our lives the way God desires in our relationships and interaction with others. Mercy is the quality in God that leads Him to desire a relationship with people who do not deserve to be in a relationship with Him. The mercy that He asks us to show to others must reflect this unconditional love to those who we may deem 'undeserving'. The prophet Isaiah sets out straightforward guidelines for this in the first chapter, verses 16-17.

> 'Wash yourselves; make yourselves clean; remove the evil of your doings from before my eyes; cease to do evil, learn to do good; seek justice, correct oppression; defend the fatherless, plead for the widow.'

How often do we 'walk by on the other side'? God's mercy, unlike human mercy, cannot be exhausted and Jesus makes us a promise – that we will receive God's divine and inexhaustible mercy. God Himself has shown His people mercy and thereby demonstrated the kind of mercy that He requires of us. Jesus Himself demonstrated God's mercy in practical ways through healing and other miracles; He did not just offer messages of consolation or sympathy or reserve mercy to those who might have been thought 'worthy'. God's love for His creation leads Him to do for it, what it cannot do for itself; He forgives and liberates those who deserve no such blessings. When we acknowledge our own status before God, our own un-deservedness; when we weep at our own spiritual poverty and acknowledge God's mercy to us, we can begin to show true mercy to others and receive God's inexhaustible mercy. As the prophet Micah says in chapter 6:8:

> 'He has shown you, O man, what is good; and what does the Lord require of you but to do justice, and to love kindness, and to walk humbly with your God.'

Matthew 5:8

The sixth blessing, or Beatitude, is in chapter 5:8; Jesus says:

'Blessed are the clean in heart, for they God shall see.'

The Greek word 'kathari' used here means clean, clear, pure and neat. It comes from a root word that means purged of undesirable elements or purified from contamination, and in other contexts sincere, genuine, blameless, and innocent. In Greece, the first Monday at the start of Lent is celebrated as 'Kathari Deftera', which means Clean Monday. It is also known as Pure Monday or Ash Monday. The set reading for Clean Monday is from Isaiah 1 including verses 16 and 18:

'Wash yourselves; make yourselves clean; remove the evil of your doings from before my eyes.'

'Come now, let us reason together, says the Lord; though your sins are like scarlet, they shall be as white as snow; though they are red like crimson, they shall become like wool.'

In this blessing, Jesus puts together the desire for a clean and pure heart with the promise that we shall see God. The parallels with the words of the psalmist, in Psalm 24:3-6, would have been obvious to His listeners.

'Who shall ascend the hill of the Lord? And who shall stand in His holy place? He who has clean hands and a pure heart, who does not lift up his soul to what is false, and does not swear deceitfully. He will receive blessing from the Lord, and vindication from the God of his salvation. Such is the generation of those who seek Him, who seek the face of the God of Jacob.'

Much of the Jewish law focussed on the outward washing and cleansing of the body and other items, in the expectation of eternal reward. But Jesus is talking about cleansing of the heart, washing the inner thoughts and desires, the purging of undesirable elements from within. Again the psalmist expresses this in Psalm 51:10 and Psalm 73:1.

'Create in me a clean heart, O God, and put a new and right spirit within me.'

'Truly God is good to the upright, to those who are pure in heart.'

Having clean hands makes us physically safe from disease, but it is also a spiritual representation of the state of our heart, expressed in Job 17: 9 and 22:30.

> 'Yet the righteous holds to his way, and he that has clean hands grows stronger and stronger'

> 'He delivers the innocent man; you will be delivered through the cleanness of your hands.'

And as with the other Beatitudes, Jesus makes a promise, that those with a clean heart shall see God. As the psalmist says in Psalm 17: 15

> 'As for me, I shall behold thy face in righteousness; when I awake, I shall be satisfied with beholding thy form.'

Matthew 5:9

The seventh blessing, or Beatitude, is in chapter 5 verse 9; Jesus says:

> 'Blessed are the peacemakers, for they sons of God shall be called.'

Jesus spoke in Aramaic, not Greek, so He would have used the well-known word 'shalom' when referring to 'peace'. The ancient Hebrew concept of peace meant wholeness, completeness, soundness, health, safety and prosperity, and had an implicit permanence. It is taken from the root word 'shalam' that means to be safe in mind, body or estate. Although it can mean an absence of war, it generally refers to an inner completeness and tranquillity; an inner peace and completeness brought on by sharing in God's presence and His protection. As it says in Isaiah 32:17-18,

> 'And the effect of righteousness will be peace; and the result of righteousness quietness and trust for ever. My people will abide in a peaceful habitation, in secure dwellings, and in quiet resting places.'

Jesus was not referring to mediators or political negotiators, but to those who have an inward sense of the completeness and safety that is only available through walking with God. The ancient Hebrew understanding of shalom was that a person could be so filled with God's peace that it would spill over towards others, making others inwardly complete, and thereby making that person a peacemaker. Psalm 34:14 is written in such a way as to suggest that being a peacemaker is not an option but a command:

> 'Depart from evil, and do good; seek peace, and pursue it.'

Jesus is called The Prince of Peace; as citizens of His Kingdom we should also be peacemakers. By sharing Christ's teaching and the Gospel, and being filled to overflowing with His peace, or shalom, we can bring peace to others; helping people to be reconciled to God. John Wesley wrote that "The peacemakers are they that out of love to God and man do all possible good to all men." The well-used Old Testament blessing from Numbers 6:24-26 is God's promise of peace to His people.

> 'The Lord bless you and keep you; The Lord make His face to shine upon you and be gracious to you; The Lord lift up His countenance upon you and give you peace.'

As with the other blessings, Jesus makes a promise, that peacemakers will be called sons of God. Since God already acknowledges Christians as heirs with Christ, this promise is to do with other people acknowledging that those who are peacemakers must be sons of God. Such was the case with Aaron. Aaron, brother of Moses was the first of the priests, from the tribe of Levi, and as such was considered to be like a son of God. Jesus may well have been alluding to the recognition of Aaron by God in the words of Malachi 2:5-6,

> 'My covenant with him [Aaron] was a covenant of life and peace [...] True instruction was in his mouth, and no wrong was found on his lips. He walked with me in peace and uprightness, and he turned many from iniquity.'

Jesus wants us to be so filled with God's peace that it will spill over to others who will then acknowledge that we must be sons of God.

Matthew 5:10

The eighth blessing, or Beatitude, is in chapter 5 verse 10; Jesus says:

> 'Blessed are the ones having been persecuted for the sake of righteousness, for of them is the kingdom of the heavens'.

The word 'persecute' means to pursue in order to harm, torment or oppress. A persecutor is one who pursues or one who starts a legal action. It comes from the Greek word 'dioko' meaning to hunt or chase after, to bring someone down like an animal, or to punish with vengeance. The Hebrew word 'radap' has the same meaning – to pursue. Both Old and New Testaments give numerous examples of physical, social, mental and spiritual persecution that God's people suffered. But persecution of itself is not worthy of blessing, only when it is 'for the sake of righteousness'. As we read in Isaiah 33:15,

> 'He who walks righteously and speaks uprightly, who despises the gain of oppressions, who shakes his hands lest they hold a bribe, who stops his ears from hearing of bloodshed and shuts his eyes from looking upon evil, he will dwell on the heights; his place of defence will be the fortresses of rocks; his bread will be given him, his water will be sure.'

We are not expected to seek persecution, but we are warned to expect it if we live according to God's commands in righteousness since the world hates righteousness. King Ahab, for example, in 2 Chronicles 18 admits that he hates the righteous prophet Micaiah because he refuses to lie about God's word. God wants us to speak His truth, to live according to His commands; to live lives of righteousness in a world that prefers sin. The prophet Jeremiah suffered persecution; we read of God's promise to him in Jeremiah 15:19-21.

> Therefore thus says the Lord: "If you return, I will restore you, and you shall stand before me. If you utter what is precious, and not what is worthless, you shall be as my mouth. They shall turn to you, but you shall not turn to them. And I will make you to this people a fortified wall of bronze; they will fight against you, but they shall not prevail over you, for I am with you to save you and deliver you, says the Lord. I will deliver you out of the hand of the wicked, and redeem you from the grasp of the ruthless".

The transliteration from the Greek of the promise in this Beatitude reads: 'for of them is the kingdom of the heavens'. This is usually translated as 'for theirs is the kingdom of heaven'. But, as we saw in chapter 4:17, Jesus spoke about bringing the Kingdom of heaven to Earth, saying 'for has drawn near the kingdom of the heavens', suggesting not that the righteous will one day go to heaven but that they are blessed by *being* the Kingdom of Heaven – in the here and now. As the psalmist writes in Psalm 31: 14-16,

> But I trust in thee, O Lord, I say, "Thou art my God". My times are in thy hand; deliver me from the hand of my enemies and persecutors. Let thy face shine on thy servant; save me in thy steadfast love.

Matthew 5:11-12

The final blessing, in chapter 5 verses 11-12, seems very much like a restatement of the previous blessing in verse 10; Jesus says:

> 'Blessed are you when they reproach you and persecute and say all evil against you, lying, for the sake of me. Rejoice and be glad, because the reward of you much in the heavens; for thus they persecuted the prophets before you.'

However, in verse 10, Jesus is indicating more of a physical persecution for the sake of righteousness, but in verse 11 He is saying that the persecution will be in the form of lies and false accusations and will be for His sake; specifically for being Christ's followers. This blessing is less general than those that went before and seems to be addressed directly to Jesus' disciples. Jesus and His disciples would have been familiar with the history of the persecution of prophets such as Isaiah, Jeremiah and Zechariah. As it says in Isaiah 51: 7-8:

> 'Hearken to me, you who know righteousness, the people in whose heart is my law; fear not the reproach of men, and be not dismayed at their reviling. For the moth will eat them up like a garment, and the worm will eat them like wool; but my deliverance will be forever, and my salvation to all generations.'

By likening the anticipated persecution of His disciples to that of the prophets, Jesus was conferring on them a similar authority; making clear that those who follow Him are to be heeded. Jesus knew that His followers would be mocked as He had been mocked, as had the prophets who had courageously spoken God's word in the past, as we read in 2 Chronicles 36:16,

> 'but they kept mocking the messengers of God, despising his words and scoffing at his prophets'.

Jesus is preparing His disciples for a persecution of ridicule, of malicious lies, and accusations of all manner of evil, that will be made as a result of violent prejudice against the message of Christ's Gospel and the Kingdom of God. Jesus' disciples are not to seek such persecution, but should be prepared to be reviled as He was, in the knowledge that God the Father will reward such faithfulness. We read about God's promise for this kind of faithfulness at the very founding of the Jewish nation in Genesis 15:1,

After these things the word of the Lord came to Abram in a vision, "Fear not Abram, I am your shield; your reward shall be very great".

Jesus tells His disciples to rejoice and be glad because their faithfulness will be rewarded. As we read in Isaiah 25:8,

'He will swallow up death for ever, and the Lord God will wipe away tears from faces, and the reproach of his people he will take away from all the earth; for the Lord has spoken.'

Matthew 5:13

In verse 13, Jesus continues to address His disciples, saying:

> 'Ye are the salt of the earth; but if the salt be tainted, by what shall it be salted? For nothing is it strong longer except being cast out to be trodden down by men.'

In its literal, form the second part is difficult to understand; it is usually translated as 'It is no longer good for anything except to be thrown out and trodden under foot by men'. But why was Jesus talking about salt? Jesus and His disciples understood that a salted sacrifice, a covenant of salt, was an agreement based on trust. We read in 2 Chronicles 13:5,

> 'Ought you not to know that the Lord God of Israel gave the kingship over Israel for ever to David and his sons by a covenant of salt?'

David received his kingdom forever from God by a "covenant of salt". Salt was very precious – there was a cost to the covenant. We read in Leviticus 2:11,

> 'You shall season all your cereal offerings with salt; you shall not let the salt of the covenant with your God be lacking from your cereal offering; with all your offerings you shall offer salt.'

Salt was regarded as a necessary ingredient of the daily food, and so of all sacrifices offered to God, salt represented the very close connection of covenant-making. Salt also represented close friendship, through partaking of hospitality which cemented that friendship. Covenants, or agreements, were generally confirmed by sacrificial meals and salt was always present. Since, too, salt is a preservative, it would easily become symbolic of an enduring covenant. So offerings to God were to be a statute forever, as we read in Numbers 18:19,

> 'All the holy offerings which the people of Israel present to the Lord I give to you, and to your sons and daughters with you, as a perpetual due; it is a covenant of salt for ever before the Lord for you and for your offspring with you.'

The same property of salt that preserves also cleanses. We read about Elijah's response when faced with bad water and an unfruitful land in 2 Kings 2: 20-21,

'He said, "Bring me a new bowl, and put salt in it." So they brought it to him. Then he went to the spring of water, threw salt in it and said "Thus says the Lord, I have made this water wholesome; henceforth neither death nor miscarriage shall come from it."

A further interesting property of salt is that it causes thirstiness. If we, as Jesus' disciples, are salty we will create a thirst in others; a thirst for knowledge of the Gospel of Christ. It has been said that there is 'no such thing as free-lance work in the Kingdom of God', nor must a Christian even consider the possibility of having a 'second string' or a 'side-line'[1]. Rather, our covenant of salt with God is a statute forever. As the psalmist writes in Psalm 141:3-4,

'Set a guard over my mouth, O Lord, keep watch over the door of my lips. Incline not my heart to any evil, to busy myself with wicked deeds in company with men who work iniquity; and let me not eat of their dainties.'

---

[1] J. Blanchard (1975) Learning and Living the Christian Life p82. Worthing: Henry Walter Ltd

Matthew 5:14-15

In verse 13, Jesus was speaking to His disciples about the internal influence they would have on others and on the world. In verses 14-15, he talks to His disciples about the external influence they would have, being like light in the world.

> 'Ye are the light of the world. Not can a city to be hid on a mountain set; nor do they light a lamp and place it under the bushel, but on the lampstand, and it lightens all the ones in the house.'

This may have been referring to the prophecy in Isaiah 49:6 that says,

> 'I will give you as a light to the nations that my salvation may reach to the end of the earth',

Jesus gave Himself this title, saying, "I am the light of the world". By telling His disciples that they were the 'light of the world', He was giving these ordinary people, such as you or I, a title normally reserved for eminent rabbis. This was right at the start of Jesus' ministry, not after three years of teaching, suggesting that being the light was not to do with knowledge, but to do with their faith in Him. He may also have been alluding to the prophecy in Daniel 12:3 that says,

> 'And those who are wise shall shine like the brightness of the firmament; and those who turn many to righteousness, like stars forever.'

When Jesus gives the disciples this title, there is a caveat; the light must be seen, and it must be seen from a height, from a central place that will light the whole house. As light dispels darkness and enables a man to see his way, so the Christian, by his teaching and example, removes ignorance and prejudice, and discloses the way of life. By His reference to a city, Jesus may have been pointing to the church, not just an individual, as needing to be a light that is seen from a height and shines light on the whole world. As it says in Psalm 97:11,

> 'Light dawns for the righteous, and joy for the upright in heart.'

In the Temple and in Jewish homes there was only one lampstand used to light the whole room. The lampstand had great significance to the Jews; it was to be placed in the Temple in the Holy Place, and tended day and night so that it never went out; it was to shine a light day and night.

In Revelation, the lampstands represent the churches, so we can see that Jesus was not just talking to individual disciples but to His church, the bride of Christ. Jesus teaches His disciples that they have been 'enlightened' for the benefit of others; that the light is not to be concealed but must show itself and shed the Lord's light into the darkness of the world. We are called to shine God's light in a dark and dangerous place where otherwise people would make a shipwreck of their lives. As it says in 2 Samuel 22:29,

> 'Yea, thou art my lamp, O Lord, and my God lightens my darkness.'

and in Psalm 119:105,

> 'Thy word is a lamp to my feet and a light unto my path.'

Matthew 5:16

In verse 16, Jesus continues to address His disciples, with reference to verses 14 and 15, making it clear that it is not sufficient to have light; we must walk in the light and by the light.

> 'Thus let shine the light of you before men, so that they may see of you the good works and may glorify the Father of you in the heavens.'

Jesus calls His disciples to be a constant witness to the truth and power of God's light. By following His commands and living holy and pure lives in all circumstances, God's light will be shed on the lives of all people. As Paul wrote to the Ephesians in chapter 5:8-9,

> 'Once you were darkness, but now you are light in the Lord; walk as children of light for the fruit of light is found in all that is good and right and true.'

As disciples, we are called to shine the light 'before men'; to shine before all people. Jesus may well have been referring to the prophecy in Isaiah 60:1-3.

> 'Arise, shine; for your light has come, and the glory of the Lord has risen upon you. For behold, darkness shall cover the earth, and thick darkness the peoples; but the Lord will arise upon you, and his glory will be seen upon you. And nations shall come to your light, and kings to the brightness of your rising.'

The disciples were to shine not to be seen themselves, but to show the glory of God. We are to reflect the light of God so that the people of the earth will see God's glory reflected in us. Our actions should not be to honour ourselves, but to bring honour to God. As we read in Habakkuk 2:14,

> 'For the earth will be filled with the knowledge of the glory of the Lord, as the waters cover the sea.'

By contrast, we read in Micah 3: 9-11, that the priests of Israel had been perverting justice and dishonouring God.

> 'Hear this, you heads of the house of Jacob and rulers of the house of Israel, who abhor justice and pervert all equity, who build Zion with blood and Jerusalem with wrong. Its heads give judgement

for a bribe; its priests teach for hire; its prophets divine for money.'

Jesus, as always, seeks to bring glory to His Father; in the good works in our lives we must seek to bring glory to our Father. As we read in Isaiah 58:8,

'Then shall your light break forth like the dawn, and your healing shall spring up speedily; your righteousness shall go before you; the glory of the Lord shall be your rear guard.'

and in 1 Chronicles 16: 23-24,

'Sing to the Lord, all the earth! Tell of his salvation from day to day. Declare his glory among the nations, his marvellous works among all the peoples!'

Matthew 5:17

In verse 17, Jesus Himself clearly states that He has not come to change or replace the law or what has been spoken by the prophets; He says,

> 'Think not that I came to destroy the law or the prophets; I came not to destroy but to fulfil.'

By these words, Jesus is upholding the law and commandments that God has given to men through the prophets that came before Him. He was making it clear that the law and the prophets should continue to be taught by His disciples. Jesus would have been familiar with the prophecy in Isaiah 2:3 in which we read,

> 'And many peoples shall come and say "Come, let us go up to the mountain of the Lord, to the house of the God of Jacob; that he may teach us his ways and that we may walk in his paths." For out of Zion shall go forth the law, and the word of the Lord from Jerusalem.'

The beatitudes that come before this statement held a challenge to the accepted teaching of the scribes and the Pharisees; Jesus' sermon encapsulated the spirit, or the intent, of the law rather than the external trappings of the law that had become prevalent. Jesus would have been familiar with the ancient command in Joshua 1:7-8 in which we read,

> 'Only be strong and very courageous, being careful to do according to all the law which Moses my servant commanded you; turn not from it to the right hand or to the left, that you may have good success wherever you go. This book of the law shall not depart out of your mouth, but you shall meditate on it day and night, that you may be careful to do according to all that is written in it.'

Jesus came to reveal the full depth of meaning in the law; to illustrate and explain it; to demonstrate the love of God that is revealed in it. As we read in Psalm 19:7-9.

> 'The law of the Lord is perfect, reviving the soul; the testimony of the Lord is sure, making wise the simple; the precepts of the Lord are right, rejoicing the heart; the commandment of the Lord is pure, enlightening the eyes; the fear of the Lord is clean, enduring for ever; the ordinances of the Lord are true, and righteous altogether.'

44

If you read Psalm 119 (all 176 verses), you will find that it encapsulates much of what Jesus said in His Sermon on the Mount. In verses 1-6 we read,

> 'Blessed are those whose way is blameless, who walk in the law of the Lord. Blessed are those who keep his testimonies, who seek him with their whole heart, who also do no wrong, but walk in his ways. Thou hast commanded thy precepts to be kept diligently. O that my ways may be steadfast in keeping thy statutes. Then I shall not be put to shame, having my eyes fixed on all thy commandments.'

Notice the blessings, or beatitudes, that we read here that suggest this psalm may have been in Jesus' mind when He spoke about blessings and the fulfilment of the law as reciprocal. Jesus did not come to abolish or change the law but to teach us its true value in Him, and to remind us that those who keep the law are blessed.

Matthew 5:18

In verse 18, Jesus continues his discourse on the law and the prophets. He makes it clear that by fulfilling the law, He has not changed the status of God's law; it remains just and true and is established for all time.

> 'For truly I say to you, until pass away the heaven and the earth, iota one or one point by no means shall pass away from the law, until all things come to pass.'

In Hebrew, the slightest change to a letter – such as a straight line into a slight curve – can completely change the meaning of a word or phrase. Jesus is saying that even the sense of a single letter will not be lost since God's designs are as unchangeable as He is. There will be no loss or change to the authority of the law, from its greatest to its least requirements. As we read in Psalm 119: 89-90,

> 'For ever, O Lord, thy word is firmly fixed in the heavens. Thy faithfulness endures to all generations; thou hast established the earth, and it stands fast.'

We also read in Psalm 111: 7-8,

> 'The works of his hands are faithful and just; all his precepts are trustworthy, they are established for ever and ever, to be performed with faithfulness and uprightness.'

Jesus was teaching His disciples that the truth and the entirety of the law is secure and will endure, and that the law will be fulfilled down to the smallest point. But He also knew that God's law is more than writing on parchment; that God's law can be written on our hearts. Jesus may well have had in mind the prophecy of Jeremiah in chapter 31: 33,

> 'This is the covenant which I will make with the house of Israel after those days, says the Lord: I will put my law within them, and I will write it upon their hearts; and I will be their God, and they shall be my people.'

Jesus affirms that the law is just as relevant for the church of the New Testament; that it will continue to be a divine revelation of God's word and His commands. So long as the earth endures, the scripture of the Old Testament remains unimpaired and continues to proclaim the Gospel of Christ, as we read in Isaiah 40:8,

'The grass withers, the flower fades; but the word of our God will stand for ever.'

Jesus teaches His disciples that the law of God is eternal and unchangeable and that following His way will not be contrary to the laws of the old covenant; nothing is added or taken away. Everything that Jesus taught was grounded in the Old Testament scripture and here He is making it crystal clear that the law and the prophets were not to be put aside. Indeed, the continuance of the law was in itself a command of the covenant between God and His people, as we read in Isaiah 59:21,

'And as for me, this is my covenant with them, says the Lord: my spirit which is upon you, and my words which I have put in your mouth, shall not depart out of your mouth, or out of the mouth of your children, or out of the mouth of your children's children, says the Lord, from this time forth and for evermore.'

Matthew 5:19

In verse 19, Jesus is giving His disciples a stark warning against setting aside even the smallest part of God's law.

> 'Whoever therefore breaks one commandments of these the least and teaches thus men, least he shall be called in the kingdom of the heavens; but whoever does and teaches, this one great shall be called in the kingdom of the heavens.'

The Greek word 'lysē', translated here as 'break', is sometimes translated as undo, annul, violate, or disobey. The meaning is clear; the commandments are not to be set aside, diminished, or disobeyed, and those who teach that any of the commandments can be put aside will bear the responsibility. It is a warning not to think that there are little sins that don't really matter; to beware of self-deceit that justifies our own behaviour. As we read in Proverbs 11: 6,

> 'The righteousness of the upright delivers them, but the treacherous are taken captive by their lust.'

Do we, in the way we act, or speak, or explain God's word, do so in such a way as to set aside His holy precepts or explain away its force and meaning? This warning extends beyond the individual to the church and even to nations. Do we as individuals set aside any of God's law for our own convenience or to justify our own behaviour? Do we do so as a church or as a nation? We read again in Proverbs 14: 34,

> 'Righteousness exalts a nation, but sin is a reproach to any people.'

Jesus teaches us that all the law of God is binding, and that the whole of it should be obeyed; that we should not suggest that some is more important than others. But He also goes on to say that those who do uphold and teach all the law, the righteous, will be worthy of His Kingdom. As we read in Psalm 118: 19-20,

> 'Open to me the gates of righteousness that I may enter through them and give thanks to the Lord. This is the gate of the Lord; the righteous shall enter through it.'

Jesus reminds those who take on the responsibility to teach others to continue in obedience to the law, and not to weaken the authority of the law, by both word and example. Jesus was familiar with the words of the prophet Isaiah who decried the deceitful teaching of his day, as we read in Isaiah 32 verses 6-8 and verse 16-17,

'For the fool speaks folly, and his mind plots iniquity: to practice ungodliness, to utter error concerning the Lord, to leave the craving of the hungry unsatisfied, and to deprive the thirsty of drink. The knaveries of the knave are evil; he devises wicked devices to ruin the poor with lying words, even when the plea of the needy is right. But he who is noble devises noble things, and by noble things he stands.'

'Then justice will dwell in the wilderness, and righteousness abide in the fruitful field. And the effect of righteousness will be peace, and the result of righteousness, quietness and trust for ever.'

Good and holy teachers exhort their flock to keep the law by words and example of their life.

Matthew 5:20

In verse 20, Jesus gives His disciples a further warning, this time about true righteousness that goes beyond following the law; a warning not to be fooled into thinking that God will be content with the outward appearance of righteousness.

> 'For I tell you that except shall exceed of you the righteousness more than that of the scribes and the Pharisees, by no means shall ye enter into the kingdom of the heavens.'

We can read elsewhere in the Gospels that the religious leaders of the day adhered to all the rules and regulations that had been passed down over the centuries that were often embellishments of the Mosaic Law. But we also read that they would pick and choose which regulations to follow to suit them, and would at times set aside the actual law. The sacrificial rituals had been followed down the generations but the vulnerable in society had been left uncared for. They offered sacrifices, fasted often and publicly, prayed often and publicly, and were rigorous about ablutions and tithes, but neglected justice, truth, purity and holiness of heart. Jesus may well have wanted to remind His disciples of how God had made it clear to His people that it is not mere religious observance that He desires from them. We read in Proverbs 21:3 and chapter 15:8,

> 'To do righteousness and justice is more acceptable to the Lord than sacrifice,'

> 'The sacrifice of the wicked is an abomination to the Lord, but the prayer of the upright is his delight.'

Perhaps Jesus had in His mind some of the words from the prophet Isaiah, in chapter 1:11, in which the Lord expresses His distaste of the empty religious offerings.

> 'What to me is the multitude of your sacrifices? says the Lord; I have had enough of burnt offerings of rams and the fat of fed beasts; I do not delight in the blood of bulls, or of lambs, or of he-goats.'

It seems that the observance of the law by the religious leaders was not motivated by a sincere desire to glorify God, but for their own public applause or to obtain eternal life. This was not a new phenomenon in Jesus' time; we read in 1 Samuel 15:22 that the Lord's desire is for obedience and for His people to listen to Him.

'Has the Lord as great delight in burnt offerings and sacrifices, as in obeying the voice of the Lord? Behold, to obey is better than sacrifice, and to hearken than the fat of rams.'

We can all probably think of people who demonstrate the outward trappings of Christianity, but their lives contradict what they profess. Can you think of things in your own Christian life that are really only the outward trappings? We know that God desires a righteousness that means obedience to Him that leads to purity of heart, steadfast love of Him and our neighbour that leads to justice, and a thirst for knowledge of Him that leads to truth. As we read in Hosea 6:6,

'For I desire steadfast love and not sacrifice, the knowledge of God rather than burnt offerings.'

Matthew 5:21-22

In verses 21-22, Jesus is setting the groundwork for His teaching about love for our neighbour.

> 'Ye heard that it was said to the ancients: Thou shalt not kill; and whoever kills, liable shall be to the judgement. But I tell you that everyone being angry with the brother of him liable shall be to the judgement; and whoever says to the brother of him raca, liable shall be to the council; and whoever says fool, liable shall be to the gehenna of fire.'

We are probably all familiar with the sixth commandment in Exodus 20:13 and reiterated in Deuteronomy 5:17,

> 'You shall not kill'.

Legal definitions of what it means 'to kill' someone were just as complicated and open to interpretation at the time of Jesus as they are now. Jesus had already told His disciples that he had not come to change or replace the law, but here He reminds them what is at the heart of the law; it is sinful even to hate another in your heart. This was not a new concept, as we read in Leviticus 19:17,

> 'You shall not hate your brother in your heart, but you shall reason with your neighbour, lest you bear sin because of him.'

The word brother used here is the same word as used elsewhere in the New Testament to mean Christian brothers, or brothers in Christ, rather than just a relative; a neighbour. It is legitimate to feel anger at sin and injustice, but Christ teaches that we are not to feel anger against a person; that God will judge and punish even concealed anger. We read in Ecclesiastes 7:9,

> 'Be not quick to anger, for anger lodges in the bosom of fools.'

The Ten Commandments do not specifically prohibit hate, even the kind of hate that leads to killing, or even that leads to a person wishing for someone's death. This is the kind of unseen anger that is often expressed in ways that show we despise or belittle our neighbour, for example in the language we use about them. We read in Proverbs 14:21 and 11:12,

> 'He who despises his neighbour is a sinner.'

'He who belittles his neighbour lacks sense, but a man of understanding remains silent.'

The progressively severe consequences that Jesus refers to, from judgment at the city court, to the council of the Sanhedrin, and finally to the awful 'gehenna' (the valley of Hinnom where fires were continually kept burning), convey the seriousness of this concealed anger. This is true because such expressions find their origin in a heart full of hatred and enmity. We must be careful to guard against allowing our anger at sin from spilling over towards our fellow human beings, as we read in Psalm 4:4,

'Be angry, but sin not; commune with your own hearts on your beds and be silent.'

Matthew 5:23-24

In verses 23 to 24, Jesus continues His teaching about what it means to love our neighbour; it is a foreshadowing of what we know as the Lord's Prayer that comes later in this Sermon on the Mount. Jesus says,

> 'Therefore if thou bringest the gift of thee to the alter and there rememberest that the brother of thee has something against thee, leave there the gift of thee before the alter, and go first to be reconciled to the brother of thee, and then coming offer the gift of thee.'

This could be interpreted as meaning that we should consider if we have wronged our neighbour before we offer our worship, and if so we need to repent and be reconciled to our neighbour first before our worship is acceptable. Of course this is something we should do to enable our neighbour the opportunity to forgive us. However, given the context of what Jesus has already said, it seems more probable that Jesus is warning us to ensure that we have forgiven our neighbour for any wrong we may think they have done to us before we bring our worship to God. As we read in Psalm 15:1-3,

> 'O Lord, who shall sojourn in thy tent? Who shall dwell on thy holy hill? He who walks blamelessly, and does what is right, and speaks truth from his heart; who does not slander with his tongue, and does no evil to his friend, nor takes up a reproach against his neighbour.'

Jesus is telling us that even religious duties are displeasing to God if we have a difference with our neighbour; that our worship is corrupted by our resentments. Jesus expects His disciples to sincerely seek reconciliation. When Jesus tells His disciples to 'leave the gift at the alter and go', He implies a sense of urgency; that no time or effort should be wasted in bringing about reconciliation. We find these words in Ecclesiasticus 28:2,

> 'Forgive thy neighbour the hurt that he hath done unto thee, so shall thy sins also be forgiven when thou prayest.'

The early church took this seriously and sought to see that all differences amongst them were settled; that they were all reconciled to each other before celebrating the Holy Communion. In the Church of England liturgy, before communion is taken, the prayer of preparation includes the words "we have sinned against you and against our neighbour, in what we have thought, in what we have said and done, through ignorance, through weakness, through our own deliberate fault.' For sacrifice or worship to be acceptable to God it must be without blemish, whether a physical defect or defects of conduct. This was made clear in the law, for example in Leviticus 22:20 we read,

> 'You shall not offer anything that has a blemish, for it will not be acceptable for you,' and in the prophets, for example in Job 11:15 'Surely then you will lift up your face without blemish; you will be secure and will not fear.'

God desires reconciliation with us; He also desires that we be reconciled with our neighbours.

> 'He who brings thanksgiving as his sacrifice honours me; to him who orders his way aright I will show the salvation of God' (Psalm 50:23)

Matthew 5:25-26

In verses 25 to 26, Jesus continues His teaching about reconciliation and the reciprocal nature of reconciliation with our neighbour. He says,

> 'Be well disposed to the opponent of thee quickly while thou art with him in the way, lest the opponent of thee deliver thee to the judge and the judge to the attendant, and into prison thou be cast; truly I say to thee, by no means shalt thou come out thence until thou repayest the last farthing.'

Clearly it is incumbent upon us to settle disagreements and heal all possible sources of friction on a daily basis so that hatred, discord and resentment cannot fester in our community; it is better to seek conciliation and fairness at the first sign of disagreement or conflict. When we have a sense of self-righteousness, or are too concerned with our own rights, we are in danger of disadvantaging others; it is so easy to justify our own actions to ourselves and believe that we are in the right. Jesus would have been familiar with the words in Proverbs 25:8-10 where we can read,

> 'What your eyes have seen do not hastily bring into court; for what will you do in the end, when your neighbour puts you to shame? Argue your case with your neighbour himself, and do not disclose another's secret; lest he who hears you bring shame on you, and your ill repute have no end.'

Jesus is warning of the consequences of delay in reconciliation. He does not indicate who has caused the disagreement; presumably that is not relevant – reconciliation must still be sought, not reluctantly, but with kindness and friendship. Jesus knows how likely it is that differences will occur; we even see them emerge amongst the first Christians in the Acts of the Apostles. He points to the remedy, that differences should be settled immediately even if this means acting to our own perceived disadvantage. He also conveys a sense of urgency; that allowing discord to fester can open the flood gates of strife, as we read in Proverbs 17:14,

> 'The beginning of strife is like letting out water; so quit before the quarrel breaks out.'

If reconciliation is not made, the heart remains unforgiving and quarrelsome, and God, the Judge, will see the offence. Jesus is warning His disciples that there will be justice against those who remain hardened and impenitent; we cannot pay our debts to God; only obtain His forgiveness through faith. In the same way that God's Kingdom is in the here and now, a place of imprisonment is in the here and now as well as in the future. A place of imprisonment need not be a place at all, but a journey in our minds as we come to face, recognise, and acknowledge our sins. Once again, Jesus is preparing the hearts of His listeners, His disciples, to accept the reciprocal nature of forgiveness as it will be taught in the Lord's Prayer, and expounding the command, yet to be mentioned in Matthew's Gospel, to love our neighbour as ourselves. We are called to forgive, to be reconciled, and to be friends, to come to agreement with our neighbour and with God, and thus be at peace. As we read in Job 22:21-22,

> 'Agree with God, and be at peace; thereby good will come to you. Receive instruction from his mouth, and lay up his words in your heart.'

Matthew 5:27-28

In verses 27 to 28, Jesus begins to teach His disciples about betrayal and temptation, saying,

> 'Ye heard that it was said: Thou shalt not commit adultery. But I tell you that everyone seeing a woman with a view to desire her already committed adultery with her in the heart of him.'

This is of course not confined to one gender; women are equally vulnerable to such temptation. We know that God tests us in the way a good teacher will test a student to help us learn to stand firm. But the devil tempts us in order to make us fall. No amount of victories won, knowledge gained, or good deeds will protect us from the frequency or ferocity of the attacks from the devil, and he targets our weaknesses. The commandment Jesus refers to from Exodus 20:14, 'You shall not commit adultery', immediately follows 'You shall not kill' that Jesus has already addressed at length. The penalties prescribed in Deuteronomy 22:22, for this crime were severe; Jesus' disciples would have been in no doubt as to the importance of His words. Once again Jesus is warning his listeners that obedience and faithfulness to God must be from the heart and not just an outward conformity to the law; betrayal and adultery result from impure thoughts. As we read in Proverbs chapter 6, verses 25 and verses 27-28,

> 'Do not lust in your heart for her beauty or let her captivate you with her eyes.'

> 'Can a man carry fire in his bosom and his clothes not be burned? Or can one walk upon hot coals and his feet not be scorched?

It is perhaps more difficult to refrain from sinful thoughts than from the act itself, especially as the opportunity for the act may not occur, but the opportunity for sinful thought is daily with us. Impure thoughts easily spring from looking, as we are warned in Proverbs, and as David's adultery with Beersheba testifies to (2 Samuel 11:2). Jesus is warning against the thought which lies at the root of the act; against indulging in thoughts that are contrary to God's ways. Scripture is unequivocal about the fact that God knows our thoughts and ways, as we read in Job 31:3-4,

> 'Does not calamity befall the unrighteous, and disaster the workers of iniquity? Does not he see my ways, and number all my steps?'

Here we again see that Jesus came not destroy the law but to fulfil it; He demonstrates that when the law is only applied to outward acts they only affect the wider society, but when the law is applied to the inner thoughts, the effect is on our hearts, minds, and souls. We are called to meditate on God's law and His words, and thereby exclude all impure thoughts, as we read in Malachi 3:16,

> 'Then those who feared the Lord spoke with one another; the Lord heeded and heard them, and a book of remembrance was written before him of those who feared the Lord and thought on his name.'

Keep your eyes and thoughts fixed firmly on Jesus, as we read also in Hosea 14:9,

> 'Whoever is wise, let him understand these things; whoever is discerning, let him know them; for the ways of the Lord are right, and the upright walk in them.'

Matthew 5:29-30

In verses 29 to 30, Jesus continues His teaching about betrayal and temptation, acknowledging our weaknesses and the dreadful consequences to ourselves, saying,

> 'So if the eye of thee right causes to stumble thee, pluck it out and cast from thee; for it is expedient for thee that perish one of the members of thee and not all the body of thee be cast into Gehenna. And if the right of the hand causes to stumble thee, cut out it and cast from thee; for it is expedient for thee that perish one of the members of the and not all the body of thee into Gehenna go away.'

The Greek word 'skandalon' that Jesus is recorded as having used here, and translated as 'causing to stumble', referred to a trap or snare laid for an enemy – a trap with a springing device. Jesus is warning His disciples that even what they choose to look on may be a trap. In today's world where we are bombarded by images in so many aspects of our lives, this warning is perhaps especially relevant. Consider, for example, the images shown in a movie; it is often said 'oh it's just a movie', but each individual is vulnerable to their own traps, and we each need to be fully aware of our own weaknesses and run from these traps, knowing that God is able to see us when we fall into them. As we read in Proverbs 5:21,

> 'For a man's ways are before the eyes of the Lord, and he watches all his paths.'

Jesus was still referring to the commandment not to commit adultery and we know that God, speaking through the prophets, referred to Israel's betrayal of Himself as adultery. As is so often the case, Jesus speaks on two levels; He is referring to the relationships between people and also to the relationship between us and God. The right eye or hand was considered to be the most important by the Jews; the disciples would have understood that Jesus was saying that even if the root of your trap – whatever is causing you to stumble – is of high value, it is of less value than your relationship with God and must be discarded. Job spoke about making a 'covenant' with his eyes, acknowledging the dangers of allowing his eyes to look on temptation, saying in chapter 31:1-2,

> 'I have made a covenant with my eyes; how then could I look upon a virgin? What would be my portion from God above, and my heritage from the Almighty on high?'

Of course, we need our eyes to prevent us from stumbling, so to some extent this is a play on words. Jesus also talks about casting the cause of temptation, be it the eye or hand or whatever, into Gehenna. The message is about putting things out of reach or onto the rubbish tip. Gehenna was a place outside the city walls where rubbish and all unclean things would be incinerated. We know that in order to prevent the spread of disease items must be thrown out, isolated, or even destroyed. We also know that if a limb is severely infected or diseased or has for example frost bite, the limb has to be removed to save the rest of the body. In essence the message is simple, if your eye or hand are tempted to do something that you wouldn't want the Lord Jesus to see you doing – then don't let yourself do it or even dwell on the thought. How? By turning our eyes on Jesus and meditating on God's word, as we read in Psalm 119: 9-10,

> 'How can a young man keep his way pure? By guarding it according to thy word. With my whole heart I seek thee; let me not wander from thy commandments.'

Matthew 5:31-32

In verses 31 to 32, Jesus continues his teaching about adultery and relationships saying,

> 'And it was said: Whoever dismisses the wife of him, let him give her a bill of divorce. But I tell you that everyone dismissing the wife of him apart from a matter of unchastity makes her to commit adultery, and whoever a dismissed woman marries, commits adultery.'

It seems that the words in Deuteronomy 24:1 that Jesus was referring to that says,

> 'When a man takes a wife and marries her, if then she finds no favour in his eyes because he has found some indecency in her, and he writes her a bill of divorce...'

was taken by some to allow Jewish men to divorce their wives simply because they no longer liked the look of her. This is an example of how, when faced with temptation, we find a means to justify our actions. Our focus is often on what we are 'allowed' to do rather than on what we 'ought' to do. Jesus may well have had in mind the words of the prophet Malachi in chapter 2:16 where we read,

> 'For I hate divorce, says the Lord God of Israel, and the covering of one's garment with violence, says the Lord of hosts. So take heed to yourselves and do not be faithless.'

Jesus is once again stressing the consequences of unfaithfulness; that it causes the breaking of a covenant, remembering that God sees His relationship with His people in the light of a marriage; a covenant whereby two become one as is clearly stated in Genesis 2:24,

> 'Therefore a man leaves his father and his mother and cleaves to his wife, and they become one flesh.'

We know from this that God instituted marriage, and is party to the marriage covenant which is in fact a covenant of three; with God as the third strand in a marriage, the cord that ties the couple together is stronger. When we break that three-fold bond, we are unfaithful not just to our spouse but also to God. When Nathan the prophet spoke to King David after he had committed adultery with Bathsheba, he acknowledged his betrayal of God in this act as he wrote in Psalm 51:4 saying,

'Against thee, thee only have I sinned, and done that which is evil in thy sight.'

Jesus is here limiting the rights of divorce to cases of unfaithfulness, or unchastity, making it clear that if there is divorce for any other reason, and either party remarries, they commit adultery. It is implied that it is unfaithfulness that breaks the marriage vows; it breaks the covenant. It is worth noting that in Biblical times, women who were divorced had no means of support unless they could remarry – the alternative was destitution or prostitution – which is why Jesus is suggesting that a divorcing husband would likely cause a woman to commit adultery even if there had been no initial unfaithfulness. Covenants, both human and divine, are not to be broken, as we read in Proverbs 5:18-19,

'Let your fountain be blessed, and rejoice in the wife of your youth, a lovely hind, a graceful doe. Let her affection fill you at all times with delight, be infatuated always with her love.'

Matthew 5:33-37

In verses 33 to 37, Jesus seems to be following up on His teaching about how the law had been interpreted in a kind of watered-down way to justify the actions of the people. Here He is referring to the third commandment that is restated in Leviticus 19:12 as 'You shall not swear by my name falsely and so profane the name of your God', saying

> 'Again ye heard that it was said to the ancients: Thou shalt not perjure, shalt repay but to the Lord the oaths of thee. But I tell you not to swear at all; neither by the heaven, because the throne it is of God; nor by the earth, because footstool it is of the feet of him; nor by Jerusalem, because city it is of the great King; nor by the head of thee swear, because thou canst not one hair white to make or black let be. But the word of you Yes yes, No no; for the excess of these of evil is.'

It seems that it was common at that time, as it is today, for people to swear on their life or something else they held to be of value, and it was thought that as long as one did not swear by God Himself they had not broken the law. The Jews habitually swore impressive sounding oaths to impress and persuade people. Jesus again highlights the hypocrisy prevalent at that time. Perhaps He was thinking of the words of the prophet Hosea in chapter 10:4,

> 'They utter mere words; with empty oaths they make covenants; so judgement springs up like poisonous weeds in the furrows of the field.'

To take the Lord's name in vain is to use it frivolously or even profanely, without acknowledging His holiness. To use His name when you do not intend to honour your words is a direct violation of the third commandment. The word of a Christian should be their bond, they should not need to reinforce their words with an oath or appeal to any other witnesses or any other means to support the truth of what they say. A person who swears by the Lord over a trivial matter, and thereby breaks the third commandment, is equally capable of swearing falsely against a neighbour and breaking the ninth. If we consider our word not enough, or expect others to question it, it is because of an expectancy of untruthfulness which is only made worse when we attempt to clear ourselves of suspicion. If we consider our word enough - that we can be trusted, others will be able to rely on our yes meaning yes and no meaning no; be careful what passes your lips, as we read in Deuteronomy 23:22-23,

'You shall be careful to perform what has passed your lips, for you have voluntarily vowed to the Lord your God what you have promised with your mouth.'

Vows that we might make in contemporary society would be for example marriage vows – a covenant with our spouse and God, or oaths in judicial courts – a covenant with the people. If we reserve truthfulness for these kinds of declarations, we run the risk of neglecting truthfulness for the rest of the time, and of course God knows the intentions of our hearts. By referring to the passages about the earth being God's footstool and Jerusalem being the city of the great King, Jesus is reminding His disciples that all of creation, including ourselves, is the footstool of God and thus to swear by anything in His creation is as sacred an oath as if swearing by God. We read in Isaiah 66:1,

'Thus says the Lord: Heaven is my throne and the earth is my footstool; what is the house which you would build for me, and what is the place of my rest?'

Matthew 5:38-39

In verses 38 to 39, we find some of the hardest of Jesus' teaching, and yet what He taught was intended by God from the beginning; it was not new.

> 'Ye heard that it was said: An eye instead of an eye, and a tooth instead of a tooth. But I tell you not to oppose an evil person; but who thee strikes on the right cheek of thee, turn to him also the other.'

It seems that the command found in Exodus 21:24 ('Eye for eye, tooth for tooth, hand for hand, foot for foot, burn for burn, wound for wound, stripe for stripe') was in fact an improvement on what had gone before, in that it required a moderate and proportionate response, an equivalent punishment, as opposed to the kind of genocidal retribution that had preceded this law and continued amongst some other people groups. Indeed history is littered with examples of this kind of retribution and hatred right up to the present day. The law was restated in Leviticus 24:20, but had already been set in the context of loving our neighbour as we read in Leviticus 19:18.

> 'You shall not take vengeance, or bear any grudge, against the sons of your own people, but you shall love your neighbour as yourself.'

At the time of Jesus, recompense could be made in financial compensation similar to our contemporary litigation, whereby the loss is given a monetary value. Rather than a just retaliation, for some it had become an opportunity for financial compensation and all that it entails as we see in contemporary litigation cases. The retribution laws were intended to take vengeance away from private individuals so that instead it should be justly administered by the courts for the good of the community. They were intended to stop excessive revenge and vendettas. As we read in Proverbs 20:22 and 24:29,

> 'Do not say 'I will repay evil', wait for the Lord, and he will help you.'

> 'Do not say 'I will do to him as he has done to me; I will pay the man back for what he has done.'

When Jesus spoke about turning the other cheek, this meant allowing yourself to be insulted. The message here is that even when pride is hurt there should be no vengeance. As we read again in Proverbs 16:32 and 24:17-18, and also in Lamentations 3:30,

> 'He who is slow to anger is better than the mighty, and he who rules his spirit than he who takes a city.'

> 'Do not rejoice when your enemy falls and let not your heart be glad when he stumbles; lest the Lord see it and be displeased, and turn away his anger from him,' and 'Let him give his cheek to the smiter and be filled with insults.'

Jesus calls His disciples to forget the wrongs that have been done to them; when injured, not to fall into hatred or ill-will, or wish for revenge; to exercise patience. Jesus' disciples are to disarm their opponents, not by any hostile act, but by generosity and kindness, and we have this promise in Isaiah 35:4,

> 'Say to those who are of a fearful heart 'Be strong, fear not. Behold, your God will come with vengeance, with the recompense of God. He will come and save you.'

Matthew 5:40-42

In verses 40 to 42, Jesus is again reminding his listeners of God's commandments, laid down at the earliest times, regarding our relationship with our neighbour, saying,

> 'And to the one wishing thee to sue and the tunic of thee to take, allow him also the outer garment; and who thee shall impress mile one to go with him two. To the one asking thee give and the one wishing from thee to borrow turn not away.'

The tunics worn at the time were ordinary undergarments with no particular value. However, the outer garment often had special value as it would have blue tassels woven in on the corners as a reminder to follow the Lord's commandments. To give up this outer garment implies a higher degree of generosity. When Christians meet with someone who seeks to take a part of their property, they should be prepared to lose more of their property rather than fight for it in court. The overcoat or outer garment was not allowed to be kept overnight as a pledge as the poor often used it as a bed covering. This is clearly stated in the law in Exodus 22:26,

> 'If ever you take your neighbour's garment in pledge, you shall restore it to him before the sun goes down.'

The word 'angari', translated here as 'impress', means to be compelled by violence to do any particular service, especially for those in authority, very much as men were at one time press-ganged into service for the army or navy. For the Christian, it is better to invest in people by helping and befriending them than to invest in treasures. Perhaps Jesus had Proverbs 21:26 in mind where we read:

> 'All day long the wicked covets, but the righteous gives and does not hold back.'

The laws relating to the poor and lending were also very clear, and again what Jesus was saying here was not new. We find it very easy to justify our actions with rational arguments such as expressing a concern that if we keep lending we will encourage dependency, or if we give all our money away we will not have enough for our own family. But God has commanded us not to harden our hearts, as we read in Deuteronomy 15:7-8,

> 'If there is among you a poor man, one of your brethren, in any of the towns within your land which the Lord your God gives you,

you shall not harden your heart or shut your hand against your poor brother, but you shall open your hand to him and lend him sufficient for his need, whatever it may be.'

As with the other commandments there are promises for our obedience. We have sayings such as 'what goes around comes around' or 'pay it forward' and this is a constant theme in God's covenant with us, as we read in Deuteronomy 15:10 and in Proverbs 11:24 and 18:17,

'You shall give to him freely, and your heart shall not be grudging when you give to him; because for this the Lord you God will bless you in all your work and in all that you undertake.'

'One man gives freely yet grows all the richer; another withholds what he should give, and only suffers want.'

'He who is kind to the poor lends to the Lord, and he will repay him for his deed.'

Matthew 5:43-45

In verses 43 to 45, Jesus is continuing His teaching about God the Father's expectation of our behaviour towards each other, saying,

> 'Ye heard that it was said: Thou shalt love the neighbour of thee and thou shalt hate the enemy of thee. I but tell you: Love ye the enemies of you and pray ye for the ones persecuting you; so that ye may become sons of the Father of you in heaven, because the sun of him he makes to rise on evil men and good and rains on just men and unjust.'

In Leviticus 19:18, the law states 'Love your neighbour as yourself', the rest had been added by generations of teachers. The teachers of the law had inferred that if a neighbour, or friend, was to be loved, then an enemy was to be hated, and not just the Gentiles. However, a neighbour is one who is 'nearby' and thus could just as easily be an enemy who is close by. Further, in the preceding verse in Leviticus, verse 17, the law states

> 'You shall not hate your brother in your heart.'

The word used here for brother also means kinsman or fellow countryman. It is worth noting that the English word 'hate' is often used as a translation of many different Hebrew words that vary in meaning and intensity according to context, such as despised, unloved, or even loved less. The idea of showing concern for your enemy is in fact well established in the law, as we read in Exodus 23:4-5,

> 'If you meet your enemy's ox or his ass going astray, you shall bring it back to him. If you see the ass of one who hates you lying under its burden, you shall refrain from leaving him with it, you shall help him to lift it up.'

Jesus reminds His listeners that the righteous treat their enemies with love. He demonstrated this Himself by loving those who opposed him and praying for them. This same teaching is also found in Proverbs 19:11 and 25:21-22 where we read

> 'A man's insight gives him patience, and his virtue is to overlook an offense.'

> 'If your enemy is hungry, give him bread to eat; and if he is thirsty, give him water to drink; for you will heap coals of fire on his head, and the Lord will reward you.'

Jesus goes on to point out that God pours out His blessings on all regardless of whether they are 'just or unjust'. His love is not dependent on our behaviour; He acts first to love and bless us. Jesus expects His disciples to treat their enemies with fairness and equity, doing to them as they would have them do to themselves. We can find practical examples in 2 Kings 6:22 and again in 2 Chronicles 28:15 where we read

'He answered, 'You shall not slay them. Would you slay those whom you have taken captive with your sword and with your bow? Set bread and water before them that they may eat and drink and go to their master.'

'They took the captives, and with the spoil they clothed all that were naked amongst them; they clothed them, gave them sandals, provided them with food and drink, and anointed them; and carrying all the feeble among them on asses, they brought them to their kinsfolk at Jericho.'

The principle of loving one's enemies is valid and binding on all who would follow Christ. In receiving His love we are enabled to love our enemies. We are not to be defined by our enemies; we are to be defined by our love for God in Jesus that also loves our neighbour.

Matthew 5:46-48

In the final verses of chapter 5, Jesus concludes His teaching about relationships between people, and He summarises by pointing to our heavenly Father as the perfect example, saying,

> 'For if ye love the ones loving you, what reward have ye? Not even the tax collectors the same do? And if ye greet the brothers of you only, what excess do ye? Not even the gentiles the same do? Be therefore ye perfect as the Father of you heavenly perfect is.'

Previously, Jesus had been teaching His disciples about God's impartial love. Here He is pointing out that there is nothing surprising about loving those that treat us well since even amongst criminals there can be mutual support and friendship. When we perceive someone as our enemy, or as someone who does not care for us, or opposes us, we are tempted to treat them with anger and hurt. It is often those who we are expected to get along with, someone in our family, or church, or at work. Jesus continually seeks to transform conflict into peace and His disciples are called to be impartial as He is. This was not new; it was God's desire from the beginning, as we read in Genesis 17:1 and Leviticus 11:44,

> 'I am God Almighty; walk before me and be blameless.'

> 'For I am the Lord your God; consecrate yourselves therefore, and be holy, for I am holy.'

If we only love our friends or those we perceive not to oppose us, we are acting only for ourselves and not for God's sake. Jesus talks about greeting, or saluting, that was, and still is, a common form of civility and friendship. The disciples of Jesus are called to greet even those who they perceive as their enemy; they are to go beyond what others might expect; they are to be perfect. Jesus calls us to be perfect like our heavenly Father. The Greek word 'teleioi' translated as perfect can also be translated as mature, full-grown, finished, complete, pure and holy. This is clearly stated in the law in Leviticus 19:2 and Deuteronomy 18:13 where we read,

> 'Say to all the congregation of the people of Israel, You shall be holy; for I the Lord your God am holy.'

> 'You shall be blameless before the Lord your God,'

The Hebrew word translated as perfect in the Old Testament can also be translated as blameless, unblemished, without defect, whole, upright, with integrity, sound, intact; it is not the same thing as 'sinless'. Job was described as perfect (blameless and upright), but he was found to have faults. His righteousness was in his desire to live according to God's laws and precepts. To be like our heavenly Father is to imitate Him, especially in our love towards our neighbour, be they friend or foe. Love that is perfect shows love to both friends and enemies; it is to be blameless and upright. We are to be as free from hate and anger as Jesus is; we are to become mature and complete in Him. When we walk with God, when we follow in His way, we choose the perfect way, and as always, we then receive the blessings that are promised alongside His commands, as we read in 2 Samuel 22:31,

> 'This God – his way is perfect; the promise of the Lord proves true; he is a shield for all those who take refuge in him.'

MATTHEW CHAPTER SIX

Matthew 6:1

In the first verse of chapter six, Jesus begins to teach His disciples about the relationship between ourselves as individuals and our heavenly Father.

> 'And take ye heed the righteous of you not to do in front of men with a view to be seen by them; otherwise, reward ye have not with the Father of you in the heavens.'

The word translated here as 'righteous' was probably understood at the time to imply the giving of alms; giving to the poor and needy was described in the Old Testament as being righteous. It is also sometimes translated as piety; praying or fasting in public. Jesus is not telling His disciples that they should seek to do things in secret, but that they should not be seeking publicity; it is about our motivation, do we seek to bring glory to ourselves or to God? As we read in Proverbs 21:14 and Proverbs 22:4,

> 'A gift in secret averts anger.'

> 'The reward for humility and fear of the Lord is riches and honour and life.'

Just as the Pharisees took great pains to be seen doing their charitable works at the time Jesus was speaking, people today often give to charity to raise their own status. Giving to charity can have many motives in our society, including the desire for public approval, ambition, salving the conscience, and even tax avoidance. If our motivation is self-interest, and not the glory of God, even if what we are doing is considered to be 'good', it does not store up for us 'treasures in heaven'. When what we do is motivated by our own acceptance of God's grace and seeks His glory, then we receive the rewards of His grace, as we read in Psalm 62:12 and also in Jeremiah 17:10,

> 'Thou dost requite a man according to his work."

> 'I the Lord search the mind and try the heart, to give every man according to his ways, according to the fruit of his doings.'

We cannot hide our motivation from God; He knows our inner most thoughts and desires. By suggesting that we give in secret, Jesus is acknowledging our weaknesses and showing us a clear path to take that will avoid the temptation to parade our giving. God knows even before we do what our desires and plans will be, as we read in Psalm 139:1-4,

'O Lord, thou hast searched me and known me. Thou knowest when I sit down and when I rise up; thou discernest my thoughts from afar. Thou searchest out my path and my lying down, and art acquainted with all my ways. Even before a word is on my tongue, lo, O Lord, thou knowest it altogether.'

We also have a responsibility to others to allow them to take the path of humility, and not judge others on their outward appearance or lack of ostentatious giving. We cannot see what is in the heart of another, only God can, and we have the assurance that He does see what we do in secret, our true motivation, and we will receive His blessings accordingly. As we read in 1 Samuel 16:7 when God rejects David's older brother as king, He says,

'Do not look on his appearance or on the height of his stature, because I have rejected him; for the Lord sees not as a man sees; man looks on the outward appearance, but the Lord looks on the heart.'

Matthew 6:2-4

In verses 2-4, Jesus reiterates His warning to His disciples not to seek the good opinion of men through public or ostentatious charitable deeds, but to give without expectation of reward and because of our love for God our Father, saying,

> 'When therefore thou doest alms, sound not a trumpet before thee, as the hypocrites do in the synagogues and in the streets, so that they may be glorified by men; truly I tell you, they have the reward of them. But thee when thou doest alms not let know the left hand of thee what does the right of thee, so that may be of thee the alms in secret; and the Father of thee, the one seeing in secret will repay thee.'

Jesus is also warning against pride, and specifically against hypocrisy. The origin of this word is from the Greek 'hypokrites' that means an actor or a stage player, who in ancient Greece wore a large mask to indicate which character they played. The word came to mean someone who was wearing a figurative mask; someone who was pretending to be someone or something they were not. It is likely that the Pharisees at the time of Jesus would have made public demonstrations of 'good deeds' to cover for their moral and spiritual misdeeds, or weaknesses, just as people have done down the ages, and many public and supposedly philanthropic people still do today. But we cannot deceive our heavenly Father, as we read in Psalm 44:21,

> 'For he knows the secrets of the heart.'

It is important to note that Jesus did not say 'if' you give alms, but 'when'; we should be mindful of this command that is enshrined in Old Testament law. So there is an expectation that God's people will give to the poor and needy, but how we do this matters. When Jesus spoke about our 'not letting our left hand know what our right hand is doing,' He was most likely indicating that we should not even allow ourselves to dwell on our own works of charity, to avoid being puffed up in our own conceit. Even when we do things in secret, there is the temptation to feel self-righteous; Jesus warns us that even in secret we can be led away from seeking God's glory in our innermost thoughts. We should give not only without ostentation but without self-consciousness. Our reward is not in self-righteous complacency but in being closer to God; closer to His presence, as we read in 1 Kings 8:39,

'Then hear thou in heaven they dwelling place, and forgive, and act, and render to each whose heart thou knowest, according to all his ways, for thou, thou only, knowest the hearts of all the children of men.'

Just as our heavenly Father sees when we do wrong, he sees when we do 'good' to others, be it giving alms or acts of mercy. As we have freely received, we should freely give; our giving should overflow from the love that we receive from our heavenly Father and not be motivated by a desire to notch up a 'good deed' tally. Our reward is the peace of knowing that we are our Father's children, as we read in 1 Chronicles 28:9 when David speaks to his son saying,

'And you Solomon my son, know the God of your father, and serve him with a whole heart and with a willing mind; for the Lord searches all hearts, and understands every plan and thought.'

Matthew 6:5-6

In verses 5-6, Jesus continues His teaching about the pitfalls of public displays of religion, this time in the context of prayer, saying,

> 'And when ye pray, be not ye as the hypocrites; because they love in the synagogues and in the corners of the open streets standing to pray, so that they may appear to men; truly I tell you, they have the reward of them. But when thou prayest, enter into the private room of thee and having shut the door of thee pray to the Father of thee, the one in secret; and the Father of thee the one seeing in secret will repay thee.'

There is a place for public prayer, after all Jesus Himself prayed aloud on several occasions with the intention that His disciples should know that He was praying for them. However, Jesus was referring not to prayer intended to benefit those who heard, but that which is used to benefit the status of the person speaking. How difficult it is for us, knowing that others might be listening, to remain truly humble and pure in prayer that is spoken aloud. Before we ever begin we would do well to consider the words in Hosea 14:2 where we read,

> 'Take with you words and return to the Lord; say to him 'Take away all iniquity; accept that which is good and we will render the fruit of our lips.'

By reminding His disciples to pray in private, Jesus is once again showing us a clear path that will avoid the temptation of ostentatious piety. The disciples would no doubt have been familiar with the account of Elisha who went into the room of the dead child and shut the door to pray, in 2 Kings 4:33, or Daniel who went alone into the upper chamber to pray and give thanks, in Daniel 6:10, or King David who sat before the Lord, in 2 Samuel 7:18. When we pray, it is not for our Father's sake but for ours; it is good for us to acknowledge our dependence on Him: that He owes us nothing but gives us everything. God Himself calls us to seek His presence in a private place, as we read in Isaiah 26:20 and 65:24,

> 'Come, my people, enter your chambers, and shut your doors behind you.'

> 'Before they call I will answer, while they are yet speaking I will hear.'

The Hebrews believed that prayer was also a time of self-judgement and self-evaluation. When we come to our Father in thanks and praise, and with supplications, we must also search our hearts, acknowledging with humility our weakness and our sanctification only through Jesus. But we can also come with the assurance that our Father hears us, as we read in Psalm 55:17 and 34:15,

> 'Evening and morning and at noon I utter my complaint and moan, and he will hear my voice.'

> 'The eyes of the Lord are toward the righteous; his ears towards their cry.'

In secret, we can seek our Father without distraction, and with all our heart, as we read in Jeremiah 29:12-14,

> 'Then you will call upon me and come and pray to me, and I will hear you. You will seek me and find me; when you seek me with all your heart, I will be found by you, says the Lord.

Matthew 6:7-8

In verses 7-8, Jesus continues His teaching about prayer and public displays of religion. He has already warned of hypocrisy and ostentation; here He warns of empty words, saying,

> 'But praying do not utter empty words as the gentiles; for they think that in the much speaking of them they will be heard. Not therefore be ye like them; for knows God the Father of you of what things need ye have before you to ask him.'

These 'empty words' can also be translated as 'vain repetitions', meaning for example to declare the same thing in many forms; to repeat a thing often; to say the same thing in different words; to repeat the same words as though God did not hear at first. This form of behaviour, that Jesus refers to as being what the gentiles do, is described in 1 Kings 18:26, when the priests of Baal called on the name of their god 'from morning until noon, saying O Baal, answer us' over and over. When we pray in public, and are tempted to pray ostentatiously, it is easy to repeat short phrases in this way. This kind of repetitious prayer can be found in many, if not most religions, and sadly in Christianity too. Many worship songs, old and new, have seemingly endless repetitions of phrases. We need to be aware that our worship is designed to give glory to God and not merely fulfil an emotional or public need, making us 'feel' better. Jesus would have been familiar with the words in Ecclesiastes 5:2 where we read,

> 'Be not rash with your mouth, nor let your heart be hasty to utter words before God, for God is in heaven, and you upon the earth; therefore let your words be few.'

Jesus was not condemning long prayers; the prayer of Daniel for example, in chapter 9:3-19, is both long and earnest. His condemnation is of prayers that are vain, unnecessary, meaningless, repetitious, or superstitious. Jesus was warning His disciples against thinking that the number of prayers, or length of prayers, or using a formula, or time spent praying, is a way to gain the Lord's favour. It is what is in the heart that matters, as John Wesley wrote, "The very best prayers are but vain repetitions if they are not the language of the heart." The advice given in Proverbs 10:19 is to restrain our lips, we read that

> 'When words are many, transgression is not lacking, but he who restrains his lips is prudent.'

Our trust and confidence ought to proceed from that which God is able to do in us, and not from that which we can say to Him. As a church, we often teach prayers that are to be said by rote. It is ironic that the teaching of Jesus about how to pray, the Lord's Prayer, has become a rote prayer itself, used in the very repetitious way that Jesus was warning His disciples against. Prayer is not about us informing God - He already knows; it is about drawing near to Him, to seek Him, to humble ourselves before Him, and share our needs with Him in the reassurance that we will receive from Him. Jesus reminds His disciples that their Heavenly Father already knows what we need and the desires of our hearts, as we read in Psalm 38:9 and Isaiah 58:9,

> 'Lord, all my longing is known to thee, my sighing is not hidden from thee.'

> 'Then you shall call, and the Lord will answer; you shall cry, and he will say, 'Here I am.'

Matthew 6:9

In verse 9, Jesus begins to teach His disciples how to pray. He did not say 'pray in these words', but was showing us the manner in which we should pray, firstly acknowledging God as our Father, saying,

> 'Thus therefore pray ye: Father of us the one in heaven; let it be hallowed the name of thee.'

We are taught to pray 'Our Father', or the 'Father of us', because we are not alone, but part of the body of the Church. By addressing God as Father, we can demonstrate our love and respect for, and confidence in Him. God is described as 'Father' in both the law and the prophets, for example in Deuteronomy 32:6, Isaiah 63:16, and Isaiah 64:8.

> 'Do you thus requite the Lord, you foolish and senseless people? Is not he your Father, who created you, who made you and established you?'

> 'For thou art our Father, though Abraham does not know us and Israel does not acknowledge us; thou, O Lord, art our Father, our Redeemer from of old is thy name.'

> 'Yet, O Lord, thou art our Father, we are the clay, and thou art our potter; we are all the work of thy hand.'

Having acknowledged God as Father, we are also to affirm our recognition that He is in Heaven and has ultimate authority over creation, as we read in Deuteronomy 4:39, Joshua 2:11, and 2 Chronicles 20:6

> 'Know therefore this day, and lay it to your heart, that the Lord is God in heaven above and on the earth beneath; there is no other.'

> 'For the Lord your God is he who is God in heaven above and on earth beneath.'

> 'O Lord, God of our fathers, art thou not God in heaven? Dost thou not rule over all the kingdoms of the nations? In thy hand are power and might, so that none is able to withstand thee.'

Once we have established our reminder that God is our Father and that He is in Heaven over all, the first petition Jesus tells us to make is that God's glory might be seen. Our great and over-riding concern is for God's glory, with honouring His name; to express reverence for His person and zeal for His honour. Our first priority must be to things of God; this priority is paralleled in the order of the Ten Commandments. His name is hallowed when His word, His Church, His Son, His laws, His commandments, and His name are honoured and treated as holy, as we read in Isaiah 5:16, Isaiah 29:23, and Ezekiel 36:23,

> 'But the Lord of hosts is exalted in justice, and the Holy God shows himself holy in righteousness.'

> 'They will sanctify my name; they will sanctify the Holy One of Jacob and will stand in awe of the God of Israel.'

> 'I will vindicate the holiness of my great name, which has been profaned among the nations, and which you have profaned among them; and the nations will know that I am the Lord, says the Lord God, when through you I vindicate my holiness before their eyes.'

The whole of Psalm 111 is a psalm that hallows the Name of our Father, as we read for example in verse 3,

> 'Full of honour and majesty is his work, and his righteousness endures forever.'

Matthew 6:10

In verse 10, Jesus is teaching His disciples that our second and third petitions should also focus on God our Father; for the coming of His kingdom and the doing of His will. He says:

> 'Let it come the kingdom of thee; let it come about the will of thee, as in heaven also on earth.'

Once again, the important principle is that God's glory is seen; that God comes first. We are to pray for the success of the Gospel whereby people will become members of God's spiritual kingdom; the Kingdom of Heaven that is in the hearts of God's people. This is a kingdom in which people from all nations, who have received His salvation, walk continually with God, serve Him, and live according to His precepts. It is a kingdom in which God dwells with people, both spiritually and physically, and was foretold by the prophet Daniel in chapter 7:13-14,

> 'There came one like a son of man, and he came to the Ancient of Days and was presented before him. And to him was given dominion and glory and kingdom, that all peoples, nations and languages should serve him; his dominion is an everlasting dominion, which shall not pass away, and his kingdom one that shall not be destroyed.'

Our prayer must be that God will reign as King in the hearts of people; that they will choose willingly to submit to His authority; that God's word will bring light to the world and by His Spirit bring justice and peace. We are to pray that the Kingdom of God will continue to advance so that His Kingdom of perfect righteousness will come, and then as we read in Psalm 145:10-12,

> 'All thy works shall give thanks to thee, O Lord, and all thy saints shall bless thee. They shall speak of the glory of thy kingdom, and tell of thy power, to make known to the sons of men thy mighty deeds and the glorious splendour of thy kingdom.'

The petition that immediately follows is for the doing of His will; that the whole of creation chooses willingly to conform to His Will without opposition, as we read in Daniel 7:27 and in Psalm 103:19-21,

> 'And the kingdom and the dominion and the greatness of the kingdoms under the whole heaven shall be given to the people of the saints of the Most High; their kingdom shall be an everlasting kingdom, and all dominions shall serve and obey them.'

'Bless the Lord, O you his angels, you mighty ones who do his word, hearkening to the voice of his word. Bless the Lord all his hosts, his ministers that do his will.'

This is a prayer that people will become like the angels in Heaven who do His will. By making this petition, we affirm our desire that God's will may rule in our own hearts, acknowledging that His eyes are watching over us, as we read in Psalm 11:4 and Nehemiah 9:6,

'The Lord is in his holy temple, the Lord's throne is in heaven; his eyes behold, his eyelids test, the children of men.'

'Ezra said 'Thou art the Lord, thou alone; thou hast made heaven, the heaven of heavens, with all their host, the earth and all that is in it, the seas and all that is in them; and thou preservest all of them; and the host of heaven worship thee.'

Matthew 6:11

In verse 11, having instructed His disciples to seek God's glory first, Jesus begins to teach His disciples how they should pray for themselves, saying,

'The bread of us daily give to us today.'

The Greek word 'epiousion' used here is most often translated as 'daily', but there is some debate about this. It is possible that a truer translation would be 'essential nourishment' that could be both physical and spiritual; that which is essential for our health and wellbeing. It is possible that Jesus was referring His disciples back to the Exodus, in that case, we could think of it as being 'bread sufficient for the coming day' as was the 'manna' in Exodus, as we read in Exodus chapter 16:4 and Numbers chapter 11:8

> 'The Lord said to Moses, 'Behold, I will rain bread from heaven for you; and the people shall go out and gather a day's portion every day, that I may prove them, whether they will walk in my law or not,'

> 'The people went about and gathered it and ground it in mills or beat it in mortars, and boiled it in pots, and made cakes of it; and the taste of it was like the taste of cakes baked with oil.'

Jesus instructs us to petition for what is necessary for the day, no more, no less. If we again look back to the Exodus, when the people of Israel were given 'manna', there was only ever enough for one day except that on the day before the Sabbath there was provision for two days so that the Israelites could rest on the Sabbath, as we read in Exodus 16:21,

> 'Morning by morning they gathered it, each as much as he could eat; but when the sun grew hot, it melted.'

This is an important Biblical principle. We are to be a people who rely on God's provision and trust in Him for our daily needs, for both bodily nourishment and spiritual nourishment. We are to ask for no more than is necessary for the day ahead and be content with what we have. Jesus may well have had the warning in Proverbs 30:8-9 in mind where we read,

> 'Remove far from me falsehood and lying; give me neither poverty nor riches; feed me with the food that is needful for me, lest I be full, and deny thee, and say 'Who is the Lord?' or lest I be poor, and steal, and profane the name of my God.'

We know we can trust God our Father to supply all our needs from the many promises and examples of His provision to His people, as we read for example in Psalm 78:25, Psalm 105:40 and Psalm 132:15,

> 'Man ate of the bread of the angels; he sent them food in abundance.'

> 'They asked, and he brought quails, and gave them bread from heaven in abundance.'

> 'I will abundantly bless her provisions; I will satisfy her poor with bread.'

We can have confidence in the promise to those who walk righteously, speak uprightly, and despise the gain of oppressions, that is given through the prophet Isaiah in chapter 33:16

> 'He will dwell on the heights; his place of defence will be the fortresses of rocks; his bread will be given him, his water will be sure.'

Matthew 6:12

In verse 12, Jesus continues His teaching about how to pray for ourselves, saying

> 'And forgive us the debts of us, as indeed we forgive the debtors of us.'

The Greek word 'aphes', used here for 'forgive', has a number of meanings, that differ somewhat from the contemporary English meaning, including: to send forth, to leave there, to let go, to let alone, to send away, to dismiss, to loose, to let go free, and to wipe away. The same root word is used in Leviticus 25:40 in the year of Jubilee when the Israelites were released from their debts. Jesus' disciples knew that forgiveness comes from the free mercy of God as we read for example in Psalm 32:1 and 5, and Daniel 9:9,

> 'Blessed is he whose transgression is forgiven; whose sin is covered.'

> 'I acknowledged my sin to thee, and I did not hide my iniquity; I said, 'I will confess my transgressions to the Lord'; then thou didst forgive the guilt of my sin.'

> 'To the Lord our God belong mercy and forgiveness.'

The Greek word 'opeilemata', used here for 'debts', also has multiple meanings beside the financial obligations, including: an offense, a moral obligation, a fault, a transgression, rebellion, and also non-fulfilment of a duty – a thing left undone. Jesus' disciples would have been familiar with the promises of God's mercy and forgiveness found for example in Micah 7:18-19,

> 'Who is a God like thee, pardoning iniquity and passing over transgression for the remnant of his inheritance? He does not retain his anger for ever because he delights in steadfast love. He will again have compassion upon us; he will tread our iniquities under foot. Thou wilt cast all our sins into the depths of the sea.'

Jesus goes on to teach that we should also forgive others in the same manner that God forgives us, not just in terms of financial obligations, but offences or injury or unkindness either by word or deed. Jesus reminds His disciples of the command to be merciful to others as God is merciful to them, as we read for example in 2 Samuel 22:26, Proverbs 3:3 and Zechariah 7:9,

'With the merciful thou dost show thyself merciful; with the blameless man thou dost show thyself blameless.'

'Let not mercy and faithfulness forsake you; bind them about your neck, write them on the tablet of your heart.'

'Thus says the Lord of hosts, render true judgements, show kindness and mercy each to his brother.'

Although the Book of Sirach (Ecclesiasticus) is not included in the Protestant Bible, it is retained in the Roman Catholic Bible and Jesus would certainly have been familiar with its content since it would have been read in the Synagogues. Jesus may well have had the words from Sirach 28:2-4 in mind that challenge us and speak directly of the requirement from us to show mercy and to forgive others, where we read

'Forgive your neighbour the wrong he has done, and then your sins will be pardoned when you pray. Does anyone harbour anger against another, and expect healing from the Lord? If one has no mercy toward another like himself, can he then seek pardon for his own sins?'

Matthew 6:13

In verse 13, Jesus reminds us of our weaknesses and teaches us to ask for God's protection against evil, saying

> 'And not bring us into temptation, but rescue us from evil.'

We are taught to pray that we will not be led into temptation, and this follows on from our acknowledgement of our own sin and the need to ask for forgiveness in the previous verse. Here we acknowledge that we need God's strength to help us lead a holy life. The Greek word 'eisenenkes' translated here as 'bring' is also often translated as 'lead', it can also mean to drag into or to announce. We know from other scripture that God Himself does not tempt us, thus we can infer that this petition is that, acknowledging our own weakness and need, God will not allow us to be led into temptation, to fall under its power and succumb to it; the second part of this verse confirms this. Allowing ourselves to indulge in temptation is not the same thing as being tested; we know that God allows His people to be tested as we read for example in Deuteronomy 8:2,

> 'And you shall remember all the way which the Lord your God has led you these forty years in the wilderness, that he might humble you, testing you to know what is in your heart, whether you would keep his commands or not.'

The Greek word 'rhysai' translated here as 'rescue' is usually translated as 'deliver', it can also mean save from or to drag out of danger. Perhaps Jesus was in fact using the juxtaposition of being dragged down by sin and being dragged to safety so that we could think of this phrase as being 'let us not be dragged down by sin, but drag us away from it', and we have promises that God will deliver us as we read for example in Psalm 91:9-10 and Jeremiah 15:21,

> 'Because you have made the Lord your refuge, the Most High your habitation, no evil shall befall you, no scourge come near your tent.'

> 'I will deliver you out of the hand of the wicked and redeem you from the grasp of the ruthless.'

It seems that in the Greek it is unclear whether the word translated as 'evil' means evil one, evil thing, or evil person. But what we do know, and Jesus Himself would have been familiar with the scripture is that we have a promise that God will keep us from all evil as we read in Psalm 121:7-8,

> 'The Lord will keep you from all evil; he will keep your life. The Lord will keep your going out and your coming in from this time forth and evermore.'

So Jesus teaches us that our first petition should be that God will be glorified, next that God will supply our earthly and spiritual needs, and then that we will be forgiven for what we have or have not done, as we forgive others, and finally that we will be dragged out of the mire of sin and temptation. And as always, we can trust in God's promises that He will deliver and save us and keep us from harm, as we read also in Proverbs 1:33,

> 'But he who listens to me will dwell secure and will be at ease, without dread of evil.'

Matthew 6:14-15

Having taught His disciples earlier, in verse 12, to pray for God's forgiveness as we forgive others, in verses 14-15, Jesus is expanding on this theme. The emphasis here is on our human forgiveness of each other; that this is not optional but a condition of our own forgiveness from God. He says,

> 'For if ye forgive men the trespasses of them, will forgive also you the Father of you heavenly; but if ye forgive not men, neither the Father of you will forgive the trespasses of you.'

The word 'paraptóma' translated here as 'trespasses' is not the same word as that used in verse 12. It can mean a false step; a falling away after being close beside; a lapse or deviation from the truth; an error or slip up. Perhaps this was meant to suggest that since these trespasses were just a failing in others of their duty to us it should be easy for us to forgive. Alternatively, the use of a different word here may have been to emphasise the more personal nature of the trespass of another person towards us, the kind that is not only hard to forgive but harder still to forget. Jesus may well have been reminding His disciples that God's forgiveness includes forgetting, as we read in Jeremiah 31:34,

> 'And no longer shall each man teach his neighbour and each his brother, saying 'Know the Lord,' for they shall all know me, from the least of them to the greatest, says the Lord; for I will forgive their iniquity, and I will remember their sin no more.'

Forgiveness of injuries is one of God's commands that we find most difficult to accept and even harder to follow. It is not that we are making some kind of bargain that if we forgive someone else that God will forgive us; the point is that if we do not forgive, then we are not following the command to love our neighbour and the enmity which we hold against them becomes a barrier to our receiving from God. God Himself demonstrates by His own example that forgiveness must have no limits, no conditions, no boundaries, and no 'get-out' clauses, as we read in Nehemiah 9:17,

> 'They refused to obey, and were not mindful of the wonders which thou didst perform among them; but they stiffened their neck and appointed a leader to return to their bondage in Egypt. But thou art a God ready to forgive, gracious and merciful, slow to anger and abounding in steadfast love, and didst not forsake them.'

In some ways this is a reflection of the Old Testament concept of 'measure for measure' in terms of retribution; here we have measure for measure in terms of forgiveness. If we refuse to forgive and forget the injuries which have been done to us, it is only us that is harmed by this. Sometimes forgiveness is only possible through the kind of deep prayer that God will forgive another as Jesus Himself prayed for His executioners. Sometimes it may feel impossible, but with God's grace, when we beg God's forgiveness, and we forgive others sincerely, fully, willingly and forget, then we can receive His grace in full pardon. We can trust in His clear promise that we read in Isaiah 43: 25,

'I, I am He who blots out your transgressions for my own sake, and I will not remember your sins.'

Matthew 6:16-18

In verses 16 to 18, Jesus is returning to the warning to His disciples not to seek human approval, but to seek always to be right with God in their devotional life, saying,

> 'And when ye fast, be not as the hypocrites gloomy, for they disfigure the faces of them so that they may appear to men fasting; truly I tell you, they have the reward of them. But thou fasting anoint of thee the head and the face of thee wash, so that thou appearest not to men fasting but to the Father of the one in secret; and the Father of the one in secret will repay thee.'

Previously, Jesus had warned against ostentation in prayer and giving of alms; here He applies this teaching to fasting. He is again cautioning against hypocrisy; the play acting of penitence and remorse, of counterfeit expressions of sorrow for our thoughts and actions. Fasting is very much a natural expression of grief; it is difficult to find the appetite to eat when one is suffering from grief whatever the reason, be it through external or internal causes. However, the Jewish people had appointed special days on which to fast in order to demonstrate their piety; it seems that it was customary for the Pharisees to fast twice a week. At these times they would cover their heads with ashes and allow their faces to become blackened by this ash in order that people could see that they were fasting; but God speaks against these superficial acts as we read in Isaiah 58:3-5,

> 'Behold, in the day of your fast you seek your own pleasure, and oppress all your workers. Behold, you fast only to quarrel and to fight and to hit with wicked fist. Fasting like yours this day will not make your voice to be heard on high.'

Jesus was not prohibiting fasting; God Himself asked His people to repent with fasting, but added the condition that this should be from the heart and not just the outward tearing of clothes, as we can read in the prophet Joel 2:12-13,

> 'Yet even now, says the Lord, return to me with all your heart, with fasting, with weeping, and with mourning; and rend your hearts and not your garments.'

Jesus teaches His disciples to conceal their fasting to avoid the temptation of ostentation and hypocrisy since fasting is intended to cultivate our humility not our pride. The fasting that God desires, rather than the outward tokens, is made clear in Isaiah 58:6-7, where we read,

'Is this not the fast that I choose: to loose the bonds of wickedness, to undo the thongs of the yoke, to let the oppressed go free, and to break every yoke? Is it not to share your bread with the hungry and bring the homeless poor into your house; when you see the naked to cover him, and not to hide yourself from your own flesh?'

When Jesus talked of anointing their head and washing their face, He was not suggesting that His disciples pretend to be joyful when they were not - this would be equally hypocritical. But as His disciples, they should have the joy of the knowledge of their salvation, and the humility to bring their secret griefs to their Father in heaven, as we read in Ecclesiastes 9:8 and Psalm 51:6,

'Let your garments be always white; let not oil be lacking on your head.'

'Behold, thou desires truth in the inward being; therefore teach me wisdom in my secret heart.'

Matthew 6:19-21

In verses 19 to 21, Jesus continues teaching His disciples to keep their eyes, and their hearts, firmly fixed on God and heavenly matters; keeping a right relationship with Him, saying,

'Do not store up for you treasures on the earth, where moth and rust removes, and where thieves dig through and steal; but store up for you treasures in heaven, where neither moth nor rust removes, and where thieves do not dig through nor steal; where for is the treasure of thee, there will be also the heart of thee.'

The word translated here as rust means something that 'eats into' or consumes. There are several similar metaphors used in Old Testament Scripture that Jesus could have been referring to, such as in Job 13:28 and 27:16-19 and also in Isaiah 50:9 where we read:

'Man wastes away like a rotten thing, like a garment that is moth eaten.'

'Though he heap up silver like dust, and pile up clothing like clay; he may pile it up, but the just will wear it, and the innocent will divide the silver. The house which he builds is like a spider's web [...]. He goes to bed rich, he opens his eyes and his wealth is gone.' 'Behold, all of them will wear out like a garment; the moth will eat them up.'

Jesus also reminds His disciples that worldly wealth is not only consumed over time but is also vulnerable to theft. He warns against seeking worldly wealth or riches that will come to nothing and leave the heavenly store house bare. Again there are many passages of scripture that Jesus could have referred to here, such as Job 24:16, Proverbs 23:4 and 11:28, and also Isaiah 51:7-8 where we read:

'In the dark they dig through houses; by day they shut themselves up.'

'Do not toil to acquire wealth; be wise enough to desist.'

'He who trusts in his riches will wither, but the righteous will flourish like a green leaf.'

'Hearken to me, you who know righteousness, the people in whose heart is my law [...] For the moth will eat them up like a garment, and the worm will eat them like wool; but my deliverance will be for ever, and my salvation to all generations.'

Jesus exhorts His disciples to store up treasure that cannot be consumed or stolen; to set their hearts on the things of God and to be true to Him as we read in Job 31:24-25 and 28, Psalm 62:10 and also in Ecclesiasticus 29:10-11:

'If I have made gold my trust or called fine gold my confidence; if I have rejoiced because my wealth was great or because my hand had gotten much [...] I would have been false to God above.'

'If riches increase, set not your heart on them.'

'Lose thy money for thy brother and thy friend, and let it not rust under a stone to be lost. Store up thy treasure according to the commandments of the Most High, and it shall bring thee more profit than gold.'

Our investment in the heavenly store house, where our heart must be, is through the act of loving our neighbour and we can trust in God's promise that heavenly treasure is the fruit of righteousness, as we read in Isaiah 3:10,

'Tell the righteous that it shall be well with them, for they shall eat the fruit of their deeds.'

Matthew 6:22-23

In verses 22 to 23, Jesus is continuing His teaching about keeping our focus on God the Father, trusting in His provision, and sharing that provision, saying

> 'The lamp of the body is the eye. If therefore be the eye of thee single, all the body of thee shining will be; but if the eye of thee evil be, all the body of thee dark will be. If therefore the light in thee darkness is, the darkness how great.'

The word 'single' used in the Greek is typically translated as sound, good, clear or healthy. However, the original use implied a single uncomplicated thread, a focus on one thing without distraction; to look in just one direction. It is also important to note that in Old Testament Scripture, the word 'eye' frequently meant the heart, often used in the context of justice for the poor. It is clear from the overall context of the Sermon on the Mount that Jesus means that our single focus should be on God and His commands, so we could read this as 'the lamp of the body is the heart and if we keep our heart focussed on God we will be filled with His light, as we read in Proverbs 4:25-26 & 23:26, and in Psalm 119:2 and verse 10,

> 'Let your eyes look directly forward, and your gaze be straight before you. Take heed to the path of your feet, then all your ways will be sure.'

> 'My son, give me your heart, and let your eyes delight in my ways.'

> 'Blessed are those who keep his testimonies, who seek him with their whole heart.'

> 'With my whole heart I seek thee; let me not wander from thy commandments.'

At the time when Jesus was speaking, the phrase having an 'evil eye' meant being miserly or begrudging, and the original Hebrew is at times translated as miserly rather than having an evil eye. This is contrasted with a 'bountiful eye' as we read in Proverbs 28:22 and 22:9,

> 'A miserly man hastens after wealth and does not know that want will come upon him.'

100

'He who has a bountiful eye will be blessed, for he shares his bread with the poor.'

Jesus is again warning against duplicity, that we should have not have multiple motives when we give alms, when we pray, when we fast, or even when we give; our heart (or eyes) should have a single motive for God's glory and purposes, as we read in Deuteronomy 15:9 and Jeremiah 13:16,

'Take heed lest there be a base thought in your heart and you say 'the seventh year, the year of release is near' and your eye be hostile to your poor brother, and you give him nothing, and he cry to the Lord against you, and it be sin in you.'

'Give glory to the Lord your God before he brings darkness, before your feet stumble on the twilight mountains, and while you look for light he turns it into gloom and makes it deep darkness.'

In humility we need to keep our eyes fixed firmly in the right direction, with pure motives and with generous hearts, remembering the words of Isaiah 5:20-21,

'Woe to those who call evil good and good evil, who put darkness for light and light for darkness, who put bitter for sweet and sweet for bitter. Woe to those who are wise in their own eyes, and shrewd in their own sight.'

Matthew 6:24

In verse 24, Jesus continues teaching His disciples about attitudes towards treasure and wealth, and keeping God as our one, true, and only master, saying

> 'No one can two lords to serve; for either the one he will hate and the other he will love, or one he will hold to and the other he will despise. You cannot God to serve and mammon.'

Jesus continues the theme of 'single-mindedness', reminding His disciples that it is not possible to serve two different masters with complete faithfulness, since the supreme service of one leaves little or no room for service of the other. His disciples, must choose whom they serve with single-minded loyalty. The attempts by the Israelites to keep one foot in each camp; attempts to serve two masters, was described by Elijah as 'limping', where we read in 1 Kings 18:21:

> 'And Elijah came near to all the people, and said, "How long will you go limping with two different opinions? If the Lord is God, follow him; but if Ba'al, then follow him." And the people did not answer him a word.'

Even where two masters may be of the same character and have the same objective; it is not possible to serve the orders of both at the same time. Further, if our affections lie with one, they cannot lie with the other; if we are determined to follow the orders of one, we must necessarily disregard the orders of the other. So God's people must choose to follow Him with their whole heart to the exclusion of all else as we read in Joshua 24:15 and 1 Samuel 7:3,

> 'And if you be unwilling to serve the Lord, choose this day whom you will serve, whether the gods your fathers served in the region beyond the River, or the gods of the Amorites in whose land you dwell; but as for me and my house, we will serve the Lord.'

> 'Then Samuel said to all the house of Israel, "If you are returning to the Lord with all your heart, then put away the foreign gods and the Ashtaroth from among you, and direct your heart to the Lord, and serve him only, and he will deliver you out of the hand of the Philistines."

The word mammon that Jesus used was from classical Hebrew; it literally meant money. Money itself has no intrinsic value of its own, only what we apportion to it. At the time Jesus was speaking, the word was probably used in the world of trade to mean gain or wealth. In this context, it clearly means riches or money, or anything loved or sought after without reference to God. It is not possible to deceive God; He knows what we have set our hearts on, as we read in Ezekiel 33:31 and in Psalm 10:3,

> 'And they come to you as people come, and they sit before you as my people, and they hear what you say but they will not do it; for with their lips they show much love, but their heart is set on their gain.'

> 'For the wicked boasts of the desires of his heart, and the man greedy for gain curses and renounces the Lord.'

In choosing the one Master, we can pray as David did in Psalm 119:36,

> 'Incline my heart to thy testimonies, and not to gain.'

Matthew 6:25-26

In verses 25-26, Jesus continues to teach His disciples about single-mindedness; about not being distracted from trusting discipleship by material anxieties, saying

> 'Therefore I say unto you; be not anxious for the life of you, what ye may eat or what ye may drink, nor for the body of you, what ye may put on, not the life more is than the food and the body than the raiment? Look ye at the birds of heaven that they sow not nor reap nor gather into barns, and the Father of you heavenly feeds them; and do not ye more excel them?'

This year we had a good crop of apples, we had done very little in contribution – just clearing of undergrowth and a small amount of pruning, yet here was food that would just fall from the tree when ready. In many ways, to doubt the Father's bounty is to betray His trust; in the beginning, God promised to provide all our food, as we read in Genesis 1:29-31,

> 'Behold I have given you every plant yielding seed which is upon the face of all the earth, and every tree with seed in its fruit; you shall have them for food. And to every beast of the earth, and to every bird of the air, and to everything that creeps on the earth, everything that has the breath of life, I have given every green plant for food.'

Jesus was not teaching His disciples not to care for themselves or others but warning against anxiety that arises from distrust; that we dishonour God our Father when we fail to trust that He will provide our food and clothing. There are specific examples in Old Testament Scripture of when God supplied food and water to His people, for example during the forty years in the wilderness with Moses, the widow's jars of flour and oil not running out when Elijah stayed with her or when the ravens fed Elijah, as we read in 1 Kings 17:5-6

> 'So he went and did according to the word of the Lord; he went and dwelt by the brook Cherith that is east of the Jordan. And the ravens brought him bread and meat in the morning, and bread and meat in the evening; and he drank from the brook.'

As God's people, it is part of our worship that we acknowledge His bountiful provision for all of His creation as we read for example in Psalm 104:14-15 and also in Psalm 147:7-11,

> 'Thou dost cause the grass to grow for the cattle, and plants for man to cultivate, that he may bring forth food from the earth, and wine to gladden the heart of man, oil to make his face shine, and bread to strengthen man's heart.'

> 'Sing to the Lord with thanksgiving; make melody to our God upon the lyre. He covers the heavens with clouds, he prepares rain for the earth, he makes grass grow upon the hills. He gives to the beasts their food, and to the young ravens which cry. His delight is not in the strength of the horse, nor his pleasure in the legs of a man; but the Lord takes pleasure in those who fear him, in those who hope in his steadfast love.'

With humility and child-like trust, we can rest in God's promises, as we read in Psalm 127:1-2

> 'Unless the Lord builds the house, those who build it labour in vain. Unless the Lord watches over the city, the watchman stays awake in vain. It is in vain that you rise up early and go late to rest, eating the bread of anxious toil; for he gives to his beloved sleep.'

Matthew 6:27-30

In verses 27-30, Jesus continues the theme of trusting in God, reminding His disciples to acknowledge their dependence on God, and to give Him the credit for what seems to be the fruit of their own labour, saying

> 'But who of you being anxious can to add to the stature of him cubit one? And concerning clothing why be ye anxious? Consider the lilies of the field, how they grow; they labour not nor spin; but I tell you that not Solomon in all the glory of him was clothed as one of these. But if the grass of the field today being and tomorrow into an oven being thrown God thus clothes, not much more you, little faiths?'

The word translated here as 'stature' meant height, but it could also mean age, likewise, the word 'cubit' used here, although it was a standard measurement of the day (the distance from the elbow to the tip of the middle finger), was also used to represent measurement of time, as was a 'handbreadth' as we read in Psalm 39:45,

> 'Lord, let me know my end, and what is the measure of my days; let me know how fleeting my life is. Behold, thou hast made my days a few handbreadths, and my lifetime is as nothing in thy sight. Surely every man stands as a mere breath.'

The fleeting nature of flowers and grass is frequently used in Old Testament Scripture and it illustrates not only the transient nature of our lives, the number of days of which are entirely in God's hands, but also contrasts with the everlasting nature of God Himself, as we read in Job 14:5 and Isaiah 40:6-8,

> 'Since his days are determined, and the number of his months is with thee, and thou hast appointed his bounds that he cannot pass.'

> 'A voice says 'cry', and I said 'what shall I cry?' All flesh is grass, and all its beauty is like the flower of the field. The grass withers, the flower fades, when the breath of the Lord blows on it; surely the people are grass. The grass withers, the flower fades; but the word of our God will stand forever.'

Jesus is again warning His disciples against immoderate anxiety about material needs that can lead to a desire to gain those things by their own efforts and lose sight of God in their undertaking. Jesus reminds His disciples that whatever we need depends on the blessing of God as we read in Jeremiah 10:23,

'I know O Lord that the way of man is not in himself, that it is not in man who walks to direct his steps.'

Alongside the warning, Jesus is also reminding His disciples to trust and have faith in God's promises to clothe and feed His people, who are more precious than flowers, as He had clothed and fed them in the wilderness like a shepherd, as we read in Deuteronomy 8:4 and Isaiah 40:11,

'Your clothing did not wear out upon you, and your foot did not swell, these forty years.'

'He will feed his flock like a shepherd, he will gather the lambs in his arms, he will carry them in his bosom, and gently lead those that are with young.'

Matthew 6:31-32

In verses 31-32, Jesus continues to teach His disciples about trust, teaching that God's people are to be different from those who do not know Him as their Father; different from those whose prayers and desires are focused on material need and gain, saying

> 'Therefore, be ye not anxious saying: what may we eat? or what may we drink? or what may we put on? All for these things the nations seek after; knows the Father of you heavenly that ye need these things of all.'

God's people, those who are in His Kingdom, are to rely on God and acknowledge His blessings. If His people do not rely on God's care, often described as being like a Father, then they behave as if they are not part of His family. It is important to note that the promises of provision in Old Testament Scripture are linked with obedience; it is also noteworthy that trusting in self-made wealth is described as iniquity, as in Psalm 49:5-6 where we read:

> 'Why should I fear in times of trouble, when the iniquity of my persecutors surrounds me, men who trust in their wealth and boast of the abundance of their riches?'

Jesus was reminding His disciples that God has promised to care for His people with abundance so long as they continued to follow His laws, to live according to His commands, and trust in His provision. This was made very clear in Leviticus 26:3-5 where we read:

> 'If you walk in my statutes and observe my commandments and do them, then I will give you your rains in their season, and the land shall yield its increase, and the trees of the field shall yield their fruit. And your threshing shall last to the time of vintage, and the vintage shall last to the time of sowing; and you shall eat your bread to the full, and dwell in your land securely.'

In fact we can read that our Heavenly Father knows so well what the needs of His people are that He even promises to make provision for our Sabbath rest. When the people were in the wilderness, enough food was provided the day before the Sabbath that the people did not need to gather on that day. God also gave His people a law to give the land a Sabbath year of rest – every seventh year - and such is His care that He promised provision even for this as we read in Leviticus 25:19-22:

'The land will yield its fruit, and you will eat your fill, and dwell in it securely. And if you say, "What shall we eat in the seventh year, if we may not sow or gather in our crop?" I will command my blessing upon you in the sixth year, so that it will bring forth fruit for three years.'

God our Heavenly Father knows all our wants and needs; a loving and wise father provides for the necessities for his children and teaches them to seek wisdom rather than things that are unnecessary. Jesus deliberately calls God Father to help His disciples understand that they need not doubt His paternal care; that He knows their everyday needs which He refers to as "all these things". It is part of our worship to trust the eyes of our Father to watch over us and the hand of our Father to provide, as we read in Isaiah 40:28-29 and Psalm 95:6-7:

'He does not faint or grow weary; His understanding is unsearchable. He gives power to the faint, and to him who has no might he increases strength.'

'O come, let us worship and bow down, let us kneel before the Lord our Maker. For he is our God, and we are the people of his pasture, and the sheep of his hand.'

Matthew 6:33-34

In verses 33-34, Jesus summarises His teaching about trust in our heavenly Father, and the direction of focus for our lives that should put first things first, saying

> 'But seek ye first the kingdom and the righteousness of Him, and these things all shall be added to you. Therefore, be ye not anxious for the morrow, for the morrow will be anxious of itself; sufficient to the day the evil of it.'

Jesus teaches His disciples that they are to put His Kingdom at the top of their list of priorities, and to do this they must seek the righteousness of Christ that is made known in God's commandments. Jesus' disciples are to put God's precepts ahead of society's norms and traditions in obedience to Him, and 'all these things', that is our material needs, will be taken care of, as we read in Lamentations 3:25 and Psalm 34:9-10,

> 'The Lord is good to those who wait for him, to the soul that seeks him.'

> 'O fear the Lord, you his saints, for those who fear him have no want. The young lions suffer want and hunger; but those who seek the Lord lack no good thing.'

King Solomon, when asked in a dream to ask anything of God, asked for wisdom to govern the Lord's people and discern between good and evil. This is a clear example from Old Testament Scripture of Solomon seeking God's righteousness first and then 'all these things' being added, as we read in 1 Kings 3:11-13,

> 'And God said to him, "Because you have asked this, and have not asked for yourself long life or riches or the life of your enemies but have asked for yourself understanding to discern what is right, behold, I now do according to your word. Behold, I give you a wise and discerning mind, so that none like you has been before you and none shall arise after you. I give you also what you have not asked, both riches and honour, so that no other king shall compare with you, all your days".'

As Jesus' disciples we should spend our life in the pursuit of His Kingdom and His righteousness, and the fruits of happiness will follow. Constantly seeking purity of heart and holiness and the fruits of righteousness will diminish cares and anxieties for the future. We have an example in Scripture of the importance of trusting in God and not worrying about tomorrow, when His people were given manna in the wilderness, as we read in Exodus 16:18-20,

> 'But when they measured it with an omer, he that gathered much had nothing over, and he that gathered little had no lack; each gathered according to what he could eat. And Moses said to them, "Let no man leave any of it till the morning." But they did not listen to Moses; some left part of it till the morning, and it bred worms and became foul.'

Our heavenly Father has our future, as well as our present, in His hands and we are to leave it in His hands; our future preparations should only be concerned with His Kingdom and His righteousness, as we read in Proverbs 27:1, and those who seek the Lord can trust in His promises, see Proverbs 8:17 and Isaiah 3:10,

> 'Do not boast about tomorrow, for you do not know what a day may bring forth.'

> 'I love those who love me, and those who seek me diligently find me.'

> 'Tell the righteous that it shall be well with them, for they shall eat the fruit of their deeds.'

MATTHEW CHAPTER SEVEN

Matthew 7:1-2

In the earlier part of the Sermon on the Mount, Jesus taught His disciples about their relationship with God their Father and with each other. In chapter 7 verses 1-2, He begins to teach His disciples about how to behave, firstly towards each other, saying

> 'Judge not, lest ye be judged; with what for judgement ye judge ye shall be judged, and with what measure ye measure it shall be measured to you'.

The Greek word that Jesus used here, krinete – translated as judge, did not refer to the kind of judgements made in court, but to criticism of another or judgments about the status of another's faith or salvation. The context makes it clear that what Jesus is warning against is our making unfavourable private judgements about another's character or actions. He is warning His disciples against fault-finding in others that may be motivated by a lack of humility in acknowledging our own faults, as we read in Isaiah 65:5,

> 'Who say, 'Keep to yourself. Do not come near me, for I am holier than you!' These are smoke in My nostrils, a fire that burns all the day.'

Jesus is not condemning His disciples from having an opinion about the conduct of others, especially when it is clearly against the law, but what He is warning against is the tendency to form hasty judgements without allowance for circumstances, and then expressing this opinion about a person. It is clear from the law that actions are to have equal consequences, and this includes intent to harm even when no actual harm has been committed, as we read in Deuteronomy 19:18-21,

> 'And the judges shall make careful inquiry, and indeed, if the witness is a false witness, who has testified falsely against his brother, then you shall do to him as he thought to have done to his brother; so you shall put away the evil from among you. And those who remain shall hear and fear, and hereafter they shall not again commit such evil among you. Your eye shall not pity: life shall be for life, eye for eye, tooth for tooth, hand for hand, foot for foot.

The principle of 'measure for measure' seems to be a fundamental principle of the universe, expressed by scientists as 'for every action there is an equal and opposite reaction', and expressed colloquially as 'what goes around comes around'. If we stand in a cavern and hurl abuse at the walls, abuse will be hurled back at us; if we whisper words of sweetness, words of sweetness will come back to us. We can choose for ourselves whether to heed Jesus' warning, whether to be severe or merciful to others, knowing that mercy will be shown to the merciful and we reap what we sow, as we read in 2 Samuel 22:27, Psalm 18:25-26, Hosea 10:12, and in Proverbs 12:14,

> 'With the pure You will show Yourself pure; And with the devious You will show Yourself shrewd,'

> 'With the merciful You will show Yourself merciful; with a blameless man You will show Yourself blameless; with the pure You will show Yourself pure; and with the devious You will show Yourself shrewd,'

> 'Sow for yourselves righteousness; reap in mercy; break up your fallow ground, for it is time to seek the Lord, till He comes and rains righteousness on you.'

> 'A man will be satisfied with good by the fruit of his mouth, and the recompense of a man's hands will be rendered to him.'

Matthew 7:3-5

In verses 3-5, Jesus continues His teaching about our behaviour towards others that is to be determined by our own self-scrutiny and self-reform, reminding His disciples of their tendency to blindness and self-deceit regarding their own faults, saying,

> 'And why seest thou the chip in the eye of the brother of thee, the but in thine eye beam thou considerest not? or how wilt thou say to the brother of thee: Allow that I may pluck out the chip out of the eye of thee and behold not the beam in the eye of thee? Hypocrite, pluck out first out of the eye of thee the beam, and then thou wilt see clearly to pluck out the chip out of the eye of the brother of thee.'

Have you ever listened to your own voice in a recording? If so, you are likely to have found that it sounds very different from what you hear in your own head. Or have you seen your mirror image in reverse so that you see how you really look to others? If someone could read your inmost thoughts what would they find? The same nature that fails to see our own faults drives envy and malice that will perceive even the smallest of faults in others, as we read in Psalm 50:16-20,

> 'But to the wicked God says: 'What right have you to declare My statutes, or take My covenant in your mouth, seeing you hate instruction and cast My words behind you? When you saw a thief, you consented with him, and have been a partaker with adulterers. You give your mouth to evil and your tongue frames deceit. You sit and speak against your brother; you slander your own mother's son.'

Before we can relate to others in Christian love, we need to clear our own vision in order properly to see and repent of our own failures. Our zeal should be directed towards reproving ourselves and knowing our own defects better than we know our neighbour's. If in humility we seek to amend our own faults, we are less likely to fall into hypocrisy. This is a constant theme of the Old Testament prophets that we can read for example in Isaiah 1:16-17, Jeremiah 25:4-5, and Zephaniah 2:1,

> 'Wash yourselves, make yourselves clean; put away the evil of your doings from before My eyes. Cease to do evil, learn to do

good; seek justice, rebuke the oppressor; defend the fatherless, plead for the widow.'

'And the Lord has sent to you all His servants the prophets, rising early and sending them, but you have not listened nor inclined your ear to hear. They say, 'Repent now everyone of his evil ways and his evil doings.'

'Seek the Lord, all you meek of the earth who have upheld His justice. Seek righteousness, seek humility.'

When we have faced, and with the help of our heavenly Father overcome, our own sins, then we shall be able, with insight and love, to help others overcome theirs, and pray along with the psalmist in Psalm 51:7-13,

'Purge me with hyssop, and I shall be clean; wash me and I shall be whiter than snow. Make me hear joy and gladness, that the bones You have broken may rejoice. Hide Your face from my sins and blot out all my iniquities. Create in me a clean heart, O God, and renew a steadfast spirit within me. Do not cast me away from Your presence, and do not take Your Holy Spirit from me. Restore to me the joy of Your salvation and uphold me by Your generous spirit. Then I will teach transgressors Your ways, and sinners shall be converted to You.'

Matthew 7:6

In verse 6, it seems at first glance that Jesus has introduced a random additional topic, but when read in the context of the previous verses, we can see that it is likely to be a continuation of His teaching about our judgement of others, saying,

> 'Not give the holy to the dogs, neither cast the pearls of you before the pigs, lest they will trample them with the feet of them and turning may rend you.'

Jesus has already taught His disciples not to sit in censorious judgment on others. Here he adds that we are to exercise discrimination in our dealings with others. His disciples are not to use censorious judgment but be discriminatingly judicious. Jesus Himself knew it was sometimes useless to tell His message to those who had hardened their hearts and we know from the Gospels that there were times when He refused to answer them. He may well have had Proverbs 9:7-8 or Proverbs 23:9 in mind, where we read,

> 'He who corrects a scoffer gets shame for himself, and he who rebukes a wicked man only harms himself. Do not correct a scoffer, lest he hate you; rebuke a wise man and he will love you. Give instruction to a wise man, and he will be still wiser; teach a just man, and he will increase in learning.'

> 'Do not speak in the hearing of a fool, for he will despise the wisdom of your words.'

These words of Jesus may also have been a warning against continually pressing the Gospel, which is holy and precious, on those who continue to reject it. Consider what the implications of this might be for evangelism and outreach. Jesus reminds His disciples that the Gospel and the things of God's Kingdom are holy and precious beyond price and must be treated as such. This is an important truth and made abundantly clear in the law and the prophets of Old Testament Scripture as we read for example in Exodus 22:31 and Leviticus 22:6-7 where we read,

> 'And you shall be holy men to Me: you shall not eat meat torn by beasts in the field; you shall throw it to the dogs.'

118

'The person who has touched any such thing shall be unclean until evening and shall not eat the holy offering unless he washes his body with water. And when the sun goes down, he shall be clean; and afterward he may eat the holy offerings, because it is his food.'

God's people are not to use anything that is holy to the Lord in anyway that might cause it to be profaned or degraded. Perhaps we need to consider this in the context of contemporary social media. We are of course called to witness and share the holy and precious Gospel but with discernment and with wise judgement, remembering that we should direct all our steps according to God's precepts. Jesus likened the beauty of God's kingdom to precious pearls worth a king's ransom, worthy of honour and majesty, as we read in Psalm 96:7-9,

'For the LORD is great and greatly to be praised; He is to be feared above all gods. For all the gods of the peoples are idols, but the Lord made the heavens. Honour and majesty are before Him; strength and beauty are in His sanctuary. Give to the Lord, O families of the peoples, give to the Lord glory and strength. Give to the Lord the glory due His name; bring an offering and come into His courts. O worship the Lord in the beauty of holiness! Tremble before Him, all the earth.'

Matthew 7:7-11

In verses 7-11, Jesus returns to the Fatherhood of God, saying,

> 'Ask, and it shall be given to you; seek, and ye shall find; knock and it shall be opened to you. For everyone asking one receives, and the seeking one finds, and to the knocking one it shall be opened. Or what is there of you man, whom will ask the son of him a loaf not a stone he will give him? Or also a fish he will ask, not a serpent he will give him? If therefore ye evil being know gifts good to give to the children of you, how much more the Father of you in the heavens will give good things to the ones asking him.'

By giving His disciples these three important directions to 'ask, seek, and knock', Jesus is reminding them that, being poor in spirit, they are in want of His spirit; that being lost from God's purposes, they must seek His peace and salvation; that being in earnest, they should knock with perseverance on the door that opens onto the true way of life. We know that we can ask, as Solomon was commanded by God to do, as we read in 1 Kings 3:5, and that He will answer as we read in Isaiah 30:19,

> 'At Gibeon, the Lord appeared to Solomon in a dream by night: and God said, "Ask! What shall I give you?" And 'He will be very gracious to you at the sound of your cry; when He hears it, He will answer you.'

Jesus had already taught His disciples that they should seek God's righteousness, here He is promising them that this search will not go unrewarded; that those who seek the true riches of His Kingdom will find them; first we are to seek, as we read in Psalm 27:78 and Isaiah 55:6,

> 'Hear, O Lord, when I cry with my voice! Have mercy also upon me, and answer me. When You said 'Seek My face,' my heart said to You 'Your face, Lord, I will seek.'

> 'Seek the Lord while He may be found, call upon Him while He is near.'

When we seek, Jesus teaches us that our Heavenly Father will give us good things as promised in the Psalms and the prophets, where we read in Psalm 37:4, Psalm 84:11, and Isaiah 63:7,

> 'Delight yourself also in the Lord, and He shall give you the desires of your heart.'

> 'For the Lord God is a sun and shield; the Lord will give grace and glory; no good thing will He withhold from those who walk uprightly.'

> 'I will mention the loving kindness of the Lord and the praises of the Lord, according to all that the Lord has bestowed on us, and the great goodness toward the house of Israel, which He has bestowed on them according to His mercies, according to the multitude of His loving kindness.'

In our daily lives we find Jesus through prayer; this is not just saying your prayers in the morning and evening and at mealtimes; it is a frequent heart-to-heart conversation with Him who we know loves us. Seeking God with all our heart involves remaining in contact with Jesus the whole day. We can do this by short prayers and meditations about everything that occurs; by being aware that in all circumstances God is present and we can discuss with Him, our best friend, what is the best thing to do and thank Him always, as we read in Jeremiah 29:11-13,

> 'For I know the thoughts that I think toward you, says the Lord, thoughts of peace and not evil, to give you a future and a hope. Then you will call upon Me and go and pray to Me, and I will listen to you. And you will seek Me and find Me, when you search for Me with all your heart.'

Matthew 7:12

In verse 12, Jesus is concluding the teachings He has given His disciples in the preceding chapters, summing them up in one straightforward rule, saying,

> 'All things therefore as many soever as ye wish that may do to you men thus also ye do to them; this for is the law and the prophets.'

These words assimilate Jesus' teaching on judging and reproving as well as His teaching about respecting our neighbour as commanded in the law; it is a summary of the whole and has been considered the 'golden rule' for two millennia. Jesus' disciples are not to act from selfishness or injustice but are to put themselves in the place of others and ask what they would expect or hope for if they were in their place. Jesus would have been familiar with the saying found in the Book of Tobit 4:15 (in the Roman Catholic Bible and in the Apocrypha to the Anglican Bible), thought to have been written about the same time as the Book of Daniel, where we read,

> 'Do to no one what you would not want done to you.'

The words in Tobit are in the negative form 'do not do'; it is a rule of not doing, rather than of doing, whereas Jesus' words are positive and proactive; His is a rule of doing, rather than not doing; He says, 'what you want men to do to you, do also to them.' In His teaching, Jesus highlights the positive commandments. The Law and the Prophets do teach what not to do, but they also teach God's people the things they ought to do. This is summed up in Leviticus 19:18 and further illustrated for example in Psalm 82:34 and Isaiah 1:17 and 58:67, where we read:

> 'You shall love your neighbour as yourself.'

> 'Defend the poor and fatherless; do justice to the afflicted and needy. Deliver the poor and needy; free them from the hand of the wicked.'

> 'Learn to do good; seek justice, rebuke the oppressor; defend the fatherless, plead for the widow.'

'Is this not the fast that I have chosen: to loose the bonds of wickedness, to undo the heavy burdens, to let the oppressed go free, and that you break every yoke? Is it not to share your bread with the hungry and that you bring to your house the poor who are cast out; when you see the naked, that you cover him, and not hide yourself from your own flesh?'

Doing to others as we would have them do to us is what is taught in the Law and the Prophets. Rather than giving His disciples a list of rules or commands by which to govern their behaviour, Jesus gave this simple principle that can be applied to every situation that involves their neighbour. This includes not just our actions, but our words, our thoughts, and even our prayers, as we read in Zechariah 8:16-17,

'These are the things you shall do: speak each man the truth to his neighbour; give judgement in your gates for truth, justice, and peace; let none of you think evil in your heart against your neighbour.'

Jesus' disciples are called to follow His 'Golden Rule', and we have the promise that the righteous will not be shaken as we read in Psalm 112:5-7,

'A good man deals graciously and lends; he will guide his affairs with discretion. Surely, he will never be shaken; the righteous will be in everlasting remembrance. He will not be afraid of evil tidings; his heart is steadfast, trusting in the Lord.'

Matthew 7:13-14

In verses 13-14, having taught His disciples about the righteousness of the Kingdom of God, Jesus now warns them that they have a choice to make. Choices must be made for which there will be consequences, good or bad, and He likens this to setting out on a journey saying,

> 'Enter ye in through the narrow gate; because wide the gate and broad the way leading away to destruction, and many are the ones going in through it; because strait the gate and made narrow the way leading away to life and few are the ones finding it.'

The Greek word 'stenēs', translated here as 'narrow', has also been translated as 'strait', meaning a narrow or cramped way through, such as a gorge, or mountain pass, where there is little room to pass by one another. Jesus speaks first of the gateway. We still use 'wicket' gates in the 21st century; these are small doorways, for a single person to enter or leave a secure area, inset into a full-size doorway or gate that would allow trucks (or carriages) and large numbers of people to go through. So, the choice is which gate to go through, the small one, through which we cannot take anything else, not even our pride, self-will, or sins; or the large one, following the crowd taking all our baggage with us. Jesus' disciples are called to choose the strait gate that leads to life, as we read in Deuteronomy 30:19 and Jeremiah 21:8,

> 'I call heaven and earth as witnesses today against you, that I have set before you life and death, blessing and cursing; therefore, choose life, that both you and your descendants may live.'

> 'Now you shall say to this people, 'Thus says the Lord: "Behold, I set before you the way of life and the way of death."

This small and narrow gate leads to a narrow path of holiness; Jesus has already taught His disciples how to follow its way. The people of God's Kingdom are not to follow the crowd, go with the flow, follow the fashions of the day, take the easy route, or even accept the majority view if it is in contravention of God's fundamental Laws and statutes. Jesus knew of the warnings in Scripture of the seductiveness of temptation, as we read for example in Proverbs 4:26-27; 7:25 and 16:25, where we read:

'Ponder the path of your feet and let all your ways be established. Do not turn to the right or the left; remove your foot from evil.'

And, referring to temptation,

'Do not let your heart turn aside to her ways, do not stray into her paths; for she has cast down many wounded, and all who were slain by her were strong men. Her house is the way to hell, descending to the chambers of death.'

'There is a way that seems right to a man, but its end is the way of death.'

Repentance, faith, humility, self-denial, and holiness of life are not, and never have been, fashionable; it is the few who take this path. Christians must search their hearts and ask themselves: which gate have they chosen; which path are they travelling? Jesus' disciples are to seek, and choose, the small, tight, narrow, doorway that leads to the Highway of Holiness, the way of righteousness, the path of justice, to find life and fulness of joy, as we read in Isaiah 35:8, Proverbs 8:20, and Psalm 16:11,

'A highway shall be there, and a road, and it shall be called the Highway of Holiness. The unclean shall not pass over it, but it shall be for others. Whoever walks the road, although a fool, shall not go astray.'

'I traverse the way of righteousness, in the midst of the paths of justice.'

'You will show me the path of life; in Your presence is fulness of joy; at Your right hand are pleasures forevermore.'

Matthew 7:15-17

In verses 15-17, Jesus' warning follows on from what He had previously been speaking about, making it clear that in the wide and easy way there will be false teachers who will try to widen the 'strait' gate, who will teach the broad path that is so much easier to travel, saying,

> 'Beware of false prophets, who come to you in clothes of sheep, but within are wolves greedy. From the fruits of them ye will know them. They do not gather from thorns grapes or from thistles figs? So every tree good fruits produces, but the corrupt tree fruits evil produces.'

The original Hebrew for the word prophet (navi) is derived from 'nabû' which means to declare or announce, to name, or to invoke, one called by God, and not necessarily speaking about the future. It was more like being a spokesperson or mouthpiece, as for example Aaron was for Moses. Prophets were also regarded as religious teachers; thus, a false prophet is a teacher of incorrect doctrine. False, or Lying prophets were well documented in Old Testament Scripture, as we read for example in 1 Kings 13:18 and Isaiah 5:20:

> 'He said to him, "I too am a prophet as you are, and an angel spoke to me by the word of the Lord, saying 'Bring him back with you to your house, that he may eat bread and drink water'." (He was lying to him)'

> 'Woe to those who call evil good, and good evil; who put darkness for light, and light for darkness; who put bitter for sweet, and sweet for bitter.'

The sheep was a symbol of innocence, sincerity, and harmlessness. To wear sheep's clothing is to assume the appearance of innocence. It seems that it was the custom for religious men to wear sheep skins or other animal skins, as did John the Baptist. False teaching is one of the ways that Jesus' disciples may be enticed away from the narrow way; it may come in the guise of innocence and harmlessness, and a pretence at gentleness; speaking words that may make us feel comfortable, but Jesus likens to greedy wolves, as we read in Jeremiah 23:16 and Ezekiel 22:27-28:

'Thus says the Lord of hosts: "Do not listen to the words of the prophets who prophesy to you. They make you worthless; they speak a vision of their own heart, not from the mouth of the Lord. They continually say to those who despise Me, 'The Lord has said, "You shall have peace", and to everyone who walks according to the dictates of his own heart, they say 'No evil shall come upon you'."'

'Her princes in her midst are like wolves tearing the prey, to shed blood, to destroy people, and to get dishonest gain. Her prophets plastered them with untempered mortar, seeing false visions, and divining lies for them, saying, 'Thus says the Lord God,' when the Lord had not spoken.'

Jesus teaches His disciples a simple rule by which they can know true from false teachers: to examine the paths they tread, the fruit they bear, the foundations on which they build what they say, and their attitude towards Jesus – do they question His authority or go beyond His words? True prophets will produce good fruit that flows from following the Father's holy laws, as we read in 1 Samuel 24:13, Proverbs 20:11 and Psalm 92:13-14,

'As the proverb of the ancients says, 'Wickedness proceeds from the wicked'.

'Even a child is known by his deeds, whether what he does is pure and right.'

'Those who are planted in the house of the Lord shall flourish in the courts of our God. They shall still bear fruit in old age; they shall be fresh and flourishing.'

Matthew 7:18-20

In verses 18-20, Jesus continues His warning that people will be recognised by their fruits, by their actions. Having been warned against false teachers, His disciples are reminded that this warning also applies in their own lives, saying,

> 'Cannot tree a good fruits evil to bear, nor tree a corrupt fruits good to bear. Every tree not producing fruit good is cut down and into fire is cast. Therefore from the fruits of them ye will know them.'

Jesus was speaking to people who would have been very familiar with the effect of disease on a fruit tree; that the fruit will be both sparse, diseased, and potentially poisonous. As our hearts are, so our actions will be; our actions cast a light on the true state of our hearts. The unrighteous, who do not follow God's laws and statutes, like the diseased tree bear only the actions of the unrighteous. The fruits of righteousness and justice, that God the Father desires His people to bear, are made clear in Old Testament Scripture, as we read for example in Isaiah 3:10 and 5:7,

> 'Say to the righteous that it shall be well with them, for they shall eat the fruit of their doings. Woe to the wicked. It shall be ill with him. For the reward of his hands shall be given him.'

> 'For the vineyard of the Lord of hosts is the house of Israel, and the men of Judah are His pleasant plant. He looked for justice, but behold, oppression; for righteousness, but behold, a cry for help.'

So, Jesus' disciples are called to bear the fruit of righteousness and justice, obeying God's teaching in the Law and the Prophets, taking the narrow path through the 'strait' gate. Often, a diseased tree must be destroyed to prevent disease spreading to other healthy trees. It is a universal reality that whatever has become useless or toxic is eventually disposed of. Jesus is echoing the warning found in Isaiah 5:4-5 where we read,

> 'What more could have been done to My vineyard that I have not done in it? Why then, when I expected it to bring forth good

128

grapes did it bring forth wild grapes? And now, please let Me tell you what I will do to My vineyard: I will take away its hedge, and it shall be burned; and break down its wall, and it shall be trampled down.'

In verse 20, Jesus is repeating what He has said before, that His disciples must be wary of those who make a pretence of holiness or religion and teach a corruption of the truth and whose actions are contrary to God's teaching; that just as plants that are nourished by unpolluted water and soil produce healthy and abundant fruit, so God's people, who feed on His word and are watered by the Spirit, will bear the fruit of righteousness. This we know from promises that we read for example in Ezekiel 47:12, Psalm 1:3, and Jeremiah 17:7-8,

'Along the bank of the river, on this side and that, will grow all kinds of trees used for food; their leaves will not wither, and their fruit will not fail. They will bear fruit every month because their water flows from the sanctuary. Their fruit will be for food, and their leaves for medicine.'

'He shall be like a tree planted by rivers of water, that brings forth its fruit in its season, whose leaf also shall not wither; and whatever he does shall prosper.'

'Blessed is the man who trusts in the Lord, for he shall be like a tree planted by the waters, which spreads out its roots by the river, and will not fear when heat comes; but its leaf will be green and will not be anxious in the year of drought, nor will cease from yielding fruit.'

Matthew 7:21

In verse 21, Jesus continues His teaching that His people will be recognised by the fruit of their lives; that profession of religion, or living a religious life, or studying and believing in the Bible, and even acknowledging God as Lord, is not sufficient to enter His Kingdom if they do not do their Father's will, saying,

> 'Not everyone saying to me Lord, Lord, will enter into the kingdom of the heavens, but the one doing the will of the Father of me in the heavens.'

Jesus is warning His disciples to beware that their actions and lifestyle do not deny what they profess with their mouth. Calling on the Lord in prayer is not of itself a special virtue; the Pharisees were devoted to prayer, as are many who profess to be religious; unless it is part of a life consistent with doing our Father's will, it is meaningless, as we read in Proverbs 1:28-31,

> 'Then they will call on me, but I will not answer; they will seek me diligently, but they will not find me. Because they hated knowledge and did not choose the fear of the Lord, they would have none of my counsel and despised my every rebuke. Therefore, they shall eat the fruit of their own way, and be filled to the full with their own fancies.'

Having taught His disciples that the entrance to the Kingdom is through the 'strait' gate, through the narrow way, Jesus teaches how this is to be done – by doing His Father's will. Those who do not obey cannot enter as we read in Isaiah 59:2, Hosea 7:14 and 8:2-3 and Micah 3:4,

> 'But your iniquities have separated you from your God; and your sins have hidden His face from you, so that He will not hear.'

> 'They did not cry to Me with their heart when they wailed upon their beds.'

> 'Israel will cry to Me 'My God, we know you!' Israel has rejected the good; the enemy will pursue him.'

'Then they will cry to the Lord, but He will not hear them; He will even hide His face from them at that time, because they have been evil in their deeds.'

Jesus' disciples must take care not to be deceived by others, but also not to deceive themselves by following their own will instead of the Father's. We know it is the Father's will to believe in His Son and to obey His statutes, being careful to observe them, as we read of Moses speaking to the Israelites in Deuteronomy 4:5-6 and 30:19-20,

'Surely I have taught you statutes and judgements, just as the Lord my God commanded me, that you should act according to them in the land which you go to possess. Therefore be careful to observe them'

"Therefore choose life, that both you and your descendants may live; that you may love the Lord your God, that you may obey His voice, and that you may cling to Him, for He is your life and the length of your days."

Here there are echoes of Jesus' earlier words about prayer, referring to God's Kingly rule, His will being done on earth as in Heaven; those who are truly His obey His will and enter into His kingdom, as we read in Ezekiel 44:5,

'And the Lord said to me, "Son of man, mark well, see with your eyes and hear with your ears, all that I say to you concerning all the ordinances of the house of the Lord and all its laws. Mark well who may enter the house and all who go out from the sanctuary.'

Matthew 7:22-23

In verses 22-23, Jesus continues His warning about the many who choose the broad way; those who are religious and may be good teachers or preachers, or great authors or theologians, but are not acting under His authority; they may have acted in His name but not according to His will accepting His grace, saying,

> 'Many will say to me in that day, 'Lord, Lord, not in thy name we prophesied, and in thy name demons we expelled, and in thy name mighty works many did?' and then I will declare to them, 'Never I knew you; depart from me the ones working lawlessness.'

Jesus is also continuing the theme that His people will be recognised by their fruits as will false prophets and hypocrites, and those who are motivated by seeing service in the church as a source of profit or public honour. Jesus' words were both prophetic, as we know from the error-strewn history of the established church, but also reflective on the past failures of some Jewish priests and teachers, as we read for example in Jeremiah 5:31, 14:14, and 27:15,

> 'The prophets prophesy falsely, and the priests rule by their own power; and My people love to have it so. But what will you do in the end?'

> 'And the Lord said to me, 'The prophets prophesy lies in My name. I have not sent them, commanded them, nor spoken to them; they prophesy to you a false vision, divination, a worthless thing, and the deceit of their heart.'

> 'For I have not sent them,' says the Lord, 'yet they prophesy a lie in My name, that I may drive you out, and that you may perish, you and the prophets who prophesy to you.'

Jesus goes on to say that He will declare, or profess, that He did not know these people; that their profession is false and deceitful. Jesus makes clear that these people are not known to Him as He knows His own disciples; their fruits condemn them. Jesus warns that prophecy, exorcism, and even miracles are nothing unless His disciples' lives bear the fruit of faith in Him. Those whose lives are based on human understanding of religion, or who are motivated by pursuing their own ends rather than seeking the narrow path that God the Father has set before them, will be ordered to depart from Jesus' presence, as we read in Psalm 5:5-6, 6:8, and 119:115,

> 'The boastful shall not stand in Your sight; You hate all workers of iniquity. You shall destroy those who speak falsehood; the Lord abhors the bloodthirsty and deceitful man.'

> 'Depart from me, all you workers of iniquity.' And 'Depart from me, you evildoers, for I will keep the commandments of my God.'

These are dire warnings, but as we have seen before, they are contrasted with wonderful promises in Scripture. These promises are for those who Jesus does know, for those who choose life, who choose the strait gate, who seek always to remain in His truth and righteousness, faithfully following His commandments and statutes, whose motivation is for His kingdom to come, as we read for example in Psalm 15:1-2 and Psalm 24:3-4,

> 'Lord, who may abide in Your tabernacle? Who may dwell in Your holy hill? He who walks uprightly, and works righteousness, and speaks the truth in his heart.'

> 'Who may ascend into the hill of the Lord? Or who may stand in His holy place? He who has clean hands and a pure heart.'

Matthew 7:24-27

In verses 24-27, Jesus concludes His 'Sermon on the Mount' by contrasting the outcomes for those who listen to His words and then do as He says with those who listen unheeding, saying,

> 'Everyone therefore who hears of me words these and does them, shall be likened man to a prudent, who built of him the house on the rock. And came down the rain and came the rivers and blew the winds and fell against house that, and not it fell; for it had been founded on the rock. And everyone hearing of me words these and not doing them shall be likened man to a foolish, who built of him the house on the sand. And came down the rain and came the rivers and blew the winds and beat against house that and it fell and was the fall of it great.'

A similar analogy to that used by Jesus is found in Ezekiel 13, in which false prophets are condemned, referring to buildings failing against the storms. The false prophets made their pronouncements seem plausible by an outward semblance of truth, using 'untempered mortar'. This is mortar that is not mixed properly with the exact ingredients and will only last a short time and wash away in heavy rain. Mortar that is brought to its proper consistency following the correct instructions will last for centuries. So, we read for example in verses 13-14,

> 'Thus says the Lord God: 'I will cause a stormy wind to break forth in My fury; and there shall be a flooding rain in My anger, and great hailstones in fury to consume it. So I will break down the wall you have plastered with untempered mortar, and bring it down to the ground, so that its foundation will be uncovered; it will fall, and you shall be consumed in the midst of it. Then you shall know that I am the Lord.'

Jesus' words also echo those found in Job and Proverbs that speak of those who are unrighteous or foolish who will fall, be overthrown or swept away, and of those who are righteous, who keep God's commands and precepts, who will stand on a firm foundation, as we read for example in Job 22:16, Proverbs 10:8, Proverbs 10:25, and Proverbs 12:7,

'Will you keep to the old way which wicked men have trod, who were cut down before their time, whose foundations were swept away by a flood?'

'The wise in heart will receive commands, but a prating fool will fall.'

'When the whirlwind passes by, the wicked is no more, but the righteous has an everlasting foundation.'

'The wicked are overthrown and are no more, but the house of the righteous will stand.'

Jesus requires that His disciple not only hear His words, but they must 'do' accordingly. Consider the words of Ezekiel 33:31-32 and ask yourself how often we go to church and enjoy the singing and the music, the fellowship, the familiar readings and yet not 'do' His word, we read,

'So they come to you as people do, they sit before you as My people, and they hear your words, but they do not do them; for with their mouth they show much love, but their hearts pursue their own gain. Indeed you are to them as a very lovely song of one who has a pleasant voice and can play well on an instrument; for they hear your words, but they do not do them.'

We have the promise that those who hear the words of Jesus and does them will stand on the rock forever, as we read for example in Psalm 125:1-2,

'Those who trust in the Lord are like Mount Zion which cannot be moved but abides forever. As the mountains surround Jerusalem, so the Lord surrounds His people from this time forth and forever.'

135

MATTHEW CHAPTER EIGHT

Matthew 8:3

At the beginning of Chapter 8, Jesus is met by a leper who says to Him "Lord, if you are willing, You can make me clean." Jesus reached out and touched the leper, saying,

> 'I am willing, be thou cleansed.'

The first words Jesus spoke were to confirm to the leper that He was indeed willing. He also confirmed His divine right to be asked. Jesus did not say 'I am sure God is willing'; but the words 'I am willing' conveyed His supreme authority, that required no supplication to a higher power, and also the will to exercise that authority on behalf of the leper who acknowledged himself to be unclean. When Jesus spoke, what He commanded was done, as we read in Psalm 33: 9 and again in Psalm 148:5,

> 'For He spoke, and it was done; He commanded, and it stood fast.'

> 'Let them praise the name of the Lord, for He commanded and they were created.'

There are examples in Old Testament Scripture when God had restored the flesh of a person. For example, Moses' hand was first made leprous and then restored by God as a sign to the people while they were still in Egypt, as we read in Exodus 4:7,

> 'And He said, 'Put your hand in your bosom again.' So he put his hand in his bosom, and drew it out of his bosom, and behold, it was restored like his other flesh.'

There is also the detailed account of Naaman, in 2 Kings chapter 5, who's skin was restored by God when he followed the instructions given to him by Elisha, as we read in verse 14,

> 'So he went down and dipped seven times in the Jordan, according to the saying of the man of God; and his flesh was restored like the flesh of a little child, and he was clean.'

It is interesting to note that the leper did not ask Jesus to heal him but used the word 'katharisai' which means 'to cleanse'. Our contemporary word 'cathartic' can be traced back to this Greek word and was introduced into English as a medical term meaning to purge the person of unwanted material both in mind and body. Jesus' reply is that the leper is cleansed – not healed. The implication is that this had significance beyond the restoration of the flesh; that the man was also restored ceremonially which meant that he would be able to participate fully in worship and Jewish ceremony; that he would no longer be 'unclean'. To be ceremonially unclean was to be separated from God's people, as we read in Numbers 19:20,

> 'But the man who is unclean and does not purify himself, that person shall be cut off from among the assembly, because he has defiled the sanctuary of the Lord. The water of purification has not been sprinkled on him; he is unclean.'

Jesus' disciples can know with confidence that God is willing to cleanse and restore, in body mind and spirit, those who seek and ask, as we read for example in Psalm 51:7 and Lamentations 5:21,

> 'Purge me with hyssop, and I shall be clean; wash me and I shall be whiter than snow.'

> 'Turn us back to You, O Lord, and we will be restored.'

Matthew 8:4

In verse 4, Jesus demonstrates the truth of His earlier assertion in Chapter 5:17 that He had not come to destroy the Law or the Prophets, but to fulfil it, when he speaks to the leper who had been cleansed, saying,

> 'See to no one thou tellest but go thyself show to the priest and offer the gift which commanded Moses, for a testimony to them.'

Jesus told the man not to talk about what had happened before he had presented himself to the priest. Since leprosy is highly contagious, the law of Moses forbade the man to break the social distancing regulations until he had obtained the testimony of the priest that he was clean, taking with him the required gifts for this purpose, as we read in Leviticus 14:2, 4, and 10,

> 'This shall be the law of the leper for the day of his cleansing: he shall be brought to the priest.' And 'Then the priest shall command to take for him who is to be cleansed two living and clean birds, cedar wood, scarlet, and hyssop.'

> 'On the eighth day he shall take two male lambs without blemish, one ewe lamb of the first year without blemish, three-tenths of an ephah of fine flour mixed with oil as a grain offering, and one log of oil.'

By insisting that the man made his offering, Jesus was confirming His relationship to the Law; that He had not come to destroy or contradict it, and we read in Psalm 19:7,

> 'The law of the Lord is perfect, converting the soul; the testimony of the Lord is sure.'

In obedience to the Law, Jesus reminded the man that the gifts should be offered as a sacrifice of thanksgiving to God. Under the Law, a sacrifice was the seal of cleansing that required the shedding of blood of an unblemished lamb. This was made perfectly clear in both the Law and the prophets, that the sacrificial lamb should be offered and that it should be without blemish, as we read in Exodus 12:5 and Malachi 1:14,

'Your lamb shall be without blemish, a male of the first year. You may take it from the sheep or the goats.'

'But cursed be the deceiver who has in his flock a male, and takes a vow, but sacrifices to the Lord what is blemished.'

The Greek word 'martyrion' used here for testimony also means witness, proof, demonstration of some fact, piece of evidence, or attestation. Our word martyr comes from this Greek word, so that a martyr is one who bears testimony to their faith or one who bears witness to their faith. It was for the priest to attest or bear testimony as to whether an individual was clean and had therefore cause to demonstrate their gratitude to God according to the Law. An individual was not legally clean until the priest had seen and agreed the evidence, and following this, the man would be restored to the community with all the associated privileges of social and religious life. Through Jesus' words, His disciples were reminded that it is an unblemished sacrificial gift that confers cleansing, and that as part of worship, God's people are called to bring offerings of thanksgiving, as we read in Psalm 96:7-9,

'Give to the Lord, O families of the peoples, give to the Lord glory and strength. Give to the Lord the glory due His name; bring an offering and come into His courts. O worship the Lord in the beauty of holiness! Tremble before Him all the earth.'

141

Matthew 8:7

In verse 7, Jesus is responding to a request for help for the paralysed servant of a centurion, a gentile, saying,

> 'I having come will heal him.'

Although the centurion was a gentile, Jesus did not hesitate, but told the man that he would come. By His action, Jesus demonstrated to His disciples that the Father cares for all His children, as we read in Job 36:5, 'Behold God is mighty, but despises no one.' He would also have been familiar with the prophecy concerning himself in Isaiah, that God's covenant was to be to all people including the gentiles, as we read in Isaiah 42:6,

> 'I will keep You and give You as a covenant to the people, as a light to the Gentiles.'

Jesus then told the centurion that He would heal the man. There was no equivocation; Jesus did not say that He would come and see what He could do, or see if He could help, or that He might help if... He makes an absolute promise that He will heal. Again, Jesus would have been familiar with the prophecy concerning Himself in Isaiah where we read in Chapter 53:5,

> 'But He was wounded for our transgressions, He was bruised for our iniquities; the chastisement for our peace was upon Him, and by His stripes we are healed.'

There are many places in Old Testament Scripture where God names Himself, including 'I Am who I Am' in Exodus 3:14. He also said that He is 'The God of all flesh' in Jeremiah 32:27 and Jesus may well have had this in mind when he spoke with a gentile. But Jesus also knew, when He said that He would heal the man, that one of the names God has given Himself is 'The Lord who heals', as we read in Exodus 15:26,

> 'If you diligently heed the voice of the Lord your God and do what is right in His sight, give ear to His commandments and keep all His statutes, I will put none of the diseases on you which I have brought on the Egyptians. For I am the Lord who heals you.'

The Greek word that Jesus used here for 'heal' is 'therapeusō', which meant to do service, take care of, provide for, attend to, or to treat. In this instance then, Jesus was not referring to spiritual or ceremonial cleansing, but the treatment of the bodily condition; to attend to the man's needs and restore his health. Jesus would have known the promises that God's people, who have a contrite heart and have been redeemed, will be healed as we read in Psalm 107:20, Isaiah 57:18, and Jeremiah 30:17,

> 'He sent His word and healed them and delivered them from their destructions.'

> 'I have seen his ways, and will heal him, and restore comforts to him and to his mourners.'

> 'For I will restore health to you and heal you of your wounds, says the Lord.'

Jesus also knew that the Father's nature is to heal when we ask, as we read for example in Psalm 30:2; 103:2-3 and Jeremiah 17:14,

> 'O Lord my God, I cried out to You, and You healed me.'

> 'Bless the Lord, O my soul, and forget not all His benefits; who forgives all your iniquities, who heals all your diseases.'

> 'Heal me, O Lord, and I shall be healed; save me, and I shall be saved.'

Matthew 8:10-12

In verses 10-12, Jesus contrasts the lack of faith, or confidence in His power to heal, that He found among the Jewish leaders with that of the centurion, and uses the opportunity to announce that the Kingdom of God would be received by the gentiles, saying,

> 'Truly I tell you, from no one such faith in Israel I found. And I tell you that many from east and west will come and will recline with Abraham and Isaac and Jacob in the kingdom of the heavens; but the sons of the kingdom will be cast out into the darkness outer; there will be weeping and gnashing of the teeth.'

The centurion did not ask for signs, or proof, but asked only for a word of command. Clearly, he was convinced that Jesus was no ordinary man, but a prophet sent from God. Jesus, acknowledging the faith of this gentile, then refers to Abraham, the first to demonstrate righteous faith in God, and He would have been perfectly familiar with the promises made by God to Abraham that through him all the people on earth would be blessed; all the nations on earth, as we read in Genesis 12:3 and 22:18,

> 'I will bless those who bless you, and I will curse him who curses you; and in you all the families of the earth shall be blessed.'

> 'In your seed all the nations of the earth shall be blessed, because you have obeyed My voice.'

The phrase 'from the east and west' was used to mean the whole world and Jesus is here making clear to His disciples that God's blessings were to be enjoyed also by the gentiles, from peoples all over the world. He also says that these people will 'recline' with Abraham, Isaac, and Jacob. This referred to the manner that people ate their meals; the way they would feast or banquet, suggesting that gentiles, who have been redeemed, would also share in the honour of feasting with the Patriarchs, as we read in Psalm 107:1-3 and Isaiah 49:11-12,

> 'Oh give thanks to the Lord, for He is good. For His mercy endures forever. Let the redeemed of the Lord say so, whom He has redeemed from the hand of the enemy and gathered out of the

lands, from the east and from the west, from the north and from the south.'

'I will make each of My mountains a road, and My highways shall be elevated. Surely these shall come from afar, look! Those from the north and the west, and these from the land of Sinim.'

Jesus declares that gentiles will also receive the same salvation with Abraham; the same promise that was formerly given to the Jewish fathers, an inheritance in common with them, if they demonstrate the same faith as Abraham, as did the centurion. Jesus' words also contain a warning that those who persist in rebellion to God's word, even if they are descendants of Abraham, will become irreconcilable in their sin and unable to enter into His presence. Jesus' message to His listeners would have been a hard one; He warns that God will exclude those who consider themselves sons of the kingdom but who do not abide by His word, and will also admit those they would have considered as outsiders, the gentiles, but who do abide by His word, into His glorious kingdom, as we read in Malachi 1:11,

'For from the rising of the sun, even to the going down, My name shall be great among the gentiles; in every place incense shall be offered to My name, and a pure offering; for My name shall be great among the nations, says the Lord of hosts.'

Matthew 8:13

In verse 13, Jesus speaks again to the centurion, the gentile, and confirms that what he has asked of Jesus will be done and that it will be done according to the confidence that the centurion has shown in Jesus, saying,

> 'Go, as thou believest let it be to thee.'

This was an example of someone being healed from a distance, without being directly in Jesus' presence, and there is no indication that it was even at the request of the servant, but of his master – the centurion. There is also no indication that the centurion lingered to ask for proof, or for some kind of demonstration, but appears to have accepted Jesus at His word and set off for home. The word that Jesus used here for 'believe', that translates into the Greek as 'pisteuó', was the same word as that used in the account of Abraham. Abraham believed God as we read in Genesis 15:6,

> 'And he believed in the Lord, and He accounted it to him for righteousness.'

This Greek word - pisteuó – means: to believe, to have faith in, to trust in, to be persuaded or to persuade oneself; to consider something to be true and worthy of one's trust; to accept as true, genuine, or real; to have a firm conviction as to the ability or efficacy of someone; to consider to be true. In secular Greek literature, as well as in the New Testament, the word had a basic meaning of intellectual assent or a belief that something is true; the word conveys the idea of being sure or persuaded that something is a fact. It can also mean to entrust oneself to an entity in complete confidence; to believe in with the implication of total commitment to the one who is trusted. Such was the faith of Abraham and such was the faith of the centurion. The same word is used when the Israelites in the wilderness failed to believe, as we read in Psalm 78:22 and 32, and in Psalm 106:24,

> 'Because they did not believe in God and did not trust in His salvation.'

'In spite of this they still sinned and did not believe in His wondrous works.' And 'Then they despised the pleasant land; they did not believe His word.'

It is interesting to note that Jesus said "*As* thou believest", not *because* thou believest. Faith, or trust, is a grace that gives glory to God; the reward of faith is not from the 'work' of believing, so that God owes His people in any way, but it is from His grace. In these words, Jesus is teaching His disciples that what will be to them will be according to their faith. When God's people believed His words, as exemplified in the Exodus, they received His mighty works. When His people believe that God can do something, He will do it, and Jesus here reminds His listeners of this truth. Time and again, His people are exhorted to trust in Him, as we read for example in Psalm 37:3, Psalm 37:5, and Psalm 84:12,

'Trust in the Lord, and do good; dwell in the land, and feed on His faithfulness.'

'Commit your way to the Lord, trust also in Him, and He shall bring it to pass.'

'O Lord of hosts, blessed is the man who trusts in You.'

Again we find that this is a promise that we can trust; that as we believe, it will be done for us, as we read also in Isaiah 26:4,

'You will keep him in perfect peace, whose mind is stayed on You, because he trusts in You. Trust in the Lord forever, for in the Lord is everlasting strength.'

Matthew 8:20

In verse 20, Jesus replied to a scribe who had just declared that he would follow Jesus wherever He would go, saying,

> "The foxes holes have and the birds of the heaven nests, but the Son of man has not where his head may lay."

This is typically thought to be a warning about the cost of discipleship; a warning that, unlike even the wild animals, Jesus did not know where He might find shelter for the night and His disciples would have to expect the same. However, it is worth noting that the Greek word translated here as fox (alōpekes) can also mean fox-like, a crafty or cunning person of uncertain origin. Also, the Greek word translated as hole or den (phōleous) can mean a lair or lurking place. This is contrasted with the birds of the air who have temporary shelter; the Greek word Jesus used (kataskēnōseis) means a perch, a shelter or even a tent. Perhaps Jesus was questioning whether there was a place for Him in the man's heart and if he truly desired to dwell with Jesus in God's house, as we read in Psalm 84:3-4,

> 'Even the sparrow has found a home, and the swallow a nest for herself where she may lay her young, at Your alters, O Lord of hosts, My King and my God. Blessed are those who dwell in Your house; ever singing Your praise.'

In His reply, Jesus refers to Himself as the 'Son of man'. In the Hebrew, this is 'ben-adam' – son of Adam. This is a title that Jesus used Himself to refer to Himself many times in the Gospels. His listeners would doubtless have been aware that this was a title given to the prophet Ezekiel by God and thus may have been a reference to His own ministry, likening it to God's commission of Ezekiel to speak to the people of Israel, as we read in Ezekiel 2:3-5,

> 'And He said to me: "Son of man, I am sending you to the children of Israel, to a rebellious nation that has rebelled against Me; they and their fathers have transgressed against Me to this very day. For they are impudent and stubborn children. I am sending you to them, and you shall say to them, 'Thus says the Lord God.' As for them, whether they hear or whether they refuse, for they are

a rebellious house, yet they will know that a prophet has been amongst them."

Jesus' disciples would also have recognised the words 'Son of Man' as a Messianic title from the vision of Daniel. The kingdom over which the Son of Man was to have dominion was not to be a fixed habitation on earth, neither would it be an earthly dwelling for those who choose to follow Him, as we read in Daniel 7:13-14,

'I was watching in the night visions, and behold, one like the Son of Man, coming with the clouds of heaven. He came to the Ancient of Days, and they brought Him near before Him. Then to Him was given dominion and glory and a kingdom, that all peoples, nations, and languages should serve Him.'

To follow Jesus, wherever He would go, is to allow Him to have a dwelling place in our hearts and not turn back from following Him and call upon His name, as we read in Psalm 80:17-18,

'Let your hand be upon the man of your right hand, upon the son of man whom You made strong for Yourself. Then we will not turn back from You; revive us, and we will call upon Your name.'

Matthew 8:22

In verse 22, Jesus responds to one of His disciples who has just said to Him that he wanted to go first to bury his father, saying,

> "Follow thou me and leave the dead to bury the of themselves dead."

Again, this is typically thought to be a warning as to the cost of discipleship. The suggestion is not that Jesus disapproved of a proper burial, but that His disciples should put their duty to God first; that the proclamation of the Kingdom of God should not be neglected because of the presumed duties of men. The Greek word that Jesus used here, 'nekros' literally meant one who had deceased, but it was also used as a metaphor for spiritual death. Jesus' listeners would have understood that in the metaphorical sense it would be possible for the spiritually dead to bury the dead; the Jews considered a person who transgressed against, or departed from, the Law to be 'dead'. It is also worth noting that to be burying the dead would have meant the disciple defiling himself and becoming ceremonially unclean for a week, as we read in Numbers 19:11,

> 'He who touches the dead body of anyone shall be unclean for seven days.'

After the seven days, the person then had to go through a ritual purification, if not they would defile the tabernacle of the Lord. When God spoke to Moses at Mount Sinai, He told him 'You shall be to Me a kingdom of priests and a Holy nation' (Exodus 19:6). Perhaps Jesus was here reminding His disciples that as a 'kingdom of priests' their actions must not in any way profane the sanctuary of God, and as a Holy nation they were to separate themselves to the Lord – to be holy to the Lord - as did the Nazirites, as we read in Numbers 6:6-7,

> 'All the days that he separates himself to the Lord he shall not go near a dead body. He shall not make himself unclean even for his father or his mother, for his brother or his sister when they die, because his separation to God is on his head.'

There are parallels in this passage with that found in 1 Kings 19, in which Elijah indicates to Elisha that he should follow him. Elisha asked to say farewell to his parents at which point Elijah makes it clear that it was not him that had called Elisha to follow him, but it was God's calling, as we read in verse 20,

> 'And he left the oxen and ran after Elijah and said, "Please let me kiss my father and my mother, and then I will follow you." And he said to him, "Go back again, for what have I done to you?"'

In this short phrase, Jesus conveys to His disciples that they are spiritually alive; that as a kingdom of priests they are to keep themselves from defiling the Kingdom, and as members of a Holy nation, they are to keep themselves from being spiritually defiled. Because of their separation to the service of God, they need to keep themselves free from distraction and to keep their obedience to Him as their first and unwavering priority, as we read for example in Psalm 115:17-18,

> 'The dead do not praise the Lord, nor any who go down into silence. But we will bless the Lord from this time forth and forevermore. Praise the Lord!'

Matthew 8:26

In verse 26, Jesus responds to His disciples who ask Him to save them from a frightening storm while they are in a boat on the Sea of Galilee, saying,

"Why fearful are ye, Little faiths?"

The Greek word 'oligopistoi', translated as little-faiths (of little faith), means incredulous or lacking in confidence. Jesus' disciples, even knowing that He was on board, still showed fear and unbelief. Time and again the Old Testament Scripture speaks of the Lord's sovereignty over His creation and man's lack of confidence in that power to redeem and deliver, even Sarah and Moses doubted His power, as we read for example in Genesis 18:14, Numbers 11:23, Isaiah 59:1, and Isaiah 50:2,

'Is anything too hard for the Lord?'

'The Lord said to Moses "Has the Lord's arm been shortened? Now you shall see whether what I say will happen to you or not."

'Behold, the Lord's hand is not shortened that it cannot save; nor His ear heavy that it cannot hear.'

'Why, when I came was there no man? Why, when I called, was there none to answer? Is My hand shortened at all that it cannot redeem? Or have I no power to deliver? Indeed, with My rebuke I dry up the sea.'

We are told that after Jesus had spoken to His disciples, He then rebuked the winds and the sea, as if treating the tempest as hostile and in need of restraint. It is interesting to note that waves are caused by the wind and Jesus addressed the cause of the storm. This incident would have had great significance for the witnesses in the boat as they would have been familiar with the references in Scripture to God's awesome power over the seas and the elements. Jesus here demonstrated His divine power and gave further proof that He is the Son of God with the same power to rule the sea, as in Job 38:8, Naham 1:4, Proverbs 8:29, & 30:4,

'Or who shut in the sea with doors when it burst forth and issued from the womb?'

'He rebukes the sea and makes it dry.'

'When He assigned to the sea its limit, so that the waters would not transgress His command when He marked out the foundations of the earth.'

'Who has ascended into heaven, or descended? Who has gathered the wind in His fists? Who has bound the waters in a garment? Who has established all the ends of the earth? What is His name, and what is His son's name, if you know?'

Jesus uses His awesome power to deliver and redeem, to calm and still, as we read in Psalm 89:9 and Psalm 107:28-30,

'You rule the raging of the sea; when its waves rise, you still them.'

'Then they cry out to the Lord in their trouble, and He brings them out of their distresses. He calms the storm, so that its waves are still. Then they are glad because they are quiet; so He guides them to their desired haven.'

Richard Wurmbrand[2] once wrote "A ship full of water sinks – but not if it is Jesus' ship. It goes forward when no wind blows in its sails; it glides on when the oarsmen have become lazy and do not row anymore. The church advances even when it is filled to the brim with heresies, schisms, and sins that make her the mockery of men. It advances contrary to the laws of hydrodynamics. It is the only ship which stays afloat and sails on though full of water, because its motivation is the right one." Jesus' disciples can have confidence in the God of our salvation as we read in Psalm 65:5-7,
'By awesome deeds in righteousness You will answer us, O God of our salvation. You who are the confidence of all the ends of the earth, and of the far-off seas; who established the mountains by His strength, being clothed with power; You who still the noise of the seas, the noise of their waves, and the tumult of the peoples.'

---

[2] Richard Wurmbrand (1977) Reaching Towards The Heights (November 6) Basingstoke: Marshall Morgan & Scott

MATTHEW CHAPTER NINE

Matthew 9:2

In verse 2, Jesus speaks to a paralytic who has been brought to Him by his friends, lying on his bed. We can assume that he has been brought to Jesus for healing and He responds saying,

> 'Be of good cheer, child, are forgiven of thee the sins.'

The Greek word 'tharseó', translated here as good cheer also means to be of good courage; to radiate warm confidence; to be emboldened from within. Jesus reminds His listeners that God emboldens those who trust in Him, empowering them with a bold inner attitude of faith. By showing an unflinching bold courage, His disciples demonstrate their inner confidence in God the Father which manifests itself as joy, as we read in Ecclesiastes 9:7,

> 'Go, eat your bread with joy, and drink your wine with a merry heart, for God has already accepted your works.'

Jesus addresses the paralytic as 'téknon'. This Greek word literally means child but can also mean a descendent or anyone living in full dependence - and in this context dependence on our heavenly Father. Jesus taught His disciples to rely on the Lord in utter dependence, and by using this word He emphasized the childlike attitude that gladly submits to the Father's plan, as we read in Proverbs 3:1-2 and 11-12,

> 'My son, do not forget my law, but let your heart keep my commands; for length of days and long life and peace they will add to you.'

> 'My son, do not despise the chastening of the Lord, nor detest His correction; for whom the Lord loves He corrects, just as a father the son in whom he delights.'

It was Jesus' next words that got Him into trouble with the religious leaders. He tells the man that his sins are forgiven, 'aphientai' – they are sent forth, sent away, permitted to depart, let go, to be disregarded. Christ here demonstrated to His disciples that the problem of sin has to be dealt with first, that it is the most important element to be dealt with, and possibly the root cause of the illness. King Hezekiah after his physical healing went on to thank God that his sins had been cast away; Scripture makes clear links between sickness and forgiveness, and that forgiveness comes first, as we read in Isaiah 38:17, 33:24, and Psalm 103:3,

'But You have lovingly delivered my soul from the pit of corruption, for You have cast all my sins behind Your back.'

'The inhabitants [of Jerusalem] will not say, "I am sick"; the people who dwell in it will be forgiven their iniquity.'

'Bless the Lord 'Who forgives all your iniquities, who heals all your diseases.'

Jesus, in these words, made it abundantly clear to His disciples that being reconciled to God is more important than anything else and that those who have confidence in the Father and call on Him will receive His mercy and blessing, as we read in Psalm 32:1-2, Psalm 86:5, and Jeremiah 31:34,

'Blessed is he whose transgression is forgiven, whose sin is covered. Blessed is the man to whom the Lord does not impute iniquity, and in whose spirit there is no deceit.'

'For You, Lord, are good and ready to forgive, and abundant in mercy to all those who call upon You.'

'They all shall know Me, from the least of them to the greatest of them, says the Lord. For I will forgive their iniquity, and their sin I will remember no more.'

Matthew 9:4-6

In verses 4-6, Jesus makes it clear that He knows the thoughts of the scribes who were present, saying,

> "Why think ye evil things in the hearts of you? For which is easier, to say: are forgiven of thee the sins, or to say: rise and walk? But in order that ye may know that authority has the Son of man on the earth to forgive sins" – then he says to the paralytic: "Rise, take of thee the mattress and go to the house of thee."

By telling the scribes what the thoughts in their hearts were, Jesus was offering proof of His divinity and was fulfilling the prophecy found in Isaiah that speaks about the Messiah who in righteousness will judge by the spirit of God, as we read in chapter 11 verse 3,

> 'His delight is in the fear of the Lord, and He shall not judge by the sight of His eyes, nor decide by the hearing of His ears.'

Jesus saw their thoughts, and His words echo those found in Zechariah 8:17, Proverbs 3:29, and Jeremiah 4:14, where we read,

> 'Let none of you think evil in your heart against your neighbour.'

> 'Do not devise evil against your neighbour, for he dwells by you for safety's sake.'

> 'O Jerusalem, wash your heart from wickedness, that you may be saved. How long will your evil thoughts lodge within you?'

Only God can search the heart; no sin escapes His notice. Jesus affirms His relationship to God by exposing the secret thoughts of the scribes. Scripture makes it clear that though sin may be unseen by other people, and as yet unacknowledged by ourselves, God searches out and knows all that we think and are both consciously and subconsciously, as we read in Psalm 44:21 and 139:2, and Jeremiah 17:10,

> 'Would not God search this out? For He knows the secrets of the heart.'

'You know my sitting down and my rising up; You understand my thought afar off. You comprehend my path and my lying down and are acquainted with all my ways.'

'I, the Lord, search the heart, I test the mind, even to give every man according to his ways, according to the fruit of his doings.'

Jesus then asks His listeners to consider which is easier, to forgive or to heal, knowing that unless He could do both, He could do neither; that neither could be done but by God. Jesus knew that His critics could not deny His right to forgive the sins of the paralytic when He restored him to health; one healing (the physical) became the proof and establishment of the other healing (the spiritual). His listeners would doubtless have been reminded of the prophecy concerning the Messiah in Isaiah 35:5-6 where we read,

'Then the eyes of the blind shall be opened, and the ears of the deaf shall be unstopped. Then the lame shall leap like a deer, and the tongue of the dumb sing.'

Finally, Jesus tells the paralytic to get up and go home as proof of his healing. He was able to rise, stand upright, and walk where Jesus told him to, knowing that his sins were forgiven as promised in Isaiah 43:25:

'I, even I, am He who blots out your transgressions for My own sake; and I will not remember your sins.'

Matthew 9:12-13

In verses 12-13, Jesus responds to the Pharisees, who question why He was eating with tax collectors and sinners, saying,

> "Not need have the ones being strong of a physician but the ones ill having. But going, learn ye what it is: Mercy I desire and not sacrifice; not for I came to call righteous but sinners."

Jesus may have been suggesting that the Pharisees, who considered themselves holy, did not need His aid. Instead, He was there for those who acknowledged their sin, their spiritual ill health, and their need to receive His mercy and healing. Jesus did not go to these people because they received Him warmly, but because they needed Him. Old Testament Scripture makes clear that spiritual healing is part of the nature of God, as we read for example in Psalm 6:2, Psalm 41:4, and Psalm 147:3,

> 'Have mercy on me, O Lord, for I am weak; O Lord heal me for my bones are troubled.'

> 'I said, "Lord be merciful to me; heal my soul, for I have sinned against you."'

> 'He heals the broken hearted and binds up their wounds.'

Jesus then recommends that the Pharisees go and read the passage from Hosea in order better to understand that He had not come for those who considered themselves righteous by virtue of their religious observance, but for those who acknowledge their sin in humility. This was a direct challenge to the insincere sacrificial rites that Hosea prophesied about, as we read in chapter 6:6, Proverbs 21:3 and 1 Samuel 15:22,

> 'For I desire mercy and not sacrifice, and the knowledge of God more than burnt offerings.'

> 'To do righteousness and justice is more acceptable to the Lord than sacrifice.'

"Has the Lord as great delight in burnt offerings and sacrifices as in obeying the voice of the Lord? Behold, to obey is better than sacrifice, and to heed than the fat of rams."

There is no virtue in sacrifice of itself; it was instituted by Moses as a sign of repentance, thankfulness, and redemption. Without these, any sacrifice would be meaningless and not what God had intended, as we read in Jeremiah 7:22-23,

'For I did not speak to your fathers, or command them in the day that I brought them out of the land of Egypt, concerning burnt offerings or sacrifices. But this is what I commanded them, saying 'Obey My voice, and I will be your God, and you shall be My people. And walk in all the ways that I have commanded you, that it may be well with you.'

It is worth considering what this may mean in contemporary life, for example, the time spent at church may have become merely a ritual sacrifice. Jesus reminds His disciples that God has also made it clear what He has intended and desires from His people: mercy, justice, righteousness, and obedience, as we read in Micah 6:8, Psalm 51:16-17, and Amos 5:22-24,

'He has shown you, O man, what is good; and what does the Lord require of you but to do justly, to love mercy, and to walk humbly with your God?'

'For You do not desire sacrifice, or else I would give it; You do not delight in burnt offering. The sacrifices of God are a broken spirit, and broken and a contrite heart – these, O God, You will not despise.'

'Though you offer Me burnt offerings and your grain offerings, I will not accept them, nor will I regard your fattened peace offerings. Take away from Me the noise of your songs, for I will not hear the melody of your stringed instruments. But let justice run down like water, and righteousness like a mighty stream.'

Matthew 9:15

In verse 15, Jesus responds to John's disciples who ask why His disciples do not fast, saying,

> 'And said to them Jesus: not can the sons of the bridechamber to mourn, so long as with them is the bridegroom? Will come but days when is taken away from them the bridegroom, and then they will fast.'

The friends of the bridegroom, also translated as sons/children of the bridechamber, were those who accompanied the bridegroom to the house of his father-in-law when he went to fetch his bride home. By having the presence of Christ, the bridegroom, with them, they would be expected to be celebrating a time of joy and feasting, not sorrow and fasting. The companions of the bridegroom were, by tradition, exempt from obligations including fasting and mourning; it was a time to rejoice, as we read in Isaiah 62:10,

> 'I will greatly rejoice in the Lord, my soul shall be joyful in my God; for He has clothed me with the garments of salvation, He has covered me with the robe of righteousness, as a bridegroom decks himself with ornaments, and as a bride adorns herself with her jewels.'

By referring to Himself as the bridegroom, Jesus was once again claiming to be the Messiah by alluding to the prophesies that talk of His relationship to Jerusalem, that is His people, and that the kingdom 'banquet' was imminent. God clearly likens His people to a bride to whom He has betrothed Himself for eternity and likens Himself to the bridegroom, or husband, who delights in His bride, as we read in Isaiah 54:5, Isaiah 62:4-5, and Hosea 1:16 and 19-20,

> 'For your Maker is your husband, the Lord of hosts is His name; and your Redeemer is the Holy One of Israel; He is called the God of the whole earth.'

> 'For the Lord delights in you and your land shall be married. For as a young man marries a virgin, so shall your sons marry you;

and as the bridegroom rejoices over the bride, so shall your God rejoice over you.'

'And it shall be in that day,' says the Lord, 'that you will call Me 'My Husband,' and no longer call Me 'My Master' [...] I will betroth you to Me forever; yes, I will betroth you to Me in righteousness and justice, in loving kindness and mercy; I will betroth you to Me in faithfulness, and you shall know the Lord.'

Jesus goes on to acknowledge that there will come a time when His disciples will fast. During the wedding celebrations there is no place for mourning or fasting, but after the feasting what is appropriate behaviour changes; there is an appropriate time for joy and sorrow as we read in Ecclesiastes 3:4 and 17,

'A time to weep, and a time to laugh; a time to mourn and a time to dance.'

'I said in my heart, 'God shall judge the righteous and the wicked, for there is a time for every purpose and for every work.'

The time for mourning that Jesus knew would come was also clearly spoken of in the prophets, as we read in Zechariah 12:10,

'And I will pour on the house of David and on the inhabitants of Jerusalem the Spirit of grace and supplication; then they will look on Me whom they pierced. Yes, they will mourn for Him as one mourns for his only son and grieve for Him as one grieves for a firstborn.'

Matthew 9:16-17

In verses 16-17, Jesus continues His teaching about appropriate response and fitness for purpose, saying,

> "No one now puts a patch cloth of unfulled on garment an old; for takes away the fullness of it from the garment, and a worse rent becomes. Neither do they put wine new into wineskins old; otherwise, are burst the wineskins, and the wine is poured out and the wineskins are destroyed. But they put wine new into wineskins fresh, and both are preserved."

The Greek word often translated as 'unshrunk', literally translates as 'unfulled'. Fulling cloth involved two processes: scouring and milling (thickening); this was done by pounding the woollen cloth with a club. In Roman times, stale urine – a source of ammonium salts – was used to cleanse and whiten the cloth. The 'thickening' gave the cloth strength and increased its waterproofing. An 'unfulled' patch would cause the whole garment to become 'unfulled', or if you think about the waterproofing of fulling, you could say that the garment that had a leak remains leaky. Jesus may have been teaching His disciples not to expect to continue with old traditions of religion (those that were additional to the Law); that He had not come to repair, improve, or update existing religious practices or put a patch on an old system that had become corrupt as we can read in the prophet Micah 3:9-11,

> 'Now hear this, you heads of the house of Jacob and rulers of the house of Israel, who abhor justice and pervert all equity, who build up Zion with bloodshed and Jerusalem with iniquity; her heads judge for a bribe, her priests teach for pay, and her prophets divine for money.'

Judaism had become inflexible from the accumulation of centuries of non-Scriptural traditions. Jesus had not come to reform the old traditions, but to teach people to have a new heart for God and His laws. Over the centuries, unscriptural man-made traditions have also established themselves in the Christian church; traditions that have become brittle and worn out; systems into which people still try to pour in new wine without bursting the old skins. New skins or bottles would yield to the fermenting wine and be strong enough to hold it from bursting. Perhaps Jesus was saying that it would not be fitting for His teaching to be attached to the old and often corrupt religious practices of the Pharisees; His disciples should not expect to fit His teaching into these old and worn-out traditions; man-made traditions that made God's Law void; man-made righteousness that cannot be mended – the old garments of sin cannot be repaired but must be thrown away in order to walk in God's ways as we read in Psalm 119:81-83,

> 'My soul faints for Your salvation, but I hope in Your word. My eyes fail from searching Your word, saying "When will You comfort me?" For I have become like a wineskin in smoke, yet I do not forget Your statutes.'

God's message of new wine is clearly revealed in Christ as the blessings of grace from God manifested in the Gospel as pardon for sin, reconciliation, atonement, justification, and sanctification. The love of God as revealed in the Gospel cannot be received by those who still wear the old garments or are like the old and brittle wine skins – the Gospel will be rejected and 'spilled out'. The new skins are those who have come to repentance and have received God's grace into new hearts and new spirits and new lives, as we read in Ezekiel 36:26-27,

> 'I will give you a new heart and put a new spirit within you; I will take the heart of stone out of your flesh and give you a heart of flesh. I will put My Spirit within you and cause you to walk in My statutes, and you will keep My judgements and do them.'

Matthew 9:22

In verse 22, Jesus had become aware that a woman in the crowd had reached out and touched the hem of His garment and had been healed, saying,

> "Be of good cheer, daughter; the faith of thee has healed thee."

Jesus, doubtless knowing that she had been healed of a condition that made her ceremonially unclean according to the rules in Leviticus 15:25, spoke with gentleness and compassion, letting her know that she need not fear to approach Him, telling her to be of good cheer or to take courage. He also referred to her as a daughter – a term of affection and tenderness. Jesus demonstrated to His disciples that even those who are 'unclean' can approach Him, knowing that God the Father promises to heal, as we read for example in Isaiah 57:19 and Jeremiah 33:6,

> 'I create the fruit of the lips; peace, peace to him who is far off and to him who is near, says the Lord, and I will heal him.'

> 'Behold, I will bring it health and healing; I will heal them and reveal to them the abundance of peace and truth.'

Jesus then immediately states that the woman had been healed because of her faith. The word faith, in Greek 'pistis', is the same word used in translation from the Hebrew in reference to the faith of Abraham – that was credited to him as righteousness. This word for faith means trust in, reliance on, belief or credence in, or confidence in God the Father. Time and again, in the Old Testament Scriptures, we can read how God's people failed to trust Him and bore the consequences; equally, we can read of His amazing miracles when they simply trusted God to save them as He has promised, as we read in Numbers 23:19 and Proverbs 3:5,

> 'God is not a man, that He should lie, nor a son of man, that He should repent. Has He said, and will He not do? Or has He spoken, and will He not make it good?'

> 'Trust in the Lord with all your heart and lean not on your own understanding; in all your ways acknowledge Him, and He shall direct your paths.'

The woman's faith – her confidence in Jesus – was the means of her restoration both physically and ceremonially; it was Jesus' power that cured her in connection with her faith; faith was the means, but the power was from Jesus. It is perhaps worth noting that the hem of the garments of the people of Israel was to have tassels attached, according to Numbers 15:39, as a reminder of the Lord's commandments and that they were to keep themselves holy, or set apart, for God, and it was the hem that the woman reached out for – a symbol of holiness. But Jesus' words make it clear that the woman's healing did not come from some sort of supernatural property of His garment, but that He, of His own will, had healed her. When people break faith with us, we lose our faith and trust in them; God promises never to break faith with us and so we can have confidence in His word and trust in Him as does the psalmist, as we can read for example in Psalm 52:8 and 84:11-12,

'But I am like a green olive tree in the house of God; I trust in the mercy of God forever and ever. I will praise You forever, because You have done it; and in the presence of Your saints, I will wait on Your name, for it is good.'

'For the Lord God is a sun and shield; the Lord will give grace and glory; no good thing will He withhold from those who walk uprightly. O Lord of hosts, blessed is the man who trusts in You!'

Matthew 9:24

In verse 24, Jesus arrived at the house of a prominent citizen, named as Jairus in the other Gospels, who had received the news that his daughter was dead. Jesus addressed the crowd of mourners, saying,

> "Depart ye; not for died the girl but sleeps."

It may be that Jesus meant that her state of death, though real, would prove to be temporary; in other words, He may have used the word 'sleep' figuratively. The Greek word that Jesus used 'katheudei' literally means sleeping but can be used figuratively for death; it was a common euphemism for death at the time. If the child had simply been sleeping – in the normal sense of the word – Matthew is unlikely to have felt compelled to record the event. We can assume that the witnesses believed her to be dead since the commotion of mourning had already begun and Jesus asked them to leave. Jesus knew what was about to happen and spoke of her being raised as a person is from natural sleep. Jesus' contemporaries spoke of death as being asleep and they would have been familiar with the prophetic words in Isaiah 26:19 where we read,

> 'Your dead shall live; together with my dead body they shall arise.
> Awake and sing, you who dwell in dust; for your dew is like the
> dew of herbs, and the earth shall cast out the dead.'

There are clear parallels with the miracles of Elijah and Elisha in this account. In both of those accounts of a child being raised from the dead, the child was treated as if they were merely sleeping and prayed for in privacy. Jesus' disciples would no doubt have been familiar with the account of Elijah that is written in 1 Kings 17:21-22 and that of Elisha in 2 Kings 4:31-33, where we read.

> 'And he stretched himself out on the child three times, and cried
> out to the Lord and said, "O Lord my God, I pray, let this child's
> soul come back to him." Then the Lord heard the voice of Elijah;
> and the soul of the child came back to him, and he revived.'

> 'Therefore he [Gehazi] went back to meet him [Elisha], and told
> him, saying "The child has not awakened." When Elisha came into

the house, there was the child, lying dead on his bed. He went in therefore, shut the door behind the two of them, and prayed to the Lord.'

According to the law found in Numbers 19:11, 'He who touches the dead body of anyone shall be unclean for seven days.' Jesus here demonstrated His divine nature in that rather than being defiled by touching the dead, the child was restored to life, and He remained clean. Jesus' prophetic words made clear to His disciples that He knew what was to be and that it was a foretaste of what was to come. The Old Testament prophets predicted that the Messiah would restore life and those witnessing this event would have been reminded of these prophecies that we can read for example in Isaiah 25:8, Daniel 12:2, Hosea 13:14 and Psalm 49:15,

> 'He will swallow up death forever, and the Lord God will wipe away tears from all faces; the rebuke of His people He will take away from all the earth; for the Lord has spoken'

> 'And many of those who sleep in the dust of the earth shall awake, some to everlasting life, some to shame and everlasting contempt.'

> 'I will ransom them from the power of the grave; I will redeem them from death.'

> 'But God will redeem my soul from the power of the grave, for He will receive me.'

Matthew 9:28-30

In verses 28-30, Jesus responds to two blind men who had been following Him and calling out, "Son of David, have mercy on us." When Jesus had reached the house and gone inside, He spoke to them saying,

> "Believe ye that I can this to do?" They say to Him: "Yes, Lord". Then He touched the eyes of them saying: "According to the faith of you let it be to you". And were opened of them the eyes. And sternly admonished them Jesus saying: "See no one let know".

We might wonder if Jesus was testing the faith of the two men by waiting until he had gone into the house before responding, He certainly asked them if they had faith in Him. By following Jesus into the house, these two men had already demonstrated perseverance and a knowledge that the prophets had foretold that the Messiah would show mercy, as we read in Psalm 31:19 and 72:12-13,

> 'Oh, how great is Your goodness, which You have laid up for those who fear You, which You have prepared for those who trust in You in the presence of the sons of men.'

> 'For He will deliver the needy when he cries, the poor also, and him who has no helper. He will spare the poor and needy.'

Blindness was common at the time and was often used figuratively to illustrate a lack of spiritual perception. These two physically blind men could not see Jesus and His miracles but could perhaps see in their understanding the true nature of Jesus. Jesus' question made it clear that the men sought Him from a confidence that He was the Messiah, it was not just a desperate cry for help. By calling Jesus Son of David, they demonstrated an expectation of the fulfilment of the prophecies found in Isaiah 29:18, 35:5 and 42:6-7 and 16 where we read,

> 'In that day, the deaf shall hear the words of the book, and the eyes of the blind shall see out of obscurity and out of darkness.'

> 'Then the eyes of the blind shall be opened, and the ears of the deaf shall be unstopped.'

'I will keep You and give You as a covenant to the people, as a light to the Gentiles, to open blind eyes, to bring out prisoners from prison, those who sit in darkness from the prison house.'

'I will bring the blind by a way they did not know; I will lead them in paths they have not known. I will make darkness light before them, and crooked places straight.'

Jesus' reply demonstrates that He knew that their faith was sincere and that He accepted and was pleased with it. These two men made a simple profession of faith; they knew that the Messiah would have the power, they believed that Jesus was the Messiah, and they trusted that He was willing and able to heal them. It may be that Jesus' subsequent request that they tell no one was to set an example of humility; that they should not boast about the mercy they had received as taught in Proverbs 20:6 and 25:27 where we read,

'Most men will proclaim each his own goodness, but who can find a faithful man?'

'It is not good to eat much honey; so to seek one's own glory is not glory.'

What is clear is that Jesus' words and actions demonstrated His divine nature, and His disciples are called to profess their faith, trusting in Jesus' power and His willingness to open our eyes as we read in Psalm 119:18 and 146:8,

'Open my eyes, that I may see wondrous things from Your law.'

'The Lord opens the eyes of the blind; the Lord raises those who are bowed down; the Lord loves the righteous.'

Matthew 9:37-38

In verses 37-38, Jesus speaks about the urgent need for the people to hear the Gospel and is about to appoint twelve of His disciples, later known as apostles (meaning 'sent'), as helpers to share the news of the Kingdom, saying,

> "Indeed, the harvest is much, but the workmen are few; pray ye therefore the Lord of the harvest so that he may thrust forth workmen into the harvest of him."

The image of a field of ripe corn that needs harvesting is a powerful one even for contemporary readers; we still sow and reap corn albeit with high-tech machinery. It seems that it was common at the time Jesus was talking for teachers to refer to their assistants as reapers and the work of their instruction as the harvest, so Jesus' imagery would have had clear implications for His listeners. The workmen that Jesus referred to were to be His disciples and would be sent out to teach the Good News, as we read in Jeremiah 3:15,

> 'And I will give you shepherds according to My heart, who will feed you with knowledge and understanding.'

Jesus goes on to teach His disciples that they should pray that there will be workers to carry out the harvest; that it is a duty of His disciples to pray for the teaching of Jesus to reach those in need – those who have not yet heard the message of salvation, as we read in Joel 3:13, Micah 5:7, and Isaiah 5:7,

> 'Put in the sickle, for the harvest is ripe. Come, go down, the vats overflow – for their wickedness is great.'

> 'Then the remnant of Jacob shall be in the midst of many peoples, like dew from the Lord, like showers on the grass, that tarry for no man nor wait for the sons of men.'

> 'For the vineyard of the Lord of hosts is the house of Israel, and the men of Judah are His pleasant plant. He looked for justice, but behold, oppression; for righteousness, but behold, a cry for help.'

Jesus words, that we should pray that God would 'thrust forth' men who could do this work, makes clear that it is God Himself who will choose and call those who are to minister in this way; that it is only God who can call and send the labourers. It is God that prepares the harvest and He who prepares the hearts of people as we read in Psalm 10:16-18,

> 'The Lord is King forever and ever; the nations have perished out of His land. Lord You have heard the desire of the humble; You will prepare their heart; You will cause Your ear to hear, to do justice to the fatherless and the oppressed, that the man of the earth may oppress no more.'

Jesus' disciples are called to pray that God will prepare hearts and open ears and that He will choose and find the labourers needed for the task, and, like Isaiah, be prepared to serve, as we read in Isaiah 7:8,

> 'I heard the voice of the Lord, saying "Whom shall I send, and who will go for Us?" Then I said, "Here I am! Send me."

MATTHEW CHAPTER TEN

Matthew 10:5-6

In verses 5-6, Jesus, having given the twelve apostles His power to heal and cast out unclean spirits, sends them out with these words:

> "Into the way of the nations go ye not, and into a city of Samaritans enter not; but go rather unto the sheep the lost of the house of Israel."

It was proper that the Gospel should be preached first to the Jews with whom God had made the ancient covenant and as the people amongst whom the Messiah was born. Jesus intended that the first offers of salvation should be made to the people of Israel and that in this first mission, no stumbling block might be cast in their way – knowing that the time would come for the Gentiles. The Samaritans had built their own temple and claimed that Moses had intended theirs as the true temple. They accepted only the five books of Moses and rejected the writings of the prophets; to be arguing these ancient disputes would doubtless have been fruitless and a waste of time. Jesus sent out the twelve knowing the time was short and that the need of the people of Israel was great as we read in Jeremiah 50:6,

> 'My people have been lost sheep. Their shepherds have led them astray; they have turned them away on the mountains. They have gone from mountain to hill; they have forgotten their resting place.'

Jesus goes on to send the apostles to the Jews; to announce the appearance of the Jewish Messiah; to announce the Jewish Kingdom; and to provide signs as proof of Jesus' divine authority – that He was the King of the Jews. By His words, referring to the lost sheep of the house of Israel, Jesus was also making clear that He had come to fulfil to prophecy that God Himself would seek out His lost sheep, as we read in Ezekiel 34:11-12,

> 'For thus says the Lord God: "Indeed I Myself will search for My sheep and seek them out. As a shepherd seeks out his flock on the day he is among his scattered sheep, so will I seek out My sheep and deliver them from all the places where they were scattered on a cloudy and dark day."

It was right that the message should go first to the people of Israel, but Jesus knew that the prophet Isaiah made it clear that once Israel had grasped the true knowledge of God it would be their privilege to share that good news – the Gospel – with the other nations, as we read in Isaiah 56:8,

> 'The Lord God, who gathers the outcasts of Israel says, "Yet I will gather to him others besides those who are gathered to him."

Having received the message of salvation and the Kingdom, it was indeed the people of Israel who then shared the message to the lost sheep in the rest of the world that all should acknowledge that they have gone astray from God's commandments as we read in Isaiah 53:6 and Psalm 119:176,

> 'All we like sheep have gone astray; we have turned, everyone, to his own way; and the Lord has laid on Him the iniquity of us all.'

> 'I have gone astray like a lost sheep; seek your servant, for I do not forget Your commandments.'

This verse reminds us of walking in the will of the Lord of the Harvest and not being diverted by our own ideas of how to share. Jesus Himself was restricted by the Father's agenda. The Lord's plan always brings the best results.

Matthew 10:7-8

In verses 7-8, Jesus continues with His commission to the apostles to go to the lost sheep of Israel, adding specific instructions, saying,

> "And going proclaim ye saying, has drawn near the kingdom of the heavens. Ailing ones heal ye, dead ones raise, lepers cleanse, demons expel; freely ye received, freely give."

The subject that they were to preach was the message that the Kingdom of Heaven was at hand; that the reign of heaven had drawn near; that it was imminent. They were to proclaim, or preach, that men should prepare for the Kingdom without delay. Jesus' own ministry began with the same message – that the Kingdom of God was at hand and the people should prepare to receive it. The message that there would be an appropriate time for this proclamation was spoken of in the prophets, as we read in Isaiah 48:16 and Isaiah 61:1, where we read,

> 'Come near to Me, hear this: I have not spoken in secret from the beginning: From the time that it was, I was there. And now the Lord God and His Spirit have sent Me.'

> 'The Spirit of the Lord God is upon Me, because the Lord has anointed Me to preach good tidings to the poor; He has sent Me to heal the broken hearted, to proclaim liberty to the captives, and the opening of the prison to those who are bound.'

The chosen twelve disciples were to be itinerant preachers, letting the people of Israel know that the kingdom of the Messiah was to be set up according to the Scriptures. Jesus had already given the disciples His power to heal and cast out unclean spirits as a gift for their service to the people. When God spoke to Aaron to appoint the Levites as priests to serve the people, He referred to this as a gift that was given freely, as we read in Numbers 18:7,

> 'Therefore, you and your sons with you shall attend to your priesthood for everything at the alter and behind the veil; and you shall serve. I give your priesthood to you as a gift for service.'

178

Gifts that are entrusted to God's people are not for their own individual benefit or renown, but that they might be a channel for the free grace and bounty of God. It is received without any merit and should flow also without merit freely to others. The prophet Elisha demonstrated this principle in his dealings with Naaman, a Syrian commander, after he had been healed of his leprosy, as we read in 2 Kings 5:15-16,

> 'And he returned to the man of God, he and his aides, and came and stood before him; and he said, "Indeed, now I know that there is no God in all the earth, except in Israel; now therefore, please take a gift from your servant." But he said, "As surely as the Lord lives, before whom I stand, I will receive nothing."

Jesus' words reminded His disciple that giving freely is a fundamental Scriptural principle that is enshrined in the Law and the prophets, as we read in Deuteronomy 15:10 and Isaiah 55:1,

> 'You shall surely give to him, and your heart should not be grieved when you give to him, because for this thing the Lord you God will bless you in all your works and in all to which you put your hand.'

> 'Ho! Everyone who thirsts, come to the waters; and you who have no money, come, buy, and eat. Yes, come, buy wine and milk without money and without price.'

Matthew 10:9-10

In verses 9-10, Jesus continues with His instruction to His disciples as they prepare for their mission to proclaim the coming of His Kingdom to the people of Israel, saying,

> "Do not provide gold nor silver nor brass in the girdles of you, not a provision-bag for the way nor two tunics nor sandals nor a staff; for worthy is the workman of the provisions of him."

Since Jesus had already given the disciples power as a sign to the people, it may have been that the instruction to take no money – of whatever value, even the smallest brass coin – was to avoid the risk that they may have been tempted to receive payment for their message, as well as to ensure that they would rely only on God the Father's providence. Neither were they to take spare tunics, footwear, or staff. It seems that they were not to spend time making preparation for their journey, but just to go as they were. This allowed them to travel lightly and unencumbered by material possessions. The disciples would have been familiar with the history of Moses in which he reminds the people of Israel in the wilderness of how God demonstrated His provision even for the basics of footwear and clothing, as we read in Deuteronomy 29:5,

> 'I have led you forty years in the wilderness. Your clothes have not worn out on you, and your sandals have not worn out on your feet.'

Jesus also reminds His disciples of the fundamental principle, enshrined in the Law, that the labourer is worthy of his provisions. Those who ministered in spiritual things had a right to expect physical recompense; special provision was made for those who served in the Temple, and they could expect to receive maintenance for their work as ministers by the altar, as we read for example in Numbers 18:31,

> 'You may eat it in any place, you and your households, for it is your reward for your work in the tabernacle of meeting.'

By referring to His disciples as workmen, Jesus was intimating that they were His labourers, working in His vineyard, discharging their duty, and entitled to all the necessities of life. The Law made it clear that those who have laboured and earned their wages must be paid their dues and without delay, as we read in Leviticus 19:13, Deuteronomy 24:15, and Deuteronomy 25:4,

'You shall not cheat your neighbour, nor rob him. The wages of him who is hired shall not remain with you all night until morning.'

'Each day you shall give him his wages, and not let the sun go down on it, for he is poor and has set his heart on it; lest he cry out against you to the Lord, and it be sin to you.'

'You shall not muzzle an ox while it treads out the grain.'

Those who are called to labour for Christ have good reason to trust in Him for all their material needs; they can expect to have special provision so that they can focus on His work and allow the Lord to provide for them as He sees fit; not that the labourer might layup wealth but that they might serve, as we read in Psalm 34:8-10,

'Oh, taste and see that the Lord is good; blessed is the man who trusts in Him! Oh, fear the Lord, you, His saints! There is no want to those who fear Him. The young lions lack and suffer hunger; but those who seek the Lord shall not lack any good thing.'

Matthew 10:11-13

In verses 11-13, Jesus instructs His disciples as to where and with whom they should stay on their mission, saying,

> "And whatever city or village ye may enter, inquire who in it worthy is; and there remain until ye may go out. And entering into the house greet it; and if indeed be the house worthy, let come the peace of you on it; but if it be not worthy, the peace of you unto you let return."

The disciples were to stay with worthy hosts, not necessarily the most convenient or appealing. They would be people who would welcome a disciple of Jesus and the message of the Kingdom. He also instructs them to remain with the same household while they are in that community. This may have been to save time, or it may have been so that they did not give offence by appearing dissatisfied, but it may have been that Jesus was reminding them to have confidence in God's provision just as He provided for Elijah on his travels as we read in 1 Kings 17:9,

> 'Arise, go to Zarephath, which belongs to Sidon, and dwell there. See, I have commanded a widow there to provide for you.'

The greeting, or salutation, that the disciples were to give the host household would have been the normal greeting of the day that extended to the whole household and estate of the person, as we find for example in 1 Samuel 25:5-6 where we read,

> 'David sent ten young men: and David said to the young men, "Go up to Carmel, go to Nabal, and greet him in my name. And thus, you shall salute him: 'Peace be to you, peace to your house, and peace to all that you have.'

If the host were to be found unworthy, the blessing could not be received in the same way a person has to receive a gift to have it. This is a Biblical principle - that God's grace, gifts, or blessings, are offered freely but His people need to be willing to receive them or they effectively return to sender, as we read in Psalm 35:13,

'But as for me, when they were sick, my clothing was sackcloth; I humbled myself with fasting; and my prayer would return to my own heart.'

One of the first uses of the Hebrew word translated as 'peace' is in Exodus 21:34 where it is translated as 'make it good' and in verse 36 as 'shall surely pay'. In Chapter 22:3 it is translated as to 'make full restitution' and in verse 4 as 'restore'. The ancient meaning was to restore or make something whole in the sense of wellbeing; it means an inward sense of completeness or wholeness, tranquillity, health, and prosperity and incorporates a blessing. This peace can apply to individuals or whole communities who are worthy and willing to receive as we read in Psalm 122:6-8 and Psalm 119:165, and of course Aaron's blessing in Numbers 6:24-26,

'Pray for the peace of Jerusalem: "May they prosper who love you. Peace be within your walls, prosperity within your palaces." For the sake of my brethren and companions, I will now say, "Peace be within you."

'Great peace have those who love Your law, and nothing causes them to stumble.'

'The Lord bless you and keep you; the Lord make His face shine upon you and be gracious to you; the Lord lift up His countenance upon you and give you peace.'

Matthew 10:14-15

In verses 14-15, Jesus' words convey the urgency and significance of the message that the apostles were charged with proclaiming, saying,

> "And whoever may not receive you nor hear the words of you, going outside house or city that shake off the dust of the feet of you. Truly I tell you, more tolerable it will be for the land of Sodom and Gomorra in the day of judgement than for city that."

According to Jewish teaching, the dust of heathen cities was defiled. To symbolically shake the dust from their feet would indicate that the household or city was no better than the heathen for rejecting the message of the Kingdom. The principle that the ground on which a person is standing may be holy or otherwise is made clear first to Moses and then Joshua, as we read in Exodus 3:5 and Joshua 5:15,

> 'Then He said, "Do not draw near this place. Take your sandals off your feet, for the place where you stand is holy ground."

> 'Then the Commander of the Lord's army said to Joshua, "Take your sandal off your foot, for the place where you stand is holy."

To shake the dust from one's clothes or feet symbolised a renunciation of all connection with them, in this instance of those who would demonstrate contempt of God's word. When Nehemiah spoke to the people about the rampant injustices that were being perpetrated against the people in Jerusalem, he describes the denunciation of these injustices in terms of being shaken out and David describes not wanting anything wicked to cling to him, as we read in Nehemiah 5:13 and Psalm 101:3,

> 'Then I shook out the fold of my garment and said, "So may God shake out each man from his house, and from his property, who does not perform this promise. Even thus may he be shaken out and emptied."

> 'I will set nothing wicked before my eyes; I hate the work of those who fall away; it shall not cling to me.'

184

By warning the apostles that those who refuse to hear the Gospel and deny the authority of God the Father, refusing to listen to His voice, and rejecting His Son, He was reflecting the words of the prophets in Scripture. God's people are compared unfavourably with the people of Sodom for their continuing rejection of His Word and His Law, as we read for example in Lamentations 4:6 and Ezekiel 16:48,

> 'The punishment of the iniquity of the daughter of my people is greater than the punishment of the sin of Sodom, which was overthrown in a moment, with no hand to help her.'

> "As I live," says the Lord God, "neither your sister Sodom nor her daughters have done as you and your daughters have done."

Jesus speaks of a day of judgement, in which all must give an account. It serves as a warning to God's people that they cannot be complacent, but must daily respond to the Gospel message in the knowledge that His judgement is both righteous and true, as we read in Psalm 9:7-8 and Psalm 96:13,

> 'But the Lord shall endure forever; He has prepared His throne for judgement. He shall judge the world in righteousness, and He shall administer judgement for the peoples in uprightness.'

> 'For He is coming, for He is coming to judge the earth. He shall judge the world with righteousness, and the peoples with His truth.'

Matthew 10:16

In verse 16, Jesus warns His disciples to be cautious on their mission, to try to avoid danger, through wisdom, and through not provoking conflict or stirring up anger, saying,

> "Behold, I send forth you as sheep in the midst of wolves; be ye therefore prudent as serpents and harmless as doves."

By calling His disciples sheep, He was not suggesting that they were mild mannered or weak willed, but that they would not be given any greater strength or resources to repel any violence that would be directed against them. Jesus echoes the words of the prophets by likening those people of Israel who have sought their own interest, and whose hearts were hardened to the message of the Kingdom, to ravening wolves. Over time, the people had twisted the interpretation of the Law, or simply ignored or disobeyed it, thereby committing injustices and violence, despising God's holy statutes, and shedding innocent blood, as we read for example in Ezekiel 22:27 and Zephaniah 3:3-4,

> 'Her princes in her midst are like wolves tearing the prey, to shed blood, to destroy people, and to get dishonest gain.'

> 'Her princes in her midst are roaring lions; her judges are evening wolves that leave not a bone till morning. Her prophets are insolent, treacherous people; her priests have polluted the sanctuary, they have done violence to the Law.'

Jesus warns the disciples to exercise the caution, or prudence, of a snake that manages to escape danger by avoiding anything that is hostile towards them or may cause them any kind of injury. The disciples were not knowingly to put themselves in danger or to be unnecessarily timid. The serpent is represented in Scripture as prudent to excess, being full of cunning, as we read in Genesis 3:1 and 13,

> 'Now the serpent was more cunning than any beast of the field which the Lord God made.'

> 'The Lord God said to the woman, "What is this you have done?" The woman said, "The serpent deceived me, and I ate."

There is a clear juxtaposition in Jesus' words, contrasting the cunning of serpents with the harmlessness of doves that are simple even to the point of stupidity, as we read in Hosea 7:11,

'Ephraim also is like a silly dove, without sense – they call to Egypt, they go to Assyria.'

Naturally timid doves, that employ no defensive strategies and appear unaware of dangers, are liable to innumerable attacks. Jesus' disciples are called to have the simplicity of doves so that no fear will hinder them from their mission, as we read in Hosea 11:11,

'They shall come trembling like a bird from Egypt, like a dove from the land of Assyria. And I will let them dwell in their houses says the Lord.'

In their mission, the apostles were to proclaim the message of the Kingdom without inciting anger and hostility, but with humility and without fear, trusting in God the Father, as we read in Psalm 56:11,

'In God I have put my trust; I will not be afraid. What can man do to me?'

187

Matthew 10:17-18

In verses 17-18, Jesus continues His warning to His disciples in words that were both prophetic of the future and an echo of prophesies from the past, saying,

> "And beware from men for they will deliver up you to councils, and in the synagogues of them they will scourge you; and before leaders and also kings ye will be led for the sake of me, for a testimony to them and to the nations."

These men, of whom Jesus spoke, who would deliver the disciples up to the councils, were it seems, men of importance and having some authority, perhaps ecclesiastical or civil governors. Perhaps also Scribes, Pharisees, elders, chief priests, judges, and other rulers. They may even have included friends and neighbours. Jesus may well have had the words of the prophet Micah in mind who spoke of the perishing of the upright and faithful from Israel, as we read in Chapter 7:3-4 and 5,

> 'The prince asks for gifts, the judge seeks a bribe, and the great man utters his evil desire; so they scheme together. The best of them is like a brier; the most upright is sharper than a thorn hedge.'

> 'Do not trust in a friend; do not put your confidence in a companion.'

Jesus specifically mentioned the synagogues, identifying the priests and teachers of the Law as being in opposition to Christ's message. The warning to the disciples is to be prepared to face those who would seek opportunities and occasions to work against them and use their power and interest to cause them harm. Those who were being challenged by the Gospel of Christ, especially the religious leaders, would not seek the truth, but actively work against it, as we read for example in Jeremiah 9:3 and 5 and in Psalm 83:2-3,

> 'And like their bow they have bent their tongues for lies. They are not valiant for the truth on the earth. For they proceed from evil to evil, and they do not know Me, says the Lord.'

188

'Everyone will deceive his neighbour and will not speak the truth; they have taught their tongues to speak lies; they weary themselves to commit iniquity.' And 'For behold, Your enemies make a tumult; and those who hate You have lifted up their head. They have taken crafty counsel against Your people and consulted together against Your sheltered ones.'

The disciples were called to bear testimony to Jesus, to bear witness and give evidence, at the highest levels of society. We know from the Acts of the Apostles that they did indeed witness before kings and emperors. Today we have a saying 'he who is forewarned is forearmed', Jesus' disciples are forewarned and need to be prepared as His soldiers wearing the full armour of God. Jesus warns the disciples that they will be called to witness not just in Judea, but in distant nations to foreign princes and this too had been forecast as we read in Isaiah 66:5, Psalm 2:1-2 and Psalm 119:46-7,

'Hear the word of the Lord, you who tremble at His word: "Your brethren who hated you, who cast you out for My name's sake, said 'Let the Lord be glorified that we may see your joy.' But they shall be ashamed."

'Why do the nations rage, and the people plot a vain thing? The kings of the earth set themselves, and the rulers take counsel together, against the Lord and against His Anointed.'

'I will speak of Your testimonies also before kings, and I will not be ashamed. And I will delight myself in Your commandments, which I love.'

Matthew 10:19-20

In verses 19-20, Jesus reminds the disciples that it is not they who will be speaking; rather they are God's messengers, and He will give them the words to speak, saying,

> "But when they deliver up you, do not be anxious how or what ye may say; it will be given for to you in that hour what ye may say; for not ye are the ones speaking, but the Spirit of the Father of you the one speaking in you."

From the earliest scriptures, we know that God used individuals from His chosen people as a mouthpiece to speak His words directly to the people. Jesus' disciples would have known from the history of Moses that he was filled with the Spirit of God so powerfully that the people could see it on his face. Moses himself was at first anxious about being called to speak the words of God, but God promised to teach both Moses and his brother Aaron what to say and promised that there would also be such a prophet in the future, as we read in Exodus 4:12 and Deuteronomy 18:18,

> 'Now therefore, go, and I will be with your mouth and teach you what you shall say.'

> 'I will raise up for them a Prophet like you from among their brethren, and will put My words in his mouth, and he shall speak to them all that I command him.'

The disciples were not to be anxious, but to continue to trust in God; trust in the Father banishes fear of the unknown, fear of danger, fear of inadequacy, and fear of failure. Those who are called by God to speak His words and His truth are told not to be afraid or dismayed, as we read for example in Jeremiah 1:7-8 and 17,

> 'But the Lord said to me: "Do not say, 'I am a youth,' for you shall go to all to whom I send you, and whatever I command you, you shall speak. Do not be afraid of their faces, for I am with you to deliver you," says the Lord.'

"Therefore, prepare yourself and arise, and speak to them all that I command you. Do not be dismayed before their faces, lest I dismay you before them."

The Spirit of God, or the Holy Spirit, has a kind of heavenly role as defence counsel for those who trust in Jesus. Jesus was able to make the promise that the Holy Spirit would give the disciples the words to speak because He knew that the Spirit of the Father speaks to and through the people He chooses to send, just as He always had done through the prophets, as we read for example in Ezekiel 2:2-4 and 6,

'Then the Spirit entered me when He spoke to me and set me on my feet; and I heard Him who spoke to me. And He said to me: "Son of man, I am sending you to the children of Israel, to a rebellious nation that has rebelled against Me; they and their fathers have transgressed against Me to this very day. For they are impudent and stubborn children. I am sending you to them, and you shall say to them, 'Thus says the Lord God.'

"And you, son of man, do not be afraid of them nor be afraid of their words, though briers and thorns are with you, and you dwell among scorpions; do not be afraid of their words or dismayed by their looks, though they are a rebellious house.'

With confidence, Jesus' disciples can join with David in his Psalm 145:21, saying,

'My mouth shall speak the praise of the Lord, and all flesh shall bless His holy name forever and ever.'

Matthew 10:21-22

In verses 21-22, Jesus warns His disciples that, like the prophets of old, those who speak up for righteousness will be hated and even martyred, saying,

> "And will deliver up brother, brother to death and father child, and will stand up children against parents and put to death them. And ye will be being hated by all men on account of the name of me; but the one enduring to the end, this will be saved."

Jesus knew that His apostles and disciples would find that even friends and relations would turn their backs on them and betray them on His account. For many of the Jews, the justification for this would be the words found in Deuteronomy 13:6, that charge those who worship other gods and lead the people of Israel astray, with death, even though these people may be 'your brother, the son of your mother, your son or your daughter the wife of your bosom, or your friend who is as your own soul.' Jesus' warning of the betrayal of friends and family is also spoken of in the prophet Micah 7:6-7 and Psalm 50:20, where we read,

> 'For son dishonours father, daughter rises against mother, daughter-in-law against mother-in-law; a man's enemies are the men of his own household. Therefore, I will look to the Lord; I will wait for the God of my salvation; My God will hear me.'

> 'You sit and speak against your brother; you slander you own mother's son.'

Those who follow Jesus, who are saved from the corruption that is in the world, who seek God's righteousness and the furtherance of His kingdom, will be hated by those who either do not yet know God or have rejected Him and His commands and ordinances. The hatred that Christ's followers were to suffer was not regarding their personality, or any particular action, but because they believe in Christ and openly profess their belief in Him, as we read in Proverbs 29:27 and 4:18,

> 'An unjust man is an abomination to the righteous, and he who is upright in the way is an abomination to the wicked.'

'But the path of the just is like the shining sun, that shines ever brighter unto the perfect day. The way of the wicked is like darkness; they do not know what makes them stumble.'

Jesus calls His disciples to endure, or persevere, with the promise that they will be saved. This was to be their goal – to endure to the end, and this is the target of those who work against the Father's kingdom. Christians, as did the saints of old such as Daniel when faced with the fiery furnace, are called to stand firm in the face of persecution and suffering, holding fast to their faith to the end in the certain knowledge of their salvation; they are called to stand firm in the face of the enemy, as we read for example in Job17:9, Habakkuk 2:1, Psalm 130:5-6, Psalm 4:3 and Isaiah 25:9,

'Yet the righteous will hold to his way, and he who has clean hands will be stronger and stronger.'

'I will stand my watch and set myself on the rampart and watch to see what He will say to me, and what I will answer when I am corrected.'

'I wait for the Lord, my soul waits, and in His word I do hope. My soul waits for the Lord more than those who watch for the morning – yes, more than those who watch for the morning.'

'But know that the Lord has set apart for Himself him who is godly; the Lord will hear when I call to Him.'

'And it will be said in that day: "Behold, this is our God; we have waited for Him, and He will save us. This is the Lord; we have waited for Him; we will be glad and rejoice in His salvation."

Matthew 10:23

In verse 23, Jesus seems to be telling His disciples to exercise prudence and humility to avoid persecution, and also makes reference to time limits and future revelation, saying,

> "But when they persecute you in city this, flee ye to another; for truly I tell you, by no means ye will complete the cities of Israel until comes the Son of man."

Previously, Jesus had told His disciples that there would be times when they would have to stand and endure persecution, but here He tells them to flee from persecution. When there is an opportunity to avoid persecution, His disciples should avail themselves of it. By this, the disciples can seek other opportunities, and in addition, deprive those who wish to persecute them the opportunity for their own sake. Where the disciples could preserve themselves without denying their Lord, they were to do so. David, already a giant slayer, when he was under threat of death from King Saul, chose to flee, as we read in 1 Samuel 19:11-12,

> 'Saul also sent messengers to David's house to watch him and to kill him in the morning. And Michal, David's wife, told him, saying, "If you do not save your life tonight, tomorrow you will be killed." So, Michal let David down through a window. And he went and fled and escaped.'

The disciples were told not just to flee, but to go to another city. If the place they were in would not allow them to preach the Gospel, then they were to go elsewhere and not give up. They were not called to avoid their work because of persecution, or to despair, but to continue with the work where they would have more success. Jesus may have had the message spoken by Isaiah in mind, in which the prophet told the people to flee from Babylon and the Chaldeans, and praising God, to declare the redemption of His people, as we read in Isaiah, 48:20,

> 'Go forth from Babylon! Flee from the Chaldeans! With a voice of singing, declare, proclaim this, utter it to the end of the earth; say, "The Lord has redeemed His servant, Jacob."

Jesus indicated that the disciples would not have time to go to all the cities and towns of Israel before He was revealed as the Son of Man; that the evangelisation of Israel would not be completed before that time. The Old Testament prophets foretold that the Messiah would bring His people back to Him; that He would gather them to Himself, as we read in Isaiah 49:5,

> 'And now the Lord says, who formed Me from the womb to be His Servant, to bring Jacob back to Him, so that Israel is gathered to Him.'

Jesus' disciples are called to proclaim God's kingdom with perseverance and humility, but also without recklessness or putting themselves needlessly in danger. They are to speak God's message of truth and salvation without fear, trusting in God's promises for the future, as we read in Isaiah 57:7-8 and Jeremiah 29:11,

> 'Listen to Me, you who know righteousness, you people in whose heart is My law; do not fear the reproach of men, nor be afraid of their insults. For the moth will eat them up like a garment, and the worm will eat them like wool; but My righteousness will be forever, and My salvation from generation to generation.'

> 'For I know the thoughts that I think toward you, says the Lord, thoughts of peace and not evil, to give you a future and a hope.'

Matthew 10:24-25

In verses 24-25, Jesus warns His disciples that they will receive the same type of opposition and persecution that He received; that they must expect the same treatment, saying,

> "Not is a disciple above the teacher nor a slave above the lord of him. Enough for the disciple that he be as the teacher of him, and the slave as the lord of him. If the housemaster Beelzebub they called, how much more the members of the household of him."

Implicit in this speech is an acknowledgement that Jesus is both a teacher - with disciples, and master of His household. His disciples were to submit to His instruction as teacher and obey His voice as master, accepting that adversity, if the teacher or master is so afflicted, will also afflict the disciple or servant, as we read in Proverbs 5:12-13 and Isaiah 30:20-21,

> 'How I have hated instruction and my heart despised correction. I have not obeyed the voice of my teachers, nor inclined my ear to those who instructed me.'

> 'Though the Lord give you the bread of adversity and the water of affliction, yet your teachers will not be moved into a corner anymore, but your eyes shall see your teachers. Your ears shall hear a word behind you saying, "This is the way, walk in it."

The pagan god of the Ekronites, referred to in 2 Kings 1:2-3 as Beel-Zebub, meaning 'Lord of the flies', was considered by the Israelites to be the worst of the pagan gods. An Aramean form of the word meant 'god of dung' or 'filth', so that the name, when given to Satan, expressed supreme contempt and aversion. By using this name against Jesus, the people were expressing the greatest possible contempt; those who follow Jesus must be prepared to share a similar contempt. By attempting to discredit Jesus, His persecutors, then and now, justify their actions to themselves; they pretend to be fighting against evil and claim the moral high ground. But Jesus' disciples, the members of His household, are to wait on the Lord and be His witnesses, as we read in Isaiah 8:16-18 and 43:10,

'Bind up the testimony, seal the law among my disciples. And I will wait on the Lord, who hides His face from the house of Jacob; and I will hope in Him. Here am I and the children whom the Lord has given me. We are for signs and wonders in Israel from the Lord of hosts who dwells in Mount Zion.'

'You are my witnesses, says the Lord, and My servant whom I have chosen, that you may know and believe Me, and understand that I am He. Before Me there was no God formed, nor shall there be after Me.'

Jesus is again calling His disciples to persevere, acknowledging the wickedness and iniquity that exists in the world, but asking them to share in His lot, to submit to the same conditions to share in the highest honour, as we read in Ecclesiastes 3:16, Isaiah 44:8, and 51:15-16,

'Moreover, I saw under the sun: in the place of judgement, wickedness was there; and in the place of righteousness, iniquity was there.'

'Do not fear, nor be afraid; have I not told you from that time and declared it? You are My witnesses. Is there a God besides Me? Indeed, there is no other Rock; I know not one.'

'But I am the Lord your God, who divided the sea whose waves roared – the Lord of hosts is His name. And I have put My words in your mouth; I have covered you with the shadow of My hand, that I may plant the heavens, lay the foundations of the earth, and say to Zion, 'You are My people.'

Matthew 10:26-27

In verses 26-27, Jesus' message to His disciples is that they are not to fear to teach publicly the things that He has taught them privately, saying,

> "Therefore, fear ye not them; for nothing is having been veiled which will not be unveiled and hidden which will not be made known. What I say to you in the darkness, say ye in the light; and what in the ear ye hear, proclaim on the housetops."

Jesus knew that the persecution and opposition that the disciples would encounter would not succeed in hiding the truth but result in its wider dissemination. History tells us that persecution intensifies the zeal of people who suffer persecution and often arouses sympathy and interest from onlookers. There are clear indications in Old Testament Scripture, that Jesus' disciples would have been familiar with, about things hidden being made known; much was veiled, or covered, under the old covenant, most importantly the Most Holy place in the Temple, as we read in Exodus 26:33, Numbers 32:23 and Ecclesiastes 12:14,

> 'You shall hang the veil from the clasps. Then you shall bring the ark of the testament in there, behind the veil. The veil shall be a divider for you between the holy place and the Most Holy.'

> 'But if you do not do so, then take note, you have sinned against the Lord; and be sure your sin will find you out.'

> 'For God will bring every work into judgement, including every secret thing, whether good or evil.'

Jesus calls His disciples to devote themselves to the message of the Gospel with boldness and perseverance, and not to be alarmed when people despise them. He knew that in time all things would be brought to light, both the wicked - including those who professed to have zeal for God's Law but rejected Christ, and the righteous who can be bold in the knowledge that they follow Jesus with integrity, as we read in Proverbs 10:9 and 28:1, and Ezekiel 13:21,

198

'He who walks with integrity walks securely, but he who perverts his ways will become known.'

'The wicked flee when no one pursues, but the righteous are bold as a lion.'

'I will also tear off your veils and deliver my people out of your hand, and they shall no longer be as prey in your hand. Then you shall know that I am the Lord.'

The Gospel message, that Jesus taught His disciples in private and through parables, is to be proclaimed openly and in public, in the synagogues and the Temple, in the streets, in the fields, and from the rooftops, wherever there are people. His disciples are to proclaim the Gospel without reserve in the same way that proclamations would be sounded out with trumpet blasts from the rooftops. Jesus' disciples are not just to whisper amongst themselves, behind closed doors, keeping the message to themselves, but to blow the trumpet of the Gospel, proclaiming the truth and wisdom of God's grace, as we read in Proverbs 1:20-21, 8:1-5, and Isaiah 25:78,

'Wisdom calls aloud outside; she raises her voice in the open squares. She cries out in the chief concourses, at the openings of the gates in the city she speaks her words.'

'Does not wisdom cry out, and understanding lift up her voice? She takes her stand on the top of the high hill, beside the way, where the paths meet. She cries out by the gates, at the entry of the city, at the entrance of the doors.' And 'He will destroy on this mountain the surface of the covering cast over all people, and the veil that is spread over all people, and the veil that is spread over all nations. He will swallow up death forever, and the Lord God will wipe away tears from all faces.'

Matthew 10:28

In verse 28, Jesus continues His teaching about faithfulness to God, His Laws and precepts, and the Gospel message, saying,

> "And do not fear the ones killing the body, but the soul not being able to kill; but fear ye rather the one being able both soul and body to destroy in Gehenna."

Jesus faced violent death Himself and warned His disciples that they might expect no less, but that those who put them to death could do them no more harm. Jesus' words indicate that the body and soul are distinct entities; that the material body may be slain but the non-material soul cannot be injured by humankind. By implication the soul is immortal; the body is unimportant compared to the soul, and Jesus' disciples ought to give greater importance to the soul that has been created for a heavenly immortality; to set a higher value on the heavenly kingdom of God than the fleeting present life. Jesus encourages His disciples not to fear mortal death, as we read in Isaiah 35:3-4 and 51:12,

> 'Strengthen the weak hands and make firm the feeble knees. Say to those who are fearful-hearted, 'Be strong, do not fear! Behold, your God will come with vengeance, with the recompense of God; He will come and save you.'

> 'I, even I, am He who comforts you. Who are you that you should be afraid of a man who will die, and of the son of a man who will be made like grass?'

There is something of a question here: who or what did Jesus mean when referring to 'one who is able to destroy both body and soul'? It is most likely that Jesus was warning His disciples to be more afraid of the condemnation of God than the death sentence of human beings. If Jesus' disciples suffer death because of their fidelity to God, they have a sure hope of eternal life; if through fear of physical death, they prove unfaithful to Him, then retribution awaits them. Jesus was not implying that His disciples might go to hell if they do not remain faithful, but that we will all be held to account for our actions as regards our eternal soul and only God has power to do so. Only the Lord of hosts can be our eternal judge as we read in Isaiah 8:12-13, 11:4, 16:5, and 33:22,

'Do not say, 'A conspiracy,' concerning all that this people call a conspiracy, nor be afraid of their threats, nor be troubled. The Lord of hosts, Him shall you hallow; let Him be your fear and let Him be your dread.'

'But with righteousness He shall judge the poor and decide with equity for the meek of the earth; He shall strike the earth with the rod of His mouth, and with the breath of His lips He shall slay the wicked.'

'In mercy the throne will be established; and One will sit on it in truth, in the tabernacle of David, judging and seeking justice and hastening righteousness.'

'For the Lord is our Judge, the Lord is our Lawgiver, the Lord is our King; He will save us.'

In the account of Daniel and the fiery furnace, we have one of the greatest examples of God's people refusing to be unfaithful, on pain of death, knowing that all will be well in eternal service to God, as we read for example in Psalm 90:11-12 and Ecclesiastes 8:12-13,

'Who knows the power of your anger? For as the fear of You, so is Your wrath. So, teach us to number our days, that we may gain a heart of wisdom.'

'Though a sinner does evil a hundred times and his days are prolonged, yet I surely know that it will be well with those who fear God, and fear before Him. But it will not be well with the wicked; nor will He prolong his days, which are as a shadow, because he does not fear before God.'

Matthew 10:29-31

In verses 29-31, Jesus encourages His disciples not to fear, saying,

> "Not two sparrows of a farthing sold? And one of them not will fall on the earth without the Father of you. But of you even the hairs of the head all having been numbered are, not therefore fear ye; many sparrows excel ye."

Jesus used two illustrations to help His disciples to understand the Father's care and providence. Firstly, that God takes care even of the sparrows, the smallest and least valuable of birds. The Greek word 'assarion', translated as farthing, was the lowest value of the Roman coins. God the Father and Creator provides for and cares for even the smallest part of His creation; He has his eye even on the sparrow, so that nothing that happens in His creation happens by chance. The whole of Psalm 104 is a psalm of praise to the Lord for His creation and providence, as we read for example in verses 27-30,

> 'These all wait for You, that You may give them their food in due season, what You give them they gather in; You open Your hand, they are filled with good. You hide Your face, they are troubled; You take away their breath, they die and return to their dust. You send forth Your Spirit, they are created; and You renew the face of the earth.'

Richard Wurmbrand[3] wrote while in prison: "Sparrows don't fall from the tree without the Father's leave; neither do Christians fall without His will [...] Falls from which we return to the Lord are sources of humility, light, strength, and comfort to others." Jesus' disciples are not even to fear to fall, as even this will not happen by chance, as we read in Daniel 11:35,

> 'And some of those understanding shall fall, to refine them, purify them, and make them white, until the time of the end; because it is still for the appointed time.'

The second illustration is the fact that God numbers even the hairs of the head. If He takes care of the birds, that are of so little value, and regards

---

[3] Richard Wurmbrand, A Meditation for Every Day on the Year, 1977

so small a thing as the hair on our heads worthy of being numbered, then He will certainly protect and provide for us. Each hair on our head has had God's attention for Him to number it; He does not think it beneath Him to determine how few or how many that will be; His wisdom and knowledge are so great that His providence descends even to the most minute particles of His creation, yet we need to grasp that His children are of greater value, as we read in Job 7:17-18 and Psalm 144:3,

'What is man that You should exalt him, that You should set Your heart on him, that You should visit him every morning, and test him every moment?'

'Lord, what is man, that You take knowledge of him? Or the son of man, that You are mindful of him?'

Throughout the Old Testament we can see that God was in control of all the little events that led for example to Joseph becoming Pharaoh's right-hand man, or Esther becoming queen in order to save His people, or Ruth who became the grandmother of King David. Jesus' disciples need not fear; valued a little lower than the angels, they can trust in God's providence as we read in Psalm 8:4-5,

'What is man that You are mindful of him, and the son of man that You visit him? For You have made him a little lower than the angels, and You have crowned him with glory and honour.'

Matthew 10:32-33

In verses 32-33, we find one of the harder sayings of Jesus, in which He makes it clear that for His disciples it is not enough to be right before God, but that there must be a true and public profession of Christ as the Messiah, the Son of the Father. He says to them,

> "Everyone therefore who shall confess me before men, will confess I also him before the Father of me in the heavens; and whoever denies me before men, will deny I also him before the Father of me in the heavens."

For many people over the last two thousand years or so, this has meant life or death, and countless faithful disciples have been martyred, but for most people it is how we respond in everyday life. It is not just one act, on one dramatic occasion, but in every act, in every circumstance of life, even in the smallest things and in the most commonplace of conversations; in the daily and minute-by-minute decisions and choices we make. We confess Christ when we own His teaching, His ministry, His servants, and when nothing hinders us from supporting and assisting His servants. Jesus' words echo those spoken to Eli the priest, a descendent of Aaron, whose sons had dishonoured God's house, as we read in 1 Samuel 2:30,

> 'Therefore, the Lord God of Israel says: 'I said indeed that your house and the house of your father would walk before Me forever.' But now the Lord says: 'Far be it from Me; for those who honour Me I will honour, and those who despise Me shall be lightly esteemed.'

Those who deny Jesus before men are those who put a greater value on earthly than on heavenly things and prefer things of human value to the things that God values. Those who renounce Jesus, will also renounce Him as Saviour, Mediator and Advocate, and to set Him as a witness against them. God warns that those who choose not to keep His ways will be made contemptible and set aside from the Father in heaven, as we read for example in Malachi 2:9 and Psalm 12:3-4,

> 'Therefore, I also have made you contemptible and base before all the people, because you have not kept My ways but have shown partiality in the law.'

204

'May the Lord cut off all flattering lips, and the tongue that speaks proud things, who have said, 'With our tongues we will prevail; our lips are our own; who is lord over us?'

There is nothing in Jesus' words to suggest that these things will only happen at the end of our earthly life. Indeed, if we assume that Jesus means that each time His disciples confess Him to men that He will confess them to God the Father, how wonderful to think that every time we do stand up for Jesus, confessing in public that He is the Son of the Living God, giving Him the glory and declaring our faith in Him, this is recorded in Heaven! This message does not just apply to individuals, but to the Church as a body. The Church itself, its ministers and congregation, must openly and publicly confess Christ as Saviour and Redeemer. The disciples of Jesus must openly declare that Jesus is the eternal Son of God by whose sacrifice they are redeemed, that He died for all, that He rose from the dead and ascended into Heaven, and that He will come again, and they must declare this in the face of hatred, opposition and persecution, knowing that God has promised those who seek Him will find Him and receive salvation, as we read in Proverbs 8:17, Psalm 50:23 and Psalm 119:46,

'I love those who love Me, and those who seek Me diligently will find Me.'

'Whoever offers praise glorifies Me; and to him who orders his conduct aright I will show the salvation of God.'

'I will speak of Your testimonies also before kings, and I will not be ashamed.'

Matthew 10:34-36

In verses 34-36, Jesus was warning His followers that their allegiance to Him might cause conflict at home, within their families, and communities, saying,

> "Do not suppose that I came to bring peace on the earth; I came not to bring peace but a sword. For I came to make hostile a man against the father of him and a daughter against the mother of her and a bride against the mother-in-law of her, and the enemies of a man the members of the household of him."

Jesus did not advocate conflict; He had already taught His disciples not to offer resistance or retaliation when they were attacked or persecuted, and in the Sermon on the Mount He had taught 'Blessed are the peacemakers, for they shall be called sons of God.' Our Father is the God of peace, and those who seek peace and pursue it reflect His character. The message that His disciples are to preach is the Gospel of peace, or reconciliation, and Jesus demonstrated peace and reconciliation in His ministry. The word sword, that Jesus used here, represented division, separation, or estrangement. He was warning His disciples that because not all would receive the message of salvation, there would be tension, conflict and betrayal within families and formerly close communities. Jesus was warning that division would be the effect of His message, certainly not the purpose. Here he quotes directly from the prophet Micah 7:5-6,

> 'Do not trust in a friend; do not put your confidence in a companion; guard the doors of your mouth from her who lies in your bosom. For son dishonours father, daughter rises against her mother, daughter-in-law against her mother-in-law; a man's enemies are the men of his own household.'

It is the unrighteousness in people that produces discord, contention, and hostility, not the message of the Gospel; the spirit in those who sin against God is opposed to the Spirit of God that is in His followers. It is a consequence of the self-seeking malice of the unrighteous that there is a separation, or division, of those who seek the Lord and those who refuse to do so. Jesus Himself was betrayed by a trusted disciple. The prophet Ezekiel, referring to Jerusalem speaks of betrayal, and Scripture warns that the unrighteous hate the righteous, as we read for example in Ezekiel 22:7 and Proverbs 29:9-10,

'In you they have made light of father and mother; in your midst they have oppressed the stranger; in you they have mistreated the fatherless and the widow."

'If a wise man contends with a foolish man, whether the fool rages or laughs, there is no peace. The bloodthirsty hate the blameless, but the upright seeks his well-being.'

We know that some of the most violent and persistent feuds in history have arisen from differences in religion, and Jesus' words were a forewarning of this. Contemporary Christians also experience discrimination, partiality, bias, and rejection from strangers but also employers, relatives, close friends and family members. Scripture equates seeking peace with righteousness, as we read for example in Psalm 34: 13-14, Isaiah 1:17, and Jeremiah 22:3, and the Gospel message, without question, is one of peace and we know that Jesus is the Prince of Peace from the words of the prophet Isaiah in chapter 9:6,

'Keep your tongue from evil, and your lips from speaking deceit. Depart from evil and do good; seek peace and pursue it.'

'Learn to do good; seek justice, rebuke the oppressor; defend the fatherless, plead for the widow.'

'Thus says the Lord: "Execute judgement and righteousness and deliver the plundered out of the hands of the oppressor. Do no wrong and do no violence to the stranger, the fatherless, or the widow, nor shed innocent blood in this place."

'For unto us a Child is born, unto us a Son is given; and the government will be upon His shoulder. And His name will be called Wonderful, Counsellor, Mighty God, Everlasting Father, Prince of Peace.'

Matthew 10:37-39

In verses 37-39, Jesus continues His teaching about the cost of discipleship; teaching about the meaning of putting God first saying,

> "The one loving father or mother beyond Me is not of Me worthy; and the one loving son or daughter beyond Me is not of Me worthy; and he who takes not the cross of him and follows after Me, is not of Me worthy. The one finding the life of him will lose it, and the one losing the life for the sake of Me will find it."

This is another hard saying; it is hard to understand and hard to reconcile with the rest of Jesus' teaching as it appears to go against the law – of loving your neighbour and honouring your parents. But what Jesus is warning His followers is, that just as property or riches can come between us and the Kingdom of God, so can family ties. The interest of God's Kingdom must be paramount for Jesus' followers; everything else must take second place, even family ties. Moses, spoke about the tribe of Levi, who were appointed as priests in the Temple, putting their service to God ahead of family ties, as we read in Deuteronomy 33:9-10,

> 'Who says of his father and mother 'I have not seen them'; nor did he acknowledge his brothers or know his own children; for they have observed Your word and kept Your covenant. They shall teach Jacob Your judgements, and Israel Your law. They shall put incense before You, and a whole burnt sacrifice on Your altar.'

A proper care for one's family is right and proper, and the sixth commandment is to 'Honour your father and mother'. Jesus Himself censured the Pharisees and teachers of the law who argued that people who had vowed to give God a sum of money could not then divert that money from religious purposes to help their parents who were in need. But Jesus is effectively reminding His disciples that the first and most important command is 'You shall have no other gods before Me', so that nothing is of greater importance than the Kingdom of God. The priest Eli allowed his corrupt sons to continue to serve in the Temple, putting his family ties first; for this he was admonished by God, as we read in 1 Samuel 2:29,

> 'Why do you kick at My sacrifice and My offering which I have commanded in My dwelling place, and honour your sons more than Me, to make yourselves fat with the best of all the offerings of the children of Israel made by fire?'

Having made clear that God the Father and His Kingdom have to have the number one place in our lives, Jesus goes on to speak about His followers taking up their cross, and the implication is that putting one's family second to God's purposes is a way of taking up the cross. Taking up the cross at the time that Jesus was speaking literally meant preparing for execution; being prepared to abandon all earthly hopes and ambitions. In Roman Palestine, a person condemned to crucifixion was forced to carry the crossbeam to the place of execution. Jesus' followers must also be prepared to put their own life second to the purposes of the Kingdom of God; to be prepared to face persecution and even death; to deny our instinctive desires, for the sake of Jesus. Denying oneself doesn't just mean giving something up for Lent or even for your whole life; it is a conscious decision to choose the plans and purposes of God rather than our own plans and ambitions. Jesus finishes with a wonderful promise, that the disciple who is willing to risk or lose their comfort or life on earth for His sake will find everlasting comfort and life and can join in praise with the psalmist in Psalm 105:1-4,

> 'Oh, give thanks to the Lord! Call upon His name; make known His deeds among the peoples! Sing to Him, sing psalms to Him; talk of His wondrous works! Glory in His holy name. Let the hearts of those rejoice who seek the Lord! Seek the Lord and His strength; seek His face evermore!'

Matthew 10:40-42

In verses 40-42, Jesus concludes His teaching about discipleship with words of encouragement that those who offer hospitality to those who proclaim the message of the Gospel in His name will receive their reward, saying,

> "The one receiving you me receives, and the one me receiving receives the one having sent me. The one receiving a prophet in the name of a prophet the reward of a prophet will receive, and the one receiving a righteous man in the name of a righteous man the reward of a righteous man will receive. And whoever gives to drink one of these little ones a cup of cold water only in the name of a disciple, truly I tell you, on no account will he lose the reward of him."

Jesus refers to a prophet, a righteous man, and the 'little ones' – those of His disciples who had no wealth or position in society - to indicate that when kindness is shown to any of His disciples, regardless of rank, it is a proof of the high estimation in which that person is held because they are a servant of Christ, and that not one kindness is ever forgotten. We can find examples in Old Testament Scripture of the prophets of God being offered hospitality in this way. The widow in Zarephath received Elijah the prophet and received a reward not only of food but the life of her son restored to her, as we read in 1 Kings 17:15 and 23-24,

> 'So she went away and did according to the word of Elijah; and she and her household ate for many days.'

> 'Elijah took the child and brought him down from the upper room into the house and gave him to his mother. And Elijah said, "See, your son lives." Then the woman said to Elijah, "Now, by this I know that you are a man of God, and that the word of the Lord in your mouth is the truth."

There is also the example of the Shunammite woman who received and welcomed the prophet Elisha, even setting aside a special room for his use whenever he came to visit. She knew he was a holy man of God and wished to care for him without thought of recompense. Elisha's servant knew that she was barren, and when Elisha was told, she received the reward of giving birth to a son, and later also had the life of her son restored, as we read in 2 Kings 4:8 and 17,

'Now it happened one day that Elisha went to Shunem, where there was a notable woman, and she persuaded him to eat some food. So it was, as often as he passed by, he would turn in there to eat some food.' And 'The woman conceived and bore a son when the appointed time had come, of which Elisha had told her.'

Jesus was teaching that those who receive with kindness Himself, His disciples, a prophet, a righteous man, or even the lowliest of His disciples, demonstrate their love for God's kingdom and deserve reward. He made it clear that although many would reject them, others would receive and welcome them. By receiving Christ's followers, people would be receiving Christ Himself, and even His Father who sent Him. The kindness done could be as simple as the offering of a cup of water; the gift having value according to the love and affection in which Christ is held by the giver and therefore worthy of reward. By this we can see that even the poorest person can demonstrate their love for Christ simply by receiving His messengers. It is a Scriptural truth that by loving our neighbour, in giving or showing mercy, we are loving God, as we read for example in Proverbs 19:17, 14:31, and Psalm 18:20,

'He who has pity on the poor lends to the Lord, and He will pay back what he has given.'

'He who oppresses the poor reproaches his Maker, but he who honours Him has mercy on the needy.'

'The Lord rewarded me according to my righteousness; according to the cleanness of my hands He has recompensed me.'

MATTHEW CHAPTER ELEVEN

Matthew 11:4-6

In verses 4-6, Jesus is replying to John the Baptist's followers who came to Jesus asking if He was the 'Coming One' that they expected. He replied saying,

> "Going report ye to John the things which ye hear and see: blind men see again and lame men walk, lepers are cleansed and deaf men hear, and dead men are raised and poor men are evangelised; and blessed is whoever is not offended in me."

Had Jesus replied simply in words, His claim could easily have been refuted, instead He kept the men with Him so they could see and hear His ministry for themselves; they were able to witness for themselves what the prophets had foretold. The principle holds true also for His disciples, that they should not be credited because they profess to know something, but because they demonstrate by their conduct that what they profess is true. Jesus referred directly to the prophecy in Isaiah that John and his followers would have been familiar with, as we read in chapter 29:18-19 and chapter 35:5-6,

> 'In that day the deaf shall hear the words of the book, and the eyes of the blind shall see out of obscurity and out of darkness. The humble also shall increase their joy in the Lord, and the poor among men shall rejoice in the Holy One of Israel.'

> 'Then the eyes of the blind shall be opened, and the ears of the deaf shall be unstopped. Then the lame shall leap like a deer, and the tongue of the dumb sing. For waters shall burst forth in the wilderness, and streams in the desert.'

Jesus included in his answer a reference to the preaching of the Gospel to 'the poor'. He knew that the very nature of the Gospel was that it was designed for all, including the poor and despised. He also knew that His purpose was to fulfil the role of spiritual as well as physical physician, to cure souls, as we read in Isaiah 61:1,

> 'The Spirit of the Lord God is upon Me, because the Lord has anointed Me to preach good tidings to the poor; He has sent Me to heal the broken-hearted, to proclaim liberty to the captives, and the opening of the prison to those who are bound.'

He also added that those who received Him would be blessed; those who did not feel let down by the manner of the coming of His Kingdom when many had assumed He would come with a mighty army to save the people of Israel as in the days of King David. Jesus was doing the things that, according to the prophets, would mark the dawn of a new age. He was actively fulfilling the prophecy in Isaiah 61. John would have understood Jesus' message to mean that he was not wrong; that He was indeed the 'Coming One' and that John need not feel let down by the fact that He was not doing the kind of things that even John had expected of Him. The word translated as 'offend' can also mean 'stumble'. Jesus may have been referring to the words in Isaiah 8, that our incorrect expectations of Jesus' true nature, or like John an erroneous concept of the kingdom, could be a stumbling block, as we read in verse 14,

> 'He will be as a sanctuary, but a stone of stumbling and a rock of offense to both the houses of Israel, as a trap and a snare to the inhabitants of Jerusalem.'

Jesus' reply to John's followers clearly informed them that what the prophets had declared respecting the reign of Christ and His kingdom, in which God had promised to be kind and gracious and grant relief and assistance for every kind of disease, both physical and spiritual, was accomplished and fulfilled, as summarised in Psalm 146:8,

> 'The Lord opens the eyes of the blind; the Lord raises those who are bowed down; the Lord loves the righteous.'

Matthew 11:7-10

In verses 7-10, as John the Baptist's disciples were leaving, Jesus challenged His listeners, including the scribes and Pharisees, about the inconsistency of their acknowledgment of John the Baptist as a divinely authorised teacher, but not believing in Himself as Christ when John had done so, saying,

> "What went ye out into the wilderness to see? A reed by wind being shaken? But what went ye out to see? A man in soft material having been clothed? Behold, the ones soft material wearing are in the houses of kings. But why went ye out? A prophet to see? Yes, I tell you, and more than a prophet. This is he concerning whom it has been written: Behold, I send forth the messenger of me before the face of thee, who will prepare the way of thee before thee."

Jesus asks if those who made the journey into the wilderness to listen to John found a wind-blown reed; someone who was irresolute or unconvinced of his testimony. Clearly someone who was unsure of his commission would not allow himself to be a martyr in prison. Jesus goes on to ask if they had gone to see someone with an attractive appearance or a great house. The very fact that John was living a simple life in the desert must have resonated with their knowledge of the prophets of old who lived simple lives and yet spoke God's word to kings, as we read for example in 2 Kings 1:7-8 when Elijah sends a message to King Ahaziah,

> 'Then he said to them, "What kind of man was it who came up to meet you and told you these words?" So they answered him, "A hairy man wearing a leather belt around his waist." And he said, "It is Elijah the Tishbite."

Finally, Jesus asks if they went to see a prophet. The people would not have flocked out to the desert to listen to an ordinary person. They understood a prophet to be a person with a message from God and the courage to deliver that message; a message that conveys God's wisdom and truth. John believed in the message he was sent to deliver, convinced of its truth, yet humbly acknowledged his own lowliness compared to the Messiah who's coming he announced. We know that it is in God's nature to send angels and prophets as messengers to reveal His intentions to both the rich and powerful and to the lowliest of people, as we read for example in Exodus 23:20 and Amos 3:7,

'Behold, I send an Angel before you to keep you in the way and to bring you into the place which I have prepared.'

'Surely the Lord God does nothing, unless He reveals His secret to His servants the prophets.'

Jesus' reference to the verses in Malachi affirm John's identity as the prophet Elijah who would return, and Himself as the Messiah. John was the first prophet to have appeared in hundreds of years, but he was also different in that he was not only a messenger from and for God, as the others were, but also, he was the fulfilment of a prophecy about himself as being the one foretold to prepare the way for the Messiah's appearing, as we read in Malachi 3:1, Malachi 4:5, and Isaiah 40:3-5,

'Behold, I send My messenger, and he will prepare the way before Me. And the Lord, whom you seek, will suddenly come to His temple, even the Messenger of the covenant, in whom you delight. Behold, He is coming, says the Lord of hosts.'

'Behold, I will send you Elijah the prophet before the coming of the great and dreadful day of the Lord.'

'The voice of one crying in the wilderness: "Prepare the way of the Lord; make straight in the desert a highway for our God. Every valley shall be exalted and every mountain and hill brought low; the crooked places shall be made straight and the rough places smooth; the glory of the Lord shall be revealed, and all flesh shall see it together; for the mouth of the Lord has spoken."

Matthew 11:11-15

In verses 11-15, Jesus continues His teaching about John the Baptist, saying,

> "Truly I tell you, there has not arisen among those born of woman a greater than John the Baptist; but the lesser in the kingdom of the heavens greater than he is. And from the days of John the Baptist until now the kingdom of the heavens is forcibly treated, and forceful men seize it. For all the prophets and the law until John prophesied; and if ye are willing to receive it, he is the Elias the one about to come. The one having ears let him hear."

These words seem paradoxical, if John was not surpassed in greatness by any human being, then how could anyone be greater than he? It may be that Jesus was referring to the fact that He was not merely born of woman but is the Son of God, as we read for example in Psalm 2:7

> 'I will declare the decree: The Lord has said to Me, You are My Son, today I have begotten You.'

In his preaching in the Jordan valley, John had called on his followers to amend their ways in preparation for the Coming One who would carry out a judgement symbolised by wind and fire. Judgement involved separation of the good from the worthless, the wheat from the chaff, as we read for example in Psalm 1:4-6,

> 'The ungodly are not so but are like the chaff which the wind blows away. Therefore, the ungodly shall not stand in the judgement, nor sinners in the congregation of the righteous. For the Lord knows the way of the righteous, but the way of the ungodly shall perish.'

The reports that had reached John in prison about Jesus' ministry bore little resemblance to the ministry of judgement that John had expected. When Jesus spoke about those in the kingdom of the heavens being greater than John, it was because those whose ministry follows the resurrection of Jesus, in the power of the Holy Spirit, would be greater than John's ministry of repentance. The early prophets pointed to the Christ who was to come, John declared that He had come, the disciples and witnesses of the resurrection declare that Jesus has come, has died, has risen and that there is salvation through Him as we can read in the whole of Isaiah Chapter 53, and particularly in verse 12,

218

'Because He poured out His soul unto death, and He was numbered with the transgressors, and He bore the sin of many, and made intercession for the transgressors.'

When Jesus spoke of the kingdom of the heavens being treated with force, this was likely a reference to John's imprisonment that marked the beginning of Jesus' ministry. Many people at the time expected the new order to be introduced through violence and the forcible expulsion of the Romans but Jesus' teaching was through suffering, and He desired that His listeners would hear His message and receive it into their hearts as we read in Ezekiel 3:10-11 and Psalm 40:6-8,

'Moreover, He said to me "Son of man, receive into your heart all My words that I speak to you, and hear with your ears. And go, get to the captives, to the children of your people, and speak to them and tell them: "Thus says the Lord God", whether they hear or whether they refuse.'

'Sacrifice and offering You did not desire; my ears You have opened. Burnt offering and sin offering You did not require. Then I said, "Behold, I come; in the scroll of the book, it is written of me, I delight to do Your will, O my God, and Your law is within my heart.'

Matthew 11:16-19

In verses 16-19, Jesus likens the people who were not willing to receive Him to children who were unhappy that He wouldn't play their game, saying,

> "But to what shall I liken generation this? Like it is to children sitting in the marketplaces who calling to the others say: We piped to you and not ye did dance; we lamented and ye did not mourn. For came John neither eating nor drinking, and they say: a demon he has. Came the Son of man eating and drinking, and they say: Behold, a man gluttonous and a wine-drinker, of tax-collectors a friend and of sinners. And is justified wisdom by the works of her."

There were people who found fault with Christ, whatever He did, since it was not what they wanted or expected from the Messiah. They wanted a King who would fit in with their traditional understanding of the Messiah. Jesus' words show that in John the Baptist and in Himself they had rejected both poles of righteous conduct. John's life was too austere for them; they did not lament or weep in repentance but remained unmoved by his message. Neither did they rejoice in the good news of Christ's message of salvation. Jesus expressed His sorrow at their unwillingness to receive Him in words that echo those in Lamentations 2:13,

> 'How shall I console you? To what shall I liken you, O daughter of Jerusalem? What shall I compare you with that I may comfort you, O virgin daughter of Zion? For your ruin is spread wide as the sea; who can heal you?'

John the Baptist lived in the wilderness and ate the most basic food, he shunned feasts and entertainments and demonstrated abstinence in his lifestyle but was rejected and accused of having a demon. Jesus by contrast was sociable, He attended weddings and ate with people from all classes and backgrounds; He was similarly rejected and accused of being a drunk and a glutton, his accusers quoting from Proverbs 23:20-21,

> 'Do not mix with winebibber, or with gluttonous eaters of meat; for the drunkard and the glutton will come to poverty.'

Jesus' answer, possibly also a reference to Proverbs, was to speak of wisdom; Christ Himself, who is the wisdom of God. There is a clear message, to receive His words and commands, that is found in the opening verses of Proverbs 1 where we read in verses 1-5,

220

'My son, if you receive my words, and treasure my commands within you, so that you incline your ear to wisdom, and apply your heart to understanding; yes, if you cry out for discernment, and lift up your voice for understanding, if you seek her as silver, and search for her as for hidden treasures; then you will understand the fear of the Lord, and find the knowledge of God.'

For some people, no matter what sort of preacher or type of preaching they hear, they will find fault with the message, since what they seek is not the wisdom of God but the perceived wisdom of their own desires. The whole of Job chapter 28 is devoted to teaching about God's gift of wisdom and her works as we read for example in verses 23-28, asking 'Where can wisdom be found? And where is the place of understanding?' the answer:

'God understands its way, and He knows its place. For He looks to the ends of the earth, and sees under the whole heavens, to establish a weight for the wind, and apportion the waters by measure. When He made a law for the rain, and a path for the thunderbolt, then He saw wisdom and declared it; He prepared it, indeed, He searched it out. And to man He said, 'Behold the fear of the Lord, that is wisdom, and to depart from evil is understanding.'

Matthew 11:21-24:

In verses 21-24, Jesus warns His listeners that in receiving His message there must be a true response, and illustrates the principle that the greater the revelation the greater the accountability, saying,

> "Woe to thee, Chorazin; woe to thee, Bethsaida; because if in Tyre and Sidon happened the powerful deeds having happened in you, long ago in sackcloth and ashes they would have repented. However, I tell you, for Tyre and for Sidon more tolerable it will be in the day of judgement than for you. And thou, Capernaum, not as far as heaven, was thou exalted? As far as Hades shalt thou descend; because if in Sodom happened the powerful deeds having happened in thee, it would have remained until today. However, I tell you that for the land of Sodom more tolerable it will be in the day of judgement than for thee."

Jesus refers to the destruction of Tyre and Sidon prophesied by the prophet Ezekiel, intimating that if, through Ezekiel, the same miracles had happened as they did with Jesus, that they would have repented. The Galilean towns that Jesus spoke of were not as immoral as the cities of Tyre, Sidon, and Sodom, but they had witnessed the ministry and miracles of Jesus, and then rejected Him, and thus would be subject to more severe judgement. The house of Israel had refused to repent at the time of Ezekiel as we read in chapter 3:5-7, and compared to the city of Sodom in chapter 16:48-49,

> 'For you are not sent to a people of unfamiliar speech and of hard language, but to the house of Israel, not unto many people of unfamiliar speech and of hard language, whose words you cannot understand. Surely, had I sent you to them, they would have listened to you. But the house of Israel will not listen to you because they will not listen to Me; for all the house of Israel are impudent and hard-hearted.'

> "As I live," says the Lord God, "neither your sister Sodom nor her daughters have done as you and your daughter have done. Look, this was the iniquity of your sister Sodom: she and her daughter had pride, fulness of food, and abundance of idleness; neither did she strengthen the hand of the needy."

Christ's warning is to the unrepentant. It will be more tolerable for those who have sinned without having witnessed the ministry of Jesus than for those who hear the Gospel message but harden their hearts. Jesus and

His disciples had preached and healed throughout Galilee but most of the people still did not repent - rejecting Jesus as they rejected God's message in the past as we read for example in Jeremiah 23:14 and Lamentations 4:6,

> 'Also, I have seen a horrible thing in the prophets of Jerusalem: they commit adultery and walk in lies; they also strengthen the hands of evildoers, so that no one turns back from his wickedness, all of them are like Sodom to Me, and her inhabitants like Gomorrah.'

> 'The punishment of the iniquity of the daughter of my people is greater than the punishment of the sin of Sodom, which was overthrown in a moment, with no hand to help her.'

Capernaum was exalted by its prosperity and privileges, and as the hometown of Jesus Christ. But because of its rejection of Him it would be brought down into Hades, that is to desolation; the loss of position and prosperity. Jesus intimates here that if He had visited Sodom in the same way that He visited the Galilean towns, the people then would have repented, and the city spared. Those who do receive Christ's message, repent, and follow Him can trust in the promise of His mercy, as we read in Psalm 103:11-12,

> 'For as the heavens are high above the earth, so great is His mercy toward those who fear Him; as far as the east is from the west, so far has He removed our transgressions from us.'

Matthew 11:25-26:

In verses 25-26, Jesus publicly spoke to God as His own Father, in words that glorified Him, giving Him praise and acknowledging His wisdom, power and grace, saying,

> "I give thanks to thee, Father, lord of the heaven and of the earth, because thou hidest these things from wise and intelligent men, and didst reveal them to infants; yes, Father, because thus good pleasure it was before thee."

In His opening phrase Jesus demonstrated how to 'hallow' God's name as He had already taught His disciples, declaring Him to be Lord of heaven and earth, being the creator, upholder, and ruler of both which are filled with His presence; the one is His throne and the other His footstool. These words echo those found in Deuteronomy 10:14 and Isaiah chapter 44 verses 24-25 in which God is declared Lord of all and then speaks of making foolishness of those who claim to have knowledge:

> 'Indeed heaven and the highest heavens belong to the Lord your God, also the earth with all that is in it.'

> "I am the Lord, who makes all things, who stretches out the heavens all alone, who spreads abroad the earth by Myself; who frustrates the signs of the babblers and drives diviners mad; who turns wise men backward and makes their knowledge foolishness."

The wise and intelligent men that Jesus spoke of were doubtless those who considered themselves to be wise and intelligent; wise in their own eyes and prudent in their own sight, such as the scribes and the Pharisees who refused to submit to the righteousness of God. Many of them had rejected Jesus and His message of salvation as foretold by the prophet Isaiah as we read in chapter 5:21, chapter 29:13-14 and also in Jeremiah chapter 8 verse 9,

> 'Woe to those who are wise in their own eyes, and prudent in their own sight.'

> 'Therefore the Lord said: "Inasmuch as these people draw near with their mouths and honour Me with their lips, but have removed their hearts far from Me, and their fear toward Me is taught by the commandment of men, therefore, behold, I will again do a marvellous work among this people, a marvellous work and a

wonder; for the wisdom of their wise men shall perish, and the understanding of their prudent men shall be hidden.'

'The wise men are ashamed, they are dismayed and taken. Behold, they have rejected the word of the Lord; so, what wisdom do they have?'

Jesus was not referring to those who seek God's wisdom, but to those who follow their own perceived wisdom as people for whom the truth remains hidden. Those whose hearts are open, and uncorrupted like an infant, are able to receive the message of salvation. The apostles were not sophisticated, learned or intellectual men wedded to preconceived ideas or doctrines, but were unspoiled by philosophy and humbly accepted Jesus' teaching. The apostle Paul, initially wise in his own eyes, was humbled to enable him to receive the message according to the Father's pleasure. Thus, Jesus clearly fulfilled what was spoken of in Isaiah 6:9-10, Psalm 8:2, and Isaiah 46:9-10, where we read:

'And He said, "Go, and tell this people: 'Keep on hearing, but do not understand; keep on seeing, but do not perceive.' "Make the heart of this people dull, and their ears heavy, and shut their eyes; lest they see with their eyes, and hear with their ears, and understand with their heart, and return and be healed."

'Out of the mouth of babes and nursing infants You have ordained strength, because of Your enemies, that You may silence the enemy and the avenger.'

'For I am God, and there is no other; I am God, and there is none like Me, declaring the end from the beginning, and from ancient times things that are not yet done, saying, 'My counsel shall stand, and I will do all My pleasure.'

Matthew 11:27

In verse 27, Jesus confirmed an important truth that all things – all power in heaven and on earth - had been delivered to Him by His Father for the good of those who follow Him, saying,

> 'All things to me were delivered by the Father of me, and no one fully knows the Son except the Father, neither the Father anyone fully knows except the Son and he to whom if wills the Son to reveal.'

We could perhaps read this as: only the Father and the Son know each other, and therefore only the Son can reveal the Father. Jesus made it clear that there is a reciprocity of personal knowledge between the Son of God and His Father. As none but the Father know the Son, so none but the Son knows the Father, but the Son shares this knowledge with those whom He chooses. Jesus' relationship to the Father as His Son is clearly established, as we can read for example in 2 Samuel 7:13-14 and Psalm 2:7-8,

> 'He shall build a house for My name, and I will establish the throne of his kingdom forever. I will be his Father, and he shall be My son.'

> 'I will declare the decree: The Lord has said to Me, 'You are My Son, today I have begotten You. Ask of Me, and I will give You the nations for Your inheritance, and the ends of the earth for Your possession.'

The Father is eternally unbegotten, while the Son is eternally begotten of the Father – eternally meaning that it never starts or stops. By saying that the Son was begotten, we can understand that the Son's divine essence is exactly like the Father's and also communicated from the Father. The Son is the image of the Father; the exact representation of His being. This relationship is expounded in Proverbs if we assume that 'wisdom', or righteousness, is a reference to God's Word and thus to Christ. According to Proverbs, divine wisdom reveals the Father, because divine wisdom is the Son – the image and only begotten of the Father. In His incarnation, the Son is the image of the invisible God, in an eternal relationship, as we read for example in Proverbs 8:22-25 and 30-31,

> 'The Lord possessed me at the beginning of His way, before His works of old, I have been established from everlasting, from the beginning, before there was ever an earth. When there were no

depths I was brought forth, when there were no fountains abounding with water, before the mountains were settled, before the hills I was brought forth.'

'Then I was beside Him as a master craftsman; and I was daily His delight, rejoicing always before Him, rejoicing in His inhabited world, and my delight was with the sons of men.'

The Father, who dwells in inaccessible light, is revealed to His people by the Son because He is the visible image of the Father, representing Him visibly in His own person, and the Son is revealed by the Father's Spirit allowing His people to discern the glory of Christ. In speaking about those to whom He chooses to reveal the Father, Jesus may have had in mind the prophetic words in Psalm 110 that says of his His people that they will be 'volunteers' and adds that the Messiah will be a priest in the order of Melchizedek. The name Melchizedek means 'King of Righteousness'. He was the first individual to be given the title of priest in the Bible; he was the king of Salem and High Priest of 'El Elyon' (most high God). Jesus' words establish Himself as the eternal Son, who receives from the Father, and in consequence of His eternal union with the Godhead becomes the eternal High Priest and Mediator who alone can approach God, as we read for example in Psalm 110:3-4,

'Your people shall be volunteers in the day of Your power; in the beauties of holiness, from the womb of the morning, You have the dew of Your youth. The Lord has sworn and will not relent, You are a priest forever according to the order of Melchizedek.'

227

Matthew 11:28-30

In verses 28-30, Jesus seems to reflect back on His teaching regarding the scribes and Pharisees and once again confirms in Himself what had been foretold by the prophets about rest for the weary from God, saying,

> "Come unto me all the ones labouring and having been burdened, and I will rest you. Take the yoke of me on you and learn from me, because meek I am and lowly in heart, and ye will find rest to the souls of you; for the yoke of me gentle and the burden of me light is."

Jesus had earlier taught about how the scribes and Pharisees, in their teaching of the law in which they focussed on their own traditions, laid a heavy burden on the people. By contrast, Jesus was inviting the people to take on His burden of fulfilling the law by loving their neighbour, that is light by comparison. He did not relax the requirements of God's law or recommend a lower standard of righteousness than that required by the teachers of the law. Rather, He taught that admittance to the kingdom of heaven called for righteousness that exceeded that of the scribes and Pharisees; that the proper way to keep any commandment was to fulfil the purpose for which it was given. One example would be the keeping of the sabbath law. Jesus taught that the sabbath, instituted for the rest, relief, and general well-being of the people, was made for the sake of humans and that therefore any action, such as a healing, that promoted rest and relief on the sabbath, rather than contravening the law would honour the day by fulfilling its purpose. This rest was clearly promised in the Scriptures as we read for example in Exodus 33:14, Psalm 116:7, Isaiah 28:12, and Isaiah 55:1,

> 'And He said, "My Presence will go with you, and I will give you rest."

> 'Return to your rest, O my soul, for the Lord has dealt bountifully with you.'

> 'To whom He said, "This is the rest with which you may cause the weary to rest," and, "This is the refreshing"; yet they would not hear.'

> 'Ho! Everyone who thirsts. Come to the waters; and you who have no money, come buy and eat.'

228

Jesus spoke about taking on His yoke and learning from Him and again we can find passages in Scripture that speak of rest and refreshment for those who accept the instruction from our heavenly Father, as we read for example in Psalm 94:13 and Sirach 51:23-24,

> 'Blessed is the man whom You instruct, O Lord, and teach out of Your law, that You may give him rest from the days of adversity.'

> 'Draw near to me, you who are uneducated, and lodge in the house of instruction. Why do you say you are lacking in these things, and why do you endure such great thirst?'

Jesus also taught that the law should be fulfilled not through ceremony, ritual, or legalistic sacrifice, but through demonstrating love towards our neighbour. He taught that the will of God the Father should be done from the heart rather than following lists of rules. Jesus described Himself as meek and lowly, or humble, and His disciples are called to be meek, lowly and humble as He is in order to receive the promises of satisfaction for the hungry and thirsty, joy in the Lord, and rest for the soul, as we read in Micah 6:8, Jeremiah 31:25, Isaiah 29:19, and Jeremiah 6:16,

> 'He has shown you, O man, what is good; and what does the Lord require of you but to do justly, to love mercy, and to walk humbly with your God.'

> 'For I have satiated the weary soul, and I have replenished every sorrowful soul.'

> 'The humble also shall increase their joy in the Lord, and the poor among men shall rejoice in the Holy One of Israel.'

> 'Thus says the Lord: "Stand in the ways and see, and ask for the old paths, where the good way is, and walk in it; then you will find rest for your souls."

MATTHEW CHAPTER TWELVE

Matthew 12:3-8

At the beginning of chapter 12, Jesus' hungry disciples were criticised for plucking ears of grain, rubbing away the husks, and eating the kernels as they walked through fields on the Sabbath. In reply Jesus said,

> "Did you not read what did David, when he hungered and the ones with him? How he entered into the house of God and the loaves of the setting forth ate, which not lawful it was for him to eat neither the ones with him, except for the priests only? Or did you not read in the law that on the sabbaths the priests in the temple the sabbath profane and guiltless are? And I tell you that the temple a greater thing is here. But if ye had known what its is: Mercy I desire and not sacrifice, ye would not have condemned the guiltless. For the Lord is of the sabbath the son of man."

In an emergency, David, as recorded in 1 Samuel 21:3-5, had been permitted by the priest in charge of the sanctuary, once he had been reassured that David's men were ritually clean, to have some of the 'shewbread' on a Sabbath although no one except the priests were supposed to eat it according to Leviticus 24:5-9. The Levitical priests had to work on the Sabbath, as do modern day clergy, but remained blameless. Just as the priests serving in the temple on the Sabbath were blameless, Jesus' disciples were also blameless. Clearly, life is more important than religious ritual. Jesus goes on to remind His listeners that God is greater than the temple as we read for example in the words of Solomon in 2 Chronicles 6:18, and in Isaiah 66:1-2,

> 'But will God indeed dwell with men on the earth? Behold, heaven and the heaven of heavens cannot contain You. How much less this temple which I have built?'

> 'Thus says the Lord, "Heaven is My throne, and earth is My footstool. Where is the house that you would build Me? And where is the place of My rest? For all those things My hand has made, and all those things exist," says the Lord. "But on this one will I look: on him who is poor and of a contrite spirit, and who trembles at My word".'

Not only is Jesus more important than the temple, by referring to the words of the prophet Hosea, He makes it clear that mercy is more important than sacrifice. God sets a higher value on mercy than sacrifice; on loving our neighbour than religious observance. Religious rites have no intrinsic value and God only demands them in the context of their intended object; they are inferior to acts of mercy as we read in Hosea 6:6, 1 Samuel 15:22, and Isaiah 1:11,

'For I desire mercy and not sacrifice, and the knowledge of God more than burnt offerings.'

'So Samuel said: "Has the Lord as great delight in burnt offerings and sacrifices, as in obeying the voice of the Lord? Behold, to obey is better than sacrifice, and to heed than the fat of rams.'

"To what purpose is the multitude of your sacrifices to Me" says the Lord. "I have had enough of burnt offerings of rams and the fat of fed cattle. I do not delight in the blood of bulls, or of lambs or goats.' [see verses 12-15]

Jesus' final point is that the Sabbath was given for our benefit not our discomfort. It was instituted by God and the Sabbath law is best kept when God's purpose in giving it is fulfilled. God blessed and hallowed the Sabbath for the sake of His creation who He knew would need it. It was instituted, as we read in Exodus 20:10-11, to meet a human need, and the law is satisfied when human need is met on it.

'The seventh day is the Sabbath of the Lord your God. In it you shall do no work; you, nor your son, nor your daughter, nor your male servant, nor your female servant, nor your cattle, nor your stranger who is within your gates. For in six days the Lord made the heavens and the earth, the sea, and all that is in them, and rested the seventh day. Therefore the Lord blessed the Sabbath day and hallowed it.'

Matthew 12:11-13

In verses 11-13, Jesus continued His teaching that the Sabbath was given for the benefit of God's creation and that Human need takes priority over ritual or religious observance, saying,

> "What will there be of you man who will have sheep one, and if fall in this on the sabbath into a ditch, will he not lay hold of it and raise? By how much then surpasses a man a sheep. So that it is lawful on the sabbath well to do." Then He says to the man, "Stretch forth of thee the hand."

Jesus had already made the point that it is always right to do good on the Sabbath and that life is more important than rules. Here He seems to take the argument further, indicating that it is better to save life than to cause harm on the Sabbath. Jesus clearly referred to the fact that the Pharisees and teachers of the law already made an exception to the Sabbath rules for an animal in distress based on Exodus 23:4-5 and Deuteronomy 22:4 where we read,

> 'If you meet your enemy's ox or his donkey going astray, you shall surely bring it back to him again. If you see the donkey of one who hates you lying under its burden, and you would refrain from helping it, you shall surely help him with it.'

> 'You shall not see your brother's donkey or his ox fall down along the road, and hide yourself from them; you shall surely help him lift them up again.'

Jesus was teaching that if it is right to save the life of a sheep then it is also right – and more so - to save a person who is made in the image of God. If an animal fell into a pit on the Sabbath, those who adhered to the strict rules of the Pharisees would not hesitate to rescue it the same day, and yet they criticized Jesus for healing a man on the Sabbath. If Jesus had simply helped a person out of a pit or a ditch, this may not have precipitated such criticism, but when Jesus commanded the man with a withered hand to stretch it out and it was healed, the leaders of the synagogue most likely felt threatened and hoped to use the Sabbath law against Jesus. Yet the law itself makes it clear not only that it is wrong to act against the law, but it is also wrong to neglect duty, as we read for example in Deuteronomy 24:19-21,

'When you reap your harvest in your field, and forget a sheaf in the field, you shall not go back to get it; it shall be for the stranger, the fatherless, and the widow, that the Lord your God may bless you in all the work of your hands.'

The man with the withered hand was obedient to Jesus' command to 'stretch out his hand'; he did as He was told, and the hand was restored. The man was healed at Jesus' word, He had not even touched him and so the law was not broken even according to the most rigid interpretation. Jesus demonstrated that in mercy the Sabbath law is met and leaves us in no doubt that God is the Lord who heals, as we can read for example in Exodus 15:26, Jeremiah 30:17, Jeremiah 33:7, Psalm 103:2-3, 147:2-3, and Isaiah 53:5,

> "If you diligently heed the voice of the Lord you God and do what is right in His sight, give ear to His commandments and keep all His statutes, I will put none of the diseases on you which I have brought on the Egyptians, for I am the Lord who heals you."

> 'For I will restore health to you and heal you of your wounds, says the Lord.'

> 'Behold, I will bring it (Jerusalem) health and healing; I will heal them and reveal to them the abundance of peace and truth.'

> 'Bless the Lord, O my soul, and forget not all His benefits: Who forgives all your iniquities, Who heals all your diseases.'

> 'The Lord builds up Jerusalem; He gathers together the outcasts of Israel. He heals the broken hearted and binds up their wounds.'

> 'But He was wounded for our transgressions, He was bruised for our iniquities; the chastisement for our peace was upon Him, and by His stripes we are healed.'

Matthew 12:25-30

In verses 11-13, we read that Jesus, having healed a man demon-possessed, blind and mute, knew the Pharisees were accusing Him of casting out demons by Beelzebub and said,

> "Every kingdom divided against itself is brought to desolation, and every city or house divided against itself will not stand. And if Satan Satan expels, against himself he is divided; how therefore will stand the kingdom of him? And if I by Beelzebub expel the demons, the sons of you by what do they expel? Therefore they judges shall be of you. But if by the Spirit of God I expel the demons, then came upon you the kingdom of God. Or how can anyone enter into the house of the strong man and the vessels of him to seize, if not first he binds the strong man? And then the house of him he will plunder. The one not being with me against me is, and the one not gathering with me scatters."

The argument is simple, if Satan was casting out Satan, he would be destroying his own kingdom. A kingdom must remain united to stand against its enemies. The Pharisees taught that Satan was the cause of demon possession, and themselves practiced the casting out of demons – why would Satan undo his own work? Jesus, we are told, knew their thoughts and this knowledge belongs to God as we read in Psalm 139:1-4 and Jeremiah 9:10,

> 'O Lord, You have searched me and known me. You know my sitting down and my rising up; You understand my thoughts afar off. You comprehend my path and my lying down, and are acquainted with all my ways. For there is not a word on my tongue, but behold, O Lord, You know it altogether.'

> 'The heart is deceitful above all things, and desperately wicked; who can know it? I, the Lord, search the heart, I test the mind, even to give every man according to his ways, according to the fruit of his doings.'

The formerly demon-possessed man was healed so that he was able to see and speak, this by its own evidence demonstrated a defeat of Satan that could not be construed as anything else. In healing the man from the physical tyranny of the devil, Jesus proclaimed that the Father had sent Him as deliverer also from spiritual tyranny. The healing was testimony to the work of the Spirit of God and Jesus declared that it was

236

a demonstration of the coming of the kingdom of God as foretold in the familiar words of the prophet Isaiah in chapter 49:25 and chapter 61:1,

> 'But thus says the Lord: "Even the captives of the mighty shall be taken away, and the prey of the terrible be delivered; for I will contend with him who contends with you, and I will save your children".'

> "The Spirit of the Lord God is upon Me, because the Lord has anointed Me to preach good tidings to the poor; He has sent Me to heal the broken-hearted, to proclaim liberty to the captives, and the opening of the prison to those who are bound."

Gathering His people is the work of God, while scattering them is the work of the devil as we read for example in 1 Chronicles 16:35 (quoted also in Psalm 106:47), and Hosea 1:11,

> "Save us, O God of our salvation; gather us together, and deliver us from the gentiles, to give thanks to Your holy name, to triumph in Your praise."
> 'Then the children of Judah and the children of Israel shall be gathered together and appoint one head; and they shall come up out of the land, for great will be the day of Jezreel.'

In the words of Thomas Manson: 'The Kingdom of God is the one constructive unifying redemptive power in a distracted world; and every man has to choose whether he will take sides with it or against it.'[4] This same choice has faced God's people since the beginning, as we find in the words of Joshua chapter 24:15,

> "And if it seems evil to you to serve the Lord, choose for yourselves this day whom you will serve, whether the gods which your fathers served that were on the other side of the River, or the gods of the Amorites, in whose land you dwell. But as for me and my house, we will serve the Lord."

---

[4] T W Manson, The Sayings of Jesus (1949), p.87.

Matthew 12:31-32

In verses 31-32, Jesus continued His teaching about choices. Previously, He had made it clear that anyone who is not with Him is against Him, but here makes it clear that to be deliberately opposed to God, to purposely turn God's light into darkness, is unforgivable, saying,

> "Therefore I tell you, all sin and blasphemy will be forgiven to men, but the of the Spirit blasphemy will not be forgiven. And whoever speaks a word against the Son of man, it will be forgiven to him; but whoever speaks against the Spirit Holy, it will not be forgiven to him neither in this age nor in the one coming."

In Judaism, blasphemy is an act of cursing or reviling God, but more than that, the crime is to ascribe to oneself, or another, the rights or qualities of God. The Hebrew word is 'na'ats' which means to spurn, have contempt for, despise, or abhor. The definitions we have for blasphemy are the actions of a person in whom God is absent from their heart. The law was unequivocal on this subject; the severest penalties were to be meted out to those who blasphemed, rebelled, or deliberately chose to defy God's word, as we read in Leviticus 24:16 and Numbers 15:30,

> 'And whoever blasphemes the name of the Lord shall surely be put to death.'

> 'But the person who does anything presumptuously, whether he is native born or a stranger, that one brings reproach on the Lord, and he shall be cut off from among his people. Because he has despised the word of the Lord, and has broken His commandment, that person shall be completely cut off; his guilt shall be upon him.'

In Hebrew, the words in Numbers 15:30 translate as 'the person who does presumptuously beguile'. The word presumption originally meant seizure or occupation without right. In this instance, we can understand it to mean to act wilfully, in bold defiance of conscience or violation of known duty, and in deception. Moses warned the people not to rebel against God's direct command for which the consequences are separation from God as we read in Deuteronomy 1:42-43 and verse 45, and also in chapter 17:12,

> 'And the Lord said to me, 'Tell them, "Do not go up nor fight, for I am not among you; lest you be defeated before your enemies".

So I spoke to you; yet you would not listen, but rebelled against the command of the Lord, and presumptuously went up into the mountain.'

'Then you returned and wept before the Lord, but the Lord would not listen to your voice nor give ear to you.'

'Now the man who acts presumptuously and will not heed the priest who stands to minister there before the Lord your God, or the judge, that man shall die. So you shall put away the evil from Israel.'

Jesus teaches that this kind of sin cannot be forgiven, but the nature of this sin is such that an individual committing this blasphemy does not repent of it. Those who could ascribe the healing work of Jesus to the prince of demons were so corrupt that light had become darkness and good had become evil. God will forgive doubt and misunderstanding, but those who maliciously make war against God have no way of receiving His forgiveness. Just as darkness cannot exist in the presence of light, forgiveness can only exist where it can be received. God the Father has no pleasure in punishment His desire is only to love and forgive as we read for example in Ezekiel 33:11 and Isaiah 55:7,

'Say to them: 'As I live,' says the Lord God, 'I have no pleasure in the death of the wicked, but that the wicked turn from his way and live. Turn, turn from your evil ways! For why should you die, O house of Israel?'

'Let the wicked forsake his way, and the unrighteous man his thoughts; let him return to the Lord and He will have mercy on him; and to our God, for He will abundantly pardon.'

Matthew 12:33-37

In verses 33-37, Jesus was teaching that the choices people make, even down to their choice of words, depend on the state of their heart – whether they have a heart for God or not, saying,

> "Either make the tree good and the fruit of it good or make the tree bad and the fruit of it bad; for by the fruit the tree is known. Offspring of vipers, how can ye good things to speak evil being? For out of the abundance of the heart the mouth speaks. The good man out of the good treasure puts forth good things, and the evil man out of the evil treasure puts forth evil things. But I tell you that every word idle which will speak men, they will render concerning it account in the day of judgement; for by the words of thee thou wilt be justified, and by the words of thee thou wilt be condemned."

I think it is important to consider this reference to the heart, remembering that it is used in the context of being the seat of the soul in Old Testament Scripture. Jesus is the incarnation of the Author of Life and knows and understands the human heart far better than even 21st century people. The ancient Egyptians observed how the heart reacts to emotion and stress and how this affects every part of the body, leading them to consider the heart to be where the human soul is located. Now, in the 21st century, scientists have discovered that the heart has more than 40,000 neurons (the same cells as in the brain), and that it has an electro-magnetic field that radiates several feet outside your body. The human heart is not merely a pump, and what resides there matters, as we read in 1 Samuel 24:13, Psalm 10:6-7, Proverbs 18:12, and Isaiah 32:6-7,

> 'As the proverbs of the ancients says, 'Wickedness proceeds from the wicked.' But my hand shall not be against you.'

> 'He has said in his heart, "I shall not be moved; I shall never be in adversity." His mouth is full of cursing and deceit and oppression; under his tongue is trouble and iniquity.'

> 'Before destruction the heart of a man is haughty, and before honour is humility.'

> 'For the foolish person will speak foolishness, and his heart will work iniquity; to practice ungodliness, to utter error against the Lord, to keep the hungry unsatisfied, and he will cause the drink

of the thirsty to fall. Also the schemes of the schemer are evil; he devises wicked plans to destroy the poor with lying words.'

The verses in Proverbs and Isaiah directly linked the heart that works iniquity with lying or foolish words. In a world of 'soundbites', posts, and blogs, we know all too well of the power of words for both good and evil. Jesus would have been very familiar with the words in the Psalms and Proverbs as we read in Psalm 52:2-4, and 37:30-31, and in Proverbs 10:19-21, 13:3, 16:23, and 4:23-24,

'Your tongue devises destruction, like a sharp razor, working deceitfully. You love evil more than good, lying rather than speaking righteousness. You love all devouring words, you deceitful tongue.'

'The mouth of the righteous speaks wisdom, and his tongue talks of justice. The law of his God is in his heart; none of his steps shall slide.'

'In the multitude of words sin is not lacking, but he who restrains his lips is wise. The tongue of the righteous is choice silver; the heart of the wicked is worth little. The lips of the righteous feed many, but fools die for lack of wisdom.'

'He who guards his mouth preserves his life, but he who opens wide his lips shall have destruction.'

'The heart of the wise teaches his mouth and adds learning to his lips.'

'Keep your heart with all diligence, for out of it spring the issues of life. Put away from you a deceitful mouth and put perverse lips far from you.'

Jesus concluded with a warning that even the simplest word or phrase could have consequences; that we should seek a new heart in which to store good treasure, as we read in Ecclesiastes 12:14 and Ezekiel 18:31,

'For God will bring every work into judgement, including every secret thing, whether good or evil.'

'Cast away from you all the transgressions which you have committed and get yourselves a new heart and a new spirit. For why should you die, O house of Israel?'

241

Matthew 12:39-42

In verses 39-42, Jesus is responding to some of the scribes and Pharisees who have requested a sign from Him, saying,

> "Generation an evil and adulterous a sign seeks, and a sign shall not be given to it except the sign of Jonas the prophet. For as was Jonas in the belly of the sea monster three days and three nights, so will be the Son of man in the heart of the earth three days and three nights. Men Ninevites will stand up in the judgement with generation this and will condemn it; because they repented at the proclamation of Jonas, and behold a greater thing than Jonas is here. The queen of the south will be raised in the judgement with generation this and will condemn it; because she came out of the limits of the earth to hear the wisdom of Solomon, and behold a greater thing than Solomon is here."

Given that Jesus had already performed many miracles and then been accused of having done this through Beelzebub, we can only wonder what sort of sign might have convinced them. As teachers of the law, they should have been able to decide whether Jesus' teaching was in line with the law and the prophets - whether it was true or not – without the need for signs. It seems unlikely that any sign would have confirmed His teaching about the Kingdom of God since they would likely have attributed any sign to the devil. To those who were determined to remain in their unbelief, no sign could suffice. However, Jesus does point to His own future resurrection and the prophetic account of Jonah in the belly of the fish as a sign, as we read in Jonah 1:17, 2:6, and Psalm 16:10,

> 'Now the Lord had prepared a great fish to swallow Jonah. And Jonah was in the belly of the fish three days and three nights.'

> 'I went down to the moorings of the mountains; the earth with its bars closed behind me forever; yet You have brought up my life from the pit, O Lord my God.' And 'For You will not leave my soul in Sheol, nor will You allow Your Holy One to see corruption.'

The sign given to the people of Nineveh, that Jesus referred to, was a statement of judgement on their sin. Unlike the men of Nineveh, the teachers of the law who heard Jesus had enjoyed centuries of teaching, of worship, and divine revelation as God's chosen people, yet when called to acknowledge Jesus as the Messiah and the Author of Salvation, chose to reject Him. By contrast, the people of Nineveh, on hearing Jonah's message acted immediately and with total commitment, as we read in Jonah 3:5 and in the king's proclamation in verses 7-8,

> 'So the people of Nineveh believed God, proclaimed a fast, and put on sackcloth, from the greatest to the least of them.'

> "Let neither man nor beast, herd nor flock, taste anything; do not let them eat, or drink water. But let man and beast be covered with sackcloth, and cry mightily to God; yes, let everyone turn from his evil way and from the violence that is in his hands."

Jesus contrasted the response of the scribes and the Pharisees with that of the pagan men of Nineveh, and then went further, contrasting them with a woman, who although she had not been taught the law, came from a great distance to receive instruction from Solomon who, though given immense wisdom, was not as great as Jesus, the Prince of all the prophets, as we read in 1 Kings 4:29 and 34, 10:1 and Psalm 72:17,

> 'And God gave Solomon wisdom and exceedingly great understanding, and largeness of heart like the sand on the seashore.'

> 'Men of all nations, from all the kings of the earth who had heard of his wisdom, came to hear the wisdom of Solomon.'

> 'Now when the queen of Sheba heard of the fame of Solomon concerning the name of the Lord, she came to test him with hard questions.'

> 'His name shall endure forever; His name shall continue as long as the sun, and men shall be blessed in Him; all nations shall call Him blessed.'

Matthew 12:43-45

In verses 43-45, Jesus continued His teaching about the willingness of the people to accept His message of salvation and the kingdom of heaven, saying,

> "Now when the unclean spirit goes out from a man, he goes through dry places seeking rest, and finds not. Then he says: Into the house of me I will return whence I came out; and coming he finds it standing empty and having been swept and having been furnished. Then he goes and takes with himself seven other spirits more evil than himself, and entering dwells there; and becomes the last things man of that worse than the first. Thus it will be also generation to this evil."

The scribes and Pharisees to whom Jesus likely addressed this speech accepted the idea of unclean spirits and so would have understood the intent of this message. As part of His ministry, Jesus had freed people from the bondage of such spirits and there are Scriptural accounts of evil spirits, as we can read for example of King Saul in 1 Samuel 16:14 and 19:9,

> 'But the Spirit of the Lord departed from Saul, and a distressing spirit from the Lord troubled him.'

> 'Now the distressing spirit from the Lord came upon Saul as he sat in his house with his spear in his hand.'

The Hebrew word rā·'āh translated as 'distressing' spirit here in Samuel is mostly translated as evil spirit, but can also be translated – depending on context- as hurtful, wild, displeasing, harmful, bad, wrong, vexatious, wicked, mischievous, adversity, trouble, affliction, treacherous, and noisome. In this parable, Jesus said that the unclean spirit, having left the man sought rest; an unclean spirit can only find rest in a corrupt human heart. The going out of the unclean spirit could refer to the repentance that followed John's baptism that left the house, that is the individual, swept and furnished but without any real change of heart. The rejection of Christ leaves the heart vulnerable to the unrelenting attacks of the forces that work against God's kingdom. For those whose goodness consists merely of not doing bad, those whose life is not dedicated to actively serving God, Jesus is warning that where God is not filling the space in their heart that evil will move into the vacuum. This is perhaps what happened in Saul's case as his paranoia deepened, he even sought out the services of the witch of En Dor as we read in 1 Samuel 28:15,

> 'The king said to her, "Do not be afraid. What did you see?" And the woman said to Saul, "I saw a spirit ascending out of the earth." So he said to her, "What is his form?" And she said, "An old man is coming up, and he is covered in a mantle."

Jesus warned of the nature of evil that never ceases to try to cause harm and is continuously busy, moving from one place to another looking to find a weakness, as we read for example in Job 1:7,

> 'And the Lord said to Satan, "From where do you come?" So Satan answered the Lord and said, "From going to and fro on the earth, and from walking back and forth on it."

It is clearly not enough to be cleansed once; Jesus' disciples need to be filled with God's Spirit so that there is no space for anything else – no opening left for evil to enter. Just as a house needs to be continually swept, cleaned, and sanitised to prevent disease and infection. It is not sufficient to know what not to do; a person must know what they must do to fill their life with the righteousness of God and not let the devil get a foothold, as we read in Proverbs 19:23 and 18:10,

> 'The fear of the Lord leads to life, and he who has it will abide in satisfaction; he will not be visited with evil.'

> 'The name of the Lord is a strong tower; the righteous run to it and are safe.'

Matthew 12:48-50

In verses 48-50, Jesus responded to being told that His mother and brothers were waiting outside to speak to him, saying,

> "Who is the mother of me, and who are the brothers of me?" And stretching forth the hand of him on the disciples of him he said: "Behold the mother of me and the brothers of me. For whoever does the will of the Father of me in heaven, he of me brother and sister and mother is."

This is very much a continuation of Jesus' teaching that whoever is not with Him is against Him; that His disciples must choose to actively follow Jesus in doing the will of God the Father. Jesus asks who His mother is, this was not to deny her role as His birth mother, but to emphasise the importance of obedience to the will of the Father. As Mary had been obedient to the Lord's will, so all those who are also obedient can claim a similar relationship. Another very important mother, and an ancestor in the genealogical listing for Jesus, was Ruth. She was born a Moabite – a gentile, but because she chose to do the will of the Lord God, she became the mother of Obed, the father of Jesse who was the father of King David – both a descendent of Abraham and an ancestor to Joseph, the earthly father of Jesus. When Naomi's son died and Ruth was widowed, Ruth chose to stay with Naomi, acknowledging the Lord as her God and determined to follow Him, as we read in Ruth chapter 1 verse 16,

> 'Ruth said: "Entreat me not to leave you, or to turn back from following after you; for wherever you go, I will go; and wherever you lodge, I will lodge; your people shall be my people, and your God, my God.'

In the same way, Jesus spoke about brothers and sister, or brethren, as those who do the will of the Father and are obedient to Him. It was usual for the words brother or brethren to include those beyond the immediate family. We find that a brother or sister included the immediate family, the extended family, fellow Israelites, and even employees, and we can trace this back to Abram in Genesis 13:8,

> 'So Abram said to Lot, "Please let there be no strife between you and me, and between my herdsmen and your herdsmen, for we are brethren.'

This is also made clear in the representation of neighbours as brethren in the law as we read in Leviticus 25:25,

> And 'If one of your brethren becomes poor, and has sold some of his possessions, and if his redeeming relative comes to redeem it, then he may redeem what his brother sold.'

Jesus' words make it clear that all His disciples, those who believe and trust in Him and do the will of His Father, are part of His family, as if they are His closest relatives, related to Him by spiritual rather than earthly ties. Christ bestows on His disciples the honour of being reckoned as His brethren. His true family are those who, like Abraham, obey the Father's voice, who demonstrate the kind of faith in Jesus that Abraham showed that was credited to him as righteousness, as we read in Genesis 22:18 and Psalm 133:1,

> "In your seed all the nations of the earth shall be blessed, because you have obeyed My voice."

> 'Behold how good and pleasant it is for brethren to dwell together in unity. It is like the precious oil upon the head, running down on the beard, the beard of Aaron, running down on the edge of his garments. It is like the dew of Hermon, descending upon the mountains of Zion; for there the Lord commanded the blessing – life forevermore.'

MATTHEW CHAPTER THIRTEEN

Matthew 13:3-9

In chapter 13, Jesus begins His teaching using parables. In verses 3-9, He tells the familiar parable of the sower, saying,

> "Behold went out the one sowing to sow and in the to sow him some indeed fell beside the way, and coming the birds devoured them. But others fell on the rocky places where not it had earth much, and immediately it sprang up on account of the not to have depth of earth; the sun but having risen it was scorched on account of the not to have root it was dried up. But others fell on the thorns and came up the thorns and choked them. And others fell on the earth good and gave fruit, the one a hundred, the other sixty, the other thirty. The one having ears let him hear."

We know that some people hear the word of God gladly, while others allow the good seed to be devoured. Jesus may have had in mind the account of Joseph, in Genesis 40:16-17, that tells of Joseph's interpretation of Pharaoh's baker's dream in which the birds devoured the food in the basket. Joseph interpreted the dream to mean that the baker would be hanged. Richard Wurmbrand suggests that Joseph understood that if the birds dared come so close to the baker, then he must be a dead man.[5] The implication here is that the seeds of the word of God cannot be devoured when the recipient is spiritually alive. It is important to note that the focus of the parable is on the quality of the soil where the seed lands rather than on the sower; on the heart of the person who hears the word of God. The stones or rocks reflect those whose hardness of heart continues without any true sense of sin and repentance for it after hearing the word of God; the heart of stone needs to become a heart of flesh as we read in Ezekiel 11:19,

> "Then I will give them one heart, and I will put a new spirit within them, and take the stony heart out of their flesh, and give them a heart of flesh, that they may walk in My statutes and keep My judgements and do them; and they shall be My people, and I will be their God."

The comparison that Jesus makes of seed that has fallen amongst thorns with seed that is fruitful can be found in Jeremiah and Genesis. Through Jeremiah, God tells His people to circumcise their hearts and not sow

---

[5] Richard Wurmbrand (1977) Reaching Towards The Heights (January 8th) Basingstoke: Marshall Morgan & Scott

among thorns, but by implication they were to cultivate the word of God by ploughing the ground. In Genesis we read that Isaac, who like his father Abraham obeyed the word of the Lord when he was told to stay in the land where God had led him and not go down to Egypt, reaped a fruitful harvest and was blessed, as we read in Jeremiah 4:3-4 and Genesis 26:12,

> 'For thus says the Lord to the men of Judah and Jerusalem: "Break up your fallow ground and do not sow among thorns. Circumcise yourselves to the Lord and take away the foreskins of your hearts."

> 'Then Isaac sowed in that land and reaped in the same year a hundredfold; and the Lord blessed him.'

At the end of the parable, Jesus used what would have been a familiar phrase to His hearers, to open their ears, that was also prophetic as to His own teaching using parables, as we read in Psalm 78:1-4,

> 'Give ear, O my people, to my law; incline your ears to the words of my mouth. I will open my mouth in a parable; I will utter dark sayings of old, which we have heard and known, and our fathers have told us. We will not hide them from their children, telling to the generations to come the praises of the Lord, and His strength and His wonderful works that He has done.'

Matthew 13:11-12

In verses 11-12, Jesus replied to His disciples who had asked Him why He spoke to the people in parables, saying,

"Because to you it has been given to know the mysteries of the kingdom of the heavens, but to those it has not been given. He who for has, it will be given to him and he will have abundance; but he who has not, even what he has will be taken from him."

Jesus had encountered considerable opposition from the Jewish leaders and teachers; it may have been partly in response to this opposition that He began teaching in parables to conceal His teaching from those who were not sincere in their seeking. The harmless stories, such as the parable of the sower, gave away nothing for spies of the Pharisees to report. The mysteries of the kingdom were not being made incomprehensible, or difficult to understand, but being concealed, or withheld, from those who would reject them; from those who would not bear fruit as was expected of God's people Israel described as His vineyard in Isaiah 5:4-6,

'What more could have been done to My vineyard that I have not done in it? Why then, when I expected it to bring forth good grapes, did it bring forth wild grapes? And now please tell me what I will do to my vineyard: I will take away its hedge, and it shall be burned; and break down its wall, and it shall be trampled down. I will lay it waste; it shall not be pruned or dug, but there shall come up briers and thorns. I will also command the clouds that they shall not rain on it.'

From Jesus' reply, we learn that He intentionally spoke in such a way, seemingly in riddles, so that the message would only be received by those to whom it had been given. Even without the use of parables, Jesus' message of redemption appeared to have been a mystery to those who had a preconceived and false idea of the purpose of the coming of the Messiah. Isaiah forewarned that the message of salvation would be like a sealed book to those who appear learned, and when the message is made visible those who are blinded by the darkness of the world, they will remain blind to it, as we read in Isaiah chapter 29:11,

'The whole vision has become to you like the words of a book that is sealed, which men deliver to one who is literate, saying "Read this, please." And he says, "I cannot, for it is sealed." Then the book is delivered to one who is illiterate, saying, "Read this, please." And he says, "I am not literate."

Jesus went on to make it clear to His disciples that those who receive God's grace will receive more, and in abundance. By contrast, those who reject God's grace will find that they do not have even have what they thought they had. A parable of this effect might be for example: when water is poured over dry earth, the water runs over and is lost and the ground remains dry, but when water is poured over already damp earth it is absorbed and seeps down into the rich soil. The principle here is that the more His disciples receive, the more they are able to receive and to understand, as we read for example in Psalm 25:2-9 and 14, Psalm 49:1-4, and Psalm 119:130,

> 'Good and upright is the Lord; therefore, He teaches sinners in the way. The humble He guides in justice, and the humble He teaches His way [...] The secret of the Lord is with those who fear Him, and He will show them His covenant.'

> 'Hear this, all peoples; give ear, all inhabitants of the world, both low and high, rich and poor together. My mouth shall speak wisdom, and the meditation of my heart shall give understanding. I will incline my ear to a proverb; I will disclose my dark saying on the harp.'

> 'Your testimonies are wonderful; therefore, my soul keeps them. The entrance of Your words gives light; it gives understanding to the simple.'

Matthew 13:13-15

In verses 13-15, Jesus, paraphrased the words of the prophet Isaiah in chapter 6:9-10, saying,

> "Therefore, in parables to them I speak, because seeing they not and hearing they hear not neither understand. And is fulfilled in them the prophecy of Isaiah saying: In hearing ye will hear and by no means understand and seeing ye will see and by no means perceive. For waxed gross the heart people of this, and with the ears heavily they heard, and the eyes of them they closed; lest they see with the eyes and with the ears hear and with the heart understand and turn back, and I will heal them."

In Hebrew there is a tendency to express a consequence as though it were a purpose. This can leave us with the impression that God has deliberately hardened hearts rather than that those hearts have become hardened as a consequence of the choices the people have made. Isaiah volunteered to be God's messenger to His people, and God effectively told him to go and deliver His message but not to expect them to pay any attention to it because they would be persistent in their refusal to accept what he said to the point where they would have become incapable of accepting it, as we read in Isaiah 6:8-9 and chapter 42:18-20

> 'I heard the voice of the Lord, saying: "Whom shall I send, and who will go for Us?" Then I said, "Here I am! Send me." And He said, "Go, tell this people: 'Keep on hearing, but do not understand; keep on seeing but do not perceive.'

> "Hear you deaf; and look, you blind, that you may see. Who is blind but My servant, or deaf as My messenger whom I send? Who is blind as he who is perfect, and blind as the Lord's servant? Seeing many things, but you do not observe; opening the ears, but he does not hear."

This refusal to accept God's message is exactly what Isaiah experienced and so did Jesus. Jesus met unbelief in the places where people had witnessed the mightiest of His works. The people remained obdurate – stubbornly refusing to change their ways or beliefs. To those of Jesus' hearers whose minds were closed, His words seemed like riddles. They could not take in His message and thus could not profit by it. The more He spoke and acted among them, the more unresponsive they seemed to become. People will instinctively cover their eyes when they have foreseen an accident or some other horror so that they do not have to see it or cover their ears so that they cannot be offended by what they might hear. People will also choose not to see or hear something that may be distasteful to them for some reason, as we say, 'bury their head in the sand'. This was spoken of frequently by the Old Testament prophets, as we read for example in Jeremiah 5:21, Jeremiah 17:9, Ezekiel 12:2 and 20:49, and Zechariah 7:11-12,

> 'Hear this now, O foolish people, without understanding, who have eyes and see not, and who have ears and hear not.'

> 'The heart is deceitful above all things, and desperately wicked; who can know it?'

> "Son of man, you dwell in the midst of a rebellious house, which has eyes to see but does not see, and ears to hear but does not hear; for they are a rebellious house."

> 'Then I said, "Ah, Lord God! They say of me, 'Does he not speak parables?'."

> 'But they refused to heed, shrugged their shoulder, and stopped their ears so that they could not hear. Yes, they made their hearts like flint, refusing to hear the law and the words which the Lord of hosts had sent by His Spirit through the former prophets.'

According to Jesus' parable, the harvest that sprang up from the good soil was so abundant that the labour of the sower was not in vain; the harvest from those who hear the Word and accept it outweighs the loss from those who turn away. The promise to those who turn back to God is of salvation and healing as we read in Jeremiah 17:14 and 33:6,

> 'Heal me, O Lord, and I shall be healed; save me and I shall be saved, for You are my praise.'

> 'Behold, I will bring it health and healing; I will heal them and reveal to them the abundance of peace and truth.'

Matthew 13:16-17

In verses 16-17, Jesus continued His teaching about those who hear and are able to understand the Gospel message of salvation, saying,

> "But of you blessed the eyes because they see, and the ears of you because they hear, truly. For I say to you that many prophets and righteous men desired to see the things which ye see and did not see, and to hear the things which ye hear and did not hear."

Jesus told His disciples that they were blessed because they lived to see and hear what many prophets and kings had longed in vain to see and hear. It was not because of any merit of theirs, that could be thought superior to the Old-Testament prophets, that they enjoyed this privilege but simply because they lived at the time when Jesus came to walk on earth and were called by Him to share the life and service of the kingdom of God. Even John, the herald of the Messiah, was not so blessed as those who participated in His ministry and were heirs of the kingdom of which John, the last of the prophets of old, foretold. The prophets had looked forward to a time when all things would be fulfilled, but also knew that The Lord's message would continue to be rejected by many as had been the case in the past, as we read for example in Isaiah 42:23 and 53:1-2, and Jeremiah 7:24-27,

> 'Who among you will give ear to this? Who will listen and hear for the time to come?'

> 'Who has believed our report? And to whom has the arm of the Lord been revealed? For He shall grow up before Him as a tender plant, and as a root out of dry ground.'

> "Yet they did not obey or incline their ear but followed the counsels and the dictates of their evil hearts and went backward and not forward. Since the day that your fathers came out of the land of Egypt until this day, I have even sent to you all My servants the prophets, daily rising up and sending them. Yet they did not obey Me or incline their ear but stiffened their neck. They did worse than their fathers. Therefore, you shall speak all these words to them, but they will not obey you. You shall also call to them, but they will not answer you."

The disciples were more blessed than the ancient prophets; a far greater distinction than simply being preferred to the unbelieving populace. Jesus' words make it clear that the disciples' eyes and ears were blessed because they perceived His true nature as the Only Begotten Son of God and Redeemer. The knowledge of Christ is a distinguishing favour to those who have it; the apostles, who were to teach others, were blessed with the clearest perception of the truth, and this also was foretold, as we read in Isaiah 11:1, 32:3 and 42:1, and Proverbs 20:12,

> 'And in that day, there shall be a Root of Jesse, who shall stand as a banner to the people; for the Gentiles shall seek Him, and His resting place shall be glorious.'

> 'The eyes of those who see shall not be dim, and the ears of those who hear will listen.'

> 'Behold! My Servant whom I uphold, My Elect One in whom My soul delights! I have put My Spirit upon Him; He will bring forth justice to the Gentiles.' And 'The hearing ear and the seeing eye, the Lord has made them both.'

The prophets and righteous men of the past looked forward to the coming of the Messiah as the fulfilment of their wishes and their prophesies; their desire, as with all the righteous people, was to witness the establishment of the kingdom of Christ. They were given a glimpse of Christ from a distance in promises and veiled prophesies, but the disciple saw Him in person, heard Him preach, and witnessed the evidence of His miracles, and understood His power and significance clearly foretold for example in Micah 5:2, and Zechariah 9:9,

> 'But you, Bethlehem Ephrathah, though you are little among the thousands of Judah, yet out of you shall come forth to Me the One to be Ruler in Israel, whose goings forth are from of old, from everlasting.'

> 'Rejoice greatly, O daughter of Zion! Shout, O daughter of Jerusalem! Behold, your King is coming to you; He is just and having salvation.'

Matthew 13:18-23

In verses 18-23, Jesus gave His disciples a clear explanation of the parable of the sower, saying,

> "Ye therefore hear the parable of the sowing one. When anyone hears the word of the kingdom and does not understand, comes the evil one and seizes the thing having been sown in the heart of him; this is the word by the wayside sown. And on the rocky places sown, this is the one the word hearing immediately with joy receiving it; but he has not root in himself but short lived is, and when tribulation or persecution occurs on account of the word immediately he is offended. But the word in the thorns sown, this is the one the word hearing, and the anxiety of the age and the deceit of riches chokes the word, and unfruitful it becomes. And the word on the good earth sown, this is the one the word hearing and understanding, who indeed bears fruit and produces one indeed a hundred, the other sixty, the other thirty."

The subject of the parable is not the person who sows the word of the kingdom, but it is those who hear the word and their response to the word in their heart. In the parable, the birds who take away the seeds before they can take root represent the evil one. The Gospel can make no impression on such people because they have hardened their heart to its message, as we read in Proverbs 17:16, Psalm 78:36-37, and Ezekiel 18:31,

> 'Why is there in the hand of a fool the purchase price of wisdom since he has no heart for it?'

> 'Nevertheless they flattered Him with their mouth, and they lied to Him with their tongue; for their heart was not steadfast with Him, nor were they faithful in His covenant.'
> 'Cast away from you all the transgressions which you have committed and get yourselves a new heart and a new spirit.'

Those whose hearts Jesus likened to rocky places are those who have the appearance of piety, who practice religion because it makes them feel better, but have not had a real change of heart; they have not repented and got themselves a new heart and a new spirit, so that they stumble (the word translated as offended means to stumble in this context) and fall away when they encounter temptation, trials, and persecution. The thorns Jesus speaks of represent the cares and anxieties of the world, and the deceitful lure of riches, wealth, and power, as we read in Psalm 52:7, 62:10, Proverbs 1:7, 2:20-22 and 11:28,

> "Here is the man who did not make God his strength, but trusted in the abundance of his riches, and strengthened himself in his wickedness."

> 'Do not trust in oppression, nor vainly hope in robbery; if riches increase, do not set your heart on them.'

> 'The fear of the Lord is the beginning of knowledge, but fools despise wisdom and instruction.'

> 'So you may walk is the way of goodness and keep to the paths of righteousness. For the upright will dwell in the land, and the blameless will remain in it; but the wicked will be cut off from the earth, and the unfaithful will be uprooted from it.'

> 'He who trusts in his riches will fall, but the righteous will flourish like foliage.'

Those with hearts that Jesus likened to good earth are those whose hearts have been prepared through the grace of God to receive the word with submission and humility to give it a full opportunity to grow. They have hearts that submit to the truth and renewal of the Gospel, allowing God's spirit to water and nourish the word, allowing it to take deep root, as we read in Proverbs 1:5-6, 2:1-5 and Psalm 1:3,

> 'A wise man will hear and increase learning, and a man of understanding will attain wise counsel, to understand a proverb and an enigma, the words of the wise, and their riddles.'

> 'My son, if you receive my words, and treasure my commands within you, so that you incline your ear to wisdom, and apply your heart to understanding; yes, if you cry out for discernment, and lift up your voice for understanding, if you seek her as silver, and search for her as for hidden treasures; then you will understand the fear of the Lord and find the knowledge of God.'

> 'He shall be like a tree planted by the rivers of water, that brings forth its fruit in its season, whose leaf also shall not wither; and whatever he does shall prosper.'

Matthew 13:24-30

In verses 24-30, Jesus gave His disciples another parable to help them understand the kingdom of God, saying,

> "Was likened the kingdom of the heavens to a man sowing good seed in the field of him. But while men slept, men came of him the enemy and over sowed tares in between the wheat and went away. But when sprouted the grass and fruit produced, then appeared also the tares. So approaching, the slaves of the housemaster said to him: Lord, not good seed sowedst thou in thy field? Whence then has it tares? And he said to them: An enemy man this did. So the slaves to him say: Willest thou then, going away we may collect them? But he says: No, lest collecting the tares you should root up together with them the wheat. Leave to grow together both until the harvest; and in time of the harvest I will say to the reapers: Collect ye first the tares and bind them in bundles to burn them, but the wheat gather ye into the barn of me."

A tare was a type of weed that was prevalent in the region of Palestine. It closely resembles wheat and is therefore hard to distinguish from wheat until it matures and bears fruit that is bitter and inedible. In some areas, the tare plant is known as poison ryegrass that is often infected with a poisonous fungus that can be dangerous to grazing animals. The inference is clear that because people have a common outward appearance, it is not possible to see their true nature just by looking at them; they will be known by the fruit of their lives, good or bad, when they are held to account by God, as we read for example in Joel 3:12-14,

> 'Let the nations be wakened and come up to the Valley of Jehoshaphat; for there I will sit to judge all the surrounding nations. Put in the sickle, for the harvest is ripe. Come, go down; for the winepress is full, the vats overflow for their wickedness is great. Multitudes, multitudes in the valley of decision. For the day of the Lord is near in the valley of decision.'

Jesus knew that the time would come when there would be a harvest, not of crops, but of people, and that just as the unwholesome weeds need to be separated from the wheat, so souls would be separated according to their true nature, not according to human judgment; only God will be the judge, as we read in Isaiah 27:12, Ezekiel 18:30 and 34:20-22,

'And it shall come to pass in that day that the Lord will thresh, from the channel of the River to the Brook of Egypt; and you will be gathered one by one, O you children of Israel,'

'Therefore, I will judge you, O house of Israel, everyone according to his ways, says the Lord God. Repent, and turn from all your transgressions, so that iniquity will not be your ruin.'

'Therefore, thus says the Lord God to them: "Behold, I Myself will judge between the fat and the lean sheep. Because you have pushed with side and shoulder, butted all the weak ones with your horns, and scattered them abroad, therefore I will save My flock, and they shall no longer be a prey; and I will judge between sheep and sheep.'

Richard Wurmbrand points out that since we cannot rid ourselves of false friends, enemies, rivals, opponents, or annoyances - the tares, we must learn to love them. He goes on to say that there is no alternative to loving your enemies unless you wish to 'kill yourself slowly by nurturing hatred'.[6] Obedience to the command to love our neighbour, enables God's people to grow together with the 'tares' without being uprooted, in the confidence that they will be harvested into His barn at the proper time, as we read in Ecclesiastes 3:14-17,

'I know that whatever God does, it shall be forever. Nothing can be added to it, and nothing taken from it. God does it, that men should fear before Him. That which is has already been, and what is to be has already been; and God requires an account of what is past. Moreover, I saw under the sun; in the place of judgement, wickedness was there; and in the place of righteousness, iniquity was there. I said in my heart, 'God shall judge the righteous and the wicked, for there is a time there for every purpose and for every work.'

---

[6] Richard Wurmbrand, Reaching Towards The Heights, 1977, February 27th

Matthew 13:31-32

In verses 31-32, Jesus used another parable to describe the growth of His kingdom, saying,

> "Like is the kingdom of the heavens to a grain of mustard, which taking a man sowed in the field of him; which less indeed is than all the seeds, but when it grows, greater than the herbs it is and becomes a tree, so as to come the birds of the heaven and dwell in the branches of it."

The disciples, who were to preach the Gospel, were simple men with no reputation or high rank; for the most part they were men belonging to the common people. The Kingdom, to all appearances, began with a tiny feeble group of timid men. There are parallels with the beginnings of the nation of Israel, that became a vast number of people, which came from the seed of one old man, long past his prime and his elderly wife who was long-past child-bearing age, as we read in Genesis 15:5-6 of God speaking to Abraham,

> 'Then He brought him outside and said, "Look now toward heaven, and count the stars if you are able to number them." And He said to him, "So shall your descendants be." And he believed in the Lord, and He accounted it to him for righteousness.'

From small beginnings, the Church has grown into a vast community that covers the earth. We have the benefit of hindsight to see that over the last two thousand years, the Gospel message of the kingdom has spread to virtually every community on the planet. Jesus doubtless knew what the future would bring but used references in His parable to Old Testament prophesies that His disciples would have recognised. In these prophesies, kingdoms were represented as trees, as we find for example in Ezekiel 17:23, Ezekiel 31:6, and Daniel 4:12,

> "I will take also one of the highest branches of the high cedar and set it out. I will crop off from the topmost of its young twigs a tender one and will plant it on a high and prominent mountain. On the mountain height of Israel, I will plant it; and it will bring forth boughs, and bear fruit, and be a majestic cedar. Under it will dwell birds of every sort; in the shadow of its branches, they will dwell."

> 'All the birds of the heavens made their nests in its boughs; under its branches all the beasts of the field brought forth their young; and in its shadow all great nations made their home.'

'Its leaves were lovely, its fruit abundant, and in it was food for all. The beasts of the field found shade under it; the birds of the heavens dwelt in its branches; all flesh was fed from it.'

In this parable, the mustard seed can be thought of as the Word of God; of Christ Himself who is the Word. The tiny mustard seed can be likened to the Kingdom of God beginning in a small town with the birth of a child to humble and obscure parents in a stable, that grew to encompass people from every nation. It seems that in the region of Palestine where Jesus was teaching, due to its warm climate and rich soil, mustard bushes grew into trees large enough to climb into, unlike the modern shrubs that we may be more familiar with today. The large plant that the seed became is a representation of the success of the kingdom as had been foretold for example in Isaiah 2:2-3 and Psalm 72:16-17,

'Now it shall come to pass in the latter days that the mountain of the Lord's house shall be established on the top of the mountains and shall be exalted above the hills; and all nations shall flow to it. Many people shall come and say, "Come, and let us go up to the mountain of the Lord, to the house of the God of Jacob; He will teach us His ways, and we shall walk in His paths".'

'There will be an abundance of grain in the earth, on the top of the mountains; its fruit shall wave like Lebanon; and those of the city shall flourish like grass of the earth. His name shall endure forever; His name shall continue as long as the sun, and men shall be blessed in Him; all nations shall call Him blessed.'

Matthew 13:33

In verse 33, Jesus used yet another parable to illustrate how the kingdom of God would grow from small beginnings, saying,

> "Like is the kingdom of the heavens to leaven, which taking a woman hid in of meal measures three, until was leavened the whole."

The leaven used to make bread rise contains yeast; only a small amount is used and kneaded into the dough mixture. Yeast is not just small like a mustard seed, it is microscopic; it is a single-celled organism that needs food, warmth, and moisture to thrive. It converts its food, the sugars and starch in the flour, through fermentation, into carbon dioxide and alcohol. It is the carbon dioxide that makes the bread rise. Jesus spoke of three measures of meal; this roughly equates to four dry gallons; the woman needed only a small amount of leaven to make a large amount of bread. Leavened bread was the usual, preferred, and more palatable way to eat bread as we read in Genesis 18:6, eating unleavened bread was intended to remind the people of their suffering as we read in Deuteronomy 16:3,

> 'So Abraham hurried into the tent to Sarah and said, "Quickly, make ready three measures of fine meal; knead it and make cakes." And 'You shall eat no leavened bread with it; seven days you shall eat unleavened bread with it, that is, the bread of affliction (for you came out of the land of Egypt in haste), that you may remember the day in which you came out of the land of Egypt all the days of your life.'

In time, yeast spreads through all the dough, working from within. It works slowly and invisibly; only the effects can be seen, just as God's Spirit works unseen but we see the effect of the inward transformation of people's hearts on their outward lives. So, we can see this as an illustration of the kingdom as it exists in the hearts of individual believers; how God's grace works through their whole being and lives, as we read in Job 17:9, Proverbs 4:18, and Daniel 12:3,

> 'Yet the righteous will hold to his way, and he who has clean hands will be stronger and stronger.'

> 'But the path of the just is like the shining sun, that shines ever brighter unto the perfect day.'

264

'Those who are wise shall shine like the bright firmament, and those who turn many to righteousness like the stars forever and ever.'

We can also see this parable as an illustration of how the Gospel message acts as an agent of change within communities of people, transforming those communities from within. The yeast works until the dough has completely risen, illustrating how the kingdom of God will ultimately spread through the whole world. Just as the kingdom began with twelve ordinary men in obscure Galilee, so it has spread throughout the world. Although yeast is easily destroyed at high temperatures, scientists have discovered that yeast cultures can also go dormant and be rejuvenated after many years, even thousands of years! Jesus knew the Old Testament prophesies that foretold a time when indeed the Kingdom of God would spread and fill the whole earth, as we read in Psalm 22:27-28, Psalm 72:18-19, Isaiah 11:9, and Habakkuk 2:14,

'All the ends of the world shall remember and turn to the Lord, and all the families of the nations shall worship before You. For the kingdom is the Lord's and He rules over the nations.'

'Blessed be the Lord God, the God of Israel, who only does wondrous things! And blessed be His glorious name forever! And let the whole earth be filled with His glory.'

'They shall not hurt nor destroy in all My holy mountain, for the earth shall be full of the knowledge of the Lord as the waters cover the sea.'

And echoed in Habakkuk, 'For the earth will be filled with the knowledge of the glory of the Lord, as the waters cover the sea.'

Matthew 13:37-43

In verses 37-43, Jesus gave His disciples a clear explanation of the parable of the sower, saying,

> "The one sowing the good seed is the Son of man; and the field is the world; and the good seed, these are the sons of the kingdom; and the tares are the sons of the evil one, the enemy and the one sowing them is the devil; and the harvest the completion of the age is, and the reapers angels are. As therefore are collected the tares and with fire are consumed, thus it will be at the completion of the age; will send forth the Son of man the angels of him, and they will collect out of the kingdom of him all the things leading to sin and the ones doing lawlessness and will cast them into the furnace of fire; there will be the wailing and the gnashing of the teeth. Then the righteous will shine forth as the sun in the kingdom of the Father of them. The one having ears let him hear."

Here Jesus described the tares, sown amongst the wheat by the enemy, as being the sons of the evil one, presumably people who have chosen not to follow God's laws, but He also refers to them as being all the things that lead people into sin. Things that lead people into sin are described in the Old Testament as stumbling blocks, or idols. Whatever has a higher priority in our lives than God our Father is an idol and becomes a stumbling block. Those who allow themselves to be led into iniquity will be separated from the righteous, as we read in Ezekiel 7:19, Zephaniah 1:3, and Psalm 92:9,

> 'They will throw their silver into the streets, and their gold will be like refuse; their silver and their gold will not be able to deliver them in the day of wrath of the Lord; they will not satisfy their souls, nor fill their stomachs, because it became a stumbling block of iniquity.'

> 'I will consume man and beast; I will consume the birds of the heavens, the fish of the sea, and the stumbling blocks along with the wicked. I will cut off man from the face of the land, says the Lord.'

> 'For behold, Your enemies, O Lord, for behold, Your enemies shall perish; all the workers of iniquity shall be scattered.'

We know from the account of Moses and the burning bush that the Spirit of God can have the appearance of fire but does not necessarily consume.

Both wind and fire are symbols of the Holy Spirit and depict what the Messiah was to do by the power of the Spirit, separating the true children of the kingdom from the chaff which the wind blows away or the fire consumes. Jesus' ministry is one of sifting and separating; the fire was already there in His ministry. The fire is in His kingdom and is an instrument of God's justice, as we read in some of the many examples in 2 Samuel 23:6, Psalm 21:9, Psalm 50:3, Psalm 97:3, Isaiah 30:27, Isaiah 31:9, and Daniel 7:10,

> 'But the sons of rebellion shall be as thorns thrust away, because they cannot be taken with hands.'

> 'You shall make them as a fiery oven in the time of Your anger; the Lord shall swallow them up in His wrath, and the fire shall devour them.'

> 'Our God shall come and not keep silent; a fire shall devour before Him, and it shall be very tempestuous around Him.'

> 'A fire goes before Him and burns up His enemies round about.'

> 'Behold, the name of the Lord comes from afar, burning with His anger, and His burden is heavy; His lips are full of indignation, and His tongue like a devouring fire.'

> 'He [Assyria] shall cross over to his stronghold for fear, and his princes shall be afraid of the banner, says the Lord, whose fire is in Zion and whose furnace is in Jerusalem.'

> 'A fiery stream issued and came forth before Him. A thousand thousands ministered to Him; ten thousand times ten thousand stood before Him. The court was seated, and the books were opened.'

Jesus concluded by reminding His disciples that whilst evil and evil doers will be separated from God's presence, the righteous will shine in His kingdom, as we read in Judges 5:31 and Psalm 68:2-3,

> 'Thus let all Your enemies perish, O Lord! But let those who love Him be like the sun when it comes out in full strength.'

> 'As smoke is driven away, so drive them away; as wax melts before the fire, so let the wicked perish at the presence of God. But let the righteous be glad; let them rejoice before God; yes, let them rejoice exceedingly.'

Matthew 13:44-46

In verses 44-46, Jesus used two similar parables to further expound on the nature of His kingdom, saying,

> "Like is the kingdom of the heavens to treasure having been hidden in the field, which finding a man hid, and from the joy of him goes and sells what things he has and buys that field. Again, like is the kingdom of the heavens to a merchant seeking beautiful pearls; and finding one valuable pearl going away and sold all things what he had and bought it."

The first parable describes someone finding treasure who was not actively looking for it, but when finding it, acknowledges its supreme value, and regardless of how they had come to find it, they made every human effort to obtain it even at the cost of all their material possessions. The teaching here is that when a person sees or hears the kingdom message of salvation, they should likewise rid themselves of all that hinders them from obtaining it with the same earnestness that people seek earthly treasure. The treasure of the kingdom is worth so much more than earthly treasure, but is hidden from many people, as we read in Proverbs 3:13-15, Proverbs 16:16, and Psalm 19:10 and 39:6,

> 'Happy is the man who finds wisdom, and the man who gains understanding; for her proceeds are better than the profits of silver, and her gain than fine gold. She is more precious than rubies and all the things you may desire cannot compare with her.'

> 'How much better to get wisdom than gold! And to get understanding is to be chosen rather than silver.'
> 'The judgements of the Lord are true and righteous altogether. More to be desired are they than gold, yea, than much fine gold; sweeter also than honey and the honeycomb.'

> 'Surely every man walks about like a shadow; surely they busy themselves in vain; he heaps up riches and does not know who will gather them.'

The second parable describes someone who is actively engaged in the search for treasure. Then when they find it, they instantly recognise its value and are prepared to let go of all obstacles to having it. The treasures of God's kingdom are a free gift from God, but a person my 'buy into' it by relinquishing all that prevents them from obtaining it. The teaching here is that the kingdom of God is a treasure worth seeking, and paying for, as we read in Proverbs 2:1-5, 8:35, and 23:23,

'My son, if you receive my words, and treasure my commands within you, so that you incline your ear to wisdom, and apply your heart to understanding; yes, if you cry out for discernment, and lift up your voice for understanding, if you seek her as silver, and search for her as hidden treasures; then you will understand the fear of the Lord, and find the knowledge of God.'

'For whoever finds me finds life and obtains favour from the Lord.'

'Buy the truth, and do not sell it, also wisdom and instruction and understanding.'

Whether we seek it or stumble on it, when we find the Gospel of God's salvation, we are expected to show total commitment in taking hold of it; absolute devotion that permits no obstacles to stand in the way of our partaking of the treasures of the kingdom. Wisdom, as described in Proverbs is a gift from God that is with Him through all eternity, as we read in Proverbs 3:19, 'The Lord by wisdom founded the earth; by understanding He established the heavens.' The whole of Job chapter 28 speaks about the value of wisdom; its value beyond any earthly treasure, as we read for example in verses 15-18 and in Isaiah 33:6,

'It cannot be purchased for gold, nor can silver be weighed for its price. It cannot be valued in the gold of Ophir, in precious onyx or sapphire. Neither gold nor crystal can equal it, nor can it be exchanged for jewellery of fine gold. No mention shall be made of coral or quartz, for the price of wisdom is above rubies.'

'Wisdom and knowledge will be the stability of your times, and the strength of salvation; the fear of the Lord is His treasure.'

Matthew 13:47-50

In verses 47-50, Jesus used a parable that seems to carry a both a warning and reassurance, saying,

> "Again like is the kingdom of the heavens to a drag-net cast into the sea and, of every kind, of gathering; which when it was filled bringing up onto the shore and sitting collected the good into vessels, but the bad out cast. Thus it will be at the completion of the age; will go forth the angels and will separate the evil men from the midst of the righteous and will cast them into the furnace of fire; there will be the wailing and the gnashing of the teeth."

The word that Jesus used for 'net' translates as drag net. This kind of net is used to catch fish by dragging them up from the bottom. As the net is dragged along, it keeps gathering everything in its path, including all the dross, big fish and small fish, and all sorts of sea creatures. When the net is emptied on shore, the catch must be sorted and separated to keep that which is wanted and remove that which isn't. The warning here is that the Church itself, represented by the net, collects all kinds of people, sadly sometimes including the dross that need to be separated out. The history of the Church as an institution has been exposed time and again for its hypocrisy, corruption, and cruelty, and Jesus, knowing the failings of human nature, knew this would happen as it had been foretold through the prophets, as we read in Isaiah 1:24-25, and 27-28, and Habakkuk 1:14-15,

> 'Ah, I will rid Myself of My adversaries, and take vengeance on My enemies. I will turn My hand against you, and thoroughly purge away your dross, and take away all your alloy.'

> 'Zion shall be redeemed with justice, and her penitents with righteousness. The destruction of transgressors and of sinners shall be together, and those who forsake the Lord shall be consumed.'

> 'Why do You make men like the fish of the sea, like creeping things that have no ruler over them? They take up all of them with a hook, they catch them in their net, and gather them in their dragnet.'

In the parable, Jesus told His disciples that it is the angels who will separate the good from the bad from those collected in the net – from those in the Church. The parable does not speak of the other fish, those not caught in the net; it is not speaking of the wider world in this context, but those who are within the net of the Church. There are good and bad even within the Church, but at the judgment even these will be separated out by the angels of God, as we read for example in Psalm 1:5-6,

> 'Therefore the ungodly shall not stand in the judgement, nor sinners in the congregation of the righteous. For the Lord knows the way of the righteous, but the way of the ungodly shall perish.'

Clearly the teaching is that a mixture of the good and bad, existing together, must be patiently endured. Jesus also makes it clear that it is not our place to make those judgements, but that the angels of God will carry out that task at the end times. Our assurance from this parable is that the righteous will be collected into their vessels; it is that a true restoration of the Church will take place when Christ's true sheep will be gathered into the fold, as we read in Isaiah 51:4-5 and Psalm 100:3-4,

> 'Listen to Me, My people; and give ear to Me, O My nation; for law will proceed from Me, and I will make My justice rest as a light to the peoples. My righteousness is near, My salvation has gone forth, and My arms will judge the people; the coastlands will wait upon Me, and on My arm they will trust.'

> 'Know that the Lord, He is God; it is He who has made us, and not we ourselves; we are His people and the sheep of His pasture. Enter into His gates with thanksgiving, and into His courts with praise.'

Matthew 13:51-52

In verses 51-52, Jesus used a short parable to emphasise the importance of sharing the good news of the kingdom of God, saying,

> "Did ye understand these things all?" "Therefore, every scribe made a disciple to the kingdom of the heavens like is to a man, a house master, who puts forth out of the treasure of him new and old things."

Jesus asked His disciples if they understood His teaching. Having affirmed that they did, Jesus taught that they were then responsible for sharing their understanding – their treasures. Jesus here makes clear that His instruction to the disciples was not solely for their benefit but that they would be able to teach others in the way that the Old Testament Scribe Ezra had done, as we read in Ezra chapter 7 verses 6 and 10,

> 'This Ezra came up from Babylon; and he was a skilled scribe in the Law of Moses, which the Lord God of Israel had given.'

> 'For Ezra had prepared his heart to seek the Law of the Lord, and to do it, and to teach statutes and ordinances in Israel.'

The teaching in this parable is that divine truths are not to be lightly glossed over but their utmost importance acknowledged and thoroughly understood. The truths declared in the Law and the Prophets should be treated by Jesus' disciples as precious treasure to be 'put forth' or 'brought out' of a disciple's store, to be shared abroad. Joshua and Hosea both warned the people to observe and understand the teaching of the Law and Isaiah foretold the treasures that would come from Jerusalem, as we read in Joshua 1:7, Hosea 4:6 and Isaiah 2:3,

> 'Only be strong and very courageous, that you may observe to do according to all the law which Moses My servant commanded you; do not turn from it to the right hand or to the left, that you may prosper wherever you go.'

> 'My people are destroyed for lack of knowledge. Because you have rejected knowledge, I will also reject you from being priest for Me; because you have forgotten the law of your God, I also will forget your children.'

> 'Many people shall come and say, "Come, and let us go up to the mountain of the Lord, to the house of the God of Jacob; He will

teach us His ways, and we shall walk in His paths." For out of Zion shall go forth the law, and the word of the Lord from Jerusalem.'

When Jesus spoke of old and new treasures, He confirmed His earlier words in Chapter 5:17 where He told the people, "Do not think that I came to destroy the Law or the Prophets. I did not come to destroy but to fulfil." These treasures, or divine truths have been made known by God to His people from of old and new truths have been declared by Christ. It is easy, for example, to think of conversion or winning souls as a new task, but we can find it spoken of in Psalm 19:7-9 and Proverbs 11:30,

> 'The law of the Lord is perfect, converting the soul; the testimony of the Lord is sure, making wise the simple; the statutes of the Lord are right, rejoicing the heart; the commandment of the Lord is pure, enlightening the eyes; the fear of the Lord is clean, enduring forever; the judgements of the Lord are true and righteous altogether.'

> 'The fruit of the righteous is a tree of life, and he who wins souls is wise.'

There are all manner of treasures in the store house of the kingdom of heaven, as we read in Song of Solomon 7:13, and Jesus' disciples are called to hear, know, and declare them, as we read in Isaiah 42:9, 43:19, and 48:6,

> 'The mandrakes give off a fragrance, and at our gates are pleasant fruits, all manner, new and old, which I have laid up for you, my beloved.'

> 'Behold, the former things have come to pass, and new things I declare; before they spring forth, I tell you of them.' And 'Behold, I will do a new thing. Now it shall spring forth; shall you not know it?'

> 'You have heard; see all this, and will you not declare it? I have made you hear new things from this time, even hidden things, and you did not know them.'

Matthew 13:57

In verse 57, we read that the people in His own country were offended at Jesus who had been teaching in the synagogue. The people who lived in his hometown, referred to Him as the carpenter's son, and expressed doubt as to His authority. Jesus responded saying,

"Not is a prophet unhonoured except in his native town and in the house of him."

It could be that this phrase was a well-known proverb or saying at the time, but it seems more likely that it was a reminder to His disciples of the prophetic words found for example in Job 19:13-15, Psalm 31:11, and Psalm 38:11,

'He has removed my brothers far from me, and my acquaintances are completely estranged from me. My relatives have failed, and my close friends have forgotten me. Those who dwell in my house, and my maidservants, count me as a stranger; I am an alien in their sight.'

'I am a reproach among all my enemies, but especially among my neighbours, and am repulsive to my acquaintances; those who see me outside flee from me.'

'My loved ones and my friends stand aloof from my plague, and my relatives stand far off.'

The Old Testament prophets such as Jeremiah suffered at the hands of the very people who knew him well. Jesus here made special reference to the town He grew up in and His countrymen, for nowhere did He receive less honour than on His native soil. As a prophet of God, whom others had warmly received as a newly arrived stranger, Jesus was despised in the place where He had lived an ordinary life before His ministry began. Jeremiah spoke of his persecutors in chapter 15:15, and David spoke of his rejection by family and neighbours in Psalm 44:13-14 and 69:7-9,

'O Lord, You know; remember me and visit me, and take vengeance for me on my persecutors. In Your enduring patience, do not take me away. Know that for Your sake I have suffered rebuke.'

'You make us a reproach to our neighbours, a scorn and derision to those all around us. You make us a byword among the nations, a shaking of the head among the peoples.'

'Because for Your sake I have borne reproach; shame has covered my face. I have become a stranger to my brothers, and an alien to my mother's children.'

History demonstrates that people look with envy on those of their own rank who have pretensions to greater wisdom or superior knowledge or power. It is likely that the people of His hometown were too proud to be taught by one who, in terms of family connections, they took to be their equal or even inferior. Knowing the obscurity of His birth, His relatives could scarcely suppose that He had these things, His wisdom and mighty works, from Heaven. Their questions reveal their denial of His claim to be the Messiah, and their belief that He should be following in His earthly father's footsteps as a carpenter. Although Jesus would not use miracles to force people to believe, out of compassion He privately healed a few sick people; but His ministry was clearly hampered by their resistance. The rejection and unbelief that He experienced in Nazareth and amongst the wider population was foretold by the prophets, as we read for example in Isaiah 8:14 and 49:7,

'He will be as a sanctuary, but a stone of stumbling and a rock of offense to both the houses of Israel, as a trap and a snare to the inhabitants of Jerusalem. And many among them shall stumble; they shall fall and be broken, be snared and taken.'

'Thus says the Lord, the Redeemer of Israel, their Holy One, to Him whom man despises, to Him whom the nation abhors, to the Servant of rulers: "Kings shall see and arise, Princes also shall worship, because of the Lord who is faithful, the Holy One of Israel; and He has chosen You."

MATTHEW CHAPTER FOURTEEN

Matthew 14:16 and 18

In verses 16 and 18, we read of Jesus' response to His disciples who had suggested that the crowd of five thousand go into the surrounding villages to buy themselves food, and then informed Him that they had five loaves and two fish available. Jesus responded saying,

> "Not need they have to go away; give them ye to eat." And "Bring to me here them."

This account reveals much of the nature of Jesus. We see His compassion and care for the people; even though He had sought rest, He did not take this opportunity to send them away. Time and again through the Old Testament God the Father demonstrated His compassion on the people with regard to their physical needs as we read for example in Exodus 16:12 and Psalm 105:40,

> "I have heard the complaints of the children of Israel. Speak to them, saying, 'At twilight you shall eat meat, and in the morning, you shall be filled with bread. And you shall know that I am the Lord you God'."

> 'The people asked, and He brought quail, and satisfied them with the bread of heaven.'

Jesus knew what He was about to do, and so the command to His disciples could be seen as a test of their faith and obedience, and perhaps also their generosity. Their first objection was a lack of resources for the task, to which Jesus asked them to bring the resources that they did have. We can also see that Jesus gave the work to His disciples to carry out; that He works through the hands of His disciples. Jesus required His disciples to do what He commanded and have no doubt that He would provide the resources to accomplish the task; to demonstrate faith that God can provide and to demonstrate their generosity, as we read in Psalm 78:19-20 and Proverbs 11:24-25,

> 'They said, "Can God prepare a table in the wilderness? Behold, He struck the rock so that waters gushed out and the streams overflowed. Can He give bread also? Can He provide meat for His people?"

> 'There is one who scatters yet increases more; and there is one who withholds more than is right, but it leads to poverty. The

278

generous soul will be made rich, and he who waters will also be watered himself.'

We are told in verse 19 that Jesus looked up to Heaven and blessed and broke the bread as was the custom at the Passover meal with the words, "Blessed are You, O Lord our God, King of the Universe, who has brought forth bread from the earth." This blessing is made at the start of the meal. Jesus, through the blessing, reminded His disciples that all good gifts are from God and that He brings God's gifts to them. It was a well-established tradition not to eat until the food had received a blessing, as we read in 1 Samuel 9:13 when the people waited for Samuel and God promised blessings from the land as we read in Deuteronomy 28:8,

'For the people will not eat until he comes, because he must bless the sacrifice; afterward those who are invited will eat.'

'The Lord will command the blessing on you in your storehouses and in all to which you set your hand, and He will bless you in the land which the Lord your God is giving you.'

There is a clear Biblical principal that when His people give, God will multiply the gift. Whatever resources we have and put into Christ's hands will be sufficient and even abundant. Jesus used what was available and, having acknowledged His Father as King of the universe, what they had was sufficient. This confirmed the principle demonstrated by Elisha in 2 Kings 4:42-43, and promised in Proverbs 3:9-10 and Malachi 3:10,

'Then a man came from Baal Shalisha and brought the man of God bread of the first fruits, twenty loaves of barley bread and newly ripened grain in his knapsack. And he said, "Give it to the people, that they may eat." But his servant said, "What? Shall I set this before one hundred men?" He said again, "Give it to the people, that they may eat; for thus says the Lord: 'They shall eat and have some left over'."

'Honour the Lord with your possessions, and with the first fruits of all your increase; so your barns will be filled with plenty, and your vats will overflow with new wine.'

"Bring all the tithes into the store house, that there may be food in My house, and try Me now in this," says the Lord of hosts, "if I will not open for you the windows of heaven and pour out for you such blessing that there will not be room enough to receive it."

Matthew 14:27-31

In verses 27-31, we read about Jesus' walking on the water. I have included Peter's words here for context although the focus of this study is on Jesus' words and how they relate to Old Testament Scripture. When the disciples saw Jesus approaching in a manner that they could not grasp they were fearful until He spoke to them, saying,

> "Be of good cheer, I am; do not fear." And answering him Peter said: "Lord, if thou art, command me to come to thee on the waters. And he said: "Come." And going down from the ship Peter walked on the waters and came towards Jesus. But seeing the wind he was afraid, and beginning to sink he cried out saying: "Lord, save me," And immediately Jesus stretching out his hand took hold of him and says to him: "Little-faith why dids't thou doubt?"

The words Jesus used, 'I am', was a term by which He claimed His deity - His relationship to God. When God spoke to Moses in Exodus 3:14, God named Himself 'I Am Who I Am'. He also echoed the words of God spoken through the prophet Isaiah that promise that those who trust in Him need not fear, as we read for example in Isaiah 41:4, 4:10, and 51:12,

> 'Who has performed and done it, calling the generations from the beginning? I, the Lord, am the first; and with the last I am He.'

> 'Fear not, for I am with you; be not dismayed, for I am your God. I will strengthen you, yes, I will help you, I will uphold you with My righteous right hand.'

> 'I, even I, am He who comforts you. Who are you that you should be afraid of a man who will die, and of the son of a man who will be made like grass?'

Jesus demonstrated that He has dominion even over the sea when he commanded Peter to come to Him. There are numerous examples in the Old Testament of God making a path through the sea, also of water and sea as metaphors for life's difficulties through which God will make a path for His people, as we read for example in Isaiah 43:16, 63:12, Job 9:8, Psalm 69:1 and 77:19,

> 'Thus says the Lord, who makes a way in the sea and a path through the mighty waters.'

'Who led them by the right hand of Moses, with his glorious arm, dividing the water before them to make for Himself an everlasting name.'

'He alone spreads out the heavens and treads on the waves of the sea.'

'Save me, O God! For the waters have come up to my neck. I sink deep in mire, where there is no standing; I have come into deep waters, where the floods overflow me.'

'Your way was in the sea, Your path in the great waters, and Your footsteps were not known.'

One Old Testament example of God's intervention that was beyond normal understanding has some similarities to this account. Elisha's servant was overwhelmed at the sight of the enemy army and feared. Elisha's servant, like Peter, looked at his situation rather than keeping his eyes on the Lord who is Master over the armies, and Master of the sea, the waves and the winds, as we read in 2 Kings 6:15-17,

'And when the servant of the man of God arose early and went out, there was an army, surrounding the city with horses and chariots. And his servant said to him, "Alas, my master! What shall we do?" So he answered, "Do not fear, for those who are with us are more than those who are with them." And Elisha prayed, and said, "Lord, I pray, open his eyes that he may see." Then the Lord opened the eyes of the young man, and he saw, and behold the mountain was full of horses and chariots of fire all around Elisha.'

Peter, like Jesus, walked on the water, which is contrary to the laws of nature; Jesus defied the laws of nature regardless of the weather conditions, as did the people of Israel in the Wilderness and as the Church has done for two thousand years. God will stretch out His hand to save His disciples even when they doubt, as we read is Psalm 138:7, 144:7, 18:16, and 34:4,

'Though I walk in the midst of trouble, You will revive me; You will stretch out Your hand against the wrath of my enemies, and Your right hand will save me.'

'Stretch out Your hand from above; rescue me and deliver me out of great waters.'

'He sent from above, He took me; He drew me out of many waters.'

'I sought the Lord, and He heard me, and delivered me from all my fears.'

MATTHEW CHAPTER FIFTEEN

Matthew 15:3-9

In verses 3-9, Jesus replied to the scribes and Pharisees who objected to His disciples disregarding the tradition of washing their hands before eating bread, saying,

> "Why indeed ye transgress the commandment of God on account of the tradition of you? For God said: Honour the father and the mother, and: The one speaking evil of father or mother by death let him die. But ye say: Whoever says to his father or to his mother: A gift whatever by me thou mightest be owed, by no means shall he honour the father of him or the mother of him; and ye annulled the word of God on account of the tradition of you. Hypocrites, well prophesied concerning you Isaiah saying: This people with the lips me honour, but the heart of them far is away from me; and vainly they worship me; teaching teachings ordinances of men."

The sacred offerings, or gifts, that Jesus refers to, were a form of payment-in-kind for the priests and were rigidly enforced. The priests had established a tradition whereby people could make a vow that when they died, their money and goods would be given to the temple, meaning that they were no longer free to give to anyone else in need, such as their parents. This enabled them to continue to enjoy their possessions while they lived, thus contradicting the Law set down in Exodus 20:12, Deuteronomy 5:16, Leviticus 19:3 and the warning in Proverbs 20:20,

> 'Honour your father and your mother, that your days may be long upon the land which the Lord your God is giving you.'
> 'Honour your father and your mother, as the Lord your God has commanded you, that your days may be long, and that it may be well with you in the land which the Lord your God is giving you.'
> 'Every one of you shall revere his mother and his father and keep My Sabbaths: I am the Lord your God.'
> 'Whoever curses his father or his mother, his lamp will be put out in deep darkness.'

The word often translated as curse in the original meant to disobey, treat with irreverence, to think evil of, or plan to do evil to a person. The law of God required that parents should be provided for when old and in distress, but the Jewish teachers taught that it was more important for a person to dedicate their property to God than to provide for the needs of

284

a parent. This false teaching was directly addressed in Proverbs 28:24 and 20:25,

'Whoever robs his father or his mother, and says, "It is no transgression", the same is companion to a destroyer.'
'It is a snare for a man to devote rashly something as holy, and afterward to reconsider his vows.'

Jesus called the scribes and Pharisees hypocrites; they concealed a basic principle under the pretence of religious observance. Their intent was to be rid of the duty of providing for needy parents whilst appearing to show piety towards God. The teachers were strict in keeping to the law outwardly but not inwardly - in their hearts; they made a pretence of godliness and turned aside to modes of worship invented by men, as we read in Isaiah 29:13-14,

'Therefore the Lord said: "Inasmuch as these people draw near with their mouths and honour Me with their lips, but have removed their hearts far from Me, and their fear toward Me is taught by the commandment of men, therefore, behold, I will again do a marvellous work among the people, a marvellous work and a wonder; for the wisdom of the wise men shall perish, and the understanding of their prudent men shall be hidden."

It is worth considering how this applies in our contemporary context; what are the hypocrisies of today? In what ways do our church traditions set aside or even contravene God's commandments and statutes? This is not to say that we should look to judge others – only God can do so – but we should look to God's word as the ultimate guide to our own behaviour. Jesus' words imply that His disciples are not bound to obey man-made traditions, and we are reminded of the words that Samuel spoke to Saul in 1 Samuel 15:22 and the warning in Deuteronomy 12: 32 and Proverbs 30:5-6,

"Has the Lord as great delight in burnt offerings and sacrifices, as in obeying the voice of the Lord? Behold, to obey is better than sacrifice, and to heed than the fat of rams."
'Whatever I command you, be careful to observe it; you shall not add to it nor take away from it.'
'Every word of God is pure; He is a shield to those who put their trust in Him. Do not add to His words, lest He rebuke you, and you be found a liar.'

Matthew 15:10-11

In verses 10-11, Jesus continues His teaching about the hypocrisy of outward observance of rules when the inner person seeks only to satisfy their own desires, saying,

> "Hear ye and understand: Not the thing entering into the mouth defiles the man, but the thing coming forth out of the mouth, this defiles the man."

The first part of this statement, to hear and understand, is an important command from Jesus. His disciples cannot be satisfied simply with hearing the words of God, they must be understood. Isaiah, when he volunteers to be God's messenger is warned that the more he preaches, the more his hearers will reject his message; they would hear the words of the prophet, but they would not understand him; they would neither believe nor regard him because they desired to continue in their iniquity, as we read in Isaiah 6:8-9,

> 'Then I said, "Here am I! Send me." And He said, "Go, and tell this people: 'Keep on hearing, but do not understand; keep on seeing, but do not perceive.'

There were indeed many rules in Old Testament Scripture about defilement from contact with unclean things; there are detailed instructions for example in Leviticus chapters 5 and 11. Today, we understand the importance of personal hygiene to our own health and the health of the community, and Jesus Himself had told the people that He had not come to destroy the Law but to fulfil it, as we saw in chapter 5:17, but the specific hand washing referred to earlier in this chapter was not a command of the law of Moses, but a tradition of the Pharisees. The Law only required that the priests washed their hands and feet when they went into the tabernacle of meeting or went near the altar (see Exodus 30:21). Isaiah spoke of the things that truly defile a person in chapter 59:1-4, where we read,

> 'Behold, the Lord's hand is not shortened, that it cannot save; nor His ear heavy, that it cannot hear. But your iniquities have separated you from your God; and your sins have hidden His face from you, so that He will not hear. For your hands are defiled with blood, and your fingers with iniquity; your lips have spoken lies, your tongue has muttered perversity. No one calls for justice, nor

does any plead for truth. They trust in empty words and speak lies; they conceive evil and bring forth iniquity.'

Jesus makes it abundantly clear that what makes a person unclean is the evil that comes out of the mouth. Sadly, the history of the church is littered with examples of those who have shown an outward piety and religious observance that has concealed evil behaviour both individually and corporately. There are many passages in Old Testament Scripture that teach of the uncleanness that comes out of a person, and that the source of that evil is a sinful heart. Here are just a few: Psalm 5:9, Psalm 12:1-2, Psalm 36:13, and Job 20:12-14.

'For there is no faithfulness in their mouth; their inward part is destruction; their throat is an open tomb; they flatter with their tongues.'

'Help, Lord, for the godly man ceases! For the faithful disappear from among the sons of men. They speak idly everyone with his neighbour; with flattering lips and a double heart they speak.'

'An oracle within my heart concerning the transgression of the wicked: There is no fear of God before his eyes, for he flatters himself in his own eyes, when he finds out his iniquity and when he hates. The words of his mouth are wickedness and deceit; he has ceased to be wise and to do good.'

'Though evil is sweet in his mouth, and he hides it under his tongue, though he spares it and does not forsake it, but still keeps it in his mouth, yet his food in his stomach turns sour; it becomes cobra venom within him.'

We can also see that just as what comes out of a person can defile them, equally what comes out can bless them if the heart is righteous, so that when His disciples pray and praise in spirit and in truth, they will be blessed by God, as we read for example in Psalm 66:17-20.

'I cried to Him with my mouth, and He was extolled with my tongue. If I regard iniquity in my heart, the Lord will not hear. But certainly, God has heard me; He has attended to the voice of my prayer. Blessed be God, who has not turned away my prayer, nor His mercy from me.'

Matthew 15:13-14

In verses 13-14, Jesus responds to the disciples who have told Him that the Pharisees had been offended by His words, saying,

> "Every plant which not planted the Father of me heavenly shall be uprooted. Leave them; blind they are leaders of blind; a blind man and a blind man if leads, both into a ditch will fall."

Jesus' words are not difficult to understand; there are many places where the people of Israel are referred to as a plant of some kind, often a vineyard. These plantations, that were to be the work of God's hands, should flourish and thereby glorify God. In this particular context, we can take plants that are not the work of God's hands to mean doctrines, philosophies, traditions, or ideologies that are not from heaven – not from God. It is these that will be utterly rooted up. We can find mention of the flourishing plants, for example in Isaiah 60:21, Isaiah 61:3, Psalm 80:8-9 and Psalm 92:13, and, by contrast, the plants that are to be uprooted are spoken of in Isaiah 5:7 and Ezekiel 19:12,

> 'Also, your people shall all be righteous; they shall inherit the land forever, the branch of My planting, the work of My hands, that I may be glorified.'
> 'That they may be called trees of righteousness, the planting of the Lord, that He may be glorified.'
> 'You have brought a vine out of Egypt; You have cast out the nations and planted it. You prepared room for it and caused it to take deep root and it filled the land.'
> 'Those who are planted in the house of the Lord shall flourish in the courts of our God. They shall still bear fruit in old age; they shall be fresh and flourishing, to declare that the Lord is upright; He is my rock, and there is no unrighteousness in Him.'

> 'For the vineyard of the Lord of hosts is the house of Israel, and the men of Judah are His pleasant plant. He looked for justice, but behold, oppression; for righteousness, but behold, a cry for help.'

> 'But she [Israel] was plucked up in fury, she was cast down to the ground, and the east wind dried her fruit. Her strong branches were broken and withered; the fire consumed them.'

We can tell from Jesus' subsequent words that when He told His disciples to leave them – the Pharisees - or, let them alone, that He was referring to those who were the plants to be uprooted. We can presume that His meaning was that they should not concern themselves over their attitude since it was only to be expected; that they should not be put off by them or deceived by their errors, as we read in Isaiah 3:12 and 9:16,

> 'O My people! Those who lead you cause you to err and destroy the way of your paths.'

> 'For the leaders of this people cause them to err, and those who are led by them are destroyed.'

Again, Jesus was quoting from Scripture when He referred to blind guides. The blind teachers would destroy their own souls but also the souls of those who follow them. If a teacher is ignorant, they cannot teach what they do not know, and the people cannot learn from them. The prophets suggests that neither do they desire to learn; that some are wilfully blind, as we read for example in Isaiah 42:19, Jeremiah 5:31 and Jeremiah 6:15, and again we can read of the contrast with those who are not blind in Malachi 4:2,

> 'Hear, you deaf; and look, you blind that you may see. Who is blind but My servants, or deaf as he to whom I have sent My messengers? Who is blind as he who is perfectly instructed and blind as the Lord's servants? Seeing many things, but you do not observe; opening the ears, but they do not hear.'

> 'The prophets prophesy falsely, and the priests rule by their own power; and My people love to have it so. But what will you do in the end?'

> 'Were they ashamed when they had committed abomination? No! They were not at all ashamed; nor did they know how to blush. Therefore, they shall fall among those who fall; at the time I punish them, they shall be cast down, says the Lord.'

> 'But to you who fear My name the Sun of Righteousness shall arise with healing in His wings; and you shall go out and grow fat like stall-fed calves.'

Matthew 15:16-20

In verses 16-20, Jesus replied to Peter's request for an explanation of the parable of the blind leading the blind, saying,

> "Thus also ye unintelligent are? Do ye not understand that everything entering into the mouth into the stomach goes and into a drain is cast out? But the things coming forth out of the mouth out of the heart comes forth, and those defile the man. For out of the heart come forth thoughts evil, murders, adulteries, fornications, thefts, false witnessing, blasphemies. These things are the ones defiling the man; but with unwashed hands to eat not defiles the man."

Jesus taught that although the food that we eat may affect the body, it does not affect the mind or the soul and therefore does not defile a person's soul. He went on to state the things that do defile a person, and He began with evil thoughts that are the source of all the others, and we know that thought precedes action. Jesus spoke of this first and this is inline with the account right at the beginning of Scripture where God saw the wickedness of the intent of the thoughts and imagination of humans, as we read in Genesis 6:5, and following the flood in 8:21,

> 'Then the Lord saw that the wickedness of man was great in the earth, and that every intent of the thoughts of his heart was only evil continually.'

> 'Then the Lord said in His heart, "I will never again curse the ground for man's sake, although the imagination of man's heart is evil from his youth."

Jesus taught that the way to keep any of God's commandments is to fulfil the purpose for which it was given. In order to keep these commands, the Pharisees had developed a set of rules to apply to practical problems that displayed a lack of understanding of the purposes behind the commands to the people of Israel such as not to be defiled, but to be a people holy to the Lord. To understand what defilement means, it is the opposite of being holy and separate for God. Through these words, Jesus made it clear that the choice of obedience or disobedience to the law was made in the inner being, in the human heart; that it is not sufficient to conform by outward actions or words, but even our thoughts and imagination must conform to God's precepts. The seat of corruption, or defilement, is the human heart itself, as we read for example in 1 Samuel 24:13, Psalm 106:39, Proverbs 4:23 and 17:20,

'As the proverb of the ancients says, 'Wickedness proceeds from the wicked.'

'Thus they were defiled by their own works and played the harlot by their own deeds.'

'Keep your heart with all diligence, for out of it spring the issues of life.'

'He who has a deceitful heart finds no good, and he who has a perverse tongue falls into evil.'

Jesus had little time for ritual purification or food regulations that had no regard for the intended purposes of God. He made it clear that the law should be fulfilled ethically not ceremonially; that it is the heart that needs to be purified and washed so that what comes forth does not defile a person. The will of God should be done from the heart. For those who set their minds and desires to do the will of God, their actions and words will not deviate from it, as we read in Isaiah 55:7, Psalm 40:8 and we can join with the words of the familiar prayer of Psalm 19:14.

'Let the wicked forsake his way, and the unrighteous man his thoughts; let him return to the Lord, and He will have mercy on him; and to our God, for He will abundantly pardon.'

'I delight to do Your will, O my God, and Your law is within my heart.'

'Let the words of my mouth and the meditation of my heart be acceptable in Your sight, O Lord, my strength and my Redeemer.'

Matthew 15:24-28

In verses 24-28, Jesus replied to a woman who had come from the region of Canaan and had asked Him for help for her daughter who was demon-possessed, saying,

> "I was not sent except to the sheep lost of the house of Israel." But she coming worshipped him saying: Lord, help me. But he answering said: "It is not good to take the bread of the children and to throw to the dogs." And she said: Yes, Lord; but even the dogs eat from the crumbs falling from the table of the masters of them. Then answering Jesus said to her: "O woman, great of thee the faith; let it be to thee as thou desirest."

The lost sheep of the house of Israel were the Jews; Jesus came first to them as their long-anticipated Messiah, to preach the Gospel to the Jews only. The blessing that was expected in the Messiah resided with the family of Abraham, the sheep of Israel that had, as spoken of by the prophets, become lost, as we read for example in Isaiah 53:6, Jeremiah 5:6, and Ezekiel 34:15-16,

> 'All we like sheep have gone astray; we have turned, everyone, to his own way; and the Lord has laid on Him the iniquity of us all.'

> 'My people have been lost sheep, their shepherds have led them astray; they have turned them away on the mountains. They have gone from mountain to hill; they have forgotten their resting place.'

> "I will feed My flock, and I will make them lie down," says the Lord God. "I will seek what was lost and bring back what was driven away, bind up the broken and strengthen what was sick; but I will destroy the fat and the strong, and feed them in judgement."

Jesus' words indicate that His healing ministry was for the children of Israel, and that it shouldn't be taken from them and given to the Gentiles. But the Canaanite woman reminded Jesus that the dogs in a household, who were not stray animals but more like pets, were commonly given what was left over by the children, and it was these leftovers she was asking for on behalf of her daughter. She did not ask for what was being offered to the children, only for what they had discarded; she came with trust in His compassion as we read in Job 23:10 and Lamentations 3:32,

'Though He slay me, yet will I trust Him. Even so, I will defend my own ways before Him. He also shall be my salvation, for a hypocrite could not come before Him.'

'Though He causes grief, yet He will show compassion according to the multitudes of His mercies.'

The woman was motivated by the conviction that Jesus was the Messiah and would therefore demonstrate kindness. Her faith demonstrated a greater understanding of Jesus' status than He often found among His own people. Her daughter was healed immediately, and without necessitating direct contact, but from a physical distance. Jesus commended the woman for her faith and then told her that it was on account of her faith that her prayer was answered. Even though a Gentile, this woman recognised Christ, and worshipped Him and petitioned Him in complete humility, acknowledging her own unworthiness. Through this conversation recorded by Matthew, His disciples can have the assurance that Jesus will answer the prayers and petitions of those who acknowledge His supreme authority, honouring Him as the Messiah, and who come to Him in humility, acknowledging their own unworthiness, as we read in 1 Samuel 2:30 and in Psalm 145:18-19,

"Therefore, the Lord God of Israel says: 'I said indeed that your house and the house of your father would walk before Me forever'. But now the Lords says: 'Far be it from Me; for those who honour Me I will honour, and those who despise Me shall be lightly esteemed'."

'The Lord is near to all who call upon Him, to all who call upon Him in truth. He will fulfil the desires for those who fear Him; He also will hear their cry and save them.'

Matthew 15:32-34

In verses 32-34, Jesus, having already demonstrated His compassion for the people through miracles of healing of those who were lame, blind, mute, maimed, and other illnesses, showed compassion for their everyday needs. He asked His disciples to feed the crowd of four thousand men, besides women and children, as on a previous occasion, saying,

> "I am filled with compassion over the crowd, because now three days they remain with me and have not anything they may eat; and to dismiss them without food I am not willing, lest they fall in the way." And say to him the disciples: Whence to us in a desert loaves so many so as to satisfy a crowd so great? And says to them Jesus, "How many loaves have ye?"

Matthew records that the people ate and were satisfied and there were seven basketfuls of left-over fragments. This account is similar to that found in chapter fourteen, however, in verse 31 of chapter 15, Matthew wrote that the people 'glorified the God of Israel', suggesting that they were not Jews on this occasion. This may account for the disciple's apparent lack of faith given their previous experience; they may not have felt that Gentiles would be eligible for a similar miracle. It may also have been that even having witnessed God's power on previous occasions it was difficult for them to believe that God's power has no limit. Even Moses, having witnessed so much of God's delivering power, questioned His ability to feed the people in the wilderness, as we read in Numbers 11:21-23,

> 'And Moses said, "The people whom I am among are six hundred thousand men on foot; yet You have said, 'I will give them meat, that they may eat for a whole month.' Shall flocks and herds be slaughtered for them, to provide enough for them? Or shall all the fish of the sea be gathered together for them, to provide enough for them?" And the Lord said to Moses, "Has the Lord's arm been shortened? Now you shall see whether what I say will happen to you or not."

The disciples reported to Jesus that there were only seven loaves and a few little fish available, but this did not matter since God's power is not restricted by quantity, whether large or small. King Saul's son Jonathan declared this to be true when speaking of his own small army that stood against a vast army, as we read in 1 Samuel 14:6,

"For nothing restrains the Lord from saving, by many or by few.'

So also, God warned His people that a great amount of food, for those who do not obey His commands, will not satisfy, as is written in Leviticus 26:26,

'When I have cut off your supply of bread, ten women shall bake your bread in one oven, and they shall bring back your bread by weight, and you shall eat and not be satisfied.'

Jesus here, once again, demonstrated the compassion of God for all the people of His creation, and that it is not limited by any restrictions of human perception, either physical, cultural, or spiritual, as we read in the words of Isaiah 59:1, Hosea 11:4, and in Psalm 145:8-9,

'Behold, the Lord's hand is not shortened, that it cannot save; nor His ear heavy, that it cannot hear.'

'I drew them with cords of compassion, with bands of love. And I was to them as those who take the yoke from their neck. I stooped and fed them.'

'The Lord is gracious and full of compassion, slow to anger and great in mercy. The Lord is good to all, and His tender mercies are over all His works.'

MATTHEW CHAPTER SIXTEEN

Matthew 16:2-4

In verses 2-4, Jesus responded to a request from the Pharisees and Sadducees, who persisted in testing Him, to show them a sign, saying,

> "When evening is coming on ye say: Fair weather, for is red the sky; and in the morning: today stormy weather, for is red being overcast the sky. The face of the sky ye know to discern, but the signs of the times can ye not? A generation evil and adulterous a sign seeks, and a sign shall not be given to it except the sign of Jonah."

Matthew recorded that the Pharisees and Saducees specifically asked for a sign in what is usually translated as heaven, although the Greek word 'ouranou' can also mean air or sky. It may have been that they hoped to tempt Jesus to attempt to work a miracle specifically in the sky, or heavens, on demand, in anticipation that He would fail. The great prophets of old, Samuel and Isaiah, had demonstrated the use of such signs in the skies, as we read in 1 Samuel 12:17-18 and Isaiah 38:7-8,

> "Is today not the wheat harvest? I will call to the Lord, and He will send thunder and rain, that you may perceive and see that your wickedness is great, which you have done in the sight of the Lord, in asking a king for yourselves." So Samuel called to the Lord, and the Lord sent thunder and rain that day.'

> "And this is the sign to you from the Lord, that the Lord will do this thing which He has spoken. Behold, I will bring the shadow on the sundial, which has gone down with the sun on the sundial of Ahaz, ten degrees backward." So the sun returned ten degrees on the dial by which it had gone down.'

The doctrine that Jesus was preaching and the miracles that He was working were in fact sure signs of the promised salvation. The Pharisees and Sadducees nevertheless wanted Jesus to produce a special sign for them, although the signs that had already been shown had been sufficient to satisfy the disciples of John the Baptist, as we read earlier at the beginning of chapter 11. Those people who are not prepared to accept a sign will never see it for what it is; a clear example of this was Pharaoh's refusal to acknowledge the signs of Moses with devastating consequences. The Pharisees seemed wise in worldly things but blind to things pertaining to the kingdom of God. Jesus knew that although they asked Him for a sign, they were resolved not to observe it. In 1 Chronicles

12:32, we read that the sons of Issachar understood the times, and by contrast, Isaiah talks of those who were considered adulterous for defying the signs in Isaiah 57:3, and Ezekiel himself was described as a sign in Ezekiel 24:24,

> 'The sons of Issachar who had understanding of the times, to know what Israel ought to do, their chiefs were two hundred; and all their brethren were at their command.'

> 'But come here, you sons of the sorceress, you offspring of the adulterer and the harlot! Whom do you ridicule? Against whom do you make a wide mouth and stick out the tongue? Are you not children of transgression, offspring of falsehood.'

> 'Thus Ezekiel is a sign to you; according to all that he has done you shall do; and when this comes, you shall know that I am the Lord God.'

Jesus called the Pharisees and Sadducees a wicked and adulterous generation, not because they had asked for a sign, but because they would not be satisfied with the signs that had already been shown, and unlike the people of Nineveh they refused to repent and accept God's word and His messengers. Jesus told them that the only sign they would have would be that of Jonah who came back to life after three days apparently dead in a fish. This was the sign that Jesus was referring to – His resurrection after three days of actual death, as we read in Jonah 1:1-2, 1:17, and 3:10,

> 'Now the word of the Lord came to Jonah the son of Amittal, saying, "Arise, go to Nineveh, that great city, and cry out against it; for their wickedness has come up before Me."

> 'Now the Lord had prepared a great fish to swallow Jonah. And Jonah was in the belly of the fish three days and three nights.'

> 'Then God saw their works, that they had turned from their evil way; and God relented from the disaster that He had said He would bring upon them, and He did not do it.'

Matthew 16:6-11

In verses 6-11, Jesus was again warning His disciples about false teaching, saying,

> "Beware and take heed from the leaven of the Pharisees and Sadducees." But they reasoned among themselves saying: Loaves not we took. But knowing, Jesus said: "Why reason ye among yourselves, little-faiths, because loaves ye have not? Do ye not yet understand, neither remember ye the five loaves of the five thousand and how many baskets ye took? Neither the seven loaves of the four thousand and how many baskets ye took? How do ye not understand that not concerning loaves I said to you? But take heed from the leaven of the Pharisees and Sadducees."

Earlier in Mathew's Gospel, in Chapter 13:33, Jesus spoke about leaven, reminding the disciples of the transformative effect of yeast; that from tiny beginnings it can work through the whole dough. This can be for good effect, as when God's grace works in a person's heart, however, false teaching can also affect and work through the soul just as leaven does in dough. Jesus was warning His disciples against the superstitions of the Pharisees and the false doctrines of the Sadducees. The prophets spoke about the corruption of the priests in Israel, as we read in Hosea 5:1 and Malachi 2:7-8,

> 'Hear this, O priests! Take heed, O house of Israel! Give ear, O house of the king! For yours is the judgement, because you have been a snare to Mizpah and a net spread on Tabor.'

> "For the lips of a priest should keep knowledge, and people should seek the law from his mouth; for he is the messenger of the Lord of hosts. But you have departed from the way; you have caused many to stumble at the law. You have corrupted the covenant of Levi," says the Lord of hosts.'

The name Pharisee means 'separated one'; the Pharisees, who saw themselves as separate from those who did not adhere to the law, were devoted to the strict observance of the Laws and strove to define what was acceptable behaviour so that there would be no ambiguity. They defined what was acceptable practice in every possible scenario, in everyday life, not just with regard to worship and the Temple, and avoided those who did not follow what they considered to be their pure behaviour. Unlike the Sadducees, they did believe that the dead would be resurrected at the end of time. However, their focus on outward, or legalistic, purity led them to neglect the inward purity of the heart. By adding to the rules and regulations for everyday life, they were placing a burden on the people rather than attending to their needs, as we read in Jeremiah 23:1-2,

> "Woe to the shepherds who destroy and scatter the sheep of My pasture!" says the Lord. Therefore thus says the Lord God of Israel against the shepherds who feed My people: "You have scattered My flock, driven them away and not attended to them. Behold I will attend to you for the evil of your doings," says the Lord.'

The Sadducees refused to acknowledge Scripture beyond the first five books of the Bible, known as the Torah, and did not believe in the resurrection, or the existence of angels or spirits. They were the governing body of the Jerusalem Temple and the Sanhedrin; the High Priest was almost always a Sadducee. Annas and Caiaphas were both Sadducees. By refusing to acknowledge the prophets, their teaching was clearly in opposition to Christ's teaching. The Sadducees lived lavish lifestyles through corruption and kept a tight grip on political power. Had the Sadducees accepted the words of the prophets, they would have found ample teaching of the resurrection of the Messiah and also the resurrection of all people, as we read in Psalm 16:10, Psalm 49:15, Isaiah 25:8 and 26:19,

> 'For You will not leave my soul in Sheol, nor will You allow Your Holy One to see corruption.'

> 'But God will redeem my soul from the power of the grave, for He shall receive me.'

> 'He will swallow up death forever, and the Lord God will wipe away tears from all faces; the rebuke of His people He will take away from all the earth; for the Lord has spoken.'

> 'Your dead shall live; together with my dead body they shall arise. Awake and sing, you who dwell in the dust; for your dew is like the dew of herbs, and the earth shall cast out the dead.'

Matthew 16:13-15

In verses 13-15, Jesus and His disciples had arrived in the region of Caesarea Philippi, when Jesus questioned the disciples, saying,

> "Whom say men to be the Son of man?" And they said: Some indeed John the Baptist, and others Elias, and others Jeremias or one of the prophets. He says to them: "But ye whom me say to be?"

It is not likely that Jesus put this question to His disciples to find out how He was doing in the public eye; how He was doing in the poll ratings of the day. It is far more probable that Jesus asked this to give them the opportunity to make a declaration of their faith; to confirm and strengthen them in it. He wasn't asking what the rumours were, but He was giving His disciples the opportunity to confirm their true faith that they wouldn't be thrown into doubt by the local speculation about Him, after all Matthew had previously recorded that Jesus had just been warning the disciples of the false teaching of the Pharisees and Sadducees. The prophet Elijah had already returned in the guise of John the Baptist and the disciples were aware of this, as we read in Malachi 4:5-6,

> 'Behold, I will send you Elijah the prophet before the coming of the great and dreadful day of the Lord. And he will turn the hearts of the fathers to the children, and the hearts of the children to their fathers, lest I come and strike the earth with a curse.'

It is probable that some of the followers of Jesus had abandoned their belief in Him as the Messiah because of His refusal to declare Himself in the way they wanted, or to gather armies together to overthrow the Romans and set up an earthly kingdom. But the Messianic Kingdom, rather than a kingdom of war, was to be one of peace and justice, as we read in the familiar words of the prophet Isaiah in chapter 9:6-7,

> 'For unto us a Child is born, unto us a Son is given; and the government will be upon His shoulder. And His name will be called Wonderful, Counsellor, Mighty God, Everlasting Father, Prince of Peace. Of the increase of His government and peace there will be no end, upon the throne of David and over His kingdom, to order it and establish it with judgement and justice from that time forward, even forever, the zeal of the Lord of hosts will perform this.'

Jesus made a distinction between His disciples and the rest of the crowd. The crowd may have had differing opinions, but His disciples must commit to a declaration of their faith. The question is one that every person must answer; we also must ask ourselves 'Who do we say He is?' If merely a good man, or even a prophet, the words of Jesus can only impact our lives at a surface level. However, if we can say that Jesus is the Messiah, the risen Son of God, the impact of His words on our lives are unfathomable; we have a King to whom we owe total allegiance and commitment, as we read in Ezekiel 37:23-26, Psalm 2:6-8, and Zechariah 9:9,

> 'David My servant shall be king over them, and they shall all have one shepherd; they shall also walk in My judgements and observe My statutes and do them. Then they shall dwell in the land that I have given to Jacob My servant, where your fathers dwelt; and they shall dwell there, they, their children, and their children's children forever; and My servant David shall be their prince forever.'

> "Yet I have set My King on My holy hill of Zion. I will declare the decree: The Lord has said to Me, 'You are My Son, today I have begotten You. Ask of Me, and I will give You the nations for Your inheritance, and the ends of the earth for Your possession."

> "Rejoice greatly, O daughter of Zion! Shout, O daughter of Jerusalem! Behold your King is coming to you; He is just and having salvation, lowly and riding on a donkey, a colt, the foal of a donkey."

Matthew 16:17-19

In verses 17-19, Jesus responds to the Apostle Peter's declaration that Jesus is 'the Christ, the Son of the Living God', saying,

> "Blessed art thou, Simon Barjonas, because flesh and blood did not reveal to thee but the Father of me in the heavens. And I also to thee say, thou art Peter, and on this rock I will build of me the church, and the gates of hades will not prevail against it. I will give thee the keys of the kingdom of the heavens, and whatever thou blindest on the earth shall be having been bound in the heavens, and whatever thou loosest on the earth shall be having been loosed in the heavens."

Peter was prepared to confess Jesus as the Messiah; a change had taken place in his thinking, and he now understood the term 'Messiah' in the light of what Jesus actually was and did, rather than as the traditional idea. Jesus, by these words, acknowledged Peter's faith and understanding and knew that a rock of faith had been found on which the foundations of the kingdom, of the Church, could be laid. Peter's declaration of faith was that rock on which the foundation of the Church was to be laid; Abraham's faith was the rock on which the foundation of a people, set aside for God, could be laid, as we read in Genesis 22:17.

> 'Blessing I will bless you, and multiplying I will multiply your descendants as the stars of the heaven and as the sand which is on the seashore; and your descendants shall possess the gate of their enemies.'

It was not Peter himself, but like Abraham, it was his faith that was the rock upon which a foundation could be laid. Where Jesus is confessed as the Messiah, the Christ, the Son of the living God, there His Church can be built. Whilst the Church maintains this confession, nothing can prevail against it. The Church will prove invincible because the truth of God, on which the faith of the Church rests – the rock, will remain unshaken, as we read in Isaiah 28:16, 51:1-2 and Psalm 129:2,

> "Behold, I lay in Zion a stone for a foundation, a tried stone, a precious cornerstone, a sure foundation; whoever believes will not act hastily.'

> "Listen to Me, you who follow after righteousness, you who seek the Lord; look to the rock from which you were hewn, and to the

hole of the pit from which you were dug. Look to Abraham your father."

'Many a time they have afflicted me from my youth; yet they have not prevailed against me.'

In ancient times, the keys of a royal establishment were entrusted to a chief steward who carried them on his shoulder, and these served as a badge of authority. Similarly, when Jews were made a Doctor of Law, they were given a key to access the sacred books and tablets in the temple. Thus, having the key meant having the authority to teach and explain scripture to the people. Peter was to be like a chief steward, with a badge of authority, who, as we know from later accounts, had a leadership role in the early Church and opened the doors to the Gentiles. Opening and shutting, or binding and loosing, was to do with authorising or forbidding activities. The authority of the keys, and the power to loose or bind, were used by the early Church in teaching, discipline and legislation. The appointment of Peter, having the keys laid on his shoulder, was likely foreshadowed in the writing of the prophet Isaiah, as we read in chapter 22:20-23,

'Then it shall be in that day, that I will call My servant Eliakim the son of Hilkiah; I will clothe him with your robe and strengthen him with your belt; I will commit your responsibility into his hand. He shall be a father to the inhabitants of Jerusalem and to the house of Judah. The key of the house of David I will lay on his shoulder; so he shall open, and no one shall shut; and he shall shut, and no one shall open.'

Matthew 16:23

In verse 23, we read Jesus' response to Peter who, despite having just made his declaration acknowledging that Jesus is the Christ, demonstrates through his genuine concern for Jesus, that he has still not understood the kind of Messiah He was and what lay at the end of the earthly road for Him, saying,

> "Go behind me, Satan; an offence thou art of me. Because thou thinkest not the things of God but the things of men."

The Hebrew word satan is not a proper name, but a noun that means adversary. When it is translated as a name, the Hebrew would be 'the adversary', and in the Greek, the word 'diabolos' means 'accuser'. In order to have the opportunity to accuse, the adversary tempted Jesus in the Wilderness and here again, through Peter, Jesus was tempted not to fulfil His life's mission. Jesus was reprimanding Peter, not for being the devil, but for speaking in opposition, as an adversary. This opposition was spoken of by David and Joshua, as we read in 1 Chronicles 21:1, 2 Samuel 19:22, and Zechariah 3:1-2.

> 'Now Satan stood up against Israel and moved David to number Israel.'

> 'And David said, "What have I to do with you, you sons of Zeruiah, that you should be adversaries to me today?"

> 'Then he showed me Joshua the high priest standing before the Angel of the Lord, and Satan standing at his right hand to oppose him. And the Lord said to Satan, "The Lord rebuke you, Satan! The Lord who has chosen Jerusalem rebuke you! Is this not a brand plucked from the fire?"

Jesus recognised, in the words Peter had spoken to Him, the same temptation that He had encountered in the Wilderness, to yield to ambition and the prospect of world domination. The temptation by the adversary aimed to weaken Christ's trusting obedience to God, to choose a destiny along the lines of common expectation, rather than humility, obedience, suffering, and death that was the way of the Father's will for Him, as we read in Isaiah 8:14 and 42:1-4,

'He will be as a sanctuary, but a stone of stumbling and a rock of offence to both the houses of Israel, as a trap and a snare to the inhabitants of Jerusalem.'

"Behold! My Servant whom I uphold, My Elect One in whom My soul delights! I have put My Spirit upon Him; He will bring forth justice to the Gentiles. He will not cry out, nor raise His voice, nor cause His voice to be heard in the street. A bruised reed He will not break, and smoking flax He will not quench; He will bring forth justice for truth. He will not fail nor be discouraged, till He has established justice in the earth; and the coastlands shall wait for His law."

Because Peter was expressing the thoughts of men rather than the thoughts of God, Peter was not on the right side; he was an offence or stumbling block to Christ's mission. When Jesus' disciples are on the side of men, they are not on the side of God and become His adversary. Peter had to choose between being a stumbling block or a foundation stone. Jesus knew that His Father's will was that He should be the sin-bearing Messiah as prophesied in Isaiah. The whole of Isaiah chapter 53 declares the prophecy of the sin-bearing Messiah, including His death, as we can read for example in verse 12,

'Therefore I will divide Him a portion with the great, and He shall divide the spoil with the strong, because He poured out His soul unto death, and He was numbered with the transgressors, and He bore the sin of many, and made intercession for the transgressors.'

Matthew 16:24-26

In verses 24-26, having earlier elicited from Peter the declaration that He is the Christ, and having rebuked Peter for trying to turn Him from His goal that would involve suffering and death, Jesus taught His disciples that if they chose to follow Him that their path was likely to lead to the same end, saying,

> "If anyone wishes after me to come, let him deny himself and let him take the cross of him, and let him follow me. For whoever wishes the life of him to save, he will lose it; and whoever loses the life of him for the sake of me, he will find it. For what will be benefitted a man, if the world whole he should gain, but the soul of him loses? Or what will give a man an exchange of the soul of him?"

People can frequently be heard to say, 'this is the cross I have to bear', often referring to something or someone they are stuck with. To better understand the implication of Jesus' words, we could render them as 'If anyone wishes to come after me, let him be prepared to be led out to public execution, following my example.' Jesus was making it quite clear what taking the same road could lead to. The Son of man faced the prospect of suffering and violent death and Jesus wanted them to be prepared to face that possibility. In the Roman world a man being taken for public crucifixion was made to carry the crossbeam. This is what Jesus meant by taking up the cross – facing persecution and possible death for Jesus' sake. The disciples would no doubt have been familiar with the account of Esther who demonstrated this preparedness to deny herself even to the point of death, as we read in Esther 4:14-16,

> "For if you remain completely silent at this time, relief and deliverance will arise for the Jews from another place, but you and your father's house will perish. Yet who knows whether you have come to the kingdom for such a time as this?" Then Esther told them to reply to Mordecai: "Go, gather all the Jews who are present in Shushan, and fast for me; neither eat nor drink for three days, night or day. My maids and I will fast likewise. And so I will go to the king, which is against the law; and if I perish, I perish!"

Jesus' disciples need to ask themselves if they wish to be good Christians only to earn a better piece of heaven. The motive that Christ asks for us being a Christian is to be able to bear a heavier beam of the cross. We

308

need to learn how to cope with a storm – as did the disciples, not escape from it, and value our soul above all earthly riches, as we read in Psalm 39:6, 49:6-8, 52:7-8, and Proverbs 11:28,

> 'Surely every man walks about like a shadow; surely they busy themselves in vain; he heaps up riches and does not know who will gather them.'

> 'Those who trust in their wealth and boast in the multitude of their riches, none of them can by any means redeem his brother, nor give to God a ransom for him. For the redemption of their souls is costly.'

> 'Here is the man who did not make God his strength, but trusted in the abundance of his riches, and strengthened himself in his wickedness. But I am like a green olive tree in the house of God; I trust in the mercy of God forever and ever.'

> 'He who trusts in his riches will fail, but the righteous will flourish like foliage.'

Denying oneself is not about giving something up such as for Lent; it is telling ourselves that we will not seek our own plans and ambitions. The soul of man was not created merely for the few days of our earthly life but for immortality; that when the earthly life is finished, we might live eternally in heaven; that the soul is of higher value than all the riches and enjoyments of the world as we read in Isaiah 26:8-9,

> 'Yes, in the way of Your judgements, O Lord, we have waited for You; the desire of our soul is for Your name and for the remembrance of You. With my soul I have desired You in the night, yes, by my spirit within me I will seek You early; for when Your judgments are in the earth, the inhabitants of the world will learn righteousness.'

Matthew 16:27-28

In verses 27-28, we read that Jesus followed up His warning to the disciples of the cost of taking up their cross to follow Him with encouragement to persevere and assurances for the future and the promised kingdom, saying,

> "For the Son of man is about to come in the glory of the Father of him with the angels of him, and then he will reward to each man according to the conduct of him. Truly I say to you. There are some of the ones here standing who by no means may taste of death until they see the Son of man coming in the kingdom of him."

These words would have encouraged the disciples not to judge Christ's kingdom based on their experiences up to that time that would have seemed to indicate failure, certainly in earthly terms. Jesus was assuring them that He would indeed be revealed in glory at the proper time. Following His humiliation and suffering, He would be vindicated and glorified and given the supreme honour of sitting at God's right hand, as we read in Daniel 7:13-14 and Psalm 110:1-2,

> 'I was watching in the night visions, and behold, One like the Son of Man, coming with the clouds of heaven! He came to the Ancient of Days, and they brought Him near before Him. Then to Him was given dominion and glory and a kingdom, that all peoples, nations, and languages should serve Him.'

> 'The Lord said to my Lord, "Sit at My right hand, till I make Your enemies Your footstool" The Lord shall send the rod of Your strength out of Zion. Rule in the midst of Your enemies!"

We are familiar with the saying 'faith not works', and we know that the followers of Jesus are freely justified through faith, but Jesus' words here reminded His followers that their good works would be recognised in addition; that God also chooses to bestow a reward according to the pattern of a person's life. This is clearly spoken of in Job 34:11, Psalm 62:12, Proverbs 24:12, Ecclesiastes 3:17, and Jeremiah 32:19,

> 'For He repays man according to his work and makes man to find a reward according to his way.'

310

'Also, to You, O Lord, belongs mercy; for You render to each one according to his work.'

'If you say, "Surely we did not know this," does not He who weighs the hearts consider it? He who keeps your soul, does He not know it? And will He not render to each man according to his deeds?' And 'I said in my heart, "God shall judge the righteous and the wicked, for there is a time there for every purpose and for every work."'

'You are great in counsel and mighty in work, for Your eyes are open to all the ways of the sons of men, to give everyone according to his ways and according to the fruit of his doings.'

Jesus then spoke of the immediate future, of the establishment of the Church that was to come after the day of Pentecost, and possibly also of the destruction of Jerusalem by the Romans that took place around forty years later when some of the disciples did survive long enough to witness this. He knew that the time was coming, and within the lifetime of His disciples, when the Kingdom of God would come with power, without limitations and would advance unchecked. He knew that His resurrection from the dead would herald the Son of man coming in His kingdom; the coming of God Himself in the power of the Spirit, as we read in Joel 2:28-29,

'And it shall come to pass afterward that I will pour out My Spirit on all flesh; your sons and your daughters shall prophesy, your old men shall dream dreams, your young men shall see visions. And also, on My menservants and on My maidservants, I will pour out My Spirit in those days.'

MATTHEW CHAPTER SEVENTEEN

Matthew 17:7-9

In verses 7-9, we read of Jesus' response to the disciples who had become afraid after witnessing the transfiguration high on a mountain. He touched them and said,

> "Rise and do not fear." And lifting up the eyes of them no one they saw except himself Jesus only. And coming down them out of the mountain enjoined them Jesus saying: "To no one tell the vision until the Son of man out of dead be raised."

Jesus raised up the disciples from where they had fallen on their faces in fear at the vision. This was an example of Christ fulfilling His purpose to raise up His followers so that they might boldly enter the presence of God. It was not only His words that comforted them but His touch also. When Christ gently raised up the disciples, they saw Him alone and their fears vanished. The three disciples who witnessed the transfiguration had a vision of the Son of man as He would be vindicated and glorified, in fulfilment of His words, and in anticipation of the advent of the kingdom coming in the power of the Holy Spirit. The vision confirmed to the disciples that the kingdom was coming in power, that Jesus was more than just a good teacher - that He was indeed the Messiah, and that the Messiah had to suffer and die. There are clear parallels with the account of Daniels' vision of Gabriel as we read in Daniel 8:17-18 and 10:12,

> 'So he came near where I stood, and when he came I was afraid and fell on my face; but he said to me, "Understand, son of man, that the vision refers to the time of the end." Now, as he was speaking with me, I was in a deep sleep with my face to the ground; but he touched me and stood me upright.'

> 'Then he said to me, "Do not fear, Daniel, for from the first day that you set your heart to understand, and to humble yourself before your God, your words were heard; and I have come because of your words."

The disciples were exhorted to keep silent about the vision so that there would be no interference in God the Father's plan, but they would be able to reflect on the vision later, recognising it as confirmation of the fulfilment of the plan. They were three witnesses as the law required. They were witnesses to the vision proclaiming that the Messiah would suffer death and then be raised to life as was foretold for example in Isaiah 25:8, 26:19, Hosea 13:14, and Psalm 16:10,

'He will swallow up death forever, and the Lord God will wipe away tears from all faces; the rebuke of His people He will take away from all the earth; for the Lord has spoken.'

'Your dead shall live; together with my dead body they shall arise. Awake and sing, you who dwell in the dust; for your dew is like the dew of herbs, and the earth shall cast out the dead.'

'I will ransom them from the power of the grave; I will redeem them from death.'

'For You will not leave my soul in Sheol, nor will You allow Your Holy One to see corruption.'

The death and suffering of Christ were part of the Father's plan, whereby sin would be defeated through His death and resurrection. Jesus knew that in time His disciples would fully understand the importance of the vision, that through His death and resurrection, they and all those who would choose to follow Christ would be redeemed and raised to eternal life as promised in Daniel 12:2 and 13, Job 19:25-26, and Psalm 49:15,

'And many of those who sleep in the dust of the earth shall awake, some to everlasting life, some to shame and everlasting contempt.'

'But you, go your way till the end; for you shall rest, and will arise to your inheritance at the end of the days.'

'For I know that my Redeemer lives, and He shall stand at last on the earth; and after my skin is destroyed, this I know, that in my flesh I shall see God.' And 'But God will redeem my soul from the power of the grave, for He shall receive me.'

Matthew 17:11-12

Following the transfiguration, during which the disciples saw a vision of the prophet Elijah, the disciples asked Jesus why the scribes said that Elijah must come first. In verses 11-12, Jesus answered the disciples' question saying,

> "Elias indeed is coming and will restore all things; but I tell you that Elias already came, and they did not recognise him, but did by him whatever things they wished; and thus also the Son of man is about to suffer by them."

By these words, Jesus made it clear that He was referring to John, known as the Baptist, as being the Elijah that had been foretold. The purpose of John's ministry was to preach a doctrine that would lead to the restoration of the people in their relationship with God, and this was recorded in the Gospels as being successfully achieved amongst the common people who flocked to listen to him and were baptised in the river Jordan. John had already laid the foundation of restoration through repentance, and then passed the work on to Christ to complete the restoration of all things that John had begun. John was the one who would go before the Christ in the spirit of Elijah as prophesied by Malachi as we read in chapter 4:5-6,

> 'Behold, I will send you Elijah the prophet before the coming of the great and dreadful day of the Lord, and he will turn the hearts of the fathers to the children, and the hearts of the children to their fathers.'

Elijah himself had been rejected by the people of Israel, as had so many of God's prophets before him, such as Jeremiah who was sent to warn the people to listen. Just as the children of Israel had sought to silence Elijah and the other prophets, so would they also seek to silence John and even the Messiah, as we read for example in Jeremiah 26:8, 1 Kings 19:10, Psalm 69:9-10 and Psalm 22:6-7,

> 'Now it happened, when Jeremiah had made an end of speaking all that the Lord had commanded him to speak to all the people, that the priests and the prophets and all the people seized him, saying, "You will surely die!"

> "I have been very zealous for the Lord God of hosts; for the children of Israel have forsaken Your covenant, torn down Your

altars, and killed Your prophets with the sword. I alone am left; and they seek to take my life."

'Because zeal for Your house has eaten me up, and the reproaches of those who reproach You have fallen on me. When I wept and chastised my soul with fasting, that became my reproach. I also made sackcloth my garment; I became a byword to them.'

'But I am a worm, and no man; a reproach of men and despised by the people. All those who see Me ridicule Me.'

Just as people had rejected the one preparing the way for the Messiah, so they would reject the Messiah. Jesus reminded His disciples of the treatment and suffering of John by the scribes and Pharisees, and warned that having rejected the servant, they would, with similar disdain, reject his Master, and that both of these rejections had been foretold. The Jewish rulers did not recognise John as the forerunner of the Messiah, although many of the ordinary people did, and neither did they recognise Jesus as the Messiah. That the Christ was to suffer and be despised was foretold by Isaiah in chapter 53:3 and chapter 49:7,

'He is despised and rejected by men, a Man of sorrows and acquainted with grief. And we hid, as it were, our face from Him; He was despised, and we did not esteem Him.'

'Thus says the Lord, the Redeemer of Israel, their Holy One, to Him whom man despises, to Him whom the nation abhors, to the Servant of rulers: "Kings shall see and arise, princes also shall worship, because of the Lord who is faithful, the Holy One of Israel; and He has chosen You."

Matthew 17:17

In verse 17, we read of Jesus' response to the request of the father of a boy to heal his son, whom the disciples had been unable to heal, saying,

> "O generation unbelieving and having been perverted, until when with you shall I be? Until when shall I endure you? Bring to me him here."

The word perverse in this context means opinions, or thoughts, that hinder a person from receiving the truth. It means that which is twisted, or turned, away from the proper direction. So perverse were many of the people, particularly amongst those who were teachers of the law, that they were unable to think or act correctly. Jesus was quoting directly from Deuteronomy, and Isaiah also spoke of the corrupting influence of perverse thinking, as we read in Deuteronomy 32:5-6 and 20, and Isaiah 19:14,

> 'They have corrupted themselves; they are not His children, because of their blemish; a perverse and crooked generation. Do you thus deal with the Lord? O foolish and unwise people? Is He not your Father, who bought you? Has He not made you and established you?'

> 'And He said, "I will hide My face from them, I will see what their end will be, for they are a perverse generation, children in whom is no faith."

> 'The Lord has mingled a perverse spirit in her midst; and they have caused Egypt to err in all her work, as a drunken man staggers in his vomit.'

Jesus asked the rhetorical question; how long it would be necessary for Him to show patience and forbearance with the unbelief of the people. It was a reproof of their slowness to believe in God's saving power that had echoed down the ages in Old Testament Scripture. The words were spoken to the disciples to warn them against unbelief, and to all the bystanders who were slow to believe in Him as the Messiah, even though they had witnessed the miracles that He had wrought in their presence. The disciples didn't lack faith in terms of quantity, but in the right kind of faith in which there would be nothing to hinder them from relying completely on the unlimited capacity of their all-powerful God the Father through sincere prayer. The reproof was not directed against ignorant or

318

weak persons, but against those who maliciously and obstinately resist God. His words warn that those who continue in their perversity of understanding will no longer be worth enduring. Jesus echoed the words spoken to Moses in Exodus 16:28, Numbers 14:11 and 27, where we read,

> 'And the Lord said to Moses, "How long do you refuse to keep My commandments and My laws?"
>
> 'Then the Lord said to Moses, "How long will these people reject Me? And how long will they not believe Me, with all the signs which I have performed among them?"
>
> "How long shall I bear with this evil congregation who complain against Me?"

Jesus did respond to the boy's father, whose own faith may have wavered at the failure of the disciples, and straight away healed the boy; He did not allow the weakness of faith in His disciples to constrain His own compassion for the boy and his father. Time and again, throughout Old Testament Scripture, God the Father demonstrated His faithfulness to His people. He promised to go before them, to provide all that they needed, to ensure that they would not have to suffer the diseases that other nations did but to heal them, and even to carry them, to carry us, as a man carries his son, as we read in Deuteronomy 1:30-33,

> 'The Lord your God, who goes before you, He will fight for you, according to all He did for you in Egypt before your eyes, and in the wilderness where you saw how the Lord your God carried you, as a man carries his son, in all the way that you went until you came to this place. Yet for all that, you did not believe the Lord your God, who went in the way before you.'

Matthew 17:20-21

In verses 20-21, Jesus replied to the disciples who had asked Him why they were not able to cast out the demon and cure the boy, saying,

> "Because of the little faith of you; for truly I say to you, if ye have faith as a grain of mustard ye will say mountain to this: Remove hence there, and it will be removed, and nothing will be impossible to you. This however kind goes not out except but by prayer and fasting."

Jesus was not suggesting that His disciples are called to move mountains; they are instead called to move God. We can see that through his prayer, Moses made God change His mind about destroying the people of Israel after they had turned away to worship a golden calf. When God's people ask for what is in keeping with His plan, they can be sure that this will happen. The mountain that Jesus spoke of may well have been the Mount of Olives. He would have been familiar with the prophesies that it would be split and moved, and we find later in Matthew's Gospel that it did indeed split open at the time of the crucifixion. According to His will, the mountains will move and melt as we read in Zechariah 14:4 and Micah 1:3-4,

> 'And in that day His feet will stand on the Mount of Olives, which faces Jerusalem on the east. And the Mount of Olives shall be split in two from east to west, making a very large valley; half of the mountain shall move toward the north and half of it toward the south.'

> 'For behold, the Lord is coming out of His place; He will come down and tread on the high places of the earth. The mountains will melt under Him, and the valleys will split like wax before the fire, like waters poured down a steep place.'

A grain of mustard seed can be living, thriving, and increasing, and become a great plant. So also, the faith of Jesus' disciples should live, thrive, and increase. The disciples in this account must have had some faith, or they would not have tried to cast out the demon and cure the boy. In the moment, perhaps they lost sight of God's power, in the face of the boy's convulsions and the destructive nature of the demon. The apostles were to understand that all things were possible through faith; that seeds of doubts and unbelief, and a lack of fervent and devoted prayer would hinder them completing God's work. Nothing will be impossible for His disciples in performing that which will glorify God, enlarge His kingdom, and confirm His truth and Salvation. Jesus illustrated the power of faith using analogies from the natural world. If faith is present at all, even if it is no bigger than a mustard seed, it can accomplish wonders. Psalm 46:2 describes an imagined natural disaster in which the people of God are unafraid, knowing that He is their refuge and strength.

> 'Therefore, we will not fear, even though the earth be removed, and though the mountains be carried into the midst of the sea.'

It is not every kind of faith that will suffice; it must be strengthened and supported by prayer, especially when going into battle, and fasting, or denying oneself, strengthens prayer; in the battle we must use all to our advantage. Jesus' words suggest that some demons are more malevolent than others; prayer is a necessity and fasting may also be needed at times. Self-denial and fasting accompanied by prayer are weapons against evil that are well established in Old Testament Scripture as we read for example in Daniel 9:3, Psalm 35:13, and Jonah 3:5,

> 'Then I set my face toward the Lord God to make request by prayer and supplications, with fasting, sackcloth, and ashes.'

> 'But as for me, when they were sick, my clothing was sackcloth; I humbled myself with fasting.'

> 'So the people of Nineveh believed God, proclaimed a fast and put on sackcloth, from the greatest to the least of them.'

Matthew 17:22-23

In verses 22-23, we read that the disciples were 'exceedingly sorrowful' after Jesus once again warned them of the impending culmination of His ministry that would involve His death, but would end in His resurrection, saying,

> "The Son of man is about to be delivered into the hands of men, and they will kill him, and on the third day he will be raised."

As the time of His death approached, Jesus warned His disciples with increasing frequency of what was to come. He knew that He was to be sacrificed at the approaching Passover. He told them that He would be delivered into the hands of men. Jesus was delivered up by the counsel of God, as a sacrifice, to be an atonement for the sin of the world just as had been foretold in Isaiah 53:10-11,

> 'Yet it pleased the Lord to bruise Him; He has put Him to grief. When You make His soul an offering for sin, He shall see His seed, He shall prolong His days, and the pleasure of the Lord shall prosper in His hand. He shall see the labour of His soul and be satisfied. By His knowledge My righteous Servant shall justify many, for He shall bear their iniquities.'

Jesus told them bluntly that once He had been delivered into the hands of men that He would be killed. He knew that the descriptions in Scripture of His death were about to come to pass; that He would suffer and suffer in silence as He was to be led to be slaughtered like a lamb, as we read for example in Psalm 22:14-15 and Isaiah 53:7,

> 'I am poured out like water, and all My bones are out of joint; My heart is like wax; it has melted within Me. My strength is dried up like a potsherd, and My tongue clings to My jaws; You have brought Me to the dust of death.'

> 'He was oppressed, and He was afflicted, yet He opened not His mouth; He was led as a lamb to the slaughter, and as a sheep before its shearers is silent; so He opened not His mouth.'

Finally, Jesus told them that He would be raised on the third day. Those of His followers who believed in resurrection at the end times may have assumed that Jesus was referring to this since we know from later in the Gospel accounts that the disciples had not expected His resurrection at that time. This may have been founded on Scripture such as Daniel 12:2, Psalm 49:15, Psalm 86:13, and Isaiah 26:19 where we read:

> 'And many of those who sleep in the dust of the earth shall awake, some to everlasting life, some to shame and everlasting contempt.'

> 'But God will redeem my soul from the power of the grave, for He shall receive me.'

> 'For great is Your mercy toward me, and You have delivered my soul from the depths of Sheol.'

> 'Your dead shall live; together with my dead body they shall arise.'

However, Jesus told them that He would be raised specifically on the third day. He had previously made mention of the sign of Jonah's three days in the fish as was discussed in Chapter 12:39, but this was not the only portent of the three-day resurrection and the declaration that His body would not see corruption. The account of Abraham and Isaac foreshadowed the significance of the third day, as did the prophet Hosea, as we read in Genesis 22:3-4, Hosea 6:1-2, and Psalm 16:9-10,

> 'So Abraham rose early in the morning and saddled his donkey, and took two of his young men with him, and Isaac his son; and he split the wood for the burnt offering, and arose and went to the place of which God had told him. Then on the third day Abraham lifted his eyes and saw the place afar off.'

> 'Come and let us return to the Lord; for He has torn, but He will heal us; He has stricken, but He will bind us up. After two days He will revive us; on the third day He will raise us up.'

> 'Therefore my heart is glad, and my glory rejoices; My flesh also will rest in hope, for You will not leave my soul in Sheol, nor will You allow Your Holy One to see corruption.'

323

Matthew 17:25-27

In verses 25-27, Jesus discusses the collection of the temple tax with Peter, aware that Peter had been questioned by the collectors of this tax, saying,

> "What to thee seems it Simon? The kings of the earth from whom do they take toll or poll-tax? From the sons of them or from strangers?" And he saying: From strangers. Said to him Jesus: "Then free are the sons. But lest we should offend them, going to the sea cast a hook and the coming up first fish take, and opening the mouth of it thou wilt find a stater; that taking give them for me and thee."

A stater was a Roman silver coin the same value as a four-drachma coin; a drachma was one quarter of a shekel; the annual temple tax was two drachmae, or half a shekel per person. Other translations refer to a half-shekel tax and the coin as a shekel. The word shekel means weight. At the time of Jesus, it was also a silver coin of a particular weight of about 4 ounces. It was also a typical wage for one day of labour. Three thousand shekels equated to one talent, the heaviest unit of measurement for weight and value. This annual temple tax had been enshrined in the Law since the days of Moses, as we read in Exodus 30:13-4,

> 'This is what everyone among those who are numbered shall give: half a shekel according to the shekel of the sanctuary (a shekel is twenty gerahs). The half-shekel shall be an offering to the Lord. Everyone included among those who are numbered, from twenty years old and above shall give an offering to the Lord.'

As citizens of God's kingdom, Jesus' followers' resources are devoted to God's purposes, but we still must give to earthly powers what is due. Christ's disciples are God's people, and just as an earthly king will not collect taxes from their family, neither does God. This principle of exemption from taxes for the King's family is found in the account of David and Goliath in 1 Samuel 17:25, where we read,

> 'So the men of Israel said, "Have you seen this man who has come up? Surely he has come up to defy Israel; and it shall be that the man who kills him the king will enrich with great riches, will give him his daughter, and give his father's house exemption from taxes in Israel."

Peter had replied to the temple tax collector that Jesus did pay His taxes, so we can safely assume that He did pay all the taxes that He was expected to pay. Paying taxes is the obligation of citizens in return for services that are rendered to those citizens by the state. Even the Roman empire provided roads, water, policing, and sometimes relief for the poor. The temple tax was for God, the King; Jesus was His Son and therefore exempt from taxes, but that does not negate a disciple choosing to make an offering in fulfilment of the law. Jesus made it clear throughout His ministry that He had not come to change, replace, or destroy the Law but to fulfil it (see Chapter 5:17). Jesus was also aware that because the Jewish officials did not recognise Him, not paying the tax would create unnecessary misunderstanding. The coinage found in the fish was neither more nor less than needed, but just as required by the Law as we read in Exodus 30:15,

> 'The rich shall not give more, and the poor shall not give less than half a shekel, when you give an offering to the Lord, to make atonement for yourselves.'

Jesus' knowledge of Peter's earlier conversation, and of the fish having the coin in its mouth, are evidence of His Messianic omniscience. It seems unlikely that Jesus was compelled by poverty to look for a coin in a fish, but rather it was to add to the record of evidence that He had power and dominion over all earthly kingdoms and even fish would bring Him their tribute.

MATTHEW CHAPTER EIGHTEEN

Matthew 18:3-4

In chapter 18 verses 3-4, Jesus responded to His disciples, who had been arguing about who would be the greatest in the Kingdom of heaven, by summoning a child to Him and saying,

> "Truly I say to you, except ye turn and become as children, by no means may ye enter into the kingdom of the heavens. Therefore, he who will humble himself as child this, this one is the greater in the kingdom of the heavens."

Jesus spoke about people turning, sometimes translated as converting, from their current trajectory. He made it clear that unless people convert, or turn, from seeking earthly gain to spiritual gain, they cannot enter into the spiritual and eternal kingdom. This turning, or conversion, means turning towards God, seeking His presence; His restoration and renewal of our own spirit; His cleansing of our hearts through the work of His Holy Spirit as we read in Psalm 51:10-13,

> 'Create in me a clean heart, O God, and renew a steadfast spirit within me. Do not cast me away from Your presence, and do not take Your Holy Spirit from me. Restore to me the joy of Your salvation and uphold me with Your generous Spirit. Then I will teach transgressors Your ways, and sinners shall be converted to You.'

Jesus told His disciples that to enter the kingdom of God, they would need to be like children. This meant that they must be without worldly ambition, just as when children play together as equals and have no appreciation of what the adult world considers to be of value. We know that very young children are still free from prejudice and are typically open to being taught; they are loving, trusting, free from anxiety, and innocent. A child-like believer should demonstrate the same innocent and unrestrained trust in the Lord. Jesus may well have had the words of the psalmist in mind as we read in Psalm 131:1-2,

> 'Lord, my heart is not haughty, nor my eyes lofty, neither do I concern myself with great matters, nor with things too profound for me. Surely, I have calmed and quieted my soul, like a weaned child with his mother; like a weaned child is my soul within me.'

Jesus made clear to His disciples that they were all equal and that any superiority could only be the result of the deepest humility; therefore,

His followers, should resist seeking worldly honours or earthly profit or seeking to rule over others. The Old Testament Scripture teaches that the way to spiritual greatness is through humbling ourselves and serving others. To enter the kingdom of God, His people must accept that they have no more status than a child. Those who seek to be disciples of Jesus must turn from their own desires and submit only to Him through serving others. Jesus' words make it clear that we do not degrade ourselves by this humility. The truly humble person claims no personal merit, nor despises others or aims at being superior, and desires nothing more than to serve and dwell with the King of Heaven, as we read for example in 2 Samuel 22:28, Zephaniah 3:12, Psalm 62:1-2, Psalm 22:27, and Isaiah 57:15,

> 'You will save the humble people; but Your eyes are on the haughty, that You may bring them down.'

> 'I will leave in your midst a meek and humble people, and they shall trust in the name of the Lord.'

> 'Truly my soul silently waits for God; from Him comes my salvation. He only is my rock and my salvation.'

> 'All the ends of the world shall remember and turn to the Lord, and all the families of the nations shall worship before You.'

> 'For thus says the High and Lofty One who inhabits eternity, whose name is Holy; "I dwell in the high and holy place, with him who has a contrite and humble spirit, to revive the spirit of the humble, and revive the heart of the contrite ones."

Matthew 18:5-7

In verses 5-7, Jesus continued His teaching about the importance of humility in discipleship, not just in our relationship to God, but in our relationship to others, saying,

> "And whoever receives one child such in the name of me, me receives; and whoever offends one little ones of these believing in me, it is expedient for him that be hanged an upper millstone round the neck of him and he be drowned in the depth of the sea. Woe to the world from offences; for it is a necessity to come offences, but woe to the man through whom the offence comes."

To receive in this context means to approve, to love, to treat with kindness, or even aid in time of need. The teaching here is that whoever receives someone, who like a child, is humble, meek and unambitious, receives Jesus Himself. In other words, whoever loves another who has the Spirit of Jesus, loves Jesus also, as we read in Zechariah 2:8,

> 'For thus says the Lord of hosts: "He sent Me after glory, to the nations which plunder you; for he who touches you touches the apple of His eye."

The Greek word 'skandalise', that we can recognise, can be translated as either to cause offence or to cause one to stumble. Jesus' meaning is clear that whoever places stumbling blocks that are causes of, or temptations to, sin, before another will face punishment. In other words, those who cause others to fall, or to sin, or place anything in the way to hinder their path of righteousness, or to stumble in their faith, or to be drawn aside from the right course, or retarded in it, will face the most serious consequences. Death by drowning using millstones around the neck was a recognised mode of capital punishment at the time by the Greeks, Syrians and Romans. Jesus was teaching that the consequences are so severe that it would be better for one to have died before committing such a sin. Jesus was teaching His followers the way that believers should treat each other by humbling themselves. We know that people who think too highly of themselves, or desire to be preferred to others, treat their neighbours, or fellow Christians, with disdain. Remembering that Jesus said that treatment of these others is treatment of Him, then if we disdain others, we hold Him in disdain too. The priestly sons of Eli fell into this trap as we read in 2 Samuel 2:22-25,

'Now Eli was very old; and he heard everything his sons did to all Israel, and how they lay with the women who assembled at the door of the tabernacle of meeting. So he said to them, "Why do you do such things? For I hear of your evil dealings from all the people. No, my sons! For it is not a good report that I hear. You make the Lord's people transgress. If one man sins against another, God will judge him. But if a man sins against the Lord, who will intercede for him?"'

The whole of Psalm 73 describes how easy it is to stumble and is worth study in this context. Such are the ways of mankind that there will always be some who are attempting to make others sin, endeavouring to lead Christians astray. Such also is our weakness that our own desires will lead us astray, however, those who lead others into sin are most guilty – those who attempt to defile the purity of others. In all ages there have been those who by persecution, threats, craftiness, allurements, and persuasion, have endeavoured to seduce Christians from the faith and to lead them into sin. Our earnest prayer must be that we neither stumble ourselves or cause others to stumble in their faith, as we read in Psalm 27:11-13 and Proverbs 4:10-13,

'Teach me Your way, O Lord, and lead me in a smooth path, because of my enemies. Do not deliver me to the will of my adversaries; for false witnesses have arisen against me, and such as breathe out violence. I would have lost heart, unless I had believed that I would see the goodness of the Lord in the land of the living.'

'Hear, my son, and receive my sayings, and the years of your life will be many. I have taught you in the way of wisdom; I have led you in right paths. When you walk your steps will not be hindered, and when you run, you will not stumble. Take firm hold of instruction, do not let go; keep her for she is your life.'

331

Matthew 18:8-9

In verses 8-9, Jesus continued His warning about stumbling blocks to faith, this time in the context of our own individual weakness to temptation, saying,

> "Now if the hand of thee or the foot of thee offends thee, cut off it and cast from thee; good for thee it is to enter life maimed or lame, than two hands or two feet having to be cast into the fire eternal. And if the eye of thee offends thee, pluck out it and cast from thee; good for thee it is one-eyed into the life to enter, than two eyes having to be cast into the Gehenna of fire."

These words are almost identical to those found in Matthew 5:29 that has already been discussed from the perspective of an individual's vulnerability to temptation. Here, the focus is on the cost of resisting temptation. This may mean, in the words of Jesus, casting things away from you that have become more precious than the pursuit of righteousness; things, be they objects or even ideas, that have become idols, as we read for example in Isaiah 2:20, Isaiah 30:22, and Ezekiel 18:31,

> 'In that day a man will cast away his idols of silver and his idols of gold, which they made each for himself to worship.'

> 'You will also defile the covering of your images of silver, and the ornament of your moulded images of gold. You will throw them away as an unclean thing; you will say to them, "Get away!"

> 'Cast away from you all the transgressions which you have committed and get yourselves a new heart and a new spirit. For why should you die, O house of Israel?'

Jesus speaks of casting away even members of one's own body if they are the root cause of temptation. Jesus was teaching His disciples that stumbling blocks to an individual's faith are so serious, so dangerous to eternal life, that they must show no pity, no opportunity, no allowances for that which causes them to stumble, or for that which entices them away from the path of righteousness. Even members of one's own family must be cast aside if they become stumbling blocks to faith as we read for example in Deuteronomy 13:6-8,

'If your brother, the son of your mother, your son or your daughter, the wife of your bosom, or your friend who is as your own soul, secretly entices you, saying, 'Let us go and serve other gods,' which you have not known, neither you nor your fathers, of the gods of the people which are all around you, near to you or far off from you, from one end of the earth to the other end of the earth, you shall not consent to him or listen to him, not shall your eye pity him, nor shall you spare him or conceal him.'

Even King David's eye led him into sin when he fell into the trap of adultery with the wife of Uriah the Hittite after he saw her bathing on the rooftop (2 Samuel 11:2). He did not pluck out his eye, but he did pay a heavy price for his error. Whatever there is in a disciple's life that may become a trap, or snare, must be thrown out, cast away onto the rubbish tip, the incinerator known as Gehenna. Jesus' disciples cannot circumnavigate or water-down God's commandments; they are non-negotiable; they are to be followed with all our heart, with all our soul, and with all our strength, as we read in 1 Kings 2:4, Isaiah 33:15 and Psalm 119:1-3,

'If your sons take heed to their way, to walk before Me in truth with all their heart and with all their soul.'

'He who walks righteously and speaks uprightly, he who despises the gain of oppressions, who gestures with his hands, refusing bribes, who stops his ears from hearing of bloodshed, and shuts his eyes from seeing evil; he will dwell on high; his place of defence will be the fortress of rocks.'

'Blessed are the undefiled in the way, who walk in the law of the Lord. Blessed are those who keep His testimonies, who seek Him with the whole heart. They also do no iniquity; they walk in His ways.'

333

Matthew 18:10-14

In verses 10-14, Jesus was teaching His disciples that not only should they beware of placing stumbling blocks in the way of faith for others, but that they should be proactively seeking out those who have gone, or are going astray, and bring them into His kingdom, saying,

> "See that ye despise not one little ones of these; for I tell you that the angels of them in heavens continuously behold the face of the Father of me in heaven. For has come the Son of Man to save that which has been lost. What do you think? If there be to any man a hundred sheep and strays one of them, will he not leave the ninety-nine on the mountains and going seeks the one gone astray? And if he happens to find it, truly I say to you that he rejoices over it more than over the ninety-nine not having gone astray. Thus, it is not the will of the Father of you in heaven that should perish one little ones of these."

Jesus spoke of the angels who beheld the face of the Father in heaven. To be able to see a king's face meant having permission or access to the presence of the king. This was an indication of the rank or stature of a person; Jesus is telling His disciples that even those with the weakest of faith have this rank in the Kingdom of Heaven. King David's son Absalom, when he was in disgrace, was not allowed to see the king's face, by contrast the men of high rank in the court of the Persian empire had access to the king's presence and the prophet Micaiah was allowed to see the Lord God on His throne, as we read in 2 Samuel 14:28, Esther 1:14, and 1 Kings 22:19,

> 'And Absalom dwelt two full years in Jerusalem but did not see the king's face.'

> 'The seven princes of Persia and Media, who had access to the king's presence, and who ranked highest in the kingdom.'

> 'Then Micaiah said, "Therefore hear the word of the Lord: I saw the Lord sitting on His throne, and all the host of heaven standing by, on His right hand and on His left."

In likening the people to sheep, and His disciples to shepherds, Jesus was using the same analogy used by the Old Testament prophets to describe how the people went astray and how those who should have been shepherding the people, that is the priests and teachers, had failed to care for those who were weak, sick, broken, lost or even driven away, as we read for example in Psalm 119:176, Ezekiel 34:4 and 6, and the well-known passage in Isaiah 53:6.

> 'I have gone astray like a lost sheep; seek Your servant, for I do not forget Your commandments.'

> 'The weak you have not strengthened, nor have you healed those who were sick, nor bound up the broken, nor brought back what was driven away, nor sought what was lost; but with force and cruelty you have ruled them.'

> "My sheep wandered through all the mountains, and on every high hill; yes, My flock was scattered over the whole face of the earth, and no one was seeking or searching for them."

> 'All we like sheep have gone astray; we have turned, every one, to his own way; and the Lord has laid on Him the iniquity of us all.'

After all the warnings, Jesus goes on to comfort His disciples, telling them that it is not the will of their heavenly Father that any should perish; that He takes pleasure in, and rejoices over those who turn to Him; that He seeks out the lost and will carry them home when found, as we read for example in Psalm 147:11, Isaiah 62:5, Ezekiel 34:12, and Isaiah 40:11,

> 'The Lord takes pleasure in those who fear Him, in those who hope in His mercy.'

> 'As the bridegroom rejoices over the bride, so shall your God rejoice over you.'

> "As a shepherd seeks out his flock on the day he is among his scattered sheep, so will I seek out My sheep and deliver them from all the places where they were scattered on a cloudy and dark day."

> 'He will feed His flock like a shepherd; He will gather the lambs in His arm, and carry them in His bosom, and gently lead those who are with young.'

Matthew 18:15-18

In verses 15-18, Jesus seems to have been continuing His teaching about stumbling blocks, but this time in the context of people's own behaviour that may be in error, and how His disciples should deal with it, saying,

> "Now if sins the brother of thee, go reprove him between thee and him alone. If thee he hears, thou gain the brother of thee; but if not he hears, take with thee more one or two, that by the mouth of two witnesses of three may be established every word; but if he refuses to hear them, tell to the church; and if even the church he refuses to hear, let him be to thee as the gentile and the tax collector. Truly I say to you, whatever things ye bind on the earth shall be having been bound in heaven, and whatever things ye loose on the earth shall be having been loosed in heaven."

The law found in Leviticus states that it is right to rebuke your neighbour without hatred, without vengeance, and without bearing a grudge. In Proverbs we find the teaching that Jesus is likely referring to whereby a complaint against a neighbour should be discussed in private and that the benefit is that a soul may be won, as we read in Leviticus 19:17-18, Proverbs 25:9, and Proverbs 11:30,

> 'You shall not hate your brother in your heart. You shall surely rebuke your neighbour and not bear sin because of him. You shall not take vengeance, nor bear any grudge against the children of your people, but you shall love your neighbour as yourself.'

> 'Debate your case with your neighbour, and do not disclose the secret to another.'

> 'The fruit of the righteous is a tree of life, and he who wins souls is wise.'

Jesus was quoting directly from the law in Deuteronomy regarding the number of witnesses required for anything to be established. The Old Testament law states explicitly that one witness is not sufficient testimony, and although much of the law relates to the crime of murder, it also refers to any iniquity or sin that a person commits, as we read in Numbers 35:30, Deuteronomy 17:6 and Deuteronomy 19:15,

'Whoever kills a person, the murderer shall be put to death on the testimony of witnesses; but one witness is not sufficient testimony against a person for the death penalty.'

'Whoever is deserving of death shall be put to death on the testimony of two or three witnesses; he shall not be put to death on the testimony of one witness.'

"One witness shall not rise against a man concerning any iniquity or any sin that he commits; by the mouth of two or three witnesses the matter shall be established."

Those who refuse to listen to the rebuke, even of the body of the Church, that is the representatives of God's kingdom on Earth, are to be treated as if they are no longer part of the Church. This separation of God's people from that which is unholy is exemplified in the account of the prophet Ezra, where we read in chapter 6:21,

'Then the children of Israel who had returned from captivity ate together with all who had separated themselves from the filth of the nations of the land in order to seek the Lord God of Israel.'

In this passage, Jesus spoke once again about binding and loosing that has already been discussed in chapter 16:17-19. Binding and loosing were expressions used in Judaism to denote the pronouncement of rulings either forbidding or authorising activities or behaviours. The authority to bind or loose was given to Peter in the earlier context, but here Jesus is giving that authority to the disciples as the body of the church. The keys of the kingdom, as we read in Isaiah 22:22-23, would enable the church to exercise the power of binding and loosing in their teaching, discipline and making of rules:

'The key of the house of David I will lay on his shoulder; so he shall open, and no one shall shut; and he shall shut, and no one shall open. I will fasten him as a peg in a secure place, and he will become a glorious throne to his father's house.'

337

Matthew 18:19-20

In verses 19-20, Jesus continued His teaching about the behaviour of His disciples as the body of the Church, that there should be a three-way agreement, between each other and between the Church and our heavenly Father, saying,

> "Again truly I say to you that if two agree of you on the earth concerning every thing whatever they ask, it shall be to them from the Father of me in heaven. For where are two or three having been assembled in my name, there I am in the midst of them."

Jesus spoke about being in perfect agreement. This can be likened to being in tune or in harmony; having the same desires and wishes. These words are for the church, the assembly, rather than an individual. Agreement in prayer is a further reminder about humility and the behaviour of disciples towards each other. It is God who governs the Church, approving and ratifying decisions of which He is the author. Jesus makes the promise that when His people are in harmony with each other and with Him, that God will hear and answer their prayer, as we read for example in 2 Chronicles 15:2, Psalm 4:3, Psalm 34:15, and Jeremiah 29:12,

> 'The Lord is with you while you are with Him. If you seek Him, He will be found by you.'

> 'Know that the Lord has set apart for Himself him who is godly; the Lord will hear when I call to Him.'

> 'The eyes of the Lord are on the righteous, and His ears are open to their cry.'

> 'Then you will call upon Me and go and pray to Me, and I will listen to you.'

The Church, or those who gather as His holy assemblies, even though there may be only two or three, must assemble in His name. This means laying aside everything that hinders His disciples from approaching Christ, in obedience to His word, and being governed by His Spirit. To assemble in the name of God, where His name is recorded and declared, is a command long established in Old Testament law as we read in Exodus 20:24, and Deuteronomy 12:5,

'An altar of earth you shall make for Me, and you shall sacrifice on it your burnt offerings and your peace offerings, your sheep and your oxen. In every place where I record My name, I will come to you and I will bless you.'

'You shall seek the place where the Lord your God chooses, out of all your tribes, to put His name for His dwelling place; and there you shall go.'

Jesus reminds His disciples that when they assemble in His name He is in their midst; He has come to dwell with them. When you say your prayers in a group setting, are they like a formal letter to a distant governor, often with no expectation of receiving a reply? Or do you realise that you are actually in the presence of the Most High God, the King of Kings, before whom, if you could see Him with your human eyes, you would fall on your knees in front of and ask Him to give you the resources and the means to carry out the work that He has already directed you to do? When Jesus' disciples pray together, He is in their midst, as we read in Ezekiel 37:26-28, Zechariah 2:5 and 10-11,

'I will make a covenant of peace with them, and it shall be an everlasting covenant with them; I will establish them and multiply them, and I will set My sanctuary in their midst forevermore. My tabernacle also shall be with them; indeed I will be their God, and they shall be My people. The nations also will know that I, the Lord, sanctify Israel, when My sanctuary is in their midst forevermore.'

'For I, says the Lord, will be a wall of fire all around her, and I will be the glory in her midst.'

'Sing and rejoice, O daughter of Zion. For behold, I am coming and I will dwell in your midst, says the Lord. Many nations shall be joined to the Lord in that day, and they shall become My people. And I will dwell in your midst. Then you will know that the Lord of hosts has sent Me to you.'

Matthew 18:22-27

In verses 22-27, Jesus responds to Peter's question about forgiveness of others, asking was seven times enough? In the first part of His reply, having told Peter that he should multiply that number by seventy, Jesus painted a picture of a king who forgave the enormous debt - into the tens of millions in today's money, of one man who pleaded for time to make reparations. This was to illustrate the forgiveness that is to be found in the kingdom of God, saying,

> "I tell not to thee until seven times, but until seventy times seven. Therefore is likened the kingdom of the heavens to a man a king, who wished to take account with the slaves of him. And as he began him to take, was brought forward one to him debtor of ten thousand talents. And as he had not him to repay, commanded him the lord to be sold and his wife and children and all things whatever he has, and to be repaid. Falling therefore the slave did obeisance to him saying: Defer anger over me, and all things I will repay thee. And filled with tenderness the lord slave of that released him, and the loan forgave him."

There are several places in the Old Testament where vengeance, or punishment, is meted out sevenfold to those who have committed offence, as we read for example in Leviticus 26:21, Psalm 79:12, and Genesis 4:24,

> 'Then, if you walk contrary to Me, and are not willing to obey Me, I will bring on you seven times more plagues, according to your sins.'

> 'Return to our neighbours sevenfold into their bosom their reproach with which they have reproached You, O Lord.'

> 'If Cain shall be avenged sevenfold, then Lamech seventy-sevenfold.'

Jesus was alluding to this account in Genesis in which Lamech claimed to have taken even more revenge on the man who struck him than God had taken on Cain for killing his brother Abel. Jesus repeatedly taught His disciples about forgiveness. Peter may have thought that forgiving someone seven times would be the limit of forbearance equating to avenging someone sevenfold. But Jesus, possibly also equating the seventy-sevenfold vengeance for Lamech, tells them that it is the greater

340

number that, rather than vengeance, is to be forgiven. Jesus turned Lamech's bad example around; over against seventy-times-sevenfold vengeance, Jesus sets the target as seventy-times-sevenfold forgiveness. Jonah, knowing the forgiving nature of God, did not want to go to Nineveh to call the people to repentance because he knew that if they did turn from their wicked ways, God would forgive them, and then he would feel foolish, as we read in Jonah 4:2,

> 'So he prayed to the Lord, and said, "Ah, Lord, was not this what I said when I was still in my country? Therefore I fled previously to Tarshish; for I know that You are a gracious and merciful God, slow to anger and abundant in lovingkindness, One who relents from doing harm.'

King David was fully aware of his debts, or iniquities, that were so enormous they rose over his head, but he also knew that God does not limit the size of the debt that He will forgive and neither, as we know from these words of Jesus, does He limit the number of times He will forgive, as we read for example in Psalm 38:4, 78:38, and Micah 7:18-19,

> 'For my iniquities have gone over my head; like a heavy burden they are too heavy for me.'

> 'But He, being full of compassion, forgave their iniquity, and did not destroy them. Yes, many a time He turned His anger away, and did not stir up all His wrath.'

> 'Who is a God like You, pardoning iniquity and passing over the transgressions of the remnant of His heritage? He does not retain His anger forever, because He delights in mercy. He will again have compassion on us and will subdue our iniquities. You will cast all our sins into the depths of the sea.'

341

Matthew 18:28-35

In verses 28-35, we read the second part of Jesus' response to Peter's question about forgiveness, in which He makes it clear that, for His disciples, forgiveness of others is not an option; that they are to forgive others just as they have been forgiven, saying,

> "But going out slave that found one of the fellow slaves of him, who owed him a hundred denarii, and seizing him throttled saying: Repay if something thou owes. Falling therefore the fellow slave of him besought him saying: Defer anger over me, and I will repay thee. But he not wished but going away threw him into prison until he should repay the thing owing. Seeing therefore the fellow slaves of him the things having taken place they were grieved exceedingly and coming narrated to the lord of themselves all the things having taken place. Then calling forward him the lord of him says to him: Slave wicked, all debt that I forgave thee, since thou besought me; did it not behove also thee to pity the fellow slave of thee, as I also thee pitied? And being angry the lord of him delivered him to the jailors until he should repay all the thing owing to him. Thus also the Father of me heavenly will do to you, unless ye forgive each one the brother of him from the hearts of you."

Jesus expects His followers, those who receive the forgiveness of God, as declared in His gospel, those who call Him their Father, to demonstrate an equally forgiving attitude to others. This restates what Jesus had already said in The Lord's Prayer, 'forgive us our debts as we forgive our debtors' discussed earlier in Chapter 6:12. The wording that Jesus gave His disciples in this prayer implies that the petitioner has already forgiven any injury received before being able to request their own forgiveness. The disciples would have doubtless been familiar with the warnings in Old Testament Scripture that speak of self-deceit and lack of empathy for others as we read for example in Proverbs 21:2 and 13, and Zechariah 7:12,

> 'Every way of a man is right in his own eyes, but the Lord weighs the hearts.'

> 'Whoever shuts his ears to the cry of the poor will also cry himself and not be heard.'

'They made their hearts like flint, refusing to hear the law and the words which the Lord of hosts had sent by His Spirit through the former prophets. Thus great wrath came from the Lord of hosts.'

By having a heart of flint, that refuses to forgive others, does the very nature of that heart of stone make it impossible for it to receive forgiveness, just as water cannot be absorbed but runs off a stone. Or put more simply, if we keep our hands in our pockets, so that we cannot shake hands or give to those in need, neither can we receive gifts offered to us. Time and again the prophets called the people to demonstrate the compassion and mercy of God, as we read for example in Zechariah 7:9-10,

'Thus says the Lord of hosts: Execute true justice, show mercy and compassion everyone to his brother. Do not oppress the widow or the fatherless, the alien or the poor. Let none of you plan evil in his heart against his brother.'

Forgiveness, or the release of debts, is a fundamental principle for the people of God, as we read in Deuteronomy 15:1-2, that carries with it promises of blessings. Jesus warned that unless we forgive others we cannot receive forgiveness, but at the same time promised that God would show mercy to those that show mercy to others as we read in 2 Samuel 22:26,

'At the end of every seven years you shall grant a release of debts. And this is the form of the release: Every creditor who has lent anything to his neighbour shall release it; he shall not require it of his neighbour or his brother, because it is called the Lord's release.' And 'With the merciful You will show Yourself merciful.'

MATTHEW CHAPTER NINETEEN

Matthew 19:4-6

At the beginning of Chapter 19 in verses 4-6, Jesus replied to the Pharisees, who wished to test Him, asking Him to judge if it is lawful for a man to divorce his wife for just any reason and wanting to know what reasons Jesus might offer, saying,

> "Did ye not read that the one creating from the beginning male and female made them? And he said: For the sake of this shall leave a man his father and his mother and shall cleave to the wife of him and shall be the two in flesh one; so as no longer are they two but one flesh. What therefore God yoked together, a man let not separate.

In His reply, Jesus did not initially concern Himself with possible reasons for divorce but made it clear that marriage was something that was instituted by God from the beginning for His purposes and that in marriage a man and woman are yoked or joined together as if they were one flesh. In the Hebrew this joining, or cleaving, was more like two things being glued, bonded or cemented together. When we try to separate two items that have been glued or bonded together, there is inevitable damage to both items. This being the case, a husband and wife should live together in such a way that they cherish the other as if they were the half of themselves. When yoked together, a married couple are closely united, pulling together equally in the concerns of life. Jesus quoted directly from the first book of the Law, as we read in Genesis 1:27, 2:24, and 5:2,

> 'So, God created man in His own image; in the image of God, He created him; male and female He created them.'

> 'Therefore, a man shall leave his father and mother and be joined to his wife, and they shall become one flesh.'

> 'He created them male and female and blessed them and called them Mankind in the day they were created.'

The institution of marriage was made in heaven, by God the Father. Jesus' answer is effectively: 'No; not for any cause.' It is by God's ordinance that the two become one; mankind is given no authority to modify that ordinance. Jesus reminded the Pharisees and His disciples of the first principles in the account of Genesis, in the book of the Law. He reminded them that laws of marriage should conform to the purpose for which marriage was instituted by God, to create a new unity of two persons; no provision was made in the Law for dissolving that unity as we read in Proverbs 2:17 and Malachi 2:14-16,

> 'To deliver you from the immoral woman, from the seductress who flatters with her words, who forsakes the companion of her youth and forgets the covenant of her God.'

> 'Yet you say, "For what reason?" Because the Lord has been a witness between you and the wife of your youth with whom you have dealt treacherously; yet she is your companion and your wife by covenant. But did He not make them one, having a remnant of the Spirit? And why one? He seeks godly offspring. Therefore, take heed to your spirit, and let none of you deal treacherously with the wife of his youth. For the Lord God of Israel says that He hates divorce, for it covers one's garment with violence.'

Jesus did not modify morality according to contemporary thinking or fashion or inclinations but referred His listeners back directly to the will, purpose, and institution of God as stated in the Law and expounded by the prophets. The two become one flesh in the children who receive an equal number of chromosomes from each parent. Marriage was instituted also that mankind could enjoy companionship and support in life, as we read in Ecclesiastes 9:9,

> 'Live joyfully with the wife whom you love all the days of your vain life which He has given you under the sun, all your days of vanity; for that is your portion in life, and in the labour which you perform under the sun.'

Matthew 19:8-9

In verses 8-9, Jesus replied to His disciples who had asked Him why, if God hates divorce, did Moses allow it, saying,

> "Moses in view of the hardness of heart of you allowed you to dismiss the wives of you; but from the beginning not it has been so. But I say now to you that whoever dismisses the wife of him not for sexual immorality and marries another, commits adultery, and he who marries her that is put away commits adultery."

The disciple's question provided Jesus with a further opportunity to teach about the consequences of the hardness of our hearts. It is when people harden their hearts that they go astray and refuse to understand the law and the words of the prophets, as we read for example in Psalm 95:8-10, and Zechariah 7:12,

> 'Do not harden your heart, as in the rebellion, as in the day of trial in the wilderness, when your fathers tested Me, though they saw My work. For forty years I was grieved with that generation, and said, 'It is a people who go astray in their hearts, and they do not know My ways.'

> 'Yes, they made their hearts like flint, refusing to hear the law and the words which the Lord of hosts had sent by His Spirit through the former prophets.'

Moses 'allowed' divorce; he did not 'command' it. Only once it had been allowed did Moses compile a law to deal with that contingency, as we read for example in Deuteronomy 24:1,

> 'When a man takes a wife and marries her, and it happens that she finds no favour in his eyes because he has found some uncleanness in her, and he writes her a certificate of divorce, puts it in her hand, and sends her out of his house,'

This law presumes that divorce is already an established practice and implies that the divorce procedure involved a man making a written declaration that the woman was no longer his wife. The law refers to finding some 'uncleanness' in the wife and the implication is that this would be a justification for divorce. In Deuteronomy 22:13-21, the law regarding premarital sexual relations led some teachers to interpret this as being the form of uncleanness referred to in the law. However, over time, others had interpreted the law more liberally to include anything that the husband may find offensive, even including her loss of beauty or poor cooking! When Israel was unfaithful to God, committing 'adultery', Jeremiah spoke of God giving Israel a divorce certificate, as we read in Jeremiah 3:8,

> 'Then I saw that for all the causes for which backsliding Israel had committed adultery, I had put her away and given her a certificate of divorce.'

In the Genesis account, Abimelech, King of Gerar, clearly believed that it was wrong to take another man's wife. This was at the time of Abraham, and some five hundred or so years before Moses and the Ten Commandments. It is interesting to note that God, when speaking to Abimelech, speaks of adultery as a sin against Him; that adultery is a sin against God, as we read in Genesis 20:6,

> 'Yes, I know that you did this in the integrity of your heart. For I also withheld you from sinning against Me; therefore, I did not let you touch her,'

The law that allowed men to divorce their wives wholly disadvantaged women; Jesus' ruling, according to God the Creator's intention, redressed the balance. Jesus' reply, as with Moses allows unfaithfulness or adultery to be a just cause for divorce. In this circumstance, the very nature of the act has already dissolved the bond of marriage. Doubtless there are circumstances when a couple did not marry with the intention to sacrifice their whole life to the earthly and eternal well-being of the spouse, or else they have abandoned this intention. Sometimes it is best for a couple to part, as Jesus, Himself concedes in the case of adultery – not a single instance of falling into sin, but a lifestyle of one partner. This does not exclude other reasons such as abuse or neglect or danger or crime. But Jesus repeatedly took His listeners back to first principles – the old paths, as we read in Jeremiah 6:16,

> 'Stand in the ways and see, and ask for the old paths, where the good way is, and walk in it; then you will find rest for your souls.'

349

Matthew 19:11-12

In verses 11-12, Jesus replied to His disciples who, having heard His teaching about divorce, suggest that given His ruling it would be better not to marry, saying,

> "Not all men grasp this saying, but those to whom it has been given. For there are eunuchs who from the womb of a mother were born so, and there are eunuchs who were made eunuchs by men, and there are eunuchs who made eunuchs themselves on account of the kingdom of the heavens. The one being able to grasp it let him grasp."

Jesus stated that some, not all, would be able to grasp His words; that a life of celibacy could only be lived successfully by those who had received the ability that had been given. Jesus goes on to refer to eunuchs who had been born that way, and then to those who had been made eunuchs by others, in other words an enforced celibacy. This was a common practice at the time and often a high position in society was conferred on the individual eunuch, as we see for example in Isaiah 39:7 and Esther 1:10,

> 'And they shall take away some of your sons who will descend from you, whom you will beget; and they shall be eunuchs in the palace of the king of Babylon.'

> 'On the seventh day, when the heart of the king was merry with wine, he commanded Mehuman, Biztha, Harbona, Bigtha, Abagtha, Zethar, and Carcas, seven eunuchs who served in the presence of King Ahasuerus,'

The third kind of eunuch that Jesus spoke of are those who choose, of their own volition, to receive the gift of celibacy from God the Father, to be able to devote themselves completely to the work of the Kingdom of God, without having responsibilities towards a spouse and children. No doubt Jesus had the fifty-sixth chapter of Isaiah in mind as He taught the disciples, knowing that God promises to those who serve Him with complete devotion a place and a name in His kingdom that is surer than sons and daughters, as we read in Isaiah 56:3-4,

> 'Do not let the son of the foreigner who has joined himself to the Lord speak saying, "The Lord has utterly separated me from His people"; nor let the eunuch say, "Here I am, a dry tree." For this

says the Lord: "To the eunuchs who keep My Sabbaths, and choose what pleases Me, and hold fast to My covenant, even to them I will give in My house and within My walls a place and a name better than that of sons and daughters; I will give them an everlasting name that shall not be cut off.'

Only a minority of Jesus' followers would be given this ability, for most marriage and family life would be the norm; God has declared it to be good that a man and woman should cleave together and become a new unity. The implication in His words is that a celibate life should not be attempted by those who have not been called, only those who have received the gift of celibacy. Celibacy in itself is not a virtue; it becomes virtuous only when it is a means by which a person can devote themselves entirely to the work of God's Kingdom. If we read further on in Isaiah chapter fifty-six, we can infer that this gift will be given also to the Gentiles. The message is clear that those who seek to serve the Lord, whoever they are, from all nations, providing that they follow His Laws and keep His covenant, will have a place in His house, on His holy mountain, in His kingdom, as we read in verses 6-7,

'also the sons of the foreigner who join themselves to the Lord, to serve Him, and to love the name of the Lord, to be His servants – everyone who keeps from defiling the Sabbath, and holds fast My covenant – even them I will bring to My holy mountain, and make them joyful in My house of prayer. Their burnt offerings and their sacrifices will be accepted on My altar; for My house shall be called a house of prayer for all nations.'

Matthew 19:14

In verse 14, Jesus rebuked the disciples who had shooed away the children who had been brought to Him for a blessing, saying,

> "Permit the children and do not prevent them to come unto me; for of such is the kingdom of the heavens."

Jesus then laid His hands on the children and blessed them. There are some parallels here to His words in chapter 18:3, discussed earlier, in which Jesus taught His disciples that they should humble themselves to be like children in order to be part of His kingdom. Children, who are not eligible to inherit, are equal before the law; they are equal in the kingdom of God. The children gathered around Jesus are an illustration that entrance to the kingdom of God is not by our own efforts; that His disciples need to acknowledge that they are as helpless and dependent as little children and that God the Father loves His children that follow in His way, and call on Him in innocence and truth, as we read in Proverbs 22:6, Psalm 103:13-14, Psalm 145:18, and Hosea 11:1,

> 'Train up a child in the way he should go, and when he is old he will not depart from it.'

> 'As a father pities his children, so the Lord pities those who fear Him, for He knows our frame; He remembers that we are dust.'

> 'The Lord is near to all who call upon Him, to all who call upon Him in truth.'

> 'Israel was a child, I loved him, and out of Egypt I called My son.'

Under the old covenant, children were brought into the family of Abraham, the earthly kingdom of the Hebrews, through circumcision as early as the eighth day. Circumcision began with Abraham and his son Ishmael who was thirteen. When Abraham's son Isaac was born, he was circumcised on the eighth day. In the account of Samson, his mother was told that the child would be set aside as holy to God even from the womb. God, the Father, has established a kingdom for His children who keep His covenant, as we read in Genesis 17:24-25, Judges 13:7, and Psalm 78:5-7,

'Abraham was ninety-nine years old when he was circumcised in the flesh of his foreskin. And Ishmael his son was thirteen years old when he was circumcised in the flesh of his foreskin.'

"Behold, you shall conceive and bear a son. Now drink no wine or similar drink, nor eat anything unclean, for the child shall be a Nazirite to God from the womb to the day of his death."

'For He established a testimony in Jacob and appointed a law in Israel, which He commanded our fathers, that they should make them known to their children; that the generation to come might know them, the children who would be born, that they might arise and declare them to their children, that they may set their hope in God, and not forget the works of God, but keep His commandments.'

As a child myself, I often asked my mother where do babies and children go when they die? Her answer was: Straight to the arms of their Father in heaven! Christ Himself was a holy child, set apart and sanctified even from the womb, and He welcomes even infants into His glorious kingdom, as we read in Psalm 145:10-12, Isaiah 65:17, and 20,

'All Your works shall praise You, O Lord, and Your saints shall bless You. They shall speak of the glory of Your kingdom, and talk of Your power, to make known to the sons of men His mighty acts, and the glorious majesty of His kingdom.'

'For behold, I create new heavens and a new earth; and the former shall not be remembered or come to mind.'

'No more shall an infant from there live but a few days, nor an old man who has not fulfilled his days; for the child shall die one hundred years old.'

Matthew 19:17-19

In verses 17-19, Jesus replied to someone's question about what good things they ought to do to gain eternal life, saying,

> "Why me ask thou concerning the good? Only One is good; but if thou desire into life to enter, keep the commandments." He says to him: Which? And Jesus said: "Thou shalt not kill; Thou shalt not commit adultery; Thou shalt not steal; Thou shalt not bear false witness; Honour thy father and thy mother; and Thou shalt love the neighbour of thee as thyself."

In the Greek transliteration, we can read that Jesus responded to the man by asking why he was questioning Him about what is good and what good things he ought to do, presumably since the man should have already known what was in Scripture, and then reminded him that there is One who is good and that He, the Holy One, had already given His people the answer in the form of His commandments. The One who is good, that is God the Father, had already stated that those who keep His commandments and statutes will enter into life by them, as we read in Leviticus 18:5 and is restated for example in Nehemiah 9:29 and Ezekiel 20:11,

> 'You shall therefore keep My statutes and My judgements, which if a man does, he shall live by them; I am the Lord.'

> 'And testified against them, that You might bring them back to Your law. Yet they acted proudly, and did not heed Your commandments, but sinned against Your judgements, 'which if a man does, he shall live by them.' And they shrugged their shoulders, stiffened their necks, and would not hear.'

> 'And I gave them My statutes and showed them My judgements, 'which if a man does, he shall live by them.'

The goodness and unique holiness of God is stated many times in Scripture; that He is good to all; that there is none other like Him; and that His judgements, commandments, statutes, and teaching are utterly good, as we read for example in Psalm 25:8, Psalm 119:66-68, Psalm 145:7-9, and 1 Samuel 2:2,

> 'Good and upright is the Lord; therefore, He teaches sinners in the way.'

354

'Teach me good judgement and knowledge, for I believe Your commandments. Before I was afflicted I went astray, but now I keep Your word. You are good and do good; teach me Your statutes.'

'They shall utter the memory of Your great goodness and shall sing of Your righteousness. The Lord is gracious and full of compassion, slow to anger and great in mercy. The Lord is good to all, and His tender mercies are over all His works.'

'No one is holy like the Lord, for there is none beside You, nor is there any rock like our God.'

Having reminded the questioner of God's goodness, Jesus then reminds him of five of the commandments of God from Exodus, and restated in Deuteronomy 5:16-20, that relate directly to people's behaviour towards each other, and He concludes with the commandment, that summarises these laws, found in Leviticus, to love our neighbour as ourselves. God has clearly shown His people what good things they are required to do, as we read for example in Exodus 20:12-16, Leviticus 19:18, and Micah 6:8,

'Honour your father and your mother, that your days may be long upon the land which the Lord your God is giving you. You shall not murder. You shall not commit adultery. You shall not steal. You shall not bear false witness against your neighbour.'

'You shall not take vengeance, nor bear any grudge against the children of your people, but you shall love your neighbour as yourself; I am the Lord.'

'He has shown you, O man, what is good; and what does the Lord require of you but to do justly, to love mercy, and to walk humbly with your God.'

Matthew 19:21

In verse 21, Jesus replied to the young man who had asked Him what he still lacked even though he had kept all the commandments since his youth, saying,

> "If thou desire perfect to be, go sell of thee the belongings and give to the poor, and thou shalt have treasure in heavens, and come follow me."

We know from the subsequent verse in Matthew's account that the young man who had asked these questions of Jesus had many possessions and went away sorrowful, presumably because he was unable to bring himself to part with them in order to be able to follow Jesus. The price of perfection for this particular person was the relinquishing of his possessions; the implication is that his earthly possessions meant more to him in his heart than to walk with God in righteousness. Jesus recognised that the young man sought to understand what was required for perfection; the answer was simple – to walk with Him, as we read in Genesis 6:9 and 17:1,

> 'Noah was a just man, perfect in his generations. Noah walked with God.'

> 'When Abram was ninety-nine years old, the Lord appeared to Abram and said to him, "I am Almighty God; walk before Me and be blameless.'

In Hebrew the word 'hem-dat' can be translated as treasure, wealth, valuables, or even desires. In Aramaic, the word that Jesus would most likely have used is 'simta'. This word means much more than the English word treasure that originally meant a storehouse in which something valuable was stored. 'Simta' expresses the idea of laying your hands upon something – something that is tangible or material. At that time, people didn't have banks or safes for keeping their valuables; they would often be buried in the walls or the ground where they were vulnerable to mould, infestation, or rust. The Scriptures warn that not only is earthly wealth perishable, but it has no true value in life and can become a stumbling block, as we read for example in Proverbs 10:2, Psalm 49:6-7, and Ezekiel 7:19,

> 'Treasures of wickedness profit nothing, but righteousness delivers from death.'

356

'Those who trust in their wealth and boast in the multitude of their riches, none of them can by any means redeem his brother, nor give to God a ransom for him.'

'They will throw their silver into the streets, and their gold will be like refuse; their silver and their gold will not be able to deliver them in the day of the wrath of the Lord; they will not satisfy their souls, nor fill their stomachs, because it became their stumbling block of iniquity.'

The rule of life for Jesus' followers is not necessarily to make themselves poor by giving away all that they possess – although that may be so for some; it is that they must be prepared to go the whole way, in whatever way they are told or shown, in fulfilling the will of God. Jesus was teaching His disciples that they must have the right priorities; to seek God's kingdom and righteousness above all else; that it is difficult to do this if one's attention is preoccupied with other desires such as material wealth. Jesus' message is clear that if His followers look for joy, comfort, and security in material things it will not last, but if they seek them in heavenly things that will be everlasting. Like Noah and Abraham, to be blameless and seek perfection, Jesus' disciples have to let go of all earthly distractions and follow Him; to walk with God and seek His face, as we read in Psalm 34:12-14 and Psalm 27:8,

'Who is the man who desires life, and loves many days, that he may see good? Keep your tongue from evil, and your lips from speaking deceit. Depart from evil and do good, seek peace, and pursue it.'

'When You said, "Seek My face," my heart said to You, "Your face, Lord, I will seek."

Matthew 19:23-24

In verses 23-24, Jesus continued His teaching to the disciples after the rich young man had left in sorrow because of his great wealth, saying,

> "Truly I tell you that a rich man hardly will enter into the kingdom of the heavens. And again I tell you, easier it is a camel through the eye of a needle to enter than a rich man into the kingdom of God."

The rich young man had wanted to know how to inherit eternal life which in Matthew's Gospel is synonymous with the kingdom of God or the kingdom of the heavens to which Jesus here referred. To illustrate how hard it is for those who have riches to enter the kingdom of God, Jesus used a scenario that would seem not merely difficult but impossible; it would be impossible for a camel to pass through the eye of a needle. Over the last two millennia there has been considerable debate over this phrase, but I will take it here simply to mean something that is impossible for humans to achieve in the light of the verses that follow. From the Gospel accounts, it seems that the disciples did not have much in the way of wealth and possessions, especially as they had left everything behind to follow Christ. But Jesus' words suggested that the terms of entry into the kingdom are even more stringent than they had perhaps imagined. The illustration of the camel was intended to make clear to Jesus' listeners that it is humanly impossible for a rich person to enter the kingdom of God. In Deuteronomy we read strong warnings about the potential pitfalls of acquiring wealth, for example in 6:10-12, 8:11 and 17:

> "So it shall be, when the Lord your God brings you into the land of which He swore to your fathers Abraham, Isaac, and Jacob, to give you large and beautiful cities which you did not build, houses full of all good things, which you did not fill, hewn-out wells which you did not dig, vineyards and olive trees which you did not plant – when you have eaten and are full – then beware, lest you forget the Lord who brought you out of the land of Egypt, from the house of bondage."

> "Beware that you do not forget the Lord your God [...] then say in your heart, 'My power and the might of my hand have gained me this wealth.'

Earlier in Matthew's Gospel (chapter 7:14), Jesus spoke about the way to enter the kingdom of God being through a narrow gate and it being a hard way, and especially difficult for the rich. The message to His disciples is that it is very difficult for people with riches not to trust in them or be ready to part with them. Those who have riches will inevitably rely on them; those with nothing will turn to God and rely on Him. King Solomon fell into this trap for which there were dreadful consequences for the kingdom, as we read in 1 Kings 10:32 and 11:11:

> 'So King Solomon surpassed all the kings of the earth in riches and wisdom'.

> "Because you have done this and have not kept My covenant and My statutes which I have commanded you. I will surely tear the kingdom away from you and give it to your servant."

The testimony of George Müller (1805-1898) comes to mind. Müller never requested financial support, or ever got into debt, but was able to build and run orphanages for hundreds of children in Bristol, England. In his memoirs he describes how many times they received unsolicited donations of food just hours before they were needed to feed the children. Müller himself owned no riches but relied totally on God for his needs. As the psalmist wrote in Psalm 84:10-12:

> 'For a day in Your courts is better than a thousand. I would rather be a doorkeeper in the house of my God than dwell in the tents of wickedness, for the Lord God is a sun and shield; the Lord will give grace and glory; no good thing will He withhold from those who walk uprightly. O Lord of hosts, blessed is the man who trusts in You!'

Matthew 19:26

In verse 26, Jesus reassured His disciples who, having heard Jesus telling them how difficult it was for the rich to enter the kingdom of God, asked who can then be saved, saying,

> "With men this impossible is, but with God all things are possible."

Jesus did not try to downplay the difficulties of following in His path, but rather, He chose to reiterate the difficulties by affirming that it is impossible for men to enter the kingdom unless they have come to the point of total trust in their heavenly Father, who alone can make it possible. Jesus' disciples are to rely on the grace of God alone. Jesus was making it clear that a person cannot save themselves; no person by good works, or wealth, can save themselves or inherit eternal life; without the grace of God it is impossible, as we read in Psalm 16:1-2,

> 'Preserve me, O God, for in You I put my trust. O my soul, you have said to the Lord, "You are my Lord, my goodness is nothing apart from You."

Nevertheless, Jesus reassured His disciples, reminding them that with God nothing is impossible; nothing is too hard for Him; He is able to do everything according to His purposes. Old Testament Scripture declares unequivocally that all things are possible with God. We can think of numerous examples of when He has demonstrated this, beginning perhaps with the birth of a son to Sarah who was barren, the deliverance of His people from Egypt, the resurrection and healing of people through the witness of the prophets. The Scripture confirms that He has the power to redeem, the power to deliver, and the power to save, as we read for example in Genesis 18:4, Job 42:2, Jeremiah 32:17 and 27, Numbers 11:23, Isaiah 50:2, and Isaiah 59:1,

> 'Is anything too hard for the Lord? At the appointed time I will return to you, according to the time of life, and Sarah shall have a son.'

> 'I know that You can do everything, and that no purpose of Yours can be withheld from You.'

> 'Ah, Lord God! Behold, You have made the heavens and the earth by Your great power and outstretched arm. There is nothing too hard for You.'

'Behold, I am the Lord, the God of all flesh. Is there anything too hard for Me?'

'And the Lord said to Moses, "Has the Lord's arm been shortened? Now you shall see whether what I say will happen to you or not."

"Is My hand shortened at all that it cannot redeem? Or have I no power to deliver?"

'Behold, the Lord's hand is not shortened, that it cannot save; nor his ear heavy, that it cannot hear.'

Richard Wurmbrand[7] recalls that when he was a child, another child, mocking the concept of God as all powerful, asked "Can He make a weight He cannot lift? If He can, He is not all-powerful. If He cannot, again He is not what He claims." Wurmbrand, when he was older and was able to read and understand the Gospel accounts, discovered that God did make a weight He couldn't lift by making Himself a babe - His incarnation as the Son of man. 'Having made a weight He could not lift, God showed His almightiness by lifting the unliftable. Jesus was resurrected in power and ascended into heaven. [,,,] He can make a weight He Himself cannot lift and is almighty notwithstanding.' Salvation is possible only through the grace of God, through trusting in His mercy, as King David wrote in Psalm 13:5-6,

'But I have trusted in Your mercy; my heart shall rejoice in Your salvation. I will sing to the Lord, because He has dealt bountifully with me.'

[7] Richard Wurmbrand (1977) Reaching Towards The Heights (July 3) Basingstoke: Marshall Morgan & Scott

Matthew 19:28-30

In verses 28-30, Jesus responded to Peter's question, asking Him, since they had left everything to follow Him, what would be their reward, saying,

> "Truly I tell you that ye the ones having followed me, in the regeneration, when sits the Son of man on the throne of glory of him, ye will sit also yourselves on twelve thrones judging the twelve tribes of Israel. And everyone who left houses or brothers or sisters or father or mother or children or fields for the sake of my name, manifold will receive and life eternal will inherit. But many will be first last and last first."

Jesus knew that from the beginning, part of God's plan was that there would be a regeneration ('palingenesia' – a new beginning) of creation, when all things would be made new. This is clearly spoken of by the prophet Isaiah, who also spoke of the joy in the new creation, as we read in Isaiah 65:17-18,

> "For behold, I create new heavens and a new earth; and the former shall not be remembered or come to mind. But be glad and rejoice forever in what I create; for behold, I create Jerusalem as a rejoicing and her people a joy."

The twelve apostles were told that they would sit on thrones as judges. The Judges, in the Old Testament were leaders or governors of the people, with distinguished positions. Contemporary equivalents might be those who, for example, have a seat in government or on a high council. Again, Jesus was echoing the voice of the prophets, as we read in Daniel 7:9-10 and Jeremiah 3:17,

> "I watched till thrones were put in place, and the Ancient of Days was seated; His garment was white as snow, and the hair of His head was like pure wool. His throne was a fiery flame, its wheels a burning fire; a fiery stream issued and came forth from before Him. A thousand thousands ministered to Him; ten thousand times ten thousand stood before Him. The court was seated, and the books were opened."

> "At that time Jerusalem shall be called The Throne of the Lord, and all nations shall be gathered to it, to the name of the Lord, to

Jerusalem. No more shall they follow the dictates of their evil hearts."

Perhaps Jesus' final comment, that the first will be last and the last first, was a warning to His disciples against pride in their own self-denial, and a supposition that their self-denial was a means of gaining a place in the Kingdom, rather than continuing in the humility of acknowledging that our salvation comes only through the grace of God. Even those who have made the greatest sacrifices are not justified through those, but justification – or salvation, is only through the sacrifice made by Jesus that was to come. Nevertheless, those who do make sacrifices for the sake of Jesus will find that what they receive, in eternity, will be far greater than what they have lost in their present life. This may also have been a reference to the fact that salvation would come also to the Gentiles from all across the globe; that those who trust in His salvation, no matter their genealogy, will enter the Kingdom of God, as we read in Isaiah 56:6-7 and 66:22,

> "Also the sons of the foreigner who join themselves to the Lord, to serve Him, and to love the name of the Lord, to be His servants – everyone who keeps from defiling the Sabbath, and holds fast to My covenant – even them I will bring to My holy mountain, and make them joyful in My house of prayer. Their burnt offerings and their sacrifices will be accepted on My altar; for My house shall be called a house of prayer for all nations."

> "For as the new heavens and the new earth which I will make shall remain before Me," says the Lord, "So shall your descendants and your name remain. And it shall come to pass that from one New Moon to another, and from one Sabbath to another, all flesh shall come to worship before Me," says the Lord.'

MATTHEW CHAPTER TWENTY

Matthew 20:1-16

In verses 1-16, Jesus told a lengthy parable as further warning to His disciples not to make assumptions about the kingdom of God based on human understanding of what is just and fair, or who would be eligible for entry into the kingdom, saying,

> "For like is the kingdom of the heavens to a man a housemaster, who went out early in the morning to hire workmen in the vineyard of him. And agreeing with the workmen for a denarius the day he sent them into the vineyard of him. And going out about the third hour he saw others standing in the marketplace idle, and to those said: Go also ye into the vineyard, and whatever may be just I will give to you. And they went. And again going out about the sixth and the ninth hour he did similarly. And about the eleventh going out he found others standing, and says to them: Why here stand ye all the day idle? They say to him: Because no one us hired. He says to them: Go also ye into the vineyard. And evening having come says the Lord of the vineyard to the steward of him: Call the workmen and pay the wage, beginning from the last ones until the first. And coming the ones about the eleventh hour received each a denarius. And coming the first supposed that more they will receive; and they received the each denarius also themselves. And receiving they grumbled against the housemaster saying: These last one hour wrought, and equal them to us thou madest the ones having borne the burden of the day and the heat. But he answering one of them said: Friend, I do not injure thee; not for a denarius thou didst agree with me? Take that which is thine and go; but I wish to the last man to give as also to thee; is it not lawful to me what I wish to do among my things? Or the eye of the evil is because I good am? Thus will be the last ones first and the first last."

The Old Testament Law was very clear about ensuring that labourers received their wages and that they should receive them in a timely way. In Jesus' parable, the workers hired at the beginning of the day struck a bargain with the owner of the vineyard; the law-abiding people of Jesus' day would no doubt have felt that they had made a bargain with God and would receive His blessings if they kept His commandments, such as those that we find for example in Leviticus 19:13 and Deuteronomy 24:15.

'You shall not cheat your neighbour, nor rob him. The wages of him who is hired shall not remain with you all night until morning.'

'Each day you shall give him his wages, and not let the sun go down on it, for he is poor and has set his heart on it; lest he cry out against you to the Lord, and it be sin to you.'

In the parable, the workers hired first clearly felt that it was unfair that those who had worked less should receive the same pay. But if we consider, for example, the Law regarding the seventh year, when all debts were released, we find that considering an early release of debt to be unfair is deemed by God to be wicked and even a sin. The account of Jonah, in which he becomes angry at the Lord's mercy, is a further example of what, with our human understanding, we perceive to be unfair, but demonstrates God's compassion, as we read in Deuteronomy 15:9 and Jonah 3:10-4:1,

'Beware lest there be a wicked thought in your heart, saying, 'The seventh year, the year of release, is at hand,' and your eye be evil against your poor brother, and you give him nothing, and he cry out to the Lord against you, and it becomes sin among you.'

'Then God saw their works, that they turned from their evil way; and God relented from the disaster that He had said He would bring upon them, and He did not do it. But it displeased Jonah exceedingly, and he became angry.'

There was a coin, called a 'pondion' that was worth one twelfth of a denarius. One can imagine that the workers hired first would have been content if those hired later had received an appropriate fraction of a denarius. Jesus' words make it clear that there is no such thing as a fraction of God's love and no human limits to His mercy, as we read in Jeremiah 18:6 and in His words to Moses in Exodus 33:19,

"O house of Israel, can I not do with you as this potter?" says the Lord. "Look, as the clay is in the potter's hand, so are you in My hand, O house of Israel."

"I will make all My goodness pass before you, and I will proclaim the name of the Lord before you. I will be gracious to whom I will be gracious, and I will have compassion on whom I will have compassion."

Matthew 20:18-19

In verses 18-19, having taken the twelve disciples aside, Jesus warned them yet again of the suffering He would endure when they arrived in Jerusalem, giving very specific details, saying,

> "Behold we are going up to Jerusalem, and the Son of man will be delivered to the chief priests and scribes, and they will condemn him to death, and they will deliver him to the Gentiles for to mock and to scourge and to crucify, and on the third day he will be raised."

Jesus, as He had done earlier in Matthew's Gospel, referred to Himself as the Son of Man. Down the millennia, there has been some controversy over this title as to its meaning. In the Old Testament, the Hebrew words 'ben adam' simply means son of a human, or a human being. In the book of Ezekiel 2:1-3, the prophet was called 'son of man' when he was called by God, perhaps emphasising his position as a created human. Jesus spoke in Aramaic and so probably used the words 'bar enash', that can mean human beings in general or a particular human. Perhaps a more accurate contemporary translation would be 'The Human', or 'The Man', or even 'The Anointed Man'. Such a title would be referring to a particular human in a position of power and authority. In Daniel 7:13-14, we can read of one 'like the Son of Man' who receives power and authority from the Ancient of Days:

> "I was watching in the night visions, and behold, One like the Son of Man, coming with the clouds of heaven! He came to the Ancient of Days, and they brought Him near before Him. Then to Him was given dominion and glory and a kingdom, that all peoples, nations and languages should serve Him."

Jesus demonstrated His Divinity in the foreknowledge of His condemnation by the chief priests and scribes, that He would suffer in Jerusalem, that He would be delivered up to the Gentiles, referring to the Romans, that He would be spat upon and mocked, scourged and then crucified. This suffering, and Jesus' willingness to suffer, was foretold in the Psalms and by the prophet Isaiah, as we read for example in Psalm 22:6-7 and 16, Isaiah 42:4, and 53:5,

> 'But I am a worm, and no man; a reproach of men, and despised by the people. All those who see Me ridicule Me.'

'For dogs have surrounded Me; the congregation of the wicked has enclosed Me. They pierced My hands and My feet.'

'He will not fail nor be discouraged, till He has established justice in the earth.'

'But He was wounded for our transgressions, He was bruised for our iniquities; the chastisement for our peace was upon Him, and by His stripes we are healed.'

But Jesus also declared with certainty His resurrection on the third day. His crucifixion was not to be the end but would lead to His rising from the dead in glory, defeating death itself. This third-day deliverance that Jesus foretold has already been discussed in chapter 12:39-40, but it is a repeating pattern in Old Testament Scripture; a pattern of deliverance of which Jesus' was the ultimate plan. For example: Abraham received back Isaac on the third day (Genesis 22:3-4); The Lord came down on Mount Sinai on the third day (Exodus 19:10-11); the healing of Hezekiah on the third day (2 Kings 20:5); during their exile in Persia the deliverance of the Jews on the third day (Esther 5:1). Third-day deliverance as resurrection is foretold in the prophets, as we read in Ezekiel 37:13, Isaiah 25:8, and Hosea 6:1-2,

> "Then you shall know that I am the Lord, when I have opened your graves, O My people, and brought you up from your graves."

> 'He will swallow up death forever, and the Lord God will wipe away tears from all faces.'

> 'Come, let us return to the Lord; for He has torn, but He will heal us; He has stricken, but He will bind us up. After two days He will revive us; on the third say He will raise us up that we may live in His sight.'

Matthew 20:21-23

In verses 21-23, we can read the conversation between Jesus and the mother of the sons of Zebedee, James and John. She asks that Jesus grant her sons the right to sit one on His right hand and one on the left in His kingdom. In Jesus' reply we can see that once again the disciples demonstrated their poor understanding of the nature of the kingdom of God:

> "What wishest thou?" [...] "Ye know not what ye ask. Can ye to drink the cup which I am about to drink? [...] "Indeed, the cup of me ye shall drink, but to sit on the right of me and on the left is not mine to give, but to whom it has been prepared by the Father of me."

The right-hand and left-hand position in Jewish society were long-established high-level positions of authority. In the Sanhedrin, the 'prince' sat in the midst of two rows of elders; on his right sat a person referred to as the 'father' of the Sanhedrin, and on his left sat the 'sage'. These two positions acted as deputies to the 'prince'. There are several references to the right-hand position in Old Testament Scripture, for example in 1 Kings 2:19, the reference to the bride of Christ in Psalm 45:9, and to Christ Himself in Psalm 110:1.

> 'Bathsheba therefore went to King Solomon, to speak to him for Adonijah. And the king rose up to meet her and bowed down to her. And sat down on his throne and had a throne set for the king's mother; so she sat at his right hand.'

> 'King's daughters are among Your honourable women; at Your right hand stands the queen in gold from Ophir.'

> 'The Lord said to my Lord, "Sit at My right hand, till I make Your enemies Your footstool.'

In Old Testament Scripture, our 'cup' is a receptacle that represents our lives. This cup can be filled with blessings, as for example in Psalm 23:5, 'My cup runs over', or Psalm 116:13, 'I will take up the cup of salvation'. But it can also represent suffering resulting from God's judgement, and it was in this context that Jesus referred to the cup that He would have to partake of. There are many references to this in Scripture, as we read for example in Psalm 75:8, Isaiah 51:17, Jeremiah 25:15, and in a prophecy against Jerusalem Ezekiel 23:31.

'For in the hand of the Lord there is a cup, and the wine is red; it is fully mixed, and He pours it out; surely its dregs shall all the wicked of the earth drain and drink down.'

'Awake, awake! Stand up, O Jerusalem, you who have drunk at the hand of the Lord the cup of His fury; you have drunk the dregs of the cup of trembling and drained it out.'

'For thus says the Lord God of Israel to me: "Take this wine cup of fury from My hand, and cause all the nations, to whom I send you, to drink it."

'You have walked in the way of your sister; therefore, I will put her cup in your hand.'

Jesus made it clear that the Father had not assigned Him the role of appointing each person to his particular place in the kingdom of heaven; that God did not intend that this information should be revealed to us by Christ. This conversation was part of Jesus' teaching about the cost of following Him. It is worth noting that the word 'minister' means one who acts upon the authority of another and is a servant, in the case of a church minister, as servant of his flock. As Christ's servants, His disciples should seek to serve others not to attain exalted positions in the kingdom, as we read for example in Proverbs 16:18-19 and Jeremiah 45:5.

'Pride goes before destruction, and haughty spirit before a fall. Better to be of a humble spirit and lowly, than to divide the spoil with the proud.'

"And do you seek great things for yourself? Do not seek them; for behold, I will bring adversity on all flesh," says the Lord. "But I will give your life to you as a prize in all places, wherever you go."

Matthew 20:25-28

In verses 25-28, Jesus continued to teach His disciples the true nature of His kingdom and the principles by which those who wish to serve God the Father are to live, saying,

> "Ye know that the rulers of the nations lord it over them and the great ones have authority over them. Not thus is it among you; but whoever wishes among you great to become, will be of you servant, and whoever wishes among you to be first, he shall be of you slave; as the Son of man came not to be served, but to serve and to give the life of him a ransom instead of many."

The Hebrew word used for leader, 'nagiyd', that would have been used in Scripture, means a person under authority who fulfils the wishes of that authority, in other words a minister or servant. During the eighteenth century, Frederick the Great of Prussia (1740-1786) is quoted as saying that the ruler of a nation should be "the first servant of the state". He has been studied as a model of 'servant leadership', a contemporary philosophy in which the goal of the leader is to serve. Instead of the people working to serve the leader, the leader exists to serve the people; the priority is to serve rather than to lead. Moses was an example of servant leadership, as we read in Exodus 32:30, and also King Asa in 2 Chronicles 15:2 and 7,

> 'Now it came to pass on the next day that Moses said to the people, "You have committed a great sin. So now I will go up to the Lord; perhaps I can make atonement for your sin."

> "Hear me, Asa, and all Judah and Benjamin. The Lord is with you while you are with Him. If you seek Him, He will be found by you; but if you forsake Him, He will forsake you." […] "But you, be strong and do not let your hands be weak, for your work shall be rewarded."

Christ appoints ministers of His Church not to rule, but to serve. The only greatness, eminence, or rank to be desired should be to submit to those they serve; to be the servant of all. The servant leaders depicted in Old Testament Scripture were seen to strengthen the weak and empower those trusted to their care, they showed compassion towards the disadvantaged and the lost. Joshua, Joseph, Nehemiah, and Esther were other examples of servant leadership. Perhaps the most common description of this type of leadership is the reference to the shepherd;

372

the shepherd who serves the flock. The prophet Ezekiel warned against the leaders of Israel who sought to be served rather than to serve, as we read for example in Ezekiel 34:2,

"Son of man, prophecy against the shepherds of Israel, prophecy and say to them, 'Thus says the Lord God to the shepherds: "Woe to the shepherds of Israel who feed themselves! Should not the shepherds feed the flocks?"

Jesus again refers here to His death, perhaps to help His disciples to see their false expectation of an earthly kingdom. He is here declaring that His life is the price of our redemption; instead of the many and repeated sacrifices required by the Law, and for the numberless multitudes of people. It is through His one sacrifice that His followers can obtain reconciliation with God. This was clearly spoken of by the prophets, as we read in Job 33:23, Psalm 49:7-8, and Isaiah 53:11-12,

'If there is a messenger for him; a mediator, one among a thousand, to show man His uprightness, then He is gracious to Him, and says, 'Deliver him from going down to the Pit; I have found a ransom.'

'None of them can by any means redeem his brother, nor give to God a ransom for him – for the redemption of their souls is costly.'

'By His knowledge My righteous Servant shall justify many, for He shall bear their iniquities. Therefore, I will divide Him a portion with the great, and He shall divide the spoil with the strong, because He poured out His soul unto death, and He was numbered with transgressors, and He bore the sin of many, and made intercession for the transgressors.'

Matthew 20:32

In verse 32, we read that as Jesus and His disciples were leaving Jericho, two blind men called out to Jesus above the noise of the crowd, asking that He, the Son of David, have mercy on them. Jesus heard them and asked,

> "What wish ye I may do unto you?"

It is stated here by Matthew that before He spoke to them, Jesus stood still. He stopped what He was doing and gave them His full attention despite the multitude of people surrounding Him and the knowledge that this journey was towards His crucifixion. He was not too busy; the needs of His individual children are just as important to Him as the needs of His people, the Church, and the whole of humanity. There are numerous examples of people crying out to the Lord in Old Testament Scripture, for example the prophet Nehemiah in chapter 1:6,

> 'Please let Your ear be attentive and Your eyes open, that You may hear the prayer of Your servant which I pray before You now, day and night, for the children of Israel Your servants, and confess the sins of the children of Israel which we have sinned against You.'

In the Gospel accounts we can see that Christ is always willing to save those who turn to Him with their whole heart. In Old Testament Scripture we find many promises that those who seek the Lord do not seek Him in vain, as we read for example in Isaiah 45:18-19, Ezekiel 36:37, Psalm 102:17, and Psalm 22:24,

> 'For thus says the Lord, who created the heavens, who is God, who formed the earth and made it, who has established it, who did not create it in vain, who formed it to be inhabited: "I am the Lord, and there is no other, I have not spoken in secret, in a dark place of the earth; I did not say to the seed of Jacob, 'Seek Me in vain'; I the Lord, speak righteousness, I declare things that are right.'

> 'Thus says the Lord God: "I will also let the house of Israel inquire of Me to do this for them: I will increase their men like a flock."

> 'He shall regard the prayer of the destitute and shall not despise their prayer.'

374

'For He has not despised nor abhorred the affliction of the afflicted; nor has He hidden His face from Him; but when He cried to Him, He heard.'

The two blind men called Jesus 'Son of David', acknowledging His authority. No doubt Jesus knew what it was they wanted, yet He asked them to tell Him. Perhaps this was as a demonstration of their faith in Him, so that they would publicly acknowledge what they believed the Messiah could do for them. The question also allowed them to demonstrate that they were not merely begging for alms, but for a cure from the Son of David. It could perhaps also be seen as symbolic of those who are blind to their own sin and cannot see their way to the kingdom of God. Jesus may also have put the question to them for the sake of the people who were witnesses to this miracle which was, in itself, a fulfilling of the prophecy in Isaiah 35:5, 'Then the eyes of the blind shall be opened, and the ears of the deaf shall be unstopped'. This question also demonstrated Jesus' power and willingness to do anything they should ask. The blind men were persistent; they did not give up when the crowd told them to be quiet. They would not be discouraged from seeking the presence of the Messiah; they were determined to act on their faith and were not afraid to bring their impossible-sounding request. Those who call on the Lord can trust in the assurances of God's promise to hear, as we read for example in Psalm 50:15, Psalm 72:12-13, Isaiah 58:9, and 55:6-7,

'Call upon Me in the day of trouble; I will deliver you, and you shall glorify Me.'

'For He will deliver the needy when he cries, the poor also, and him who has no helper. He will spare the poor and needy and will save the souls of the needy.'

'Then you shall call, and the Lord will answer; you shall cry, and He will say, 'Here I am.'

'Seek the Lord while He may be found, call upon Him while He is near. Let the wicked forsake his way, and the unrighteous man his thoughts; let him return to the Lord, and He will have mercy on him; and to our God, for He will abundantly pardon.'

MATTHEW CHAPTER TWENTY-ONE

Matthew 21:2-3

In verses 2-3, we read that Jesus gave two of His disciples instructions as they approached the Mount of Olives on their way to Jerusalem, saying,

> "Go ye into the village opposite you, and at one ye will find an ass having been tied and a colt with her; loosening bring to me. And if anyone to you says anything, ye shall say, The Lord of them need has; and immediately he will send them."

Jesus clearly knew that preparation had been made for a donkey to be available for Him. It is not clear if this had been prearranged by Jesus or was a divine provision. Either scenario was possible; there are many accounts of God's provision for His prophets' and people's approaching needs, as we read for example in 1 Kings 17:19,

> "Arise, go to Zarephath, which belongs to Sidon, and dwell there. See, I have commanded a widow there to provide for you."

In his Gospel account, Matthew himself reminds the reader that what was happening here was the literal fulfilling of the prophecy of the coming of the king in Zechariah, and the work of salvation that was to follow prophesied in Isaiah, and was even prophesied far earlier by Jacob, as we read in Genesis 49:11, Zechariah 9:9, Isaiah 40:10, Isaiah 49:6 and Isaiah 62:11,

> 'Binding his donkey to the vine, and his donkey's colt to the choice vine, he washed his garments in wine, and his clothes in the blood of grapes.'

> 'Rejoice greatly, O daughter of Zion! Shout, O daughter of Jerusalem! Behold, your King is coming to you; He is just and having salvation, lowly and riding on a donkey, a colt, the foal of a donkey.'

> 'Behold, the Lord God shall come with a strong hand, and His arm shall rule for Him; Behold, His reward is with Him, and His work before Him.'

> 'Indeed He says, 'It is too small a thing that You should be My servant to raise up the tribes of Jacob, and to restore the

378

preserved ones of Israel; I will also give You as a light to the Gentiles, that You should be My salvation to the ends of the earth.'

'Indeed the Lord has proclaimed to the end of the world: "Say to the daughter of Zion, 'Surely your salvation is coming; behold, His reward is with Him, and His work before Him.'"

It is understood that in Old Testament times for a leader to ride on a donkey, ass, or a colt, it was considered an emblem of peace. Kings and princes would exchange their war horses for donkeys in times of peace. To ride on a donkey was also a mark of rank, as can be seen in the account of the Judges of Israel, as we read for example in Judges 12:14,

'He had forty sons and thirty grandsons, who rode on seventy young donkeys. He judged Israel eight years.'

In this context, Christ could be seen as entering Jerusalem as the Judge of Israel. Solomon, when he was taken to be anointed king over Israel, rode on King David's own mule. For Jesus to ride a donkey into the sacred city of Jerusalem, would have been a sign to the Jews that this was the arrival of the King, the Messiah, and Salvation. Riding on a donkey was the well-established way a king should enter the city of Jerusalem, as we read in 1 Kings 1:38-40,

'So Zadok the priest, Nathan the prophet, Benaiah the son of Jehoiada, the Cherethites, and the Pelethites went down and had Solomon ride on King David's mule and took him to Gihon. Then Zadok the priest took a horn of oil from the tabernacle and anointed Solomon. And they blew the horn, and all the people said, "Long live King Solomon!" And all the people went up after him; and the people played the flutes and rejoiced with great joy, so that the earth seemed to split with their sound.'

Matthew 21:13

After Jesus' triumphal ride into Jerusalem, He went into the temple and drove out the traders and overturned the tables of the money changers, saying, in verse 13,

> "It has been written: The house of me a house of prayer shall be called, ye but it are making a den of robbers."

Jesus was quoting directly from Isaiah when He spoke about the temple as a house of prayer. The temple was a place where God's people could pour out their soul before the Lord who would hear them as in the example of Hannah, the mother of Samuel, who prayed for a child, in 1 Samuel 1:12. The passage in Isaiah 56:7 also prophesied the calling of the Gentiles; that His house, the Church of God would be a house of prayer for all nations.

> 'And it happened, as she continued praying before the Lord, that Eli watched her mouth. Now Hannah spoke in her heart; only her lips moved, but her voice was not heard.'

> "Even them I will bring to My holy mountain and make them joyful in My house of prayer. Their burnt offerings and their sacrifices will be accepted on My altar; for My house shall be called a house of prayer for all nations."

The moneychangers in the temple grounds exchanged the Roman currency into temple shekels because, according to Jewish law, Roman currency could not be given to God. Knowing that the people had to have the temple shekel, these men charged exorbitant prices for the conversion, making a profit for themselves. They also inflated the price of the doves that were for sale, since only doves that had been approved by the priests would be accepted. This act of Jesus, driving out the money changers, was a cleansing of the temple. This was in keeping with what was expected of the Messiah as prophesied in Malachi 3:1-3 and Hosea 9:15,

> "Behold, I send My messenger, and he will prepare the way before Me. And the Lord, whom you seek, will suddenly come to His temple. Even the Messenger of the covenant, in whom you delight. Behold, He is coming," says the Lord of hosts. "But who can endure the day of His coming? And who can stand when He appears? For He is like a refiner's fire and like launderer's soap.

He will sit as a refiner and a purifier of silver; He will purify the sons of Levi, and purge them as gold and silver, that they may offer to the Lord an offering in righteousness."

"All their wickedness is in Gilgal, for there I hated them. Because of their evil deeds I will drive them from My house; I will love them no more."

When Jesus spoke of the den of robbers, He was quoting from the prophet Jeremiah who spoke against the hypocrites of the day who were content to rely on outward signs and ceremonies in the temple. Jeremiah called them thieves or robbers in their den since they trusted that they would escape the consequences of their behaviour by their false religious practices as if God could be deceived, as we read in Jeremiah 7:11,

"Has this house, which is called by My name, become a den of thieves in your eyes? Behold, I, even I, have seen it," says the Lord.

How does this affect our contemporary attitude to buying and selling on church premises? Does that kind of activity detract from the purpose of God's house? Are there other activities that detract from God's purposes? For example, do musical events become mere performances rather than true worship? Those who follow the teaching of Christ may join with the psalmist in celebration that the Lord's house is a holy house, a house of prayer in which all peoples may dwell, as we read in Psalm 93:5 and 23:6,

'Your testimonies are very sure; holiness adorns Your house, O Lord, forever.'

'Surely goodness and mercy shall follow me all the days of my life, and I will dwell in the house of the Lord forever.'

Matthew 21:16

In verse 16, Jesus echoed the words He had spoken earlier in chapter 11:25, when He had thanked His Father for revealing His purposes not to the wise but to 'babes'. Here we read that the chief priests and scribes were indignant at the sound of children calling out 'Hosanna to the Son of David', and that they asked Jesus if He heard what was being said. His reply was unequivocal, saying,

> "Yes. Never did ye read: out of the mouth of infants and sucking ones thou didst prepare praise?"

Those who should have praised the Messiah refused to do so and the children took up the cry; the temple rang with the sound of their praise. The chief priests and scribes saw this as an opportunity to condemn Jesus because He allowed Himself to be called a King by the children. In their minds, for Jesus to accept the title 'Son of David', it was blasphemy, and they clearly wanted Jesus to put a stop to the shouts of the children in the temple. These teachers of the Law could not see what the children could see, as prophesied in Isaiah 29:10-11,

> 'For the Lord has poured out on you the spirit of deep sleep, and has closed your eyes, namely, the prophets; and he has covered your heads, namely, the seers. The whole vision has become to you like the words of a book that is sealed.'

The prophet Isaiah went on to foretell that there would be those who could read the words of the book and that the humble would rejoice in the Holy One of Israel. Christ quoted directly from King David in the Psalms whose words foretold that even infants would be the heralds of the glory of God, as we read in Isaiah 29:18-19 and Psalm 8:2,

> 'In that day the deaf shall hear the words of the book, and the eyes of the blind shall see out of obscurity and out of darkness. The humble also shall increase their joy in the Lord, and the poor among men shall rejoice in the Holy One of Israel.'

> 'Out of the mouth of babes and nursing infants You have ordained strength, because of Your enemies, that You may silence the enemy and the avenger.'

The Hebrew word 'oz', translated here as strength in the Psalm, can also mean strong, mighty, loud, and power; where it is used in Chronicles, it is associated with singing, joy, and gladness, and in 2 Samuel with dancing. David, writing that God had 'ordained strength', meant that He had ordained strong glory, or glory and praise expressed with a strong voice - expressed vehemently. The Lord's strength is made perfect in the weakness of babes and infants and is thus more glorious. God can take even the babblings of babies to prepare praise for Himself. The words of the Psalm mean that, though other tongues were silent, God needs nothing more than infants, even nursing infants, to proclaim His power. The Lord God is worthy at all times of praise, and Creation itself will praise the glory of God, as we read in Psalms 29:1-2 and 19:1,

> 'Give unto the Lord, O you mighty ones, give unto the Lord glory and strength. Give unto the Lord the glory due to His name; worship the Lord in the beauty of holiness.'

> 'The heavens declare the glory of God; and the firmament shows His handiwork.'

Jesus' words not only declared His deity by accepting praise reserved for the Messiah, but it reinforced His earlier teaching that those who are humble and receive Him like a child, will perceive God's truth more clearly than those who purport to be wise. It is perhaps worth asking ourselves if the children in our communities are given opportunity to praise God. Christ's followers, like the children, should praise God, the creator of the heavens and earth, with vehemence, as in the words of King Hezekiah's prayer in 2 Kings 19:15,

> "O Lord God of Israel, the One who dwells between the cherubim, You are God, You alone, of all the kingdoms of the earth. You have made heaven and earth."

Matthew 21:19

In verse 19, we read of Jesus' response to finding that a fig tree by the road, although it was in leaf, had no fruit on it, when, according to Matthew, He was hungry, saying,

> "Never of thee fruit may be to the age."

If a fig tree has nothing on it but leaves, as in this account, then it does not have on it the small edible fruits that appear more than a month before the figs themselves. If there were only leaves on the tree, then it was a sure sign that the tree was not going to produce any figs. Thus, when Jesus said that no one would eat fruit from the fig tree, it was a statement of fact. The fig tree that withered away was not fulfilling its purpose. It is likely, since Jesus and His disciples were on their way to Jerusalem, that this was a parable about the city of Jerusalem, representing the nation of Israel, that was not fulfilling its holy purpose. Hosea spoke of Israel as being like the first fruits of the fig tree that had turned away from its purpose, as we read in Hosea 9:10,

> 'I found Israel like grapes in the wilderness; I saw your fathers as first fruits on the fig tree in its first season. But they went to Baal Peor, and separated themselves to that shame; they became an abomination like the thing they loved.'

When the source of life, such as a supply of water, is removed, a plant will speedily wither from the root. It is likely that Matthew included this account in his Gospel because Jesus was using the unfruitful fig tree as a symbol of the unfruitful Jewish nation. Despite its outward appearance and trappings of religion, the leaders of the Jewish nation were not producing the intended fruit; it did not thrive but would wither like the fig tree as prophesied in Isaiah 5:4-6 and Jeremiah 8:13,

> 'What more could have been done to My vineyard that I have not done in it? Why then, when I expected it to bring forth good grapes, did it bring forth wild grapes? And now, please let Me tell you what I will do to My vineyard: I will take away its hedge, and it shall be burned; and break down its wall, and it shall be trampled down. I will lay it waste; it shall not be pruned or dug, but there shall come up briers and thorns. I will also command the clouds that they rain no rain on it.'

"I will surely consume them," says the Lord. "No grapes shall be on the vine, nor figs on the fig tree, and the leaf shall fade; and the things I have given them shall pass away from them."

These words of Jesus, unlike the healings and blessings that we read elsewhere, demonstrated something of the judgement of God; that God will judge mankind and punish wickedness. The withering of the fig tree could be seen as a warning; that the tree was made to wither in order to serve as a parable. The fig tree in the account appeared to be healthy because it was in leaf, but the lack of fruit was evidence that something was not right. The message in Scripture is a consistent one, that those who are rooted in God's law and statutes, those who recognise and trust in Him, those who worship Him in truth, will indeed bear fruit and flourish, as we read for example in Psalm 92:12-14 and Jeremiah 17:7-8,

'The righteous shall flourish like a palm tree, he shall grow like a cedar in Lebanon. Those who are planted in the house of the Lord shall flourish in the courts of our God. They shall bear fruit in old age; they shall be fresh and flourishing.'

'Blessed is the man who trusts in the Lord, and whose hope is in the Lord, for he shall be like a tree planted by the waters, which spreads out its roots by the river, and will not fear when heat comes; but its leaf will be green, and will not be anxious in the year of drought, nor will cease from yielding fruit.'

Matthew 21:21-22

In verses 21-22, we read of Jesus' response to the disciples who asked Him how the fig tree had withered so soon, saying,

> "Truly I say to you, if you have faith and do not doubt, not only the sign of the fig tree ye will do, but also if mountain to this ye say: Be thou taken and cast into the sea, it shall be; and all things whatever ye may ask in prayer believing ye shall receive."

The withered fig tree was perhaps intended as a lesson on effective prayer since this is what Jesus was teaching His disciples here. These words are an echo of His words recorded in chapter 17:20-21, when He talked about moving mountains. Mountains were, and still are today, used to signify great difficulties; it was a form of speech used in proverbs. Mountains represent immovable objects that we can climb over, go around, or tunnel under, but not simply remove. Taken in this context, Jesus was promising that apparently immovable moral, spiritual, and physical difficulties would be removed for those who prayed in faith, asking, and believing. Jesus used the same form of words as found in the Psalms to describe the power of faith in God as our refuge and strength, as we read for example in Psalm 46:1-2,

> 'God is our refuge and strength, a very present help in trouble, therefore we will not fear, even though the earth be removed, and though the mountains be carried into the midst of the sea.'

The healings by God, recounted in both Old Testament Scripture, and here in Matthew's Gospel, demonstrated the use of tangible objects through which He could reach people, such as water in the case of Naaman the leper in 2 Kings chapter 5. But, as noted by Trevor Dearing, 'The grace of God in all its operations had to be appropriated by faith on the part of the seeker.'[8] It is up to His people to call on Him and seek Him in that faith, as we read in Deuteronomy 4:7 and Jeremiah 29:12-13,

> 'For what great nation is there that has God so near to it, as the Lord our God is to us, for whatever reason we may call upon Him?'

---

[8] Trevor Dearing (2001) Total Healing p35 Mohr Books

'Then you will call upon Me and go and pray to Me, and I will listen to you. And you will seek Me and find Me, when you search for Me with all your heart.'

Jesus' words 'whatever you ask *in prayer*' suggest that Jesus' promise refers to those desires that arise whilst *in prayer* rather than a list of requests that we may have before we come to prayer. Fully in His presence, in prayer of adoration, our desire will be in accordance with His perfect will. To have faith in God, is to expect and have assurance of obtaining what we need from God, and Jesus adds prayer with humility to faith. Jesus demanded an undoubting confidence in an answer, provided that His disciples remained within the will of God. The promise is made to those who deny themselves to follow Christ. Faith is not about forcing oneself to believe that something will or will not happen, but it is a complete trust in, and obedience to, God within a discernment of His will, as we read in Proverbs 15:29, 11:8, Psalm 145:18-19, and 37:3-5,

'The Lord is far from the wicked, but He hears the prayer of the righteous.'

'The righteous is delivered from trouble, and it comes to the wicked instead.'

'The Lord is near to all who call upon Him, to all who call upon Him in truth. He will fulfil the desire of those who fear Him; He also will hear their cry and save them.' And 'Trust in the Lord, and do good; dwell in the land and feed on His faithfulness. Delight yourself also in the Lord and He shall give you the desires of your heart. Commit your way to the Lord, trust also in Him, and He shall bring it to pass.'

Matthew 21:24-25

In verses 24-25, Jesus responded to the chief priests and elders of the people who questioned His authority, saying,

> "Will question you I also word one, which if ye tell me, I also you will tell by what authority these things I do: The baptism of John whence was it? From heaven or from men?"

By this time, Jesus had already performed many miracles that should have been sufficient evidence of His divine authority. The question was doubtless intended to trap Jesus into saying something for which they could bring a charge against Him. Rather than answering directly, He asked them instead about the authority of John the Baptist. Jesus asked if they acknowledged that John was a prophet with authority from heaven, and by implication that John's baptism of repentance was from God? If John was the fulfilment of the prophecies, then there would be no doubt that he was a messenger from Jehovah, a messenger of the covenant, that is the Christ, and that he spoke, as did Elijah, in the spirit of God and with divine authority, against unrighteousness and evil, as we read in Isaiah 40:3, Malachi 3:1 and 4:5,

> 'The voice of one crying in the wilderness: "Prepare the way of the Lord; make straight in the desert a highway for our God."

> "Behold, I send My messenger and he will prepare the way before Me. And the Lord, whom you seek, will suddenly come to His temple, even the Messenger of the covenant, in whom you delight. Behold, He is coming," says the Lord of hosts.'

> "Behold, I will send you Elijah the prophet before the coming of the great and dreadful day of the Lord."

The chief priests and elders had shown themselves unworthy of divine authority by rejecting God's holy prophet and they subsequently pretended ignorance. John himself proclaimed that he had been sent to herald the arrival of the Messiah. John had even pointed directly to Jesus at His baptism in the Jordan, declaring Him to be the only Son of God, thus, Jesus' authority had already been attested to by John. Although their first king, Saul, had been anointed by God, because of his unrighteousness, his authority was taken from him, and just as the chief priests of Jesus' day had rejected John, so their predecessors had also rejected the prophets who spoke with the authority of Jehovah, as we read in 1 Samuel 15:22-23 and Jeremiah 7:25-26,

> "Has the Lord as great delight in burnt offerings and sacrifices, as in obeying the voice of the Lord? Behold, to obey is better than sacrifice, and to heed than the fat of rams. For rebellion is as the sin of witchcraft, and stubbornness is as iniquity and idolatry. Because you have rejected the word of the Lord, He also has rejected you from being king."

> "Since the day that your fathers came out of the land of Egypt until this day, I have even sent to you all My servants the prophets, daily rising up early and sending them. Yet they did not obey Me or incline their ear but stiffened their neck. They did worse than their fathers."

Had they given the true answer to Jesus' question they would have had the true answer to their own. In effect, Jesus did answer them, since if John came as God's messenger to announce the arrival of the Messiah, then it followed that Jesus was Himself the Messiah. Those who had rejected John as a true prophet had been trapped by their own question; if they acknowledged John, they would have to acknowledge Jesus' authority. Their answer was not the truth, but what they believed was safe for them to say because they feared the crowd. John's baptism of repentance was from heaven, therefore Jesus' authority also came from heaven, the Lord's throne, as we read in Psalm 11:4, Psalm 103:19, and Isaiah 66:1,

> 'The Lord is in His holy temple, the Lord's throne is in heaven; His eyes behold, His eyelids test the sons of men.'

> 'The Lord has established His throne in heaven, and His kingdom rules over all.'

> "Heaven is My throne, and earth is My footstool. Where is the house that you will build Me? And where is the place of My rest?"

Matthew 21:27-31

In verses 27-31, we read of Jesus' response to the chief priests and elders, who had challenged His authority and claimed not to know whence John the Baptist had his authority, saying,

> "Neither I tell you by what authority these things I do. But what to you seems it? A man had children two; approaching to the first he said: Child, go today work in the vineyard. But he answering said: I go, Lord, and went not. And approaching to the second he said similarly. And answering said: I will not, later repenting he went. Which of the two did the will of the father?"

There would have been little point in Jesus proclaiming the source of His authority at this time since the chief priests had already made up their mind to refute His divine authority. Instead, Jesus tells a parable in which the owner of a vineyard has two children who are given a command by their father. Israel is represented as a vineyard in many places in Old Testament Scripture and as God's child, as we read for example in Jeremiah 2:21 and Hosea 11:1,

> "Yet I planted you a noble vine, a seed of highest quality. How then have you turned before Me into the degenerate plant of an alien vine?'

> "When Israel was a child, I loved him, and out of Egypt I called My son."

There are textual variations in the ancient Greek manuscripts. The main translations place in first position the son who initially refused to go and then went – so the first son was the one who did the father's will. In other translations the order is reversed and so the latter son is identified as the one who did the father's will. The latter tradition suggests that the Christian church is associated with the second, obedient son who repented of his initial response, and the first disobedient son has been associated with the Jewish community that repeatedly failed to listen and obey God's commands, refusing to repent, as we read for example in Jeremiah 8:4-6 and 11:7-8,

> "Will they fall and not rise? Will one turn away and not return? Why has this people slidden back, Jerusalem , in a perpetual backsliding? They hold fast to deceit, they refuse to return. I listened and heard, but they do not speak aright. No man repented

of his wickedness, saying, 'What have I done?' Everyone turned to his own course, as the horse rushes into the battle.'

'For I earnestly exhorted your fathers in the day I brought them up out of the land of Egypt, until this day, rising early and exhorting, saying, "Obey My voice." Yet they did not obey or incline their ear, but everyone followed the dictates of his evil heart.'

One son was disobedient and insolent but afterwards changed his ways; the other son was a hypocrite who courteously promised obedience but did nothing. Both were imperfect; both were unsatisfactory; the one who obeyed in the end was better, but neither was perfect. The people had repeatedly failed to match their actions to their words as we read in Ezekiel 33:31-32 and Psalm 78:36-37,

"So they come to you as people do, they sit before you as My people, and they hear your words but they do not do them; for with their mouth they show much love, but their hearts pursue their own gain. Indeed you are to them as a very lovely song of one who has a pleasant voice and can play well on an instrument; for they hear your words but they do not do them."

'They flattered Him with their mouth, and they lied to Him with their tongue; for their heart was not steadfast with Him, nor were they faithful in His covenant.'

The two sons were neither entirely disobedient nor entirely obedient. True obedience requires both the right belief or speech and the right action. Right belief and attitude must produce right speech and action. Both sons demonstrated a measure of obedience and disobedience. The righteous response is gracious, courteous obedience, and with this comes a promised reward as we read in Proverbs 6:20-22,

'My son, keep your father's command, and do not forsake the law of your mother. Bind them continually upon your heart; tie them around your neck. When you roam, they will lead you; when you sleep, they will keep you; and when you awake, they will speak with you.'

Matthew 21:31-32

In verses 31-32, Jesus continued His teaching about obedience to the will of our Father in heaven, about believing what has been taught through the law and the prophets, and of repentance, saying,

> "Truly I tell you, the tax collectors and the harlots are going before you into the kingdom of God. For came John to you in a way of righteousness, and ye believed not him; but the tax collectors and the harlots believed him; but ye seeing, not repented later so as to believe him."

This would have been a hard saying for those who heard it and who must have regarded it as an insult, and there are doubtless present-day counterparts for whom this would be true. The Jews, as God's chosen people, were supposed to be those who walked in the way of righteousness. Both Isaiah, prophesying of John the Baptist, and Jeremiah spoke about a way of righteousness, a highway, the way of the Lord, where the unclean could not pass, as we read in Isaiah 35:8 and 40:3, and Jeremiah 6:16 and 18:15,

> 'A highway shall be there, and a road, and it shall be called the Highway of Holiness. The unclean shall not pass over it, but it shall be for others. Whoever walks the road, although a fool, shall not go astray.'

> 'The voice of one crying in the wilderness: "Prepare the way of the Lord; make straight in the desert a highway for our God."

> 'Thus says the Lord: "Stand in the ways and see, and ask for the old paths, where the good way is, and walk in it; then you will find rest for your souls. But they said, "We will not walk in it."

> "Because My people have forgotten Me, they have burned incense to worthless idols, and they have caused themselves to stumble in their ways, from the ancient paths, to walk in pathways and not on a highway."

Jesus reminded His listeners that tax collectors and harlots had gone out into the wilderness to John for the baptism of repentance. He emphasised their belief in John's call to repentance, teaching that their entry into the kingdom of God was not due to any preference towards them, but was the result of their response, their hearing, believing, and repentance, as

392

evidenced by their baptism. Faith in God requires more than a verbal assent to religious doctrine; it requires that the hearer of His word repents of their sins, and instead of devoting their lives to themselves, that they devote their lives wholly to God, as even the outcast tax collectors and harlots had done. The refusal to repent or heed the voice of God is a recurring theme throughout the Old Testament Scripture, as we read for example in Psalm 81:11-12, Zechariah 7:11-12, and Jeremiah 5:3,

> "But My people would not heed My voice, and Israel would have none of Me. So I gave them over to their own stubborn heart, to walk in their own counsels."

> "But they refused to heed, shrugged their shoulders, and stopped their ears so that they could not hear. Yes, they made their hearts like flint, refusing to hear the law and the words which the Lord of hosts had sent by His Spirit through the former prophets."

> 'But they have refused to receive correction. They have made their faces harder than rock; they have refused to return.'

The chief priests and elders of the people fell into the trap of paying lip service to the way of righteousness; they refused to repent from the heart as had the sinners who sought John's baptism of repentance. The highway to the kingdom of God is attained through repentance from the heart; it is not through righteous deeds, but through the Father's mercy, as we read in Jeremiah 31:21, Joel 2:12-13, and Daniel 9:18-19,

> "Set up signposts, make landmarks; set your heart toward the highway, the way in which you went. Turn back, O virgin of Israel."

> "Now, therefore," says the Lord, "Turn to Me with all your heart, with fasting, with weeping, and with mourning. So rend your heart, and not your garments; return to the Lord your God."

> "We do not present our supplications before You because of our righteous deeds, but because of Your great mercies. O Lord, hear! O Lord, forgive!"

Matthew 21:33-40

In verses 33-40, Jesus used a parable to continue His teaching about obedience to the will of God the Father and also to foretell His own treatment at the hands of the chief priests, saying,

> "Another parable hear ye. A man there was a housemaster who planted a vineyard, and a hedge it put round and dug in it a winepress and built a tower, and let it to husbandmen, and departed. And when drew near the time of the fruits, he sent the slaves of him to the husbandmen to receive the fruits of it. And taking the husbandmen the slaves of him this one they flogged, that one they killed, another they stoned. Again he sent other slaves, more than the first ones, and they did to them similarly. But later he sent to them the son of him saying: They will reverence the son of me. But the husbandmen seeing the son said among themselves: This is the heir; come, let us kill him and let us possess the inheritance of him; and taking him they cast outside the vineyard and killed. When therefore comes the lord of the vineyard, what will he do husbandmen to those?"

In these words, Jesus used the Old Testament symbolism of a vine to represent Israel, God's people, as it is used, for example, by the prophet Isaiah and in the Psalms. The vineyard is expected to be fruitful, and the fruit collected and given to the owner of the vineyard. In Isaiah we can read almost the identical words to those found in the parable, and Isaiah goes on to speak of the wild grapes whose fruit instead of righteousness are injustice and oppression, as we read in Psalm 80:8, Isaiah 5:1-2 and 7,

> 'You have brought a vine out of Egypt; You have cast out the nations and planted it.'

> 'Now let me sing to my Well-beloved a song of my Beloved regarding His vineyard: My Well-beloved has a vineyard on a very fruitful hill. He dug it up and cleared out its stones and planted it with the choicest vine. He built a tower in its midst, and also made a winepress in it; so He expected it to bring forth good grapes, but it brought forth wild grapes.'

> 'For the vineyard of the Lord of hosts is the house of Israel, and the men of Judah are His pleasant plant. He looked for justice, but behold oppression; for righteousness, but behold, a cry for help.'

There seem to be two clear messages to this parable. The first is to reproach the chief priests and elders for their treatment of messengers sent from God - from the Old Testament prophets to John the Baptist, and to foretell His own coming treatment at their hands, as the Son of the Lord of hosts. By sending a multitude of prophets, God evidently had to contend with the obstinate disobedience of the priests. Despite the cruelty of the priests, God continued to send prophets to speak against their malice, as we read for example in 1 Chronicles 36:15 and Jeremiah 26:8,

> 'And the Lord God of their fathers sent warning to them by His messengers, rising up early and sending them, because He had compassion on His people and on His dwelling place.'

> 'Now it happened, when Jeremiah had made an end of speaking all that the Lord had commanded him to speak to all the people, that the priests, and the prophets and all the people seized him, saying, "You will surely die!"'

By killing the son, the keepers of the vineyard hoped to take possession of material wealth and privileges, leadership, power, prestige, and economic wealth. The religious leaders of the day, and since, were reluctant to relinquish their position, not even for the sake of the vineyard owner's son. By rejecting Jesus, they were bringing punishment on themselves. It is interesting to note that in Jesus' parable, and in the passage in Isaiah, there is mention of a tower that God, when He established His vineyard, set up in the midst to protect His vine; a strong tower, as we read in Psalm 61:3-4.

> 'For You have been a shelter for me, a strong tower from my enemy. I will abide in Your tabernacle forever; I will trust in the shelter of Your wings.'

Matthew 21:42-44

In verses 42-44, Jesus followed up His parable about the vinedressers who rebelled against the vineyard owner and rejected and killed his son, warning the people that the builders had rejected the foundation of God's building, quoting from the Psalms and the prophets, saying,

> "Did ye never read in the scriptures: A stone which rejected the building ones, this became head of the corner; from the Lord became this, and it is marvellous in the eyes of us? Therefore, I tell you, will be taken from you the kingdom of God and will be given to a nation producing the fruits of it. [And the one falling on stone this will be broken in pieces; but on whomever it falls, it will crush to powder him]."

The psalm foretold that Jesus would not be received with favour and applause, but that He would be rejected. It was also the same psalm from which the people had quoted when Jesus had ridden into Jerusalem on a donkey. The psalm also emphasises that God's plan cannot be thwarted by human endeavour, saying: 'This was the Lord's doing' – meaning that the Messiah would be placed on His throne by the power of God Himself, as foreshadowed by King David, who though rejected by those in power at that time, was raised up by God, as we read in Psalm 118:22-23 and Isaiah 28:16,

> 'The stone which the builders rejected has become the chief cornerstone. This was the Lord's doing; it is marvellous in our eyes.'

> 'Therefore, thus says the Lord God: "Behold, I lay in Zion a stone for a foundation, a tried stone, a precious cornerstone, a sure foundation; whoever believes will not act hastily.'

Jesus is the stone over which the Jews stumbled and were broken, and He is the stone that will smash all earthly kingdoms in the process of establishing God's kingdom. The cornerstone is the stone that supports the whole weight of the building, similarly, the salvation of the Church rests on Jesus. The stone of stumbling was clearly foretold by the prophets as we read in Isaiah 8:13-15, 28:13 and Daniel 2:44-45

> 'The Lord of hosts, Him you shall hallow; let Him be your fear and let Him be your dread. He will be as a sanctuary, but a stone of stumbling and a rock of offence to both the houses of Israel, as a

trap and a snare to the inhabitants of Jerusalem. And many among them shall stumble; they shall fall and be broken, be snared and taken.'

'But the word of the Lord was to them, "Precept upon precept, precept upon precept, line upon line, line upon line, here a little, there a little," that they might go and fall backward, and be broken and snared and caught.' And 'And in the days of these kings the God of heaven will set up a kingdom which shall never be destroyed; and the kingdom shall not be left to other people; it shall break in pieces and consume all these kingdoms, and it shall stand forever. Inasmuch as you saw that the stone was cut out of the mountain without hands, and that it broke in pieces the iron, the bronze, the clay, the silver, and the gold – the great God has made known what will come to pass after this.'

Jesus' words did not imply a stone hurling itself, or the people inadvertently tripping over a stone. To fall upon the enemy is a military term meaning to rush forward with the intent to destroy. The Jewish priests and elders dashed themselves against the stone – against Jesus. Having raised Jesus up, God placed Him high up in the corner of the building, the Church; by pulling the stone from its exalted position, it would fall and crush the person trying to pull it down. The Church cannot afford to be complacent, if God was prepared to take His kingdom from His chosen people when they strayed, they need to remain vigilant, producing the expected fruit for the kingdom and not returning to former ways – those who profane the kingdom of God will not enter, as we read in Isaiah 60:12 and 26:2,

'For the nation and kingdom which will not serve you shall perish, and those nations shall be utterly ruined.'

'Open the gates, that the righteous nation which keeps the truth may enter in.'

The authority of God will prevail so that Christ will be the precious stone that supports the Church of God and His kingdom, as the Psalmist continued in Psalm 118 in verse 24,

'This is the day the Lord has made; we will rejoice and be glad in it.'

MATTHEW CHAPTER TWENTY-TWO

Matthew 22:2-7

In verses 2-7, Jesus used a further parable to warn His listeners not to reject the call, the invitation, to the kingdom of God, saying,

> "Is likened the kingdom of the heavens to a man a king, who made a wedding feast for the son of him. And he sent the slaves of him to call the ones having been invited to the feast, and they wished not to come. Again, he sent other slaves saying: Tell the ones having been invited: Behold, the supper of me I have prepared, the oxen of me and the fatted beasts having been killed, and all things are ready; come to the feast. But they not caring went off, one to his own field, another to the trading of him; and the rest seizing the slaves of him insulted and killed. So, the king became angry, and sending the armies of him destroyed murderers those and the city of them burned."

There are many depictions of wedding feasts and banquets in Old Testament Scripture, that represent God's relationship with His people and His kingdom. Jesus' listeners would have been familiar with these passages and understood the references, as we read for example in Psalm 45:13-15, Psalm 81: 10, Song of Solomon 2:4, and Song of Solomon 5:1,

> 'The royal daughter is all glorious within the palace; her clothing is woven with gold. She shall be brought to the King in robes of many colours; the virgins, her companions who follow her, shall be brought to You. With gladness and rejoicing they shall be brought; they shall enter the King's palace.'

> 'I am the Lord your God, who brought you out of the land of Egypt; open your mouth wide, and I will fill it.'
> 'He brought me to the banqueting house, and his banner over me was love.'

> 'I have come to my garden, my sister, my spouse; I have gathered my myrrh with my spice; I have eaten my honeycomb with my honey; I have drunk my wine with my milk. Eat, O friends! Drink, yes, drink deeply, O beloved ones.'

In the parable, Jesus said that the King's messengers were to 'call the ones having been invited.' In other words, the guests had already been invited and should have been ready to come when the king's messengers arrived; preparations for this event should already have been made in anticipation, as we read in Zephaniah 1:7,

> 'Be silent in the presence of the Lord God; for the day of the Lord is at hand, for the Lord has prepared a sacrifice; He has invited His guests.'

The Jews professed to desire the kingdom of God, but when invited, they rejected God's grace with disdain. God chose to bestow an honour on the Jewish people, but they despised that which was conferred upon them. Despite having boasted about receiving the invitation to attend the banquet of the Messiah, when the call came, they didn't want to attend. Not only did they refuse to attend, but they treated the call with contempt and the messengers were abused or even slain. By choosing rather to attend to their farms or business, those invited demonstrated a devotion to worldly material things, rather than a devotion to God and the things of His heavenly kingdom. The rejection of God's call and the consequences are foretold, for example, in Psalm 81:11-12, Psalm 106:24-25, Proverbs 1:24-27, and Zechariah 14:1-2,

> 'But My people would not heed My voice, and Israel would have none of Me. So, I gave them over to their own stubborn heart, to walk in their own counsels.'

> 'Then they despised the pleasant land; they did not believe His word, but complained in their tents, and did not heed the voice of the Lord.'

> 'Because I have called and you refused, I have stretched out my hand and no one regarded, because you disdained all my counsel, and would have none of my rebuke, I also will laugh at your calamity; I will mock when your terror comes, when your terror comes like a storm, and your destruction comes like a whirlwind, when distress and anguish come upon you.'

> 'Behold, the day of the Lord is coming, and your spoil will be divided in your midst. For I will gather all the nations to battle against Jerusalem.'

Jesus calls His people to the banquet, and His people, who have been invited, must be ready to accept the invitation as in Proverbs 9:5-6,

> 'Come, eat of my bread and drink of the wine I have mixed. Forsake foolishness and live and go in the way of understanding.'

Matthew 22:8-14

In verses 8-14, Jesus told the second part of the parable about the wedding feast in which others are invited to replace those who had rejected the invitation, saying,

> "Then he says to the slaves of him: Indeed, the feast ready is, but the ones having been invited were not worthy; go ye therefore onto the partings of the ways, and as many as ye find call to the feast. And going forth slaves those into the ways, assembled all whom they found, both bad and good; and was filled the wedding chamber with reclining ones. But entering the king to behold the reclining ones, he saw there a man not having been dressed in a dress of wedding; and he says to him: Comrade, how enterest thou here not having a dress of wedding? And he was silenced. Then the king said to the servants: Binding of him feet and hands and throw out him into the darkness outer; there will be the wailing and the gnashing of teeth. For many are called, but few are chosen."

In most modern translations, the word 'highways' is used; the Greek literally says, 'parting of the ways', meaning a confluence of roads and pathways, a crossroad, where many people would be found, both 'bad and good', including the outcasts of society. The religious people who regularly attended the synagogue were not interested in what Jesus had to say and despised His message, whereas the outcasts of society eagerly accepted His message with all its blessings and forgiveness, as we read for example in Psalm 107:40-42,

> 'He pours contempt on princes and causes them to wander in the wilderness where there is no way; yet He sets the poor on high, far from affliction, and makes their families like a flock. The righteous see it and rejoice, and all iniquity stops its mouth.'

Those who are 'called' are those who were invited; those who are 'chosen' are those who accept the invitation. The message of the Gospel is preached to all and sundry, but not everyone who hears it responds and so it was in Jesus' day. The Jewish people heard God's message, spoken through the Law and the prophets, regularly in the synagogues and the Temple, but not all then responded to its message. The implication of Jesus' words in the parable are that the person who was not suitably dressed could have been properly attired if he had chosen to do so if he had requested them from the host of the feast. According to some

402

translations the person was 'speechless'; in the Greek, it simply says that he was silenced or gagged. According to Scripture, sin silences and takes the wicked captive, as we read in Job 5:16 and 1 Samuel 2:9, Psalm 112:10, Wisdom 17:2, and Psalm 37:12,

> 'So, the poor have hope, and injustice shuts her mouth.'

> 'He will guard the feet of His saints, but the wicked shall be silent in darkness.'

> 'The wicked will see it and be grieved; he will gnash his teeth and melt away; the desire of the wicked shall perish.'

> 'For when lawless people supposed that they held the holy nation in their power, they themselves lay as captives of darkness and prisoners of long night, shut in under their roofs, exiles from eternal providence.'

> 'The wicked plots against the just, and gnashes at him with his teeth.'

The appropriate clothes, the robes for the wedding, that are given to those who ask, are worn by those who do the will of the heavenly Father. The garment is holiness. Jesus made it clear through this parable that not all those who profess to have received the message will be found worthy, but only those who have put on the garments that befit the heavenly kingdom. The clothes of sin are described as filthy garments in Zechariah and as foreign garments in Zephaniah, but the robes of righteousness are rich and beautiful, as we read in Zephaniah 1:8, Isaiah 52:1, and Zechariah 3:3-4,

> 'And it shall be, in the day of the Lord's sacrifice, that I will punish the princes and the king's children, and all such as are clothed with foreign apparel.'

> 'Awake, awake! Put on your strength, O Zion; put on your beautiful garments, O Jerusalem, the holy city!'

> 'Now Joshua was clothed with filthy garments and was standing before the Angel. Then He answered and spoke to those who stood before Him, saying, "Take away the filthy garments from him." And to him He said, "See, I have removed your iniquity from you, and I will clothe you with rich robes."

Matthew 22:18-21

In verses 18-21, Jesus answers the disciples of the Pharisees and the Herodians who have asked Him if it was lawful for them to pay taxes to Caesar, saying,

> "Why me tempt ye, hypocrites? Show me the money of the tribute." And they brought to him a denarius. And he says to them: "Of whom image this and superscription?" They say: Of Caesar. Then he says to them: "Render then the things of Caesar to Caesar and the things of God to God."

Jesus' opening words here demonstrate His knowledge of the inner thoughts of His questioners; this was doubtless another sign of His divine knowledge or discernment. He spoke also of their hypocrisy; this was evidenced by their corrupt service to God, which was spoken of in the prophets, as we read for example in Malachi 1:7-8,

> "You offer defiled food on My altar, but say, 'In what way have we defiled You?' By saying, 'The table of the Lord is contemptible.' And when you offer the blind as a sacrifice, is it not evil? And when you offer the lame and sick, is it not evil? Offer it then to your governor! Would he be pleased with you? Would he accept you favourably?"

Their question asked if it was lawful to pay taxes to Caesar, in other words, was it in accordance with the law of God. Given Jesus' words, we can presume that He knew that they wanted to entrap Him so that they could hand Him over to the Roman governor or prefect for defying Caesar. The Jewish kingdom had earlier been divided into three provinces by the Romans, each governed by one of three sons of Herod the Great, and taxes were paid to these sons of Herod. However, Archelaus Herod, in southern Judea, which included Jerusalem, had been so oppressive to the population that the Romans, fearing a revolt, had removed him and installed a Roman prefect to govern the province. Thus, taxes would be paid instead to the Roman emperor. At that time, many considered it to be treason against God for the people to recognise a Gentile ruler in Jerusalem by paying him tribute. Was it right, they asked, for God's people, living on God's land, to give a proportion of its produce to a Gentile ruler? The question did not arise in Galilee, only in Judea which was governed by the Roman prefect. The Law was clear about not serving graven images, as was summed up by Daniel speaking to King

Nebuchadnezzar in chapter 3:18, and the distribution of tithe giving was also detailed in Deuteronomy 26:12-13, where we read,

> "Let it be known to you, O king, that we do not serve your gods, nor will we worship the gold image which you have set up." And "When you have finished laying aside all the tithe of your increase in the third year – the year of tithing – and have given it to the Levite, the stranger, the fatherless, and the widow, so that they may eat within your gates and be filled, then you shall say before the Lord your God: 'I have removed the holy tithe from my house, and also have given them to the Levite, the stranger, the fatherless, and the widow, according to all Your commandments which You have commanded me; I have not transgressed Your commandments, nor have I forgotten them."

The passage in Deuteronomy makes clear that offerings to God were not just for the support of the temple and the priests, but was also to provide for strangers, refugees, asylum-seekers, orphans, and widows; any who were in need. The denarius was a Roman coin and the Roman taxes had to be paid in Roman currency. The Roman coin was not the sacred shekel that was to be paid for the maintenance of the temple. Clearly the denarius belonged to Caesar, so Jesus was saying that he could have it back; God is not interested in coins. Jesus was making a clear distinction between the heavenly and the earthly kingdoms. The tribute sought by the Kingdom of God is something worth far in excess of mere coins, and its offering comes with a sure promise, as we read in Psalm 40:6 and Malachi 3:10,

> 'Sacrifices and offering You did not desire; my ears You have opened. Burnt offering and sin offering You did not require.'

> "Bring all the tithes into the storehouse, that there may be food in My house, and try Me now in this," says the Lord of hosts, "if I will not open for you the windows of heaven and pour out for you such blessing that there will not be room enough to receive it."

Matthew 22:29-32

In verses 29-32, Jesus replied to the question of the Sadducees, who believed neither in the resurrection nor in angels, saying,

> "Ye err not knowing the scriptures nor the power of God. For in the resurrection neither they marry nor are given in marriage, but as angels in heaven are. But concerning the resurrection of the dead did ye not read the thing said to you by God saying: I am the God of Abraham and the God of Isaac and the God of Jacob? He is not the God of dead men but of living ones."

The lack of knowledge of the Scriptures, through which God makes known His will, led to the false understanding and errors made by the Sadducees. The implication of Jesus' words is that by knowing the Scriptures – and by this He was referring to Old Testament Scripture, God's people are less likely to fall into error. Jesus was also teaching that the Scriptures demonstrate the power of God. The concept of resurrection may be beyond human understanding but not beyond the power of God, as we read for example in Jeremiah 32:17,

> 'Ah, Lord God! Behold, You have made the heavens and the earth by Your great power and outstretched arm. There is nothing too hard for You.'

Jesus referred to the Old Testament Scripture as having been spoken by God; it is the word of God and to be received by His people as such. He then quoted from the account, found in the book of Exodus, of the meeting between Moses and God through the burning bush. When God spoke to Moses, He named Himself 'I AM', saying, 'I AM the God of your father', not 'I was', meaning that Abraham, Isaac, and Jacob must still exist, as we read in Exodus 3:5-6 and in verse 15, and this is repeated by Elijah in 1 Kings18:36,

> 'Then He said, "Do not draw near this place. Take your sandals off your feet, for the place where you stand is holy ground." Moreover, He said, "I am the God of your father – the God of Abraham, the God of Isaac, and the God of Jacob."

> 'Moreover God said to Moses, "Thus you shall say to the children of Israel: 'The Lord God of your fathers, the God of Abraham, the God of Isaac, and the God of Jacob, has sent me to you. This is My name forever, and this is My memorial to all generations.'

'Elijah the prophet came near and said, "Lord God of Abraham, Isaac and Israel, let it be known this day that You are God in Israel, and I am Your servant, and that I have done all these things at Your word."

Jesus' reply was unequivocal in stating that both resurrection and angels are true in the kingdom of heaven. His answer made clear that the law only applied to life in this present world, not to the life to come. In that future life, Scripture teaches that people will be like the angels, having their existence in God without the constraints of a perishable human body; having relationships that transcend the physical world and even time, as we read for example in Psalm 16:9-11, 103:20, 34:7, Daniel 6:22, and Job 19:25-27,

'Therefore, my heart is glad, and my glory rejoices; my flesh also will rest in hope. For You will not leave my soul in Sheol, nor will You allow Your Holy One to see corruption. You will show me the path of life; in Your presence is fullness of joy; at Your right hand are pleasures forevermore.'

'Bless the Lord, you His angels, who excel in strength, who do His word, heeding the voice of His word.'

'The angel of the Lord encamps all around those who fear Him and delivers them.'

"My God sent His angel and shut the lions' mouths, so that they have not hurt me, because I was found innocent before Him; and also, O king, I have done no wrong before you."

'For I know that my Redeemer lives, and He shall stand at last on the earth; and after my skin is destroyed, this I know, that in my flesh I shall see God, whom I shall see for myself, and my eyes shall behold, and not another.'

Matthew 22:37-40

In verses 37-40, Jesus replied to a lawyer who, testing Him, asked which is the greatest commandment, saying,

"Thou shalt love the Lord the God of thee with all the heart of thee and with all the soul of thee and with all the understanding of thee. This is the great and first commandment. The second is like to it: Thou shalt love the neighbour of thee as thyself. On these two commandments all the law hangs and the prophets."

Jesus' words were not a summary of all the commandments, but these two commandments are the foundation of all the other commandments and the Gospel. To love with the whole heart means that nothing else can be loved in comparison. To love with all the soul means to devote all one's life, even, if necessary, unto death. With all one's strength means all one's ability. To love with all the mind means to devote all one's intellect and thought. Those who love God are those who obey Him. Jesus quoted from the law in Deuteronomy, as we read in chapter 6:5, 10:12, and 30:6.

> "You shall love the Lord your God with all your heart, with all your soul, and with all your strength."

> "And now, Israel, what does the Lord your God require of you, but to fear the Lord your God, to walk in all His ways and to love Him, to serve the Lord your God with all your heart and with all your soul."

> "And the Lord your God will circumcise your heart and the heart of your descendants, to love the Lord your God with all your heart and with all your soul, that you may live."

Richard Wurmbrandt wrote, "Everyone walks to the music he hears. Let him hear from you a more beautiful melody. It might change his pace."[9]

---

[9] Richard Wurmbrand (1977) Reaching Towards The Heights (January 3) Basingstoke: Marshall Morgan & Scott

The second command that Jesus quoted is entirely practical. The love spoken of in the law that He was referring to was not sentimental emotion or feelings; it is about a practical attitude towards others that means giving to others what they need regardless of our own feelings, treating others as you would a best friend. It is not a 'thou shall not' command, but a command to do something. To understand what one must do for others, we only must consider what we do for ourselves, so that others have the same status as ourselves. This is made clear in the Scriptures, as we read in Leviticus 19:18 and 34, Deuteronomy 10:18-19, and Proverbs 25:21.

> 'You shall not take vengeance, nor bear any grudge against the children of your people, but you shall love your neighbour as yourself.'

> 'The stranger who dwells among you shall be to you as one born among you, and you shall love him as yourself; for you were strangers in the land of Egypt.'

> 'He administers justice for the fatherless and the widow, and loves the stranger, giving him food and clothing. Therefore, love the stranger, for you were strangers in the land of Egypt.'

> 'If your enemy is hungry, give him bread to eat; and if he is thirsty, give him water to drink.'

The law, and God's word spoken by the prophets, hang like a peg on these two commandments – take away the peg and all falls. Jesus Himself is the peg, the embodiment of these two commands and His people are to love the Lord with all that is in them, as we read in Isaiah 22:23 and Psalm 103:1,

> 'I will fasten him as a peg in a secure place, and he will become a glorious throne to his father's house.'

> 'Bless the Lord, O my soul; and all that is within me, bless His holy name!'

Matthew 22:42-45

In verses 42-45, Matthew recounts that Jesus addressed the Pharisees, questioning their understanding of the Messiah, saying,

> "What to you seems it concerning the Christ? Of whom son is he?" They say to him: Of David. He says to them: "How then David in spirit calls him Lord saying: Said the Lord to the Lord of me: Sit on the right of me until I put the enemies of the underneath the feet of thee? If then David calls him Lord, how son of him is he?"

The psalm that Jesus quoted from, although written by King David, was not in reference to the person of David, but was a prophecy of the future reign of Christ, and goes on to describe Him as an eternal priest, as we read in Psalm 110 verses 1 and 4,

> 'The Lord said to my Lord, "Sit at My right hand, till I make Your enemies Your footstool."

> 'The Lord has sworn and will not relent, "You are a priest forever according to the order of Melchizedek."

David had written the words of the psalm under the inspiration of the Spirit of God the Holy Spirit, David himself declared this to be so at the end of his life, as we read in 2 Samuel 23:2-4,

> "The Spirit of the Lord spoke by me, and His word was on my tongue. The God of Israel said, the Rock of Israel spoke to me: 'He who rules over men must be just, ruling in the fear of God. And he shall be like the light of the morning when the sun rises, a morning without clouds, like the tender grass springing out of the earth, by clear shining after rain."

The genealogy recounted in the gospels proved that Jesus was born into a family descended from David. If the Pharisees had been able to cast doubt on this, it is highly likely that they would have done so. The pharisees were in error, thinking that the Messiah would have only a human lineage. Jesus' teaching was that the Messiah was far more than a mere descendant of David. The Messiah, who would be the descendant of David, was also his divine Lord, worthy of homage, fully man and fully divine, as we read for example in Psalm 2:7-8,

> 'I will declare the decree: The Lord has said to Me, 'You are My Son, today I have begotten You. Ask of Me, and I will give You the nations for Your inheritance, and the ends of the earth for Your possession.'

To sit at the Lord's right hand is to hold the highest position and power of government in the name of God, so that both heaven and earth are under the governance of Christ and that His enemies will ultimately be defeated. Ezekiel, writing probably four hundred years after King David's death, prophesied the coming of David, in reference to Christ, as shepherd and prince, as we read in Ezekiel 34:22-24 and 37:24-25,

> 'Therefore, I will save My flock, and they shall no longer be a prey; and I will judge between sheep and sheep. I will establish one shepherd over them, and he shall feed them – My servant David. He shall feed them and be their shepherd. And I, the Lord, will be their God, and My servant David a prince among them; I, the Lord, have spoken.'

> 'David My servant shall be king over them, and they shall all have one shepherd; they shall also walk in My judgements and observe My statutes and do them. Then they shall dwell in the land that I have given to Jacob My servant, where your fathers dwelt; and they shall dwell there, they, their children, and their children's children, forever; and My servant David shall be their prince forever.'

MATTHEW CHAPTER TWENTY-THREE

Matthew 23:2-3

In verses 2-3, Jesus addressed the people and His disciples, reminding them that the scribes and the Pharisees were appointed to act as deputies for Moses, and that they, the people, and His disciples, are to follow the teaching of the Law, saying,

> "On the seat of Moses sat the scribes and the Pharisees. All things therefore whatever they may tell you do ye and keep, but according to the works of them do ye not; for they say and do not."

The Law was given to the Jews through Moses and the task of teaching the Law was passed down to the scribes and Pharisees. In the synagogue the teachers sat while expounding the law; sitting in the seat of Moses means to have authority to teach the Law by explaining it. To sit in the chair of Moses is to teach, according to the Law of God, how we ought to live. This succession to Moses was given through the words of Moses' father-in-law as we read in Exodus 18:20-21,

> "You shall teach them the statutes and the laws and show them the way in which they must walk and the work they must do. Moreover, you shall select from all the people able men, such as fear God, men of truth, hating covetousness, and place such over them to be rulers of thousands, rulers of hundreds, of fifties, and rulers of tens."

At the end of his life, Moses exhorted the people to continue to act according to the Lord's statutes and judgements, as we read in Deuteronomy 4:5-6,

> "Surely, I have taught you statutes and judgements, just as the Lord my God commanded me, that you should act according to them in the land which you go to possess. Therefore, be careful to observe them; for this is your wisdom and your understanding in the sight of the peoples who will hear all these statutes, and say, 'Surely this great nation is a wise and understanding people'."

The highest-ranking scribes were the Pharisees, and their teaching was highly esteemed. Ezra was described as a scribe who was skilled in the Law of Moses and was sent to teach the people by Artaxerxes, king of Babylon, as we read in Ezra 7:6 and 25,

> 'This Ezra came up from Babylon; and he was a skilled scribe in the Law of Moses, which the Lord God of Israel had given.'

> 'And you, Ezra, according to your God-given wisdom, set magistrates and judges who may judge all the people who are in the region beyond the river, all such as know the laws of your God; and teach those who do not know them.'

It was the chair of Moses – the teaching of God's laws, not men's laws, that should be obeyed. The scribes and the Pharisees added laws of their own in spite of Moses' specific instruction not to do so (Deuteronomy 4:2). Instead of lightening people's load, they made it heavier. They wanted to make a display of their religious devotion to win praise and adoration from others, and, by paying attention to small details of the law, they ignored its real meaning. Jesus warned His disciples not to conform to the unrighteous conduct of the scribes, but to regulate their lives by the rule of the Law which they heard out of the mouths of the scribes. The unrighteous behaviour in contemporary church leaders, that is sadly so often in the press, should not hinder His disciples from living a righteous life themselves and from seeking the Law, as we read in Malachi 2:7-8,

> "For the lips of a priest should keep knowledge, and people should seek the law from his mouth; for he is the messenger of the Lord of hosts. But you have departed from the way; you have caused many to stumble at the law. You have corrupted the covenant of Levi," says the Lord of hosts.

Matthew 23:4-7

In verses 4-7, Jesus directly criticised those who should be teachers of the law and shepherds of the flock for seeking their own self-interest rather than the interest of the people, and speaks of the hypocrisy of the phylacteries worn by the scribes and Pharisees, saying,

> "And they bind burdens heavy and put on the shoulders of men, but they with the finger of them not are willing to move them. But all the works of them they do for to be seen by men; for they broaden the phylacteries of them and enlarge the fringes, and they like the chief seats in the synagogues, and the greetings in the marketplaces and to be called by men rabbi."

The teachers of the law had, over generations, with the intention of expounding the law, added rites and rituals and other religious observances that were a burden to the people. This was in direct contradiction to the command of Moses not to do so, as we read in Deuteronomy 4:2,

> "You shall not add to the word which I command you, nor take from it, that you may keep the commandments of the Lord your God which I commanded you."

The words Jesus spoke, of the teachers laying heavy burdens but not lifting a finger to help them, echo the words of Ezekiel in chapter 34:4,

> "The weak you have not strengthened, nor have you healed those who were sick, nor bound up the broken, nor brought back what was driven away, nor sought what was lost; but with force and cruelty you have ruled them."

The phylacteries, mentioned here by Jesus, were strips of parchment on which were written four passages of Scripture (Exodus 13:2-10, 11-17, Deuteronomy 6:4-9 and 13-23), that were rolled up and placed in four small cases and worn either on the arm or the forehead. These emerged from a literal interpretation of the command in Exodus to bind the Law on the hand and before the eyes, and the fringe, or tassel, refers to the command in Numbers, as we read in Exodus 13:9, Deuteronomy 6:8 and 11:18, and Numbers 15:38-39,

> "It shall be as a sign to you on your hand and as a memorial between your eyes, that the Lord's law may be in your mouth."

> "You shall bind them as a sign on your hand, and they shall be as frontlets between your eyes."

> "Therefore, you shall lay up these words of mine in your heart and in your soul, and bind them as a sign on your hand, and they shall be as frontlets between your eyes."

> "Tell them to make tassels on the corners of their garments throughout their generations, and to put a blue thread in the tassels of the corners. And you shall have the tassel, that you may look upon it and remember all the commandments of the Lord and do them."

Moses' intention was that the people should keep the laws in view, not perch them literally in front of their eyes. Moses used the analogy of frontlets; these are used in guiding a horse, to prevent distraction from the road ahead, to prevent biting, and to keep the mouth closed so the bit can be controlled. Frontlets had been used for horses since ancient times, they formed part of a horse's armour and were multi-functional. They could represent status, gave protection, and were the means for guiding the horse – the symbolism used by Moses is clear: having the Lord's commandments give status - as God's children, protection, and guidance. Rabbi was a formal term of respect given by Jewish disciples to their teacher, rather as some might refer to a teacher as 'Sir' today, although that person has not been knighted. The Law is not to be put somewhere on show but written on the heart from where it will light the way, as we read in Proverbs 3:3 and 6:23,

> 'Let not mercy and truth forsake you; bind them around your neck, write them on the tablet of your heart.'

> 'For the commandment is a lamp, and the law a light; reproofs of instruction are the way of life.'

417

Matthew 23:8-12

In verses 8-12, having expressed His disapproval of the liking of the scribes and Pharisees for honorary titles, Jesus went on to warn His disciples not to be like them, saying,

> "But ye be not called rabbi; for One is of you the teacher, and all ye brothers are. And father call ye not of you on earth; for One is of you the Father heavenly. Neither be ye called leaders, because leader of you is one the Christ. And the greater of you shall be of you servant. And he who will exalt himself shall be humbled, and he who will humble himself shall be exalted."

The Pharisees assumed the title Rabbi and expected their followers to address them by it. Jesus taught His disciples that they were to refuse such titles as rabbi and remember that they had only one teacher and were all members of His family, and that family members do not address each other by their formal titles. He used the Greek word 'kathegetai', often translated as leader or instructor and sometimes teacher, but also as master. God called Himself Father and Master, accusing the priests of despising His name at the time of Malachi, as we read in Malachi 1:6,

> "A son honours his father and a servant his master. If then I am the Father, where is My honour? And if I am a Master, where is My reverence? Says the Lord of hosts to you priests who despise My name. Yet you say, 'In what way have we despised Your name?'"

It is unlikely that Jesus meant that His disciples should not recognise the relationship of their parent as their father, especially as the fifth commandment is to honour your mother and father. It is more likely that His meaning is that His disciples should not give to others the spiritual designation of Father that belongs exclusively to God, or to claim that title for themselves. Only God has supreme authority and the right to give the Law and is the Father of all. God alone rules over us with the power and authority of a father, and Christ is the only head of the whole church. Jesus echoed the words of the prophets when He spoke of the

418

One teacher and the brotherhood of His disciples, as we read in Isaiah 54:13 and Jeremiah 31:34,

> 'All your children shall be taught by the Lord, and great shall be the peace of your children.'

> 'No more shall every man teach his neighbour, and every man his brother, saying, 'Know the Lord,' for they all shall know Me, from the least of them to the greatest of them, says the Lord. For I will forgive their iniquity, and their sin I will remember no more.'

The highest honour in the Church is not through position, but service. Jesus' disciples must beware of taking on any title – even if, through false humility, it be Servant, that diminishes the authority of Christ as Master. To will something implies choice, when it is said that something shall happen, it implies an inevitability. This distinction is made in the original Greek; Jesus said that those who will – or choose, to exalt themselves shall be humbled; those who will – or choose, to humble themselves shall be exalted, as we read in Proverbs 29:23, 16:5, 18:12, and 22:4,

> 'A man's pride will bring him low, but the humble in spirit will retain honour.'

> 'Everyone proud in heart is an abomination to the Lord; though they join forces, none will go unpunished.'

> 'Before destruction the heart of a man is haughty, and before honour is humility.'

> 'By humility and the fear of the Lord are riches and honour and life.'

Matthew 23:13-15

In verses 13-15, Jesus warned His listeners against religious hypocrisy, of religious pretension that was motivated by self-interest rather than the desire to further the kingdom of heaven, saying,

> "But woe to you, scribes and Pharisees, hypocrites, because ye shut the kingdom of the heavens before men; for you do not enter, not the ones entering do ye allow to enter. Woe to you, scribes, and Pharisees hypocrites, for you devour the houses of widows and as a pretext at great length are praying. Because of this ye shall receive greater condemnation. Woe to you scribes and Pharisees, hypocrites, because you go about the sea and the dry land to make one proselyte, and when he becomes, ye make him a son of Gehenna twofold more than you."

The word hypocrites referred to play actors, people acting a part. Jesus wasn't saying that all scribes and Pharisees were hypocrites, but that there were people who played the role of being a scribe or Pharisee, as an actor would do, without actually loving God. There were hypocrites who played the role for their own benefit who merely acted the role of scribe or Pharisee. By taking the place of a genuine teacher, these actors effectively prevented the people gaining the knowledge that was the key to the kingdom. The Pharisees who would not receive the message of the Gospel, also hindered the people from receiving it. These false teachers would utter long prayers for several hours and expect gifts or payment from widows in return for their prayers; they sold their prayers for personal gain. Some even persuaded widows to allow them to be executors of their property and then defrauded them. The people were led astray as prophesied in Isaiah 9:14-16, and widows were afflicted in contravention of the law in Exodus 22:22-23,

> 'Therefore, the Lord will cut off head and tail from Israel, palm branch and bulrush in one day. The elder and honourable, he is the head; the prophet who teaches lies, he is the tail. For the leaders of this people cause them to err, and those who are led by them are destroyed.'

"You shall not afflict any widow or fatherless child. If you afflict them in any way, and they cry at all to Me, I will surely hear their cry."

Jesus spoke of the proselyte. In Old Testament times, this referred to a stranger or newcomer to Israel, a sojourner in the land. A righteous proselyte was a gentile convert, circumcised and considered a full member of the Jewish people; a gate proselyte followed some of the laws and were not circumcised – they conformed to the Seven Laws of Noah, found in Genesis chapter nine, to be assured of a place in the world to come. The Pharisees made converts not to the Jewish faith but to their own sect, putting their own opinions above the word of God as we read in Isaiah 59:12-19,

> 'For our transgressions are with us, and as for our iniquities, we know them: In transgressing and lying against the Lord, and departing from our God, speaking oppression and revolt, conceiving, and uttering from the heart words of falsehood. Justice is turned back, and righteousness stands afar off; for truth is fallen in the street, and equity cannot enter.'

It has often been observed that converts to a religion are the most extreme and zealous; it seems that the proselytes at this time where the most vociferous against Christ and often carried out the plans of the scribes and Pharisees to prevent the spread of the Gospel message. Christ's followers are to have zeal for the word of God, as we read in Psalm 119:139-142,

> 'My zeal has consumed me because my enemies have forgotten Your words. Your word is very pure; therefore, Your servant loves it. I am small and despised, yet I do not forget Your precepts. Your righteousness is an everlasting righteousness, and Your law is truth.'

Matthew 23:16-22

In verses 16-22, Jesus continued His warnings to the teachers of the law who, motivated by self-interest, had put earthly wealth above the things of heaven and even above the holiness of God, saying,

> "Woe to you, leaders blind the ones saying: Whoever swears by the shrine, nothing it is; but whoever swears by the gold of the shrine, he owes. Fools and blind, for which greater is, the gold or the shrine sanctifying the gold? And: Whoever swears by the altar, nothing it is; but whoever swears by the gift upon it, he owes. Blind, for which is greater, the gift or the altar sanctifying the gift? Therefore, the one swearing by the altar swears by it and by all things upon it; and the one swearing by the shrine swears by it and the one inhabiting it; and the one swearing by the heaven swears by the throne of God and by the one sitting upon it."

Here Jesus called the teachers, or leaders, blind and foolish; this was the kind of strong language used by the prophets and would have been familiar terms of admonition to His listeners. Jesus, like the prophets, did not mince His words or speak in ambiguities that were open to interpretation, rather, He made it very clear that it is folly for them blindly to follow their own path, as we read for example in Isaiah 56:10-11 and Psalm 94:8,

> 'His watchmen are blind, they are all ignorant; they are all dumb dogs, they cannot bark; sleeping, lying down, loving to slumber. Yes, they are greedy dogs which never have enough. And they are shepherds who cannot understand; they all look to their own way, everyone for his own gain, from his own territory.'

> 'Understand, you senseless among the people; and you fools, when will you be wise?'

Moses gave clear instructions regarding the sanctification and holiness of the altar and its utensils, the tabernacle, the ark of the Testimony, the table, its utensils, and the lampstand, as we read in Exodus 29:37, 30:29, and Numbers 16:38. We can also read the words of the prophet Haggai who addressed the question of what makes an object holy in chapter 2:12,

> "Seven days you shall make atonement for the altar and sanctify it. And the altar shall be most holy. Whatever touches the altar must be holy."

> "You shall consecrate them, that they may be most holy; whatever touches them must be holy."

> "Because they presented them [the censers] before the Lord, therefore they are holy."

> "If one carries holy meat in the fold of his garment, and with the edge he touches bread or stew, wine or oil, or any food, will it become holy?" Then the priests answered and said, "No."

The Greek word naou or naos used here in Matthew's Gospel, is typically translated as temple, however, it can also mean shrine, which in this context is more likely, since it refers to that part of the temple where God Himself resides. Jesus was reminding His listeners that the temple is the place that God Himself chose to inhabit; His holy presence sanctifies everything that is in it; it is only this heavenly presence that can sanctify earthly things. It is perhaps worth considering if there are objects in contemporary church life that have acquired, through tradition, an assumption of holiness in their own right. Jesus echoed the words of Isaiah, reminding His listeners that heaven is God's throne, and that it is His glory that fills the temple, as we read in Isaiah 66:1, Psalm 26:8, 11:4, and 132:13, and 2 Chronicles 7:1-2,

> 'Heaven is My throne, and earth is My footstool.'
> 'Lord, I have loved the habitation of Your house, and the place where Your glory dwells.'

> 'The Lord is in His holy temple; the Lord's throne is in heaven.'
> 'For the Lord has chosen Zion; He has desired it for His dwelling place.'
> 'the glory of the Lord filled the temple, and the priests could not enter the house of the Lord, because the glory of the Lord had filled the Lord's house.'

Matthew 23:23-24

In verses 23-24, Jesus warned the teachers of the law against focusing on trifles, such as exactly how a law ought to be observed, rather than focusing on the principal provisions of the law and ensuring that the whole law was observed, saying,

> "Woe to you, scribes, and Pharisees hypocrites, because ye tithe the mint and the dill and the cumin, and ye have left aside the weightier provisions of the law, judgement and mercy and faith; but these things it behoved to do and those not to leave aside. Leaders blind, the ones straining the gnat, but the camel swallowing."

It is evident from His words that Jesus considered particular aspects of the law to have greater importance. This was in keeping with the clear intent behind the law for tithing, that made provision for the vulnerable in society, as we read in Deuteronomy 14:28-29,

> 'At the end of every third year you shall bring out the tithe of your produce for that year and store it up within your gates. And the Levite, because he has no portion or inheritance with you, and the stranger and the fatherless and the widow who are within your gates, may come and eat and be satisfied, that the Lord you God may bless you in all the work of your hand which you do.'

In Jesus' eyes, justice, mercy, and faithfulness were of much greater importance. The law is to be fulfilled according to ethics or morality not ceremony or ritual. It is human beings, not inanimate objects, that matter. Jesus echoed the prophets in stating that ceremonial observance is pointless if the people observing those ceremonies or sacrifices neglect to do justice, to show kindness, or to walk humbly with God, as we read for example in Isaiah 3:12, Jeremiah 5:28 and 22:17.

> "O My people! Those who lead you cause you to err and destroy the way of your paths."

'They have grown fat, they are sleek; yes, they surpass the deeds of the wicked; they do not plead the cause, the cause of the fatherless; yet they prosper, and the right of the needy they do not defend.'

"Yet your eyes and your heart are for nothing but your covetousness, for shedding innocent blood, and practicing oppression and violence."

The comparison of a gnat and a camel highlighted the unbalanced thinking of these scribes and Pharisees who were scrupulous in tithing sprigs of herbs of little value but were prepared to shed the blood of innocent men such as Jesus Himself. The prophets made it clear what the Lord requires, as we read for example in Micah 6:8, Jeremiah 21:12 and 22:3.

'He has shown you, O man, what is good; and what does the Lord require of you but to do justly, to love mercy, and to walk humbly with your God?' And "Execute judgement in the morning; and deliver him who is plundered out of the hand of the oppressor, lest My fury go forth like fire and burn so that no one can quench it, because of the evil of your doings."

"Execute judgement and righteousness and deliver the plundered out of the hand of the oppressor. Do no wrong and do no violence to the stranger, the fatherless, or the widow, nor shed innocent blood in this place."

The law was an expression of God's unchangeable will; Jesus had said that He had not come to make any changes to the law – the will of God, but to fulfil it. The fulfilment of God's will – the law, was to be done from the heart. Jesus' life and teaching was the perfect demonstration of having the law within His heart, and like King David, those who love God should seek to obey what is at the heart of the law, as we read in Psalm 40:8,

'I delight to do Your will, O my God, and Your law is within my heart.'

425

Matthew 23:25-26

In verses 25-26, Jesus continues His warnings to those who focus on the outward appearance of religious observance whilst not merely neglecting the inner thoughts but behaving in a manner utterly out of keeping with the religion they purported to practice, saying,

> "Woe to you, scribes and Pharisees hypocrites, because ye cleanse the outside of the cup and the dish, but within they are full of robbery and intemperance. Pharisee blind, cleanse thou first the inside of the cup that may be also the outside of it clean."

When Jesus spoke of the intemperance and robbery of those who would have been expected to have fully observed the law, He echoed the words of the prophet Isaiah who spoke about the overindulgence with alcohol by the priests and prophets that led to intoxication and corruption, as we read in Isaiah 5:11, 21-23, and 28:7-8,

> 'Woe to those who rise early in the morning, that they may follow intoxicating drink, who continue until night, till wine inflames them!'

> 'Woe to those who are wise in their own eyes, and prudent in their own sight! Woe to men mighty at drinking wine, woe to men valiant for mixing intoxicating drink, who justify the wicked for a bribe, and take away justice from the righteous man!'

> 'But they also have erred through wine, and through intoxicating drink are out of the way; the priest and the prophet have erred through intoxicating drink. They are swallowed up by wine, they are out of the way through intoxicating drink; they err in vision, they stumble in judgement. For all tables are full of vomit and filth; no place is clean.'

The Pharisees were exceedingly meticulous in observing all the ceremonial washing and purifications prescribed by the law, but there were clearly those who paid no attention to inward purity. No amount of ritual washing of the hands or other parts of the body will make a person clean in the spiritual sense, if the heart is not pure. The cleansing of the inside of a cup or dish is far more important than the outside; inward cleansing is essential rather than meticulous observance of external rituals. Jesus reproved their hypocrisy in regulating only the outward appearance of their life that was visible to the people. God had commanded the people to wash their inner selves, their hearts, through the prophets, as we read for example in Isaiah 1:16 and Jeremiah 4:14,

> 'Wash yourselves, make yourselves clean; put away the evil of your doings from before My eyes. Cease to do evil, learn to do good; seek justice, rebuke the oppressor; defend the fatherless, plead for the widow.'

> 'O Jerusalem, wash your heart from wickedness, that you may be saved. How long will your evil thoughts lodge with you?'

Jesus told the people that they should first cleanse the inside; first things first. Jesus was not condemning outward cleanliness or the washing of cups and plates, but He was making it clear that these things were secondary. The giving of alms was considered to be a form of cleansing; Jesus juxtaposed robbery and intemperance with cleansing that includes giving of alms and temperance. Only those who have been cleansed of the sin of their hands and heart can enter the presence of God who promises that cleansing, as we read for example in Psalm 24:3-4, 51:2-3, and Ezekiel 35:25,

> 'Who may ascend into the hill of the Lord? Or who may stand in His holy place? He who has clean hands and a pure heart.'

> 'Wash me thoroughly from my iniquity and cleanse me from my sin. For I acknowledge my transgressions, and my sin is always before me.'

> "Then I will sprinkle clean water on you, and you shall be clean; I will cleanse you from all your filthiness and from all your idols."

Matthew 23:27-28

In verses 27-28, Jesus, echoing the woes listed by the prophet Habakuk, speaks of yet further failings of the scribes and Pharisees, saying,

> "Woe to you, scribes and Pharisees hypocrites, because ye resemble graves having been whitewashed, which outwardly indeed appear beautiful, but within they are full of bones of dead men and of all uncleanness. Thus also ye outwardly indeed appear to men righteous, but within ye are full of hypocrisy and of lawlessness."

It seems that tombs, that were often by the roadside, were, and still are, whitewashed to make them more visible so that they were more easily avoided to reduce the risk of passers by being made unclean by inadvertently touching a tomb. The tombs were whitewashed for the benefit of unwary travellers, especially at the time of the Passover. At that time, there was of course no street lighting, so it was rather like painting white lines on our modern roads. The law considered persons to be unclean who had touched anything belonging to the dead, including graves, as we read in Numbers 19:16,

> 'Whoever in the open field touches one who is slain by a sword or who has died, or a bone of a man, or a grave, shall be unclean seven days.'

Jesus' words suggested that, on the inside, the Pharisees were like dead men, being spiritually and morally dead, and that this was concealed by a veneer of respectability. The piety of the Pharisees that Jesus addressed went no deeper than the whitewashed façade of the tombs. The Pharisees prided themselves on their strict observance of the Law, so that their failure to apply the Law correctly was, according to Jesus, lawlessness, or wickedness. The uncleanness of the inner person is described in similar terms in the Psalms and Proverbs, as we read in Psalm 5:9, 28:3 and 41:6, and Proverbs 26:23-26,

'For there is no faithfulness in their mouth; their inward part is destruction; their throat is an open tomb; they flatter with their tongue.'

'Do not take me away with the wicked and with the workers of iniquity, who speak peace to their neighbours, but evil is in their hearts.'

'And if he comes to see me, he speaks lies; his heart gathers iniquity to itself.'

'Fervent lips with a wicked heart are like earthenware covered with silver dross. He who hates, disguises it with his lips, and lays up deceit within himself; when hatred is covered by deceit, his wickedness will be revealed before the assembly.'

Jesus was making it clear that His followers, the children of God, should desire to be pure, not to appear so. When Samuel was sent to Jesse by God to find a king for the people, he thought Eliab looked a kingly specimen, but God told Samuel that He looks not at the outward appearance of people, but at the heart; David told his son Solomon the same; and Solomon later reminded the people, as we read in 1 Samuel 16:7, 1 Chronicles 28:9, Psalm 51:6, and 1 Kings 8:39,

'The Lord said to Samuel, "Do not look at his appearance or at his physical stature, because I have refused him. For the Lord does not see as a man sees; for man looks at the outward appearance, but the Lord looks at the heart."

"As for you, my son Solomon, know the God of your father, and serve Him with a loyal heart and with a willing mind; for the Lord searches all hearts and understands all the intent of the thoughts."

'Behold, You desire truth in the inward parts, and in the hidden part You will make me to know wisdom.'

'Then hear in heaven Your dwelling place, and forgive, and act, and give to everyone according to all his ways, whose heart You know (for You alone know the hearts of all the sons of men).

Matthew 23:29-33

In verses 29-33, we read the last of the woes recorded by Matthew in which Jesus warned of the hypocrisy of self-righteousness, saying,

> "Woe to you scribes and Pharisees, hypocrites, because ye build the graves of the prophets and adorn the monuments of the righteous and say: If we were in the days of the fathers of us, we would not have been of them partakers in the blood of the prophets. So ye witness to yourselves that sons ye are of the ones having killed the prophets. And ye fulfil the measure of the fathers of you. Serpents, offspring of vipers, how escape ye from the judgement of Gehenna?"

The Pharisees traced their group origins back approximately a hundred and sixty years, to a time when Judea was under the control of a Greek state. The Greek king began a campaign of repression against the Jewish religion; all Jewish practices were banned, and the Temple was made into the site of a pagan-Jewish cult. These groups of priests resisted all attempts to assimilate their faith and practice to paganism and many suffered martyrdom rather than betray their religious heritage. They came together for mutual support and brotherhood in defence of each other and of the practice of the law. They became especially defensive of the role of ceremonial purity which led them in time to forbid contact with Gentiles and Jews who were not as fastidious. They had become convinced of their own self-righteousness to the extent that they could no longer hear the truth, as prophesied by Jeremiah in chapter 7:28,

> "This is a nation that does not obey the voice of the Lord their God nor receive correction. Truth has perished and has been cut off from their mouth."

The decoration of the monuments was a further example of an empty display of religion; it was a hypocrisy – a play acting, to profess to honour those who were now silent; those whose doctrine they would not have embraced. The public ornamenting of the tombs was meant to show their piety, but Jesus showed them it was merely pretence. They were already, during Holy Week, plotting to kill Jesus as their forefathers had killed

God's messengers; messengers that had been sent by God out of compassion for His people as we read in 2 Chronicles 36:15 and Jeremiah 7:25-26,

> 'And the Lord God of their fathers sent warnings to them by His messengers, rising up early and sending them, because He had compassion on His people and on His dwelling place.'

> "Since the day that your fathers came out of the land of Egypt until this day, I have even sent to you all My servants the prophets, daily rising up early and sending them. Yet they did not obey Me or incline their ear but stiffened their neck. They did worse than their fathers."

Those who pay no heed to impending disaster cannot escape it. Jesus was simply stating that if these scribes and Pharisees would not listen to the warning that judgement was coming, that they could not escape it. Jesus uttered these words not in condemnation but in sorrow that those who should have been trustworthy guides for the people were in fact leading them to judgement and were like snakes trying to slither away from fire. Those who follow Jesus, especially those who are teachers, must beware of being complacent, remembering that the Lord knows all our ways, as we read in Jeremiah 32:19, and pray in humble repentance as did David in Psalm 51:1-2,

> 'You are great in counsel and mighty in work, for your eyes are open to all the ways of the sons of men, to give everyone according to his ways and according to the fruit of his doings.'

> 'Have mercy upon me, O God, according to Your loving kindness; according to the multitude of Your tender mercies, blot out my transgressions. Wash me thoroughly from my iniquity and cleanse me from my sin.'

Matthew 23:34-36

In verses 34-36, Jesus spoke about the prophets of ages past but indicated that they were part of a continuum; that God would continue to send His messengers and that they would be treated with similar contempt, saying,

> "Therefore behold I send to you prophets and wise men and scribes; of them ye will kill and will crucify, and of them ye will scourge in the synagogues of you and will persecute from city to city; so comes on you all blood righteous being shed on the earth from the blood of Abel the righteous until the blood of Zacharias son Barachias, whom ye murdered between the shrine and the altar. Truly I tell you, will come all these things on generation this."

Here Jesus was foretelling a future that reflects the past, referring to the coming evangelists, apostles, and wise men who would proclaim His Gospel and be persecuted just as He described; people, like the ancient prophets, who are filled with God's holy Spirit. By using the words 'behold I send', Christ identified Himself with God the Father. Since He Himself was crucified by the Pharisees, we can infer that Christ was referring to Himself as both the Sender and the One sent, as both God and man. In the account of Cain and Abel, we read that God spoke directly to Cain, warning him that 'sin lies at the door', but Cain allowed sin to rule over him, as we read in Genesis 4:7-8,

> "If you do well, will you not be accepted? And if you do not do well, sin lies at the door. And its desire is for you, but you should rule over it." Now Cain talked with Abel his brother; and it came to pass, when they were in the field, that Cain rose up against Abel his brother and killed him.'

Having spoken about the righteous blood of Abel, Jesus went on to speak about Zechariah son of Barachias. Since the names Jehoiada and Barachias both mean 'blessed of Jehovah', it is likely that they are the same person, the prophet Zachariah and the Zachariah recorded in 2 Chronicles who was murdered in the temple court, which would have put him between the shrine, or sanctuary, and the altar. This murder was especially heinous because of its location, profaning the house of the Lord, as we read in 2 Chronicles 24:20-21,

> 'Then the Spirit of God came upon Zechariah the son of Jehoida the priest, who stood above the people, and said to them, "Thus says God: 'Why do you transgress the commandments of the Lord, so that you cannot prosper? Because you have forsaken the Lord, He also has forsaken you.'" So they conspired against him, and at the command of the king they stoned him with stones in the court of the house of the Lord.'

The effect of the disobedience of their forefathers was to have consequences in their own generation in as much as they had only unrighteous examples to follow. The consequences of their disobedience, the destruction of Jerusalem, occurred about forty years later, during the lifetime of that generation. The approaching onslaught was prophesied in Ezekiel 12:27-28,

> "Son of man, look, the house of Israel is saying, 'The vision that he sees is for many days from now, and he prophesies of times far off.' Therefore, say to them, 'Thus says the Lord God: "None of My words will be postponed any more, but the word which I speak will be done," says the Lord God'."

Remembering God's warning that sin, which desires to rule over us, lies in wait at our door, we can pray for God's salvation and deliverance in the words of Psalm 79:8-9,

> 'Oh, do not remember former iniquities against us! Let your tender mercies come speedily to meet us, for we have been brought very low. Help us, O God of our salvation, for the glory of Your name; and deliver us, and provide atonement for our sins, for Your name's sake!'

Matthew 23:37-39

In verses 37-39, we read Jesus' conclusion to the foregoing verses addressed to the scribes and Pharisees who had rejected God's messengers, sent out of compassion to warn the people to return to the security of His presence, saying,

> "Jerusalem, Jerusalem, the one killing the prophets and stoning the ones sent to her, how often I wished to gather the children of thee, as a bird gathers the young of her under her wings, and ye wished not. Behold is left to you the house of you desolate. For I tell you, by no means me ye see from now until ye say: Blessed the one coming in the name of the Lord."

Jesus' expression of both indignation and sorrow here was made because His people, time and again, both in the past and future, killed and persecuted the Lord's messengers, and when offered the protection of the Lord, rejected it, exposing themselves to the ravages of their enemies. The analogy of gathering up the young under His wings is used repeatedly in Old Testament Scripture, for example Boaz speaking to Ruth, Moses speaking about the Lord's people personified as Jacob, and in the Psalms, as we read in Ruth 2:12, Deuteronomy 32:11-12, and Psalm 17:8,

> "The Lord repay your work, and a full reward be given you by the Lord God of Israel, under whose wings you have come for refuge."

> 'As an eagle stirs up its nest, hovers over its young, spreading out its wings, taking them up, carrying them on its wings, so the Lord alone led him, and there was no foreign God with him.'

> 'Keep me as the apple of Your eye; hide me under the shadow of Your wings.'

Although since the nineteenth century considered apocryphal in Protestant Bibles, Jesus would have had access to the writings found in 2 Esdras 1:30, that express the same sorrow of His rejection and it is easy to imagine that Jesus had it in mind when He uttered similar words:

"Thus says the Lord Almighty: Have I not entreated you as a father entreats his sons or a mother her daughters or a nurse her children, so that you should be my people and I should be your God and that you should be my children and I should be your father? I gathered you together, as a hen gathers her chicks under her wings: but now, what shall I do unto you? I will cast you out from my presence. When you offer oblations to me, I will turn my face from you, for I have rejected your festal days and new moons and circumcisions of the flesh. I sent you my servants the prophets, but you have taken and killed them and torn their bodies in pieces."

Jesus told them 'The house is left to you' because He would no longer be there; He would never again teach publicly; having rejected Him, the house was no longer God's but theirs. This was clearly spoken of by the prophets as we read in Jeremiah 6:8 and 22:5 and Hosea 7:13-14,

"Be instructed, O Jerusalem, lest My soul depart from you; lest I make you desolate, a land not inhabited."

"But if you will not hear these words, I swear by Myself," says the Lord, "that this house shall become a desolation."

"Woe to them, for they have fled from Me! Destruction to them because they have transgressed against Me! Though I redeemed them, yet they have spoken lies against Me. They did not cry out to Me with their heart when they wailed upon their beds."

If we read on from Jesus' quote of Psalm 118:26, that was to be shouted on His entry into Jerusalem on Palm Sunday, we find that Jesus' coming sacrifice is also prophesied in verse 27,

'Blessed is he who comes in the name of the Lord! We have blessed you from the house of the Lord. God is the Lord, and He has given us light; bind the sacrifice with cords to the horns of the altar.'

MATTHEW CHAPTER TWENTY-FOUR

Matthew 24:2

In verse 2, we read Jesus' response to His disciples' admiration of the temple building, saying,

> "See ye not all these things? Truly I tell you, by no means will be left here stone on stone which shall not be overthrown."

Jesus asked His disciples to consider, or reflect on, the buildings they were admiring and then told them that the temple would be taken apart literally stone by stone. When Solomon had finished building the first temple, God had promised the people of Israel that if they turned away from Him that the temple would be cast from His sight as we read in 1 Kings 9:6-8,

> "If you or your sons at all turn from following Me, and do not keep My commandments and My statutes which I have set before them, but go and serve other gods and worship them, then I will cut off Israel from the land which I have given them; and this house which I have consecrated for My name I will cast out of My sight. Israel will be a proverb and a byword among all peoples. And as for this house, which is exalted, everyone who passes by it will be astonished and will hiss, and say, 'Why has the Lord done thus to this land and to this house?"

This prophecy was fulfilled at the time of the exile to Babylon. Subsequently, the temple, known as the second temple, was rebuilt. Again, the people were warned, through Jeremiah, to follow God's commands to be able to dwell in the promised land, as we read in Jeremiah 7:5-7,

> "For if you thoroughly amend your ways and your doings, if you thoroughly execute judgement between a man and his neighbour, if you do not oppress the stranger, the fatherless, and the widow and do not shed innocent blood in this place, or walk after other gods to your hurt, then I will cause you to dwell in this place, in the land that I gave to your fathers forever and ever."

Jeremiah went on to prophecy the destruction of the second temple because the people had once again turned away and refused to repent, as we read in Jeremiah 7:13-14,

> "And now, because you have done all these works," says the Lord, "and I spoke to you, rising up early and speaking, but you did not hear, and I called you, but you did not answer, therefore I will do to the house which is called by My name, in which you trust, and to this place which I gave to you and your fathers, as I have done to Shiloh."

Jesus knew that these prophesies would soon be fulfilled in the lifetime of many of His listeners. Although the destruction of the temple occurred during the war with Rome in AD 70, according to the records of the Jewish historian Josephus, who was employed by the Romans, the Roman army had orders not to destroy the temple as it was to be kept as a testament to Roman valour. Josephus recorded that the fire in the temple was in fact begun by Jewish zealots who had themselves committed atrocities on their own people during the siege of Jerusalem, and thereby bringing the prophecy to fruition themselves. The very foundations of the temple were dug up according to Roman custom. Josephus had formerly described the temple as being constructed of immense green and white marble blocks and covered with golden plates. The fire, that was assisted by the Roman soldiers, caused the gold covering to melt in between the stones of the temple, so that the Roman soldiers literally took the temple apart stone by stone to retrieve the gold as plunder. Josephus also recorded that Jerusalem was levelled to the ground so that nothing was left to believe that it had ever been inhabited; that the war had laid it completely waste and unrecognisable. Thus, was fulfilled the prophecy, addressed to the rulers of Israel, that had been spoken of in Micah 3:12,

> 'Therefore because of you Zion shall be ploughed like a field, Jerusalem shall become heaps of ruins, and the mountain of the temple like the bare hills of the forest.'

Matthew 24:4-6

In verses 4-6, Jesus responds to the disciples' question about signs of His coming and the end of the age, saying,

> "See ye lest anyone you cause to err. For many will come in the name of me saying: I am the Christ, and many will cause to err. But ye will be about to hear of wars and rumours of wars; see not ye are disturbed; for it behoves to happen, but not yet is the end."

Jesus began with a warning not to let others lead His disciples into error. It is only by holding firm to the teaching of Christ that His followers can see through the deception and misleading claims of others. Much of Old Testament Scripture is a litany of examples of the people being deceived or deceiving themselves, as we read for example in Jeremiah 29:8,

> 'For thus says the Lord of hosts, the God of Israel: Do not let your prophets and your diviners who are in your midst deceive you, nor listen to your dreams which you cause to be dreamed.'

Jesus also foresaw the coming of imposters, claiming to be the real Christ. The historical records, such as those of Josephus, show that after the time of Jesus that many claimed to be the real Christ, the Anointed One, deceiving large numbers of people. There have been many such imposters, and down the millennia there have been numerous others who have claimed to be the one to show mankind the way. Again, we find the prophet Jeremiah speaking against these false prophets, for example in chapter 14:14 and 23:25,

> 'And the Lord said to me, 'The prophets prophesy lies in My name. I have not sent them, commanded them, nor spoken to them; they prophesy to you a false vision, divination, a worthless thing, and the deceit of their heart.'

> "I have heard what the prophets have said who prophesy lies in My name, saying, 'I have dreamed, I have dreamed.'"

Jesus was also warning His disciples that they shouldn't expect wars to cease or be less frequent than before He, the Messiah, had come. Neither should they deceive themselves into thinking that wars and rumours of wars indicate the imminent return of the Messiah. When Jesus spoke of 'the end', this may well have been in reference to the end of the Jewish state and the temple, rather than the end of the world. Not all wars, famines, earthquakes, or plagues would be sure signs that the end of the world is nigh. Patient perseverance is expected of Christ's followers – their focus should be on their own part in communicating the Gospel, not listening to the predictions of others or even their own imaginings, so as not to be put off from their commission to the share the Gospel. Christ's disciples are to beware of this kind of false teaching and not be frightened by the evils that they will be exposed to, but be prepared to endure and remain faithful in the face of trials because this is the will of God in whom we have confidence as we read in Psalm 27:1-3 and 46:1-3,

'The Lord is my light and my salvation; whom shall I fear? The Lord is the strength of my life; of whom shall I be afraid? When the wicked came against me to eat up my flesh, my enemies and foes, they stumbled and fell. Though an army may encamp against me, my heart shall not fear; though war may rise against me, in this I will be confident.'

'God is our refuge and strength, a very present help in trouble. Therefore, we will not fear, even though the earth be removed, and though the mountains be carried into the midst of the sea; though its waters roar and be troubled, though the mountains shake with its swelling.'

Matthew 24:7-13

In verses 7-13, Jesus continued His warnings about future false prophets and the need for His disciples to hold fast to His teaching, saying,

> "For will be raised nation against nation and kingdom against kingdom, and there will be famines and earthquakes throughout places; but all these things are beginning of birth-pangs. Then they will deliver you to affliction and will kill you, and ye will be being hated by all the nations because of the name of me. And then will be offended many and one another will deliver up and they will hate one another; and many false prophets will be raised and cause them to err many; and because to be increased the lawlessness will grow cold the love of the many. But the one enduring to the end, this will be saved."

The events Jesus described as the beginnings of birth pains did in fact occur before the Roman destruction of Jerusalem, described in detail by Josephus (in Wars of the Jews, VI.5:3), and of course they have continued since. Moses warned the Israelites that such things would come upon them if they did not continue to follow the Lord's commands and precepts, as we read in Deuteronomy 28:59,

> "If you do not carefully observe all the words of this law that are written in this book, that you may fear this glorious and awesome name, The Lord your God, then the Lord will bring upon you and your descendants extraordinary plagues – great and prolonged plagues – and serious and prolonged sickness."

The denunciation of Christians by others began with the commencement of their public persecution and continues to this day in many places around the world. Friends and members of the same family have been turned against each other in betrayal and hate as people have sought to save their own skin. A culture of denunciation has been fostered especially in societies where there is authoritarian rule or dictatorship that relies on fear and repression to maintain control of populations. There are numerous recorded examples of family members betraying each other, of sons and daughters betraying their parents, in places that have been subject to this kind of regime. The Christian church should expect persecution as it stands firm for Christ, and His disciples need to be prepared to suffer and not to yield. The first persecutions are recorded in the Acts of the Apostles; those who called themselves Christians, bearing the name of Christ, were considered to have committed a crime deserving of death, by both Gentiles and Jews. This was clearly spoken of by the prophets, as we read for example in Isaiah 9:19 and Micah 7:5-6,

'Through the wrath of the Lord of hosts the land is burned up, and the people shall be   as fuel for the fire; no man shall spare his brother.'

'Do not trust in a friend; do not put your confidence in a companion; guard the doors of your mouth from her who lies in your bosom. For son dishonours father, daughter rises against her mother, daughter-in-law against her mother-in-law; a man's enemies are the men of his own household.'

Those who suffer in prisons for Christ's sake need to be prepared to be hated; to be lonely and forsaken by friends and family as Jesus Himself was. Jesus was warning His disciples that the message of the gospel would never be agreeable to the world, and that all nations would oppose them; that they ought to prepare to endure against all kinds of temptation; that false teachers would arise to corrupt sound doctrine and lead people astray. Some would desert their faith, others corrupt it, and others would become indifferent. Christ's followers are to courageously strive to overcome temptation, continue to demonstrate His love to others and persevere to the end, remembering His words spoken in Isaiah 41:10,

"Fear not, for I am with you; be not dismayed, for I am your God. I will strengthen you, yes, I will help you, I will uphold you with My righteous right hand."

443

Matthew 24:14-18

In verses 14-18, Jesus reminded His disciples of the Old Testament prophecies that all nations would be gathered to Him, saying,

> "And will be proclaimed this gospel of the kingdom in all the inhabited earth for a testimony to all the nations, and then will come the end. When therefore ye see the abomination of desolation spoken through Daniel the prophet stand in place holy, the one reading let him understand, then the ones in Judea let them flee to the mountains, the one on the housetop let him not come down to take the things out of the house of him, and the one in the field let him not turn back behind to take the garment of him."

Within the lifetime of the apostles, the Gospel message had already spread east as far as India, north as far as Scythia (modern-day Ukraine), south as far as Ethiopia, and, since the Roman Empire had by this time reached the Atlantic Ocean, west as far as Spain and Britain, thus fulfilling the prophecies as we read for example in Isaiah 11:45, 42:1 and 4, 45:22-23, 66:18, and Jeremiah 3:17,

> "And in that day there shall be a Root of Jesse, who shall stand as a banner to the people; for the Gentiles shall seek Him. And His resting place shall be glorious."

> 'Behold! My servant whom I uphold. My Elect One in whom My soul delights! I have put My Spirit upon Him; He will bring forth justice to the Gentiles.'

> 'He will not fail nor be discouraged, till He has established justice in the earth; and the coastlands shall wait for His law.'

> "Look to Me, and be saved, all you ends of the earth! For I am God and there is no other. I have sworn by Myself; the word has gone out of My mouth in righteousness, and shall not return, that to Me every knee shall bow, and every tongue shall take an oath."

"For I know their works and their thoughts. It shall be that I will gather all nations and tongues; and they shall come and see My glory."

"At that time Jerusalem shall be called The Throne of the Lord, and all the nations shall be gathered to it, to the name of the Lord, to Jerusalem. No more shall they follow the dictates of their evil hearts."

The 'abomination' that Jesus spoke of likely refers to the Roman desecration, or profanation, of the temple before its destruction in AD 70. However, it may also have been a prophecy of the time when 'the abomination of desolation' was set up on the altar in Jerusalem by Antiochus Epiphanes, recorded in the first book of Maccabees, and of course it may also refer to something yet to come, as we read in Daniel 11:31 and 12:11-12,

'And forces shall be mustered by him, and they shall defile the sanctuary fortress; then they shall take away the daily sacrifices, and place there the abomination of desolation.'

'And from the time that the daily sacrifice is taken away, and the abomination of desolation is set up, there shall be one thousand two hundred and ninety days. Blessed is he who waits and comes to the one thousand two hundred and ninety days.'

By referencing Daniel, Jesus is again calling on His disciples to be patient and persevere to the end. His words are very much like a modern fire drill – taking the fastest route without any kind of hesitation. Jesus was perhaps also warning His followers not to cling to earthly things and not to give up when faced with earthly calamities. God promises to light the way and be a shield to those who trust Him, as we read in Psalm 18:28-30,

'For You will light my lamp; the Lord my God will enlighten my darkness. For by You I can run against a troop, by my God I can leap over a wall. As for God, His way is perfect; the word of the Lord is proven; He is a shield to all who trust in Him.'

Matthew 24:19-22

In verses 19-22, Jesus continues to warn His disciples of the prophecies of the coming tribulation, saying,

> "Woe to the pregnant women and to the ones giving suck in those days. And pray ye lest happen the flight of you in winter nor on a sabbath; for will be then affliction great, such as not has happened from the beginning of the world until now neither by no means may happen. And except were cut short days those, not was saved all flesh; but on account of the chosen will be cut short days those."

The wording used by Jesus suggests that this was not a warning of something that could be averted, but a clear prediction of what would in fact come to pass. The horrors, destruction, and immense death toll, that the Romans inflicted on Jerusalem in AD 70 could easily have been the tribulation to which these prophecies related, but there have been horrors since and there may yet be such in the future. Again, Jesus was referring to the prophecies of Daniel and Joel, as we read in Daniel 12:1 and Joel 2:1-2,

> "At that time Michael shall stand up, the great prince who stands watch over the sons of your people; and there shall be a time of trouble, such as never was since there was a nation, even to that time. And at that time your people shall be delivered, everyone who is found written in the book."

> 'Blow the trumpet in Zion and sound an alarm in My holy mountain! Let all the inhabitants of the land tremble; for the day of the Lord is coming, for it is at hand: A day of darkness and gloominess, a day of clouds and thick darkness, like the morning clouds spread over the mountains. A people come, great and strong, the like of whom has never been; nor will there ever be any such after them, even for many successive generations.'

Jesus told His disciples to pray that when the day came for them to flee that it would be neither in Winter, that would make travel harder, nor on the Sabbath. This was not because He was concerned that they may contravene the Sabbath law, but that people would feel constrained to remain in their place and also because it was the custom for the gates of Jerusalem to be shut and guarded so no one could enter or leave, as we read in Exodus 16:29, Nehemiah 13:19,

> "See! For the Lord has given you the Sabbath; therefore He gives you on the sixth day bread for two days. Let every man remain in his place; let no man go out of his place on the seventh day."

> 'So it was, at the gates of Jerusalem, as it began to be dark before the Sabbath, that I commanded the gates to be shut, and charged that they must not be opened till after the Sabbath.'

Jesus spoke about the chosen, or the elect, saying that it was on account of the elect that God intended to restrain the fierceness of this tribulation. Those who remain servants of the Lord, the remnant, those who are refined and tested, will inherit the Lord's mountains, as we read in Isaiah 1:9, 65:8-9, and Zechariah 13:8-9,

> 'Unless the Lord of hosts had left to us a very small remnant, we would have become like Sodom, we would have been made like Gomorrah.'

> "As the new wine is found in the cluster, and one says, 'Do not destroy it, for a blessing is in it,' so will I do for My servants' sake, that I may not destroy them all. I will bring forth descendants from Jacob, and from Judah an heir of My mountains; My elect shall inherit it, and My servants shall dwell there."

> "And it shall come to pass in all the land," says the Lord, "that two-thirds in it shall be cut off and die. But one-third shall be left in it: I will bring the one-third through the fire, will refine them as silver is refined, and test them as gold is tested. They will call on My name, and I will answer them. I will say, 'This is My people'; and each one will say, 'The Lord is my God.'

Matthew 24:23-28

In verses 23-28, Jesus was again warning His disciples against the false prophets and others who would falsely claim to be the one to redeem the nation, saying,

> "Then if anyone to you says: Behold here the Christ or: Here, do not believe; for will be raised false Christs and false prophets, and they will give signs great and marvels, so as to cause to err, if possible, even the chosen. Behold I have before told you. If therefore they say to you: Behold in the desert he is, go not ye forth; Behold in the private rooms, do not ye believe; for as the lightening comes forth from the east and shines forth unto the west, so will be the presence of the Son of Man; wherever may be the carcass, there will be assembled the eagles."

The false Christs may have been those people who gathered men to themselves in secret or distant places such as deserts or caverns or inner rooms, to rid themselves from the yoke of the Roman empire by force. Jesus had already spoken of the tribulation that was to come and knew that when people feel devoid of direction in the face of adversity, they are vulnerable to deception, to lies and untruths that would blind them to the way of repentance and increase unrighteousness. Long before, Moses had given the people a similar warning, as we read in Deuteronomy 13:1-3,

> "If there arises among you a prophet or a dreamer of dreams, and he gives you a sign or a wonder, and the sign or the wonder comes to pass, of which he spoke to you, saying, 'Let us go after other gods' – which you have not known – 'and let us serve them.' You shall not listen to the words of that prophet or that dreamer of dreams, for the Lord your God is testing you to know whether you love the Lord your God with all your heart and with all your soul."

In former times, people have been persuaded by 'signs and wonders'; in contemporary society people can be persuaded by 'science' and 'rationality' and their own interpretation of God's command to love. To guard against imposters and false doctrine, it is essential for Christians to confirm 'signs and wonders' by the word of God and remain attentive to potential snares. Christ has forewarned His disciples to anticipate temptation and to stand fast against the stumbling blocks of false prophets and doctrines. Jesus stated clearly that He had told His disciples what would happen as God Himself declares the end from the beginning, as we read in Isaiah 46:9-11,

> "Remember the former things of old, for I am God, and there is no other; I am God, and there is none like Me, declaring the end from the beginning, and from ancient times things that are not yet done, saying, 'My counsel shall stand, and I will do all My pleasure,' calling a bird of prey from the east, the man who executes My counsel, from a far country."

It is interesting to note that the Greek word 'parousia', although often translated as 'coming' in this context the coming of the Son of Man, can also be translated as presence, the presence of the Son of Man. In the proverbial utterance that Jesus used about the gathering of birds of prey around a carcass, the word eagle may have been deliberately substituted for vulture as a reference to the eagle-bearing standard of the Roman legions. Vultures, or eagles, will descend swiftly on a potential feast; the day when the Son of Man is revealed with judgement, will be swift. Jesus' words may also have been intended to remind the disciples that the Redeemer should no longer be sought within the confines of Judea because His kingdom would extend to the uttermost ends of the world as we read in Job 37:2-3,

> "Hear attentively the thunder of His voice, and the rumbling that comes from His mouth. He sends it forth under the whole heaven, His lightening to the ends of the earth."

Matthew 24:29-31

In verses 29-31, Jesus continued His teaching about the coming tribulation that had been foretold, saying,

> "And immediately after the affliction days of those the sun will be darkened, and the moon will not give the light of her, and the stars will fall from heaven, and the powers of the heavens will be shaken. And then will appear the sign of the Son of man in heaven, and then will bewail all the tribes of the land and they will see the Son of man coming on the clouds of heaven with power and glory much; and he will send the angels of him with trumpet a great, and they will assemble the chosen of him out of the four winds from the extremities of the heavens unto the extremities of them."

The language of darkness and stars falling that Jesus used was typically used to mean great upheavals or turmoil on earth. Similar language was used to foretell the destruction of Babylon and of Tyre, Egypt and other nations including Israel. The language was intended to convey the coming of terrible calamities, such as the destruction of Jerusalem and the slaughter of more than a million Jews by the Roman legions in AD 70, as we read for example in Isaiah 13:9-10 and Joel 2:10-11,

> 'Behold, the day of the Lord comes, cruel, with both wrath and fierce anger, to lay the land desolate; and He will destroy its sinners from it. For the stars of heaven and their constellations will not give their light; the sun will be darkened in its going forth, and the moon will not cause its light to shine.'

> 'The earth quakes before them, the heavens tremble; the sun and moon grow dark, and the stars diminish their brightness.'

When Jesus spoke of the wailing or mourning of the people when they would see the sign of the Son of Man, it is likely to have been a reference to the prophecy of His crucifixion; that the people would mourn for Him whom they had pierced, as prophesied in Zechariah 12:10,

450

"And I will pour on the house of David and on the inhabitants of Jerusalem the Spirit of grace and supplication; then they will look on Me whom they pierced. Yes, they will   mourn for Him as one mourns for his only son, grieve for Him as for a firstborn."

Jesus went on to describe the Son of Man coming on clouds of heaven, using the imagery we find in the prophecies of Daniel. It is most likely that clouds are an indication of power and judgement rather than a visible object – similar imagery is also used in the Psalms, as we read in Daniel 7:13-14 and Psalm 104:3,

"I was watching in the night visions, and behold, One like the Son of Man, coming with the clouds of heaven! He came to the Ancient of Days, and they brought Him near before Him. Then to Him was given dominion and glory and a kingdom, that all peoples, nations, and languages should serve Him. His dominion is an everlasting dominion, which shall not pass away, and His kingdom the one which shall not be destroyed."

'He lays the beams of His upper chambers in the waters, who makes the clouds His chariot, who walks on the wings of the wind.'

But Jesus didn't return in AD 70 – this is yet to come. The early Church began in tribulation and so it has continued, but there will be an end and there will be signs of an end. The Lord will send His angels, to gather His Church as we read in Joel 2:30-32 and Psalm 22:27,

"And I will show wonders in the heavens and in the earth; blood and fire and pillars of smoke. The sun shall be turned into darkness, and the moon into blood, before the coming of the great and awesome day of the Lord. And it shall come to pass that whoever calls on the name of the Lord shall be saved."

'All the ends of the world shall remember and turn to the Lord, and all the families of the nations shall worship before You.'

451

Matthew 24:32-35

In verses 32-35, Jesus reiterated the Prophecy of the coming destruction of the temple and of Jerusalem, and that this would happen within the lifespan of their generation. He also reaffirmed His own infinite status as the Son of God saying,

> "From now the fig tree learn ye the parable: When now the branch of it becomes tender and the leaves it put forth, ye know that near is the summer; so also, ye when ye see all these things, know that near it is at the doors. Truly I tell you that by no means passes away generation this until all these things happen. The heaven and the earth will pass away, but the words of me by no means may pass away."

In the foregoing verses, Jesus had spoken about the rise of false prophets; we can presume that the appearance of these false messiahs, like the first fig leaves, would be an indication of what was coming. We humans can recognise the signs of impending changes in nature; in the same way, Jesus' followers would be able to recognise the signs that the prophecy was about to be fulfilled since He had told them what they would be. The loss of their inheritance following the destruction of the temple was foretold in Isaiah 63:18-19,

> 'Your holy people have possessed it but a little while; our adversaries have trodden down Your sanctuary. We have become like those of old, over whom You never ruled, those who were never called by Your name.'

It is interesting to note that the destruction of the temple occurred exactly forty years from this prophecy. Forty years was considered to be a generation and Jesus' reference to 'this generation' echoes that of the generation that had to wander through the wilderness for forty years because of their disobedience, as we read for example in Psalm 95:10,

> 'For forty years I was grieved with that generation, and said, 'It is a people who go astray in their hearts, and they do not know My ways.'

452

Having declared this prophecy, Christ then reminded His listeners that creation, both visible and invisible, is time-limited and will pass away, as we read in Isaiah 51:6,

> "Lift up your eyes to the heavens and look on the earth beneath. For the heavens will vanish away like smoke, the earth will grow old like a garment, and those who dwell in it will die in like manner; but My salvation will be forever, and My righteousness will not be abolished."

Jesus then stated that His words will endure beyond time, thereby putting Himself on a par with God the Father. For the present generation this is the enduring message, that the word of God stands forever, that it will not alter or change, and that it will achieve all that the Father desires, as we read for example in Isaiah 40:8, 55:10-11, Numbers 23:19, Psalm 89:34, and Psalm 102:25-27,

> "The grass withers, the flower fades, but the word of our God stands forever."

> "For as the rain comes down, and the snow from heaven, and do not return from there, but water the earth, and make it bring forth and bud, that it may give seed to the sower and bread to the eater, so shall My word be that goes forth from My mouth; it shall not return to Me void, but it shall accomplish what I please, and it shall prosper in the thing for which I sent it."

> "God is not a man, that He should lie, nor a son of man, that He should repent. Has He said, and will He not do? Or has He spoken, and will He not make it good?"

> 'My covenant I will not break, nor alter the word that has gone out of My lips.'

> 'Of old You laid the foundation of the earth, and the heavens are the work of Your hands. They will perish, but You will endure; yes, they will all grow old like a garment; like a cloak You will change them, and they will be changed. But You are the same, and Your years will have no end.'

453

Matthew 24:36-39

In verses 36-39, Jesus answered the second of the disciples' questions, in which they had asked Him what the sign of His coming and the end of the age would be, saying,

> "But concerning that day and hour no one knows, neither the angels of the heavens not the Son, except the Father only. For as the days of Noah, so will be the presence of the Son of man. For as they were in days those the ones before the flood eating and drinking, marrying and being given in marriage, until which day entered Noah into the ark, and knew not until came the flood and took all, so will be the presence of the Son of man."

Here Jesus clearly stated that no one knows the day or hour of the end of the age except the Father. The first disciples wanted to know when the completion of the age in His presence would be, and Christians have pondered this question ever since that first generation. This knowledge, Jesus told them, is kept even from the angels, but is known to the Father, as we read in Zechariah 14:5-7,

> 'Thus, the Lord my God will come, and all the saints with You. It shall come to pass in that day that there will be no light; the lights will diminish. It shall be one day which is known to the Lord – neither day nor night. But at evening time it shall happen that it will be light.'

When He referred to the time of Noah, Jesus was not condemning the people for eating and drinking etc, but for their obstinacy and self-absorption that led to them failing to heed the warnings of imminent destruction. They were living in a state of indifference, thinking only of the cares and desires of their every-day life, out of touch with their heavenly maker. Speaking through Isaiah, the Lord used the account of Noah to remind the people of His covenant with them that would remain beyond the completion of the age as we read in Isaiah 54:9-10,

> "For this is like the waters of Noah to Me; for as I have sworn that the waters of Noah would no longer cover the earth, so I have

454

sworn that I would not be angry with you, nor rebuke you. For the mountains shall depart and the hills be removed, but My kindness shall not depart from you, nor shall My covenant of peace be removed," says the Lord, who has mercy on you.'

In Genesis 15:6, we read that Abraham believed in the Lord and that He accredited it to him as righteousness. Before Abraham, Noah was seen by God as righteous; Noah listened to and believed God and was, therefore, delivered from trouble. We cannot know if God sent messages of warning to others at that time, or since, but we do know that Noah listened, obeyed, and was thus saved from destruction. What we do know for sure is that for everyone there will be a final day to our earthly life when we will be in His presence, and for that we must be ready minute-by-minute since only God knows when that will be. In His presence, the righteous, like Noah, will be delivered, as we read in Genesis 7:1, Proverbs 11:5-6 and 8, and Psalm 1:5-6,

> 'Then the Lord said to Noah, "Come into the ark, you and all your household, because I have seen that you are righteous before Me in this generation."

> 'The righteousness of the blameless will direct his way aright, but the wicked will fall by his own wickedness. The righteousness of the upright will deliver them, but the unfaithful will be caught by their lust.'

> 'The righteous is delivered from trouble, and it comes to the wicked instead.'

> 'Therefore, the ungodly shall not stand in the judgement, nor sinners in the congregation of the righteous. For the Lord knows the way of the righteous, but the way of the ungodly shall perish.'

Matthew 24:40-44

In verses 40-44, Jesus continued His warning regarding the end of the age and the reference to the time of Noah when the people were going about their daily lives, saying,

> "Then will be two men in the field, one is taken, and one is left; two women grinding at the mill, one is taken, and one is left. Watch ye therefore, because ye know not on what day the Lord of you is coming. And that know ye if knew the housemaster in that watch the thief is coming, he would have watched and would not have allowed to be dug through the house of him. Therefore, also ye be ready, because in which ye think not hour the Son of man comes."

People who are going about their daily routine cannot escape the inevitable judgement that will come to each individual; we are all bound together in this inevitability. Scripture makes it clear that each person will be judged on their own merits, not on the merits of others. The ones left standing will be those who have remained faithful to Christ. There are echoes in these words of Jesus with those of Moses at the time of the Exodus, as we read in Exodus 11:5,

> 'And all the firstborn in the land of Egypt shall die, from the firstborn of Pharaoh who sits on his throne, even to the firstborn of the female servant who is behind the hand mill, and all the firstborn of the animals.'

If, for example, you are waiting for a message or a call, you don't stop everything and just sit about waiting, you would typically get on with whatever you would normally do during the day but keep your ears and eyes open so that you would hear, for example, the beep or buzz of a device or the sound of a vehicle on the driveway, so that even while you are carrying out your daily routine part of your mind is occupied with that expected connection. In the same way, if a person remains aware of the presence of the Lord throughout their day, they stand a greater chance of receiving His connection, as we read in Proverbs 4:23-27 and Deuteronomy 4:9,

'Keep your heart with all diligence, for out of it spring the issues of life. Put away from you a deceitful mouth and put perverse lips far from you. Let your eyes look straight ahead, and your eyelids look right before you. Ponder the path of your feet and let all your ways be established. Do not turn to the right or the left; remove your foot from evil.'

'Take heed to yourself, and diligently keep yourself, lest you forget the things your eyes have seen, and lest they depart from your heart all the days of your life. And teach them to your children and your grandchildren.'

The word 'watch' means uninterrupted attention on the focus of interest, which in this case, is the coming presence of Christ. As with a police stake-out, a distraction of even the most mundane nature, can lead to the failure to capture the target moment. The Christian must keep diligent watch without distraction for even a single hour. The lesson for those listening to this discourse is that they should keep on the alert and be ready for that day when it comes. They must continue to trust in Christ and demonstrate constancy in faith, to not hesitate or give way, and not lose heart; they must continue faithfully in the work assigned to them, whether working in the field or the mill. Jesus' disciples are to maintain faithful obedience, waiting for the time when they will all have to render an account of the stewardship to which they were called, as we read in Proverbs 8:33-35, Psalm 130:5-6 and Micah 7:7,

'Hear instruction and be wise, and do not disdain it. Blessed is the man who listens to me, watching daily at my gates, waiting at the posts of my doors. For whoever finds me finds life and obtains favour from the Lord.'

'I wait for the Lord, my soul waits, and in His word I do hope. My soul waits for the Lord more than those who watch for the morning.'

'Therefore I will look to the Lord; I will wait for the God of my salvation; my God will hear me.'

457

Matthew 24:45-51

In verses 45-51, having taught that all His followers should remain alert, faithful, and obedient, Jesus continued His warning to those appointed to positions of responsibility, saying,

> "Who then is the faithful slave and prudent whom appointed the lord over the household of him to give them the food in season? Blessed is slave that whom coming the lord of him will find so doing; truly I tell you that over all the goods of him he will appoint him. But if says wicked slave that in the heart of him: Delays of me the lord, and begins to strike the fellow slaves of him, and eats and drinks with the ones being drunk, will come the lord slave of that on a day on which he does not expect and in an hour in which not he knows, and will cut asunder him, and the portion of him with the hypocrites will place; there will be the wailing and the gnashing of teeth."

In these days of awareness about climate change and the impact of pollution on the environment, it is perhaps worth remembering that God appointed mankind as stewards over all creation. The household and all the goods in this parable may apply to both humanity and all of creation. Jesus' words echoed those found in Psalm 104:24-27,

> 'O Lord, how manifold are Your works! In wisdom You have made them all. The earth is full of Your possessions – this great and wide sea, in which are innumerable teeming things, living things both small and great. There the ships sail about; there is that Leviathan which You have made to play there. These all wait for You, that You may give them their food in due season.'

Those who trust to a long delay to the day of judgement – a day that maybe never comes, under the pretext of Christ's absence, deceive themselves into believing that they will remain unpunished and justify their own actions to themselves, as we read in Ecclesiastes 8:11 and as a warning in Deuteronomy 15:9,

'Because the sentence against an evil work is not executed speedily, therefore the heart of the sons of men is fully set in them to do evil.'

'Beware lest there be a wicked thought in your heart, saying, 'The seventh year, the year of release, is at hand,' and your eye be evil against your brother, and you give him nothing, and he cry out to the Lord against you, and it becomes sin amongst you.'

Jesus elaborated on the way that sin grows so that not only does the wicked servant fail to do good, but actively wastes his master's property and demonstrates cruelty to those he should care for. There are clear warnings to those who are leaders in Isaiah 56:12 and Ezekiel 34:2,

'His watchmen are blind, they are all ignorant; they are all dumb dogs, they cannot bark; sleeping, lying down, loving to slumber. Yes, they are greedy dogs which never have enough. And they are shepherds who cannot understand; they all look to their own way, everyone for his own gain, from his own territory. "Come," one says, "I will bring wine, and we will fill ourselves with intoxicating drink; tomorrow will be as today, and much more abundant."

'You eat the fat and clothe yourselves with the wool; you slaughter the fatlings, but you do not feed the flock.'

The punishment Jesus referred to was the most severe that was customary at that time. Those who have been appointed to positions of greater responsibilities bear a greater burden of service, but those who remain faithful will also receive the Lord's blessings promised for example in Psalm 112:1 and 10 and Daniel 12:3,

'Blessed is the man who fears the Lord, who delights greatly in His commandments. [...] The wicked will see it and be grieved; he will gnash his teeth and melt away; the desire of the wicked shall perish.'

'Those who are wise shall shine like the brightness of the firmament, and those who turn many to righteousness like the stars forever and ever.'

MATTHEW CHAPTER TWENTY-FIVE

Matthew 25:1-13

In verses 1-13, we read the parable of the ten virgins, in which Jesus used local customs to demonstrate what happens to those who are unprepared, saying,

> "Then shall be likened the kingdom of the heavens to ten virgins, who taking the lamps of them went forth to a meeting of the bridegroom. Now five of them were foolish and five prudent. For the foolish ones taking the lamps did not take with them oil. But the prudent ones took oil in the vessels with the lamps of them. But delaying the bridegroom slumbered all and slept. And in the middle of the night a cry there has been: Behold, the bridegroom, go ye forth to a meeting. Then were raised all virgins those and trimmed the lamps of them. So, the foolish ones to the prudent said: Give us of the oil of you, because the lamps of us are being quenched. But answered the prudent saying: Lest by no means it suffices to us and to you; go ye rather to the ones selling and buy for yourselves. And as they were going away to buy came the bridegroom, and the ready ones went in with him to the wedding festivities and was shut the door. Then later come also the remaining virgins saying: Lord, Lord, open to us.   But   he answering said: Truly I say to you, I know not you. Watch ye therefore, because ye know not the day nor the hour."

Wedding feasts at the time of Jesus were public events for the neighbourhood where all were welcome. It seems this wedding custom was still in existence in Galilee at least up to the 20th century, including the custom of the bridegroom deliberately appearing at an unexpected hour, even in the middle of the night. This perhaps has some significance given that it was in the middle of the night that at the time of Moses the firstborn of the Egyptians died, but the firstborn of the Israelites were passed over, and they subsequently received their freedom. It was also at midnight that Samson tore down the gates to the city of Gaza (Judges 16:3), and at midnight that Boaz awoke and made his promise to Ruth (Ruth 3:11). Even at midnight God's people are not afraid of the darkness in the world, as we read in Psalm 119:62,

'At midnight I will rise to give thanks to You, because of Your righteous judgements.'

None of the virgins in the story were in positions of responsibility, but ordinary members of the community; we can take this to mean that here Jesus was addressing all His children in general. The prudent could not give their oil to the others; this is a reminder that a person cannot borrow their character or relationship with God from another; each person must acquire this for themselves, as we read in Psalm 49:7 and Ezekiel 14:20,

> 'None of them can by any means redeem his brother, nor give to God a ransom for him.'

> 'Even though Noah, Daniel, and Job were in it [Jerusalem], as I live" says the Lord God, "They would deliver neither son nor daughter; they would deliver only themselves by their righteousness."

The imprudent virgins were not punished as such but were excluded from the feast. They had oil initially but not enough for their needs. The prudent had oil in reserve for any eventuality. Jesus' teaching is that it is not enough to have been ready and prepared at one time in your life but then to let this preparedness lapse or leave things to the last minute; the Christian must persevere, wait, and trust in the Lord's salvation, as we read in Isaiah 25:9, Psalm 45:14-15 and Psalm 50:4-5,

> 'And it will be said in that day: "Behold, this is our God; we have waited for Him, and He will save us. This is the Lord; we have waited for Him; we will be glad and rejoice in His salvation."

> 'The virgins, her companions who follow her, shall be brought to You. With gladness and rejoicing they shall be brought; they shall enter the King's palace.'

> 'He shall call to the heavens from above, and to the earth, that He may judge His people: "Gather My saints together to Me, those who have made a covenant with Me by sacrifice." Let the heavens declare His righteousness, for God Himself is Judge.'

463

Matthew 25:14-18

In verses 14-18, we read Jesus' opening sentences of what is known as the parable of the talents.

> "For as a man going from home called his own slaves and delivered to them the goods of him, and to one he gave five talents, to another two, to another one, to each according to his own ability, and went from home. Immediately going the one the five talents receiving traded in them and gained other five; similarly, the one receiving two gained another two. But the one the one receiving going away dug earth and hid the silver of the lord of him."

The word talent has in recent times been used to mean some kind of ability that a person is born with - a gift, something in a person's genetic makeup. This concept of the word can allow people a kind of way out by claiming that they do not have a 'talent' for doing a particular thing, therefore they cannot be expected to do it. Furthermore, people who have worked hard to develop a skill are spoken of as having a 'talent' as if they have been blessed with a gift that did not require any effort on their part. A talent was a weight, often of silver or other precious metals that represented a person's wealth as we read for example in 1 Chronicles 29:6-7 when the people of Israel offered their wealth towards the construction of the temple.

> 'Then the leaders of the fathers' houses, leaders of the tribes of Israel, the captains of thousands and of hundreds, with the officers over the king's work, offered willingly. They gave for the work of the house of God five thousand talents and ten thousand darics of gold, ten thousand talents of silver, eighteen thousand talents of bronze, and one hundred thousand talents of iron.'

In this parable, the master of the servants apportioned various sums into their care. The Greek word 'dynamin' is typically translated as ability, leading us to presume that these servants had differing abilities. However, the word can also be translated as power, strength, nature, or virtue, in other words what kind of person they were. It could have been their business acumen, or perhaps their conscientiousness in this context, since later the one is referred to as being lazy or slothful. From this perspective, the servants were not given the talents according to some innate ability, according to their genetic makeup, but according to their service record. The contrast between the two who made good use of the talents and the one who buried the silver is spoken of in Proverbs 3:9-10, 27:18, 18:9, and 26:13-16.

> 'Honour the Lord with your possessions, and with the first fruits of all your increase; so your barns will be filled with plenty, and your vats will overflow with new wine.'

> 'Whoever keeps the fig tree will eat its fruit; so he who waits on his master will be honoured.'

> 'He who is slothful in his work is a brother to him who is a great destroyer.'

> 'The lazy man says, "There is a lion in the road! A fierce lion is in the streets!" As a door turns on its hinges, so does the lazy man on his bed. The lazy man buries his hand in the bowl; it wearies him to bring it back to his mouth. The lazy man is wiser in his own eyes than seven men who can answer sensibly.'

Whatever has been entrusted into the care or keeping of God's people, they are expected to use and be productive – not to bury or hide it, or even just store it away, but to increase it. That which we have stewardship over need not be just material but also spiritual. The reward for faithful stewardship is to receive double what has been given and a place in the kingdom. The message in the earlier parable about the ten virgins was about preparedness, the message here is about service; making a spiritual profit from the deposit that God has made with us, and receive the promised reward as we read in 1 Chronicles 29:12,

> 'Both riches and honour come from You. And You reign over all. In Your hand is power and might; in Your hand it is to make great and to give strength to all.'

465

Matthew 25:19-23

In verses 19-23, we find the next part of the parable of the talents, in which Jesus foretells His return after what He describes as 'much time', saying,

> "Then after much time comes the lord slaves of those and takes account with them. And approaching the one the five talents receiving brought other five talents saying: Lord, five talents to me thou deliveredst; behold other five talents I gained. Said to him the lord of him: Well, slave good and faithful, over a few things thou wast faithful, over many thee will I set; enter thou into the joy of the lord of thee. Approaching also the one having received the two talents said: Lord, two talents to me thou deliveredst; behold other two talents I gained. Said to him the lord of him: Well, slave good and faithful, over a few things thou wast faithful, over many thee will I set; enter thou into the joy of the lord of thee."

In the parable, and we can presume therefore also in the heavenly Kingdom, the settling of accounts was on an individual basis. Each individual received their own reward; it was not considered to have been a team effort where there might be a joint reward. It will not be the church congregation, but each individual that makes up a congregation whose accounts will be settled. It is also worth noting that their reward was that more work, or responsibility, was given. It is also significant that the second man received the same commendation as the first, making it clear that it is not the amount of service that counts but its quality. Those who demonstrate wisdom, righteousness and faithfulness will reap the king's reward as we read in Proverbs 14:35, 16:13, and 28:20,

> 'The king's favour is toward a wise servant, but his wrath is against him who causes shame.'

> 'Righteous lips are the delight of kings, and they love him who speaks what is right.'

'A faithful man will abound with blessings, but he who hastens to be rich will not go unpunished.'

The virgins in the previous parable were expected to wait; the three in this parable were employed and expected to work until their master's return – it was their outward activity, not their inner spiritual life, that was to be reckoned. The implication is that God expects His employees to advance the work of His kingdom and make the most of every opportunity. Faithfulness, according to this parable, is using what God has entrusted to advance His interests in the world. An Old Testament example of faithfulness was Hezekiah, as we read in 2 Chronicles 31:20-21,

> 'Thus Hezekiah did throughout all Judah, and he did what was good and right and true before the Lord his God. And in every work that he began in the service of the house of God, in the law and in the commandment to seek his God, he did it with all his heart. So he prospered.'

The two faithful servants were invited to enter the joy of the master. The words Jesus used, "Enter into the joy of your Lord" are not the words of an earthly master when rewarding servants, but clearly the language of the heavenly kingdom. It is also the language we find in the Psalms and the prophets, as we read for example in Psalm 16:11, 43:3-4, and Isaiah 35:10,

> 'You will show me the path of life; in Your presence is fullness of joy; at Your right hand are pleasures forevermore.'

> 'Oh, send out Your light and Your truth! Let them lead me; let them bring me to Your holy hill and to Your tabernacle. Then I will go to the altar of God, to God my exceeding joy; and on the harp I will praise You, O God, my God.'

> 'And the ransomed of the Lord shall return, and come to Zion with singing, with everlasting joy on their heads. They shall obtain joy and gladness, and sorrow and sighing shall flee away.'

Matthew 25:24-30

In verses 24-30, we read the final part of the parable of the talents in which the accounts were settled for the third servant whom Jesus contrasted with the faithful servants, saying,

> "And approaching also the one the one talent having received said: Lord, I knew thee that a hard man thou art, reaping where thou didst not sow, and gathering whence thou did not scatter; and fearing, going away I hid the talent of thee in the earth; behold thou hast the thine. And answering, the lord of him said to him: Evil slave and slothful, thou knowest that I reap where I sowed not, and I gather whence I did not scatter? It behoved thee therefore to put the silver pieces of me to the bankers, and coming I would have received the mine with interest. Take therefore from him the talent and give to the one having the ten talents, for to having everyone will be given and he will have abundance; but from the one not having even what he has will be taken from him. And the useless slave cast ye out into the darkness outer; there will be the wailing and the gnashing of the teeth."

According to the parable, the one-talent servant had done no harm through his actions, but neither had he done any good with what was entrusted to him. His actions sprang from a distrust of his master, from the conviction that his master would not be fair. God does not judge His people by what they don't have, only by the use of what they have been entrusted with. The talent of silver was buried in the ground where it was useless; the religious leaders of the day effectively buried the Law in a myriad of rules and regulations so that the Law was made useless. That which was given to the people of Israel, and subsequently to the Christian Church, is to be used to profit the kingdom or, we can conclude, it risks falling into spiritual poverty as we read in Proverbs 6:6-11,

> 'Go to the ant, you sluggard! Consider her ways and be wise, which, having no captain, overseer or ruler, provides her supplies in the summer, and gathers her food in the harvest. How long will you slumber, O sluggard? When will you rise from your sleep? A little sleep, a little slumber, a little folding of the hands to sleep –

so shall your poverty come on you like a prowler, and your need like an armed man.'

Banquets were, and still are, usually held at night, so that there is a contrast between the light and illumination within the banqueting hall and the darkness outside to where those who are not welcome are cast out. The gnashing of teeth was an expression of anger, as we read for example in Psalm 112:10 that contrasts the righteous man with the wicked,

> 'He has dispersed abroad; he has given to the poor; his righteousness endures for ever; his horn will be exalted with honour. The wicked will see it and be grieved; he will gnash his teeth and melt away; the desires of the wicked shall perish.'

The master in the parable had in fact lost out because of this servant's failure to deposit the silver to at least gain interest. Jesus was not approving of usury, He would have been well aware of the law found in Deuteronomy 23:19-20,

> "You shall not charge interest to your brother – interest in money or food or anything that is lent out at interest. To a foreigner you may charge interest, but to your brother you shall not charge interest."

Rather, the message is that there is no excuse for indolence and idleness. It is often the lazy children in a classroom that fear their teacher. The third servant was described as lazy, or slothful. Clearly, he did not serve his master with his whole heart and strength. By contrast those who are faithful and work for the Lord with all their heart, soul, and strength will receive blessings in abundance, as we read in Proverbs 22:13, 20:4, and Job 42:10,

> 'The lazy man says, "There is a lion outside! I shall be slain in the streets!"'
> 'The lazy man will not plough because of winter; he will beg during harvest and have nothing.'

> 'And the Lord restored Job's losses when he prayed for his friends. Indeed, the Lord gave Job twice as much as he had before.'

469

Matthew 25:31-33

In verses 31-33, Jesus spoke to His disciples about His coming and the judgement to come that had long been prophesied, saying,

> "And when comes the Son of man in the glory of him and all the angels with him, then he will sit on a throne of glory of him; and will be assembled before him all the nations, and he will separate them from one another, as the shepherd separates the sheep from the goats, and will set the sheep on the right of him, but the goats on the left."

Jesus told the disciples that He would come in glory and with all the angels, echoing the words found in the prophet Zechariah 14:5,

> 'Thus the Lord my God will come, and all the saints with You.'

Once on His throne, the nations will be assembled before Him. The Greek words 'panta ta ethnē' is translated here as all the nations. It is the plural, and can also mean peoples or people groups, pagans, tribes, Gentiles, or a body of persons united by kinship, culture, and common traditions. Clearly no one is exempt from this judgement. There is a common theme throughout Scripture that there are two kinds of people: the wheat and the chaff; the wise and the foolish; the righteous and the wicked; God's people and those who are not. Sheep in Scripture represent innocence and harmlessness deserving of honour; goats represent greed, selfishness and disobedience, deserving of dishonour, as we read for example in Psalm 78:52, Ezekiel 34:17-18 and 20,

> 'But He made His own people go forth like sheep and guided them in the wilderness like a flock.'

> 'And as for you, O My flock, thus says the Lord God: "Behold, I shall judge between sheep and sheep, between rams and goats. Is it too little for you to have eaten up the good pasture, that you must tread down with your feet the residue of your pasture – and to have drunk of the clear waters, that you must foul the residue with your feet?'

'Therefore thus says the Lord God to them: "Behold, I Myself will judge between the fat and lean sheep."'

The throne of judgement and the judgement of all people in righteousness had long been prophesied, so that those listening to Jesus would have been familiar with the Scriptures on this, as we read for example in 1 Samuel 2:10, Psalm 9:7, and 98:9,

'The adversaries of the Lord shall be broken in pieces; from heaven He will thunder against them. The Lord will judge the ends of the earth.'

'But the Lord shall endure forever; He has prepared His throne for judgement. He shall judge the world in righteousness, and He shall administer judgement for the peoples in uprightness.'

'For He is coming to judge the earth. With righteousness He shall judge the world, and the peoples with equity.'

In Jewish and many other cultures, the right hand signifies approval and eminence; the left hand signifies rejection and disapproval. In many ways this is like the Roman thumbs up or thumbs down by which a person in an amphitheatre was reprieved or condemned. To sit at the right hand was more than a reprieve; it was to be elevated as Jesus Himself is elevated to the highest throne, as we read for example in 1 Kings 2:19, Psalm 45:9 and 110:1

'And the king rose up to meet her [Bathsheba] and bowed down to her, and sat down on his throne and had a throne set for the king's mother; so she sat at his right hand.'

'King's daughters are among Your honourable women; at Your right hand stands the queen in gold from Ophir.'

'The Lord said to my Lord, "Sit at My right hand, till I make Your enemies Your footstool.'

Matthew 25:34-40

In verses 34-40, Jesus made it clear who will be on His right, who are the blessed ones of the Father, saying,

> "Then will say the king to the ones on the right of him: Come the ones blessed of the Father of me, inherit ye the having been prepared for you kingdom from the foundation of the world. For I hungered and ye gave me to eat, I thirsted and ye gave drink me, a stranger I was and ye entertained me, naked and ye clothed me, I ailed and ye visited me, in prison I was and ye came to me. Then will answer him the righteous saying: Lord, when thee saw we hungering and fed, or thirsting and gave drink? And when thee saw a stranger and entertained, or naked and clothed? And when thee saw we ailing or in prison and came to thee? And answering the king will say to them: Truly I tell you, inasmuch as ye did to one of these brothers of me the least, to me ye did."

A person can only move in one direction at a time, left or right, up or down; a choice has to be made. Those who have made the right choices in life are the blessed of the Father, the ones who are dear or beloved by God. His people have been given clear guidance as to what are the right choices, as we read for example in Isaiah 1:16-17 and 58:6-7,

> "Wash yourselves, make yourselves clean; put away the evil of your doings from before My eyes. Cease to do evil, learn to do good; seek justice, rebuke the oppressor; defend the fatherless, plead for the widow."

> 'Is this not the fast that I have chosen: to loose the bonds of wickedness, to undo the heavy burdens, to let the oppressed go free, and that you break every yoke? Is it not to share your bread with the hungry and that you bring to your house the poor who are cast out; when you see the naked that you cover him, and not hide yourself from your own flesh?'

The list of kindnesses that Jesus gave here were some of those listed in Scripture, but perhaps more importantly, Jesus' words also acknowledge the acts of kindness that have been performed without any expectation of reward. In his own defence, Job helpfully lists his own acts of kindness or mercy to others, as we read in Job 31:16-20 and 32,

> 'If I have kept the poor from their desire, or caused the eyes of the widow to fail, or eaten my morsel by myself, so that the fatherless could not eat of it [...]; if I have seen anyone perish from lack of clothing, or any poor man without covering; if his heart has not blessed me, and if he was not warmed with the fleece of my sheep.'

> 'But no sojourner had to lodge in the street, for I have opened my doors to the traveller.'

Our treatment of others determines our relationship to God the Father. If we defraud another, we defraud God. Jesus wasn't speaking about something that was new, the knowledge that the way we treat others is the way we treat the Lord was made clear in Scripture, acknowledging that God has created all things and is in all things, as is the promise of life to those who make the right choices, as we read for example in Ezekiel 18:5-9, Proverbs 14:31, 19:17, and in the words of David in 1 Chronicles 29:14,

> 'If a man is just and does what is lawful and right; [...] if he has not oppressed anyone, but has restored to the debtor his pledge; has robbed no one by violence, but has given his bread to the hungry and covered the naked with clothing [...] if he has walked in My statutes and kept My judgements faithfully – he is just; he shall surely live!'

> 'He who oppresses the poor reproaches his Maker, but he who honours Him has mercy on the needy.'

> 'He who has pity on the poor lends to the Lord, and He will pay back what he has given.'

> 'But who am I, and who are my people, that we should be able to offer so willingly as this? For all things come from You, and of Your own we have given You.'

473

Matthew 25:41-46

In verses 41-46, Jesus explained who will be on His left at the judgement, those who have become cursed, saying,

> "Then he will say also to the ones on the left: Go from me having been cursed ones into the fire eternal having been prepared for the devil and the angels of him. For I hungered and ye gave not me to eat, I thirsted and ye gave not drink me, a stranger I was and ye entertained not me, naked and ye clothed not me, ill and in prison and ye visited not me. Then will answer also they saying: Lord, when thee saw we hungering or thirsting or a stranger or naked or ill or in prison and did not minister to thee? Then he will answer them saying: Truly I tell you, inasmuch as ye did not to one of these least ones, neither to me ye did. And will go away these into punishment eternal, but the righteous into life eternal."

The devil and his angels were condemned, and a place prepared for them, before creation; those who are put on the left hand are cursed, which is the opposite of being blessed, and condemned to exclusion from the kingdom of heaven because they refuse to receive God's blessing and salvation as we read in Psalm 119:21, Proverbs 22:8, and Isaiah 66:24,

> 'You rebuke the proud – the cursed, who stray from Your commandments.'

> 'He who sows iniquity will reap sorrow, and the rod of his anger will fail.'

> 'And they shall go forth and look upon the corpses of the men who have transgressed against Me. For their worm does not die, and their fire is not quenched. They shall be an abhorrence to all flesh.'

Jesus was teaching about the sin of neglect and indifference; about those who have no compassion for others. Having rejected mercy towards others, they are unable to receive it themselves since they have demonstrated disdain for mercy itself. Clearly, they have deceived

474

themselves into thinking that they will not be held to account for despising others since they seem to have no awareness of their own failings. Refusing to do what God commands by neglect is as much a sin as a violation of the law, as we read in Ezekiel 34:4, Psalm 82:3-4, Jeremiah 22:3,

> "The weak you have not strengthened, nor have you healed those who were sick, nor bound up the broken, nor brought back what was driven away, nor sought what was   lost; but with force and cruelty you have ruled them."

> 'Defend the poor and the fatherless; do justice to the afflicted and needy; deliver the poor and needy; free them from the hand of the wicked.'

> "Thus says the Lord: "Execute judgements and righteousness and deliver the plundered out of the hand of the oppressor. Do no wrong and do no violence to the stranger, the fatherless, or the widow, nor shed innocent blood in this place."

All people have a conscience by which they will be judged, so that even those who have not heard the law will be judged on their actions. Although the Old Testament doesn't mention conscience, the heart is clearly where the conscience resides, as we read for example in Proverbs 2:1-9, Jeremiah 17:10 and 31:34,

> 'My son, if you receive my words, and treasure my commands within you, so that you incline your ear to wisdom and apply your heart to understanding [...] Then you will understand righteousness and justice, equity and every good path.'

> 'I the Lord search the heart, I test the mind, even to give every man according to his ways, according to the fruit of his doings.'

> 'No more shall every man teach his neighbour, and every man his brother, saying, 'Know the Lord,' for they shall all know Me, from the least of them to the greatest of them, says the Lord.'

475

MATTHEW CHAPTER TWENTY-SIX

Matthew 26:2

In verse 2, having concluded His teaching about the time of judgement, Jesus reminded His disciples about His own death that had long been foretold, saying,

> "Ye know that after two days the Passover occurs, and the Son of man is delivered to be crucified."

Jesus was very specific as to the day of His crucifixion – that it would take place after two days, suggesting that this was said on a Wednesday, and clearly linking His death with the Passover. The Passover always began at sundown on the 14th day of the first moon, in the first month, Nisan, which means that it came on a different day of the week each year. In this particular year it fell on the sabbath. The Passover represented the deliverance of Israel from the slavery of Egypt, as we read in Exodus 12:12-14; Jesus also referred to Himself as the Son of man as we read in Psalm 80:17,

> 'For I will pass through the land of Egypt on that night and will strike all the firstborn in the land of Egypt, both man and beast; and against all the gods of Egypt I will execute judgement: I am the Lord. Now the blood shall be a sign for you on the houses where you are. And when I see the blood, I will Passover you; and the plague shall not be on you to destroy you when I strike the land of Egypt. So this day shall be to you a memorial; and you shall keep it as a feast to the Lord throughout your generations. You shall keep it as a feast by an everlasting ordinance.'

> 'Let Your hand be upon the man of Your right hand, upon the son of man whom You made strong for Yourself.'

Jesus would die as the true Passover lamb to effect deliverance from the slavery of sin. He proved his prophetic knowledge, correctly predicting his crucifixion. Crucifixion was a Roman, not a Jewish punishment, and the circumstances of betrayal and delivery were in accordance with the prophecies. To be hanged on a tree was to be accursed of God - Jesus took upon Himself the curse; He would be crucified by the Gentiles – the

Roman 'congregation of the wicked'; His hands and feet would be pierced and none of His bones broken; He would be flogged and insulted, as we read in Deuteronomy 21:23, Psalm 22:16-17 and Isaiah 50:6,

> 'for he who is hanged is accursed of God.'

> 'For dogs have surrounded Me; the congregation of the wicked has enclosed Me. They pierced My hands and My feet; I can count all My bones.'

> 'I gave My back to those who struck Me, and My cheeks to those who plucked out the beard; I did not hide My face from shame and spitting.'

We know from the verses following this prophecy that the chief priests and scribes were plotting to kill Jesus after the feast and in secret. Given that Jerusalem would be packed for the Passover feast, likely with between two and three million people according to the historian Josephus, they wanted to wait until the city was quieter so there would be less likelihood of any riots or disturbances. It was Christ Himself, according to the perfect will of the Father, who chose the hour and manner of His death, to coincide with the Passover as He was the true Passover lamb. Psalms 113-118 are read during the Passover meal, including Psalm 113:4-8 and 118:22-24,

> 'The Lord is high above all nations, His glory above the heavens. Who is like the Lord our God, who dwells on high, who humbles Himself to behold the things that are in the heavens and in the earth? He raises the poor out of the dust, and lifts the needy out of the ash heap, that He may seat him with princes – with the princes of His people.'

> 'The stone which the builders rejected has become the chief cornerstone. This was the Lord's doing; it is marvellous in our eyes. This is the day the Lord has made; we will rejoice and be glad in it.'

Matthew 26:10-13

In verses 10-13, we read Jesus' response to His disciples' complaint that a woman had wasted valuable ointment that could have been sold and the money given to the poor, saying,

> "Why trouble ye the woman? For work a good she wrought to me; for always the poor ye have with yourselves, but me not always ye have; for putting this woman ointment this on the body of me for to bury me she did. Truly I tell you, wherever is proclaimed gospel this in all the world, will be spoken also what did this woman for a memorial of her."

Jesus referred to the woman's sacrificial giving as being a good work. The ointment was probably the most precious thing that she had, and this was a demonstration of her love – it was probably worth more than she could afford. Jesus was not downplaying the needs of the poor but was teaching about priorities. He knew there was little time left for them to serve Him while He was still in His bodily form; they would not always have the incarnate Son of Man with them, but there would be all the time in the world to care for the poor as commanded in Deuteronomy 15:11,

> 'For the poor will never cease from the land; therefore, I command you, saying, 'You shall open your hand wide to your brother, to your poor and your needy, in your land.'

The woman, referred to as Mary in Luke's and John's Gospels anointed Jesus to prepare Him for burial. The ointment had value to Jesus in reference to His burial; that His grave would accompany a sweet odour as it would lead to salvation. Jesus took this opportunity to once again prepare His disciples for His imminent death. King Asa, who did what was good and right in the eyes of God, was prepared for burial with fragrant ointments, as we read in 2 Chronicles 16:14,

> 'They buried him in his own tomb, which he had made for himself in the City of David; and they laid him in the bed which was filled with spices and various ingredients prepared in a mixture of ointments.'

480

Priests and kings had been anointed since the time of Moses. Mary was evidently moved to anoint Christ; this was in keeping with His being both priest as Aaron was anointed, and king as Saul was anointed, as we read in Leviticus 8:12, 1 Samuel 9:16, and Isaiah 61:1,

> 'And he poured some of the anointing oil on Aaron's head and anointed him, to consecrate him.'

> 'I will send you a man from the land of Benjamin, and you shall anoint him commander over My people Israel that he may save My people from the hand of the Philistines.'

> 'The Spirit of the Lord God is upon Me, because the Lord has anointed Me to preach good tidings to the poor; He has sent Me to heal the broken-hearted, to proclaim liberty to the captives, and the opening of the prison to those who are bound.'

Mary's action remains as a memory of a loving deed. The works of Jesus' disciples should be valued not by the opinion of men, but by the testimony of the word of God. The value of an object is dependent on what value we humans put on it at any one time; a sacrificial gift has eternal value. Jesus took the opportunity to remind the disciples that the gospel of salvation was to be proclaimed to the ends of the earth, as we read in Psalm 98:2-3, Isaiah 49:6, and Micah 5:4,

> 'The Lord has made known His salvation; His righteousness He has revealed in the sight of the nations. He has remembered His mercy and His faithfulness to the house of Israel; all the ends of the earth have seen the salvation of our God.'

> 'It is too small a thing that You should be My servant to raise up the tribes of Jacob, and to restore the preserved ones of Israel; I will also give You as a light to the Gentiles, that You should be My salvation to the ends of the earth.'

> 'He shall stand and feed His flock in the strength of the Lord, in the majesty of the name of the Lord His God; and they shall abide, for now He shall be great to the ends of the earth; and this One shall be peace.'

Matthew 26:18

In verse 18, we find Jesus responding to His disciples' request to know where He wanted them to prepare for Him to eat the Passover, saying,

> "Go ye into the city to such a one and say to him: The teacher says: The time of me near is; with thee I make the Passover with the disciples of me."

In His reply, Jesus did not name the person but referred to him as 'such a one'; it is likely that he would have been someone known to them. Jesus had presumably previously made secret arrangements for this meal because He knew that the Jewish leaders were plotting His arrest. This way, Judas would have been unable to betray Jesus before the appointed time. Jesus' precise knowledge of events that were to unfold here again point to His divine nature that differed from the rest of mankind, as we read in Ecclesiastes 9:12,

> 'For man also does not know his time: like fish taken in a cruel net, like birds caught in a snare, so the sons of men are snared in an evil time, when it falls suddenly upon them.'

The disciples were told to give the message 'My time is near'. The Greek word 'kairos', translated simply as time, can also mean season, appointed time, or special time. Jesus clearly knew that His time had come. Again, looking at the Greek, the word 'engys', translated here as near, also means at hand, nigh, nearby, close or ready, indicating that Jesus knew that His death was imminent and would happen exactly at the appointed time, knowing that time itself is in God's hands as we read in Ecclesiastes 3:17 and Psalm 31:14-15,

> "God shall judge the righteous and the wicked, for there is a time there for every purpose and for every work."

> 'But as for me, I trust in You, O Lord; I say, "You are my God." My times are in Your hand; deliver me from the hand of my enemies, and from those who persecute me.'

Jesus knew He was to die as the sacrificial lamb on the day of Passover, so He made preparations to eat the meal the evening before. Jesus told the disciples that He would make, or keep, the Passover, not eat it. Jesus knew He was to be killed at the time when the Passover lamb was due to be slaughtered. The Sabbath begins at sundown on Friday night – the Jewish day begins at sundown. The time of slaughter was to be in the late afternoon, typically translated as twilight, as we read in Exodus 12:6,

> 'Your lamb shall be without blemish, a male of the first year. You may take it from the sheep or from the goats. Now you shall keep it until the fourteenth day of the same month [the tenth month]. Then the whole assembly of the congregation shall kill it at twilight.'

With this simple statement, Jesus demonstrated His divine nature and His obedience to His heavenly Father to become the final embodiment of the sacrificial Passover Lamb, the Lamb of Salvation, as prophesied in Isaiah 53:7,

> 'He was oppressed, and He was afflicted, yet He opened not His mouth; He was led as a lamb to the slaughter, and as a sheep before its shearers is silent, so He opened not His mouth.'

Matthew 26:21-25

In verses 21-25, we read that Jesus told His disciples that one of their number was about to betray Him, saying,

> "Truly I tell you that one of you will betray me." And grieving exceedingly they began to   say to him one each: Not I am Lord? And he answering said: "The one dipping with me   his hand in the dish, this man me will betray. Indeed the Son of man goes as it has been written concerning him, but woe man to that through whom the son of man is betrayed; good were it for him if was not born man that." And answering Judas the one betraying him said: Not I am, rabbi? He says to him: "Thou said it."

Jesus spoke these words aloud knowing that what had been written was about to be fulfilled, making the disciples witnesses to this knowledge. The prophet Zechariah foretold this betrayal in detail, including the making of a financial bargain. The payment was to be specifically in silver. The precise number of coins, thirty pieces of silver, was the price that was to be paid in recompense for damage done to a slave that had been gored by a neighbour's ox; the price being that for a mere servant. The prophecy also indicated that the silver coins would be returned to the house of God, as we read in Zechariah 11:12-13 and Exodus 21:32,

> 'Then I said to them, "If it is agreeable to you, give me my wages; and if not, refrain." So they weighed out for my wages thirty pieces of silver. And the Lord said to me, "Throw it to the potter" – that princely price they set on me. So I took the thirty pieces of silver and threw them into the house of the Lord for the potter.'

> 'If the ox gores a male or female servant, he shall give to their master thirty shekels of silver.'

In Matthew's Gospel, the only disciple to call Jesus 'rabbi' is Judas, firstly here when he asked Jesus if he was the traitor and later at Gethsemane at the point of betrayal. The other disciples called Jesus Lord; only Judas called Him rabbi. Members of a family would not address each other so formally; the implication is that Judas had already distanced himself from

Jesus' family. If a stranger had done this, it would have been more easily endured; instead, it was one of His intimate friends who had made the treacherous bargain, fulfilling the prophesies in Psalm 41:7-9 and 55:12-14,

> 'All who hate me whisper together against me; against me they devise my hurt. "An evil disease," they say, "clings to him. And now that he lies down, he will rise up no more." Even my own familiar friend in whom I trusted, who ate my bread, has lifted up his heel against me.'

> 'For it is not an enemy who reproaches me; then I could bear it. Nor is it one who hates me who has exalted himself against me; then I could hide from him. But it was you, a man my equal, my companion and my acquaintance. We took sweet counsel together and walked to the house of God in the throng.'

Jesus said, 'The Son of Man goes' – in Hebrew this often meant to death as we read for example in Psalm 39:13, 'Remove Your gaze from me, that I may regain strength, before I go away and am no more.' By once again foretelling His own immediate future, Jesus was reinforcing the understanding in the disciples that what was happening was not determined by chance but part of God's perfect plan – the sacrifice had long been appointed by God. Even the betrayal was anticipated as part of the ultimate plan. The apostles asked, 'Is it I Lord?' It has been said that we are all potential Judases, and it is only the grace of God that can keep us loyal to God and to our fellow men. We don't have a choice about being born, but we have choice about how we live that life. Judas paid the price for his choice, as we read in Psalm 55:15 and 23,

> 'Let death seize them; let them go down alive into hell, for wickedness is in their dwellings and among them.'

> 'But You, O God, shall bring them down to the pit of destruction; bloodthirsty and deceitful men shall not live out half their days; but I will trust in You.'

Matthew 26:26

In verse 26, we read that as they were eating the Passover meal, Jesus took bread, blessed and broke it, and gave it to the disciples, saying,

> "Take ye, eat ye; this is the body of me."

Even before the Exodus and the institution of the Passover memorial, there was a Scriptural reference in Genesis to bread and wine being offered by the priest and king, Melchizedek. The name Melchizedek means king of righteousness, he was also called priest of the Most High God – a king and priest, ruling over the city of Salem (shalom) – the city of peace. The kings descended from King David undertook priestly roles, but Jesus, at what we can think of as the first Holy Communion, was officiating as a priest of a higher order, as we read in Genesis 14:17 and Psalm 110:4,

> 'Then Melchizedek king of Salem brought out bread and wine; he was the priest of God Most High.'

> "You are a priest forever according to the order of Melchizedek."

Jesus referred to the bread as His body. He knew what would happen to His body down to the last detail that had been stipulated at the time of Moses regarding the sacrificial lamb. Even the fact that none of His bones would be broken – despite the legs being broken on the others being crucified to hasten their death, as we read in Numbers 9:12, Exodus 12:46 and Psalm 34:20,

> 'They shall eat it with unleavened bread and bitter herbs. They shall leave none of it until morning, nor break one of its bones.'

> "In one house it shall be eaten; you shall not carry any of the flesh outside the house, nor shall you break one of its bones."

> 'He guards all his bones; not one of them is broken.'

The paschal or Passover lamb represented, and was a memorial of, the saving from slavery of the Israelites. Jesus said, 'This is my body'; since He was still alive this was clearly meant to be that the bread was representative of His body in the same way that one might point to a portrait and say 'This is my ancestor'. The bread eaten at Passover would have been unleavened (without yeast) as there should have been no other bread available at that time – all the leaven should have been purged from their houses as stipulated in Exodus 12:15,

> 'Seven days you shall eat unleavened bread. On the first day you shall remove leaven from your houses. For whoever eats leavened bread from the first day until the seventh day, that person shall be cut off from Israel.'

It is worth noting that the disciples were told to take – not merely receive; to eat – not merely to taste. The bread, which is intended as nourishment for the body, is sanctified by Christ to be nourishment for the spirit. The Passover meal was symbolic of the salvation of the people of Israel from Egypt. So, the bread is symbolic of the body of the sacrificial lamb which Jesus here declared Himself to be. The meal was a memorial of the deliverance from Egypt which was a foreshadowing of the greater deliverance that was about to be accomplished. The Passover meal begins with the words: "This is the bread of affliction our ancestors ate in the land of Egypt. Let all who are hungry come and eat." At the beginning of the meal, it is the bread of affliction; later it is called the bread of freedom that was eaten as they were leaving Egypt as there was no time to wait for the dough to rise. The bread that represented Jesus body that would become the bread of freedom had first to undergo suffering as the bread of affliction in which His disciples were to share, as we read in Deuteronomy 16:3,

> 'You shall eat no leavened bread with it; seven days you shall eat unleavened bread with it, that is the bread of affliction (for you came out of the land of Egypt in haste), that you may remember the day in which you came out of the land of Egypt all the days of your life.'

Matthew 26:27-29

In verses 27-29, we read that Jesus, have previously blessed the bread and given it to His disciples, took the cup, saying,

> "Drink ye of it all; for this is the blood of me of the covenant the blood concerning many being shed for forgiveness of sins. I tell and you, by no means will I drink from now of this fruit of the vine until day that when it I drink with you new in the kingdom of the Father of me."

At the end of the Passover meal, a cup of wine was shared by the family. This cup, the 'cup of blessing' was the third cup of four that were used at the meal. This is the cup at which Jesus said, "This is my covenant blood, which is poured out for many." At the time of Moses, the blood of the sacrificed animal was sprinkled partly on the altar, representing the presence of God, and partly on the people, as we read in Exodus 24:6-8,

> 'And Moses took half the blood and put it in basins, and half the blood he sprinkled on the altar. Then he took the Book of the Covenant and read in the hearing of the people. And they said, "All that the Lord has said we will do and be obedient." And Moses took the blood, sprinkled it on the people, and said, "This is the blood of the covenant which the Lord has made with you according to all these words."

There are many examples in Old Testament Scripture in which a cup symbolised the Lord's judgement or His blessing or was used as a metaphor for an individual's lot in life, as for example the overflowing cup in Psalm 23, or the 'portion of my inheritance and my cup' in Psalm 16. The cup symbolised both warnings and promise of salvation as we read for example in Isaiah 51:17, Jeremiah 16: 7, and Psalm 116:12-13,

> 'Awake, awake! Stand up, O Jerusalem, you who have drunk at the hand of the Lord the cup of His fury; you have drunk the dregs of the cup of trembling.'

'Nor shall men break bread in mourning for them, to comfort them for the dead; nor shall men give them the cup of consolation to drink for their father or their mother.'

'What shall I render to the Lord for all His benefits toward me? I will take up the cup of salvation and call upon the name of the Lord.'

When the blood of a sacrificial animal was poured out, it was believed to be the life of the sacrifice; it was this life by which sins could be atoned for. It was the blood that sealed the covenant or contract; for those who broke such a covenant, their blood would be on their own head. When His followers take the cup of wine they enter into the covenant of blood by faith as members of God's covenant community - the covenant of Salvation through Jesus Christ. Jesus said that all are called to drink it and seal the contract of forgiveness of sins, as we read in Leviticus 17:11, Isaiah 53: 12 and 42:6,

'For the life of the flesh is in the blood, and I have given it to you upon the altar to make atonement for your souls; for it is the blood that makes atonement for the soul.'

'Because He poured out His soul unto death, and He was numbered with the transgressors, and He bore the sin of many, and made intercession for the transgressors.'

"I, the Lord, have called You in righteousness, and will hold Your hand; I will keep You and give You as a covenant to the people, as a light to the Gentiles."

Jesus said that He would not drink again until He would do so in the new kingdom. We know from the Acts of the Apostles that the risen Christ ate and drank with His disciples, so we could presume that His resurrection was the inauguration of the new kingdom; an everlasting kingdom as we read in Psalm 145:13,

'Your kingdom is an everlasting kingdom, and Your dominion endures throughout all generations.'

Matthew 26:31-32

In verses 31-32, after they had finished their supper, Jesus spoke to His disciples on the Mount of Olives, saying,

> "All ye will be offended in me tonight; it has been written for: I will strike the shepherd, and will be scattered the sheep of the flock; but after I am raised I will go before you to Galilee."

The Greek word, 'skandalisthēsesthe' translated here as stumble or offend, can also mean to fall away, or be scattered, and it was in this last sense that Jesus used the word as He then quoted directly from the prophet Zechariah. Once again, Jesus demonstrated His divine knowledge of the events leading up to and including His death, perhaps even down to the detail of a sword being used at the moment of His betrayal, as we read in Zechariah 13:7 and Psalm 38:11-12,

> "Awake, O sword, against My Shepherd, against the Man who is My Companion," says the Lord of hosts. "Strike the Shepherd, and the sheep will be scattered."

> 'My loved ones and my friends stand aloof from my plague, and my relatives stand afar off. Those also who seek my life lay snares for me; those who seek my hurt speak of destruction, and plan deception all the day long.'

Jesus knew that His disciples would fall away and forsake Him; that they would lose confidence in Him. He told them in advance so that later they would remember what He had said - that it would happen like a flock of sheep whose shepherd has been killed and the sheep are scattered and become vulnerable to their predators. In Zechariah's prophecy, it is God Himself who would smite the shepherd – the crucifixion was God's doing; Jesus was not a victim, at every stage He had choice, and He chose to obey His Father. Those who sought to take Jesus' life were instruments of God's divine purpose. God the Father gave Jesus up to be smitten for the sins of the world, as we read for example in Isaiah 53:10,

'Yet it pleased the Lord to bruise Him; He has put Him to grief. When You make His soul an offering for sin, He shall see His seed, He shall prolong His days, and the pleasure of the Lord shall prosper in His hand.'

Jesus went on to predict His resurrection, letting His disciples know that they need not lose confidence in Him. He also told them that He would go before them; like a shepherd He would collect His scattered flock and lead them again. Christ even made an appointment to meet up with His disciples after His death and resurrection, naming the place and even which hill on which they were to meet. He promised the disciples that He would meet them in Galilee – and we know from later in the Gospel that this happened as He said it would. Jesus was likened to a shepherd many times in Old Testament Scripture; King David had already been dead four hundred years when Ezekiel spoke of David as being their shepherd, clearly it was a reference to Christ. Jesus promised that after He had risen, He would meet His disciples at the designated place and gather them to Him, as we read in Isaiah 40:11, Ezekiel 34:23-24, and Micah 5:4,

'He will feed His flock like a shepherd; He will gather the lambs with His arm, and carry them in His bosom, and gently lead those who are with young.'

'I will establish one shepherd over them, and he shall feed them – My servant David. He shall feed them and be their shepherd. And I, the Lord, will be their God, and My servant David a prince among them; I, the Lord, have spoken.'

'And He shall stand and feed His flock in the strength of the Lord, in the majesty of the name of the Lord His God; and they shall abide, for now He shall be great to the ends of the earth; and this One shall be peace.'

Matthew 26:34

In verse 34, we read Jesus' response to Peter's statement that even if the others fell away that he wouldn't, saying,

> "Truly I tell thee that tonight before a cock to crow three times thou wilt deny me."

Again, we find that Jesus' knowledge of the future is accurate down to the smallest detail; he knew by what time Peter would have made his third denial. He knew Peter would deny Him that very night and not just once but three times before the cock had crowed. This was in some ways a continuation of the prophecy in Zechariah 13:7 that the sheep would be scattered. Although cockerels, or roosters, occasionally crow at any time of day, most of their crowing is like clockwork – triggered by the sunlight at dawn. The third part of the night was called cock crow, between the third and fourth watch. This suggests that all this happened within the space of just a few hours. It is also worth noting that Jesus was replying to Peter's statement of overconfidence for which we find warnings for example in Proverbs 16:18 and 27:1,

> 'Pride goes before destruction, and a haughty spirit before a fall.'

> 'Do not boast about tomorrow, for you do not know what a day may bring forth.'

Jonah is an Old Testament example of a person who fled from his obligations to God through pride. He knew that God would have mercy on the people of Nineveh if they repented and didn't want to look foolish when the doom and destruction, he was to pronounce on them, didn't happen. Instead, he fled to sea, eventually finding himself thrown overboard and being swallowed by a fish. But God, rather than condemn him, raised him from the deep, as we read in Jonah 1:3 and 2:4-6,

> 'But Jonah arose to flee to Tarshish from the presence of the Lord.'

> 'Then I said, 'I have been cast out of Your sight; yet I will look again toward Your holy temple.' The waters surrounded me, even

to my soul; the deep closed around me; weeds were wrapped around my head. I went down to the moorings of the mountains; the earth with its bars closed behind me forever; yet You have brought up my life from the pit, O Lord, my God.'

There does not seem to be any direct or specific Old Testament prophecy about Peter's denial. What is perhaps more important here is that Jesus was speaking to Peter without condemnation, but with compassion, with a total understanding of human weakness. Time and again in the Old Testament, the Lord's people betrayed and forsook Him, yet He continued to show compassion and understanding of their failings. Jesus revealed to His disciples the weakness of their own bodies – the lesson being that they had to learn to rely completely on Him in their weakness, as we read for example in Psalm103:13-14 and 78:38-39, Malachi 3:17, and Zechariah 13:9,

'As a father pities his children, so the Lord pities those who fear Him. For He knows our frame; He remembers that we are dust.'

'But He, being full of compassion, forgave their iniquity, and did not destroy them. Yes, many a time He turned His anger away, and did not stir up all His wrath. For He remembered that they were but flesh, a breath that passes away and does not come again.'

"They shall be Mine," says the Lord of hosts, "On the day that I make them My jewels. And I will spare them as a man spares his own son who serves him."

'I will bring the one-third through the fire, will refine   them as silver is refined, and test them as gold is tested. They will call on My name, and I will answer them. I will say, 'This is My people', and each one will say, 'The Lord is my God.'

Matthew 26:36-38

In verses 36-38, we read that Jesus took the disciples to a place called Gethsemane, the garden or orchard where there was likely an olive press at the base of the Mount of Olives, where He intended to pray saying,

> "Sit ye here until going away there I may pray." And taking Peter and the two sons of Zebedee he began to grieve and to be distressed. Then he says to them, "Deeply grieved is the soul of me unto death; remain ye here and watch ye with me."

By going to the garden of Gethsemane, Jesus had gone to a place that He was regularly accustomed to going. It was clearly not His intention to conceal Himself; instead, He chose to go where He was sure to be found by His enemies. Jesus told most of His disciples to sit in one place in the garden and then, taking just three, went a distance away, most likely beyond an arrow shot for their own safety. Jesus knew that He was about to be separated from His friends and loved ones, as we read for example in Psalm 88 verses 8 and 18,

> 'You have put away my acquaintances far from me; You have made me an abomination to them; I am shut up, and I cannot get out. [...] Loved one and friend You have put far from me, and my acquaintances into darkness.'

Jesus was probably only within earshot of the chosen three disciples when He began to express His deep anguish and distress which He likened to being as extreme as death itself; an agony foretold at length in the Psalms, as we read for example in Psalm 69:1-3 and 13-15, Psalm 88:1-7, and Psalm 55:4-5,

> 'Save me, O God! For the waters have come up to my neck. I sink in deep mire, where there is no standing; I have come into deep waters, where the floods overflow me. I am weary with my crying; my throat is dry; my eyes fail while I wait for my God.'

> 'But as for me, my prayer is to You, O Lord, in the acceptable time; O God, in the multitude of Your mercy, hear me in the truth

of Your salvation. Deliver me out of the mire and let me not sink; let me be delivered from those who hate me, and out of the deep waters. Let not the flood water overflow me, nor let the deep swallow me up; and let not the pit shut its mouth on me.'

'O Lord, God of my salvation, I have cried out day and night before You. Let my prayer come before You; incline Your ear to my cry. For my soul is full of troubles, and my life draws near to the grave. I am counted with those who go down to the pit; I am like a man who has no strength. Adrift among the dead, like the slain who lie in the grave, whom You remember no more, and who are cut off from Your hand. You have laid me in the lowest pit, in darkness, in the depths. Your wrath lies heavy upon me, and You have afflicted me with all Your waves.'

'My heart is severely pained within me, fearfulness and trembling have come upon me, and horror has overwhelmed me.'

Jesus asked Peter, James, and John to stay near Him and watch. The word 'watch' literally means to stay awake, to be vigilant or to guard against danger, just as a person might take the first watch of the night. Jesus was perhaps reminding the disciples of the importance of facing temptation with vigilance and prayer; the importance of watching and waiting on the Lord, as we read for example in Lamentations 3:25-26, Psalm 27:14, and Psalm 37:7,

'The Lord is good to those who wait for Him, to the soul who seeks Him. It is good that one should hope and wait quietly for the salvation of the Lord.'

'Wait on the Lord; be of good courage, and He shall strengthen your heart; wait, I say, on the Lord!'

'Rest in the Lord and wait patiently for Him; do not fret because of him who prospers in his way, because of the man who brings wicked schemes to pass.'

Matthew 26:39

In verse 39, we read that Jesus went a little further from His disciples and fell on His face, and prayed, saying,

> "Father of me, if possible it is, let pass from me cup this; yet not as I will but as thou."

By falling on His face to pray, Jesus was demonstrating His complete and utter humility before God the Father. It was the custom at that time to fall into this posture when asking for a favour that demanded complete humility, as we read for example in Genesis 17:3, Numbers 14:5 and 16:22,

> 'Then Abram fell on his face, and God talked to him.'

> 'Then Moses and Aaron fell on their faces before all the assembly of the congregation of the children of Israel.'

> 'Then they fell on their faces, and said, "O God, the God of the spirits of all flesh, shall one man sin, and You be angry with all the congregation?'

Jesus asked if it was possible for the cup to pass from Him. Of course, for God, all things are possible, but our redemption was only possible through the sacrifice and death of Christ. The cup, as has previously been discussed, as used in the Old Testament denoted the providence of God in which would be given the measure of affliction or reward due to each person. In ancient times, it was also a means of inflicting punishment; a cup of poison was a method for punishing criminals or traitors – a poisoned chalice, as we read for example in Isaiah 51:17,

> 'Awake, awake! Stand up, O Jerusalem, you who have drunk at the hand of the Lord the cup of His fury; you have drunk the dregs of the cup of trembling and drained it out.'

We can only imagine the depth of humiliation and temptation that Jesus endured in that garden. He experienced fear and anguish and, with it, temptation. Given the evidence we have already seen of His foreknowledge of events down to the most minute detail, He would have known exactly what was going to happen to Him. Although not recorded in Matthew's Gospel, Luke wrote that while Jesus was praying 'His sweat became as drops of blood falling down to the ground.' (Luke 22:44) Luke, who is believed to have been a physician, by including this detail adds weight to the witness accounts. There is a recognised very rare condition, known as hematidrosis, in which an individual literally sweats blood when they are suffering from extreme levels of stress or fear. The blood vessels around the sweat glands rupture and the blood is forced out in droplets mixed with sweat. Reported examples in modern times have included men condemned to execution and other cases of extreme fear. Jesus knew what He was facing, as we read for example in Isaiah 50:5-6,

> 'The Lord God has opened My ear; and I was not rebellious, nor did I turn away. I gave My back to those who struck Me, and My cheeks to those who plucked out the beard; I did not hide My face from shame and spitting.'

But having initially prayed to be freed from His death, Jesus immediately submitted His will to the will of His Father. Calvin wrote: 'for the modesty of faith consists in permitting God to appoint differently from what we desire.' Even Jesus had to set aside His own desires and subordinate them to the perfect desire of His Father. Jesus' disciples are called to do likewise; to pray for what we think is right but like King David to say, 'Here I am, do to me as seems good to You', as we read in 2 Samuel 15:25-26,

> 'Then the king said to Zadok, "Carry the ark of God back into the city. If I find favour in the eyes of the Lord, He will bring me back and show me both it and His dwelling place. But if He says thus: 'I have no delight in you,' here I am, let Him do to me as seems good to Him."

Matthew 26:40-41

In verses 40-41, we read that Jesus returned to where He had left His disciples, at a safe distance from Him in the Garden of Gethsemane, and found them sleeping and spoke to Peter, saying,

> "So were ye not able one hour to watch with me? Watch ye and pray, lest ye enter into temptation; indeed the spirit is eager, but the flesh is weak."

It is tempting to think that the disciples showed a lack of concern for Jesus by falling asleep, but it is recognised that profound grief or distress can cause drowsiness and deep sleep. This has been observed, for example, on the battlefield where soldiers have fallen asleep and not even been woken by exploding shells that have thrown them from their sleeping place. In this sense, the body is indeed weak by naturally seeking to avoid suffering. Jesus did not condemn His disciples but was reminding them that they needed to pray and watch, seeking strength from God, as we read for example in Habakkuk 2:1, Psalm 145:18-19, Proverbs 15:29, and 2 Chronicles 7:14,

> 'I will stand my watch and set myself on the rampart and watch to see what He will say to me, and what I will answer when I am corrected.'

> 'The Lord is near to all who call upon Him, to all who call upon Him in truth. He will fulfil the desire of those who fear Him; He also will hear their cry and save them.'

> 'The Lord is far from the wicked, but He hears the prayer of the righteous.'

> 'If My people who are called by My name will humble themselves, and pray and seek My face, and turn away from their wicked ways, then I will hear from heaven, and will forgive their sin and heal their land.'

Jesus exhorted His disciples to watch and pray to resist falling into the way of temptation that stems from human weakness; not just physical weakness such as the fear of pain and suffering but the weakness of disobedience, pride, and other demonstrations of self-interest that stem from not following the commands and statutes of God, as we read in Proverbs 4:14-15, Psalm 1:1-2, and Psalm 119:4-5 and 35-37,

> 'Do not enter the path of the wicked, and do not walk in the way of evil. Avoid it, do not travel on it; turn away from it and pass on.'

> 'Blessed is the man who walks not in the counsel of the ungodly, nor stands in the path of sinners, nor sits in the seat of the scornful; but his delight is in the law of the Lord, and in His law, he meditates day and night.'

> 'You have commanded us to keep Your precepts diligently. Oh, that my ways were directed to keep Your statutes!'

> 'Make me walk in the path of Your commandments, for I delight in it. Incline my heart to Your testimonies, and not to covetousness. Turn away my eyes from looking at worthless things and revive me in Your way.'

Whilst warning His disciples of their human frailties, Jesus also acknowledged their eager willingness to follow Him, and to seek to follow the Lord their God in righteousness, as we read in Isaiah 26:8-9, and Psalm 119:32,

> 'Yes, in the way of Your judgements, O Lord, we have waited for You; the desire of our soul is for Your name and for the remembrance of You. With my soul I have desired You in the night, yes by my spirit within me I will seek You early; for when Your judgements are in the earth, the inhabitants of the world will learn righteousness.'

> 'I will run the course of Your commandments, for You shall enlarge my heart.'

Matthew 26:42

In verse 42, we read that Jesus again went a distance away from the disciples to pray, saying,

> "Father of Me, if cannot this to pass away except I drink it, let be done the will of thee."

Christ's humanity can be seen in His human suffering – without this record of His suffering, it would be tempting to dismiss the sacrifice that He made to atone for the sins of mankind. But the Gospel makes it clear that He lived and suffered as other people do, taking none of the advantages of His divine nature for Himself. Jesus' cries to His Father are foretold in Psalm 22:2-3 and 10-11, and Psalm 69: 16-18,

> 'O My God, I cry in the daytime, but You do not hear; and in the night season and am not silent. But You are holy, enthroned in the praises of Israel.'

> 'I was cast upon You from birth, from My mother's womb You have been My God. Be not far from Me, for trouble is near; for there is none to help.'

> 'Hear me, O Lord, for Your loving   kindness is good; turn to me according to the multitude of Your tender mercies. And do not hide Your face from Your servant, for I am in trouble; hear me speedily. Draw near to my soul and redeem it; deliver me because of my enemies.'

Christ demonstrated that He was resigned to His impending suffering. Without this clarification it would be possible to suppose that His sacrifice had been imposed by God the Father rather than being a free-will offering. Jesus' words show that He had overcome the temptation to avoid the suffering, that He had won the battle and was ready to offer Himself for sacrifice according to His Father's will. In His earlier prayer, found in verse thirty-nine, Jesus had asked if it would be possible to avoid the cup; in this prayer Christ acknowledges that it was not possible to avoid the cup for God's will to be done. As Isaiah had done before Him, Jesus was willing to say, "Here I am. Send Me," as we read in Isaiah 6:8,

> 'I heard the voice of the Lord, saying: "Whom shall I send, and who will go for Us?" Then I said, "Here I am! Send me."

Jesus was obedient to God's will. The account of Daniel and his friends Shadrach, Meshach, and Abed-Nego, is full of examples of God's people demonstrating their obedience to His will even when it would cost their life. Daniel showed his obedience initially by refusing to eat the defiling food they were offered, which we read in chapter 1 verse 8. His friends refused to bow down to a golden image for which they would be thrown into the fiery furnace, giving their explanation to the king as we read in Daniel Chapter 3:17-18,

> "Our God whom we serve is able to deliver us from the burning fiery furnace, and He will deliver us from your hand O King. But if not, let it be known to you, O king, that we do not serve your gods, nor will we worship the gold image which you have set up."

Later Daniel continued to pray to God even when it had been decreed that it was against the law of Nebuchadnezzar. For this he was thrown into the den of hungry lions, as we read in chapter 6 verses 13-17. One of the central messages of the Old Testament is that God simply asks for obedience from His people, as we read for example in 1 Samuel 15:22 and Jeremiah 7:23,

> 'Has the Lord as great delight in burnt offerings and sacrifices, as in obeying the voice of the Lord? Behold, to obey is better than sacrifice.'

> 'Obey My voice, and I will be your God, and you shall be My people, and walk in all the ways I have commanded you, that it may be well with you.'

Matthew 26:45-46

In verses 45-46, we read that Jesus, having spent more time in prayer, returned again to where He had left His disciples in the Garden of Gethsemane, saying,

> "Sleep ye now and rest; behold has drawn near the hour and the Son of man is betrayed into the hands of sinners. Rise ye, let us be going; behold has drawn near the one betraying me."

There has been some debate about the interpretation of Jesus' opening remark, for example suggesting that He was speaking with irony or disappointment at having found the disciples still sleeping. However, the Greek word 'loipon', usually translated as 'now', has also been translated in other contexts as: 'later on', 'then', 'from now', 'finally', 'furthermore', and 'henceforth'. If we use the translation 'later on', it makes sense in this context, so that Jesus would have been saying, 'You can sleep and rest later because now is the time of My betrayal.' Jesus knew that His accusers were on their way and may well have been able to see their torchlight and heard the approach of those for whom He had only love, as we read in Psalm 109:1-5 and Psalm 55:20-21,

> 'Do not keep silent, O God of my praise! For the mouth of the wicked and the mouth of the deceitful have opened against me; they have spoken against me with a lying tongue. They have also surrounded me with words of hatred and fought against me without a cause. In return for my love, they are my accusers, but I give myself to prayer. Thus, they have rewarded me evil for good, and hatred for my love.'

> 'He has put forth his hands against those who were at peace with him; he has broken his covenant. The words of his mouth were smoother than butter, but war was in his heart; his words were softer than oil, yet they were drawn swords.'

Jesus had spoken earlier about His betrayal that had been written about, most likely in Psalm 41 that speaks of the treachery of a familiar friend in verse 9. When Psalm 41 was originally written, it referred to the betrayal of David. It was a foreshadowing of what was to come, just as David himself was a foreshadowing of Jesus, the Messiah. David's betrayal by his friend Ahithophel was a parallel to the betrayal by Judas, including an account of the consequences of that betrayal leading to a similar death, as we read in 2 Samuel 15:12 and 17:23.

'Then Absalom sent for Ahithophel the Gilonite, David's counsellor, from his city – from Giloh – while he offered sacrifices. And the conspiracy grew strong, for the people with Absalom continually increased in number.'

'Now when Ahithophel saw that his advice was not followed, he saddled a donkey, and arose and went home to his house, to his city. Then he put his household in order and hanged himself and died.'

The Old Testament has plenty of warnings about the consequences of those who practice deceit and lies and are self-seeking. By contrast, blessings are promised to those who trust the Lord, who do not turn aside from the truth, those who are faithful to the Lord, as we read for example in Psalm 101:7, Proverbs 13:7, Proverbs 19:5, Psalm 40:4, and Psalm 101:6,

'He who works deceit shall not dwell within my house; he who tells lies shall not continue in my presence.'

'There is one who makes himself rich yet has nothing; and one who makes himself poor yet has great riches.'

'A false witness will not go unpunished, and he who speaks lies will not escape.'

'Blessed is that man who makes the Lord his trust, and does not respect the proud, nor such as turn aside to lies.'

'My eyes shall be on the faithful of the land, that they may dwell with me; he who walks in a perfect way, he shall serve me.'

Matthew 26:50

In verse 50, we read Jesus' response to the arrival of a 'great multitude with swords and clubs' with Judas leading them and who greeted Jesus with a kiss, saying,

"Friend, do that on what thou art here."

In the Authorised and Revised Standard Version translations of this text, the rendering is as a question: 'Friend, why are you here?'. However, a more literal translation renders this passage as 'Friend, do what you are here to do', and this makes far more sense in the context since Jesus has already made it very clear that He knew exactly what Judas intended, and here He effectively tells Judas that He knows why here is there and tells him to get on with it – there was by this time no turning back. Judas had taken the bribe and had to face the consequences as we read in Exodus 23:7-8 and Deuteronomy 16:19,

> 'Keep yourself far from a false matter; do not kill the innocent and righteous. For I will   not justify the wicked. And you shall take no bribe, for a bribe blinds the discerning and perverts the words of the righteous.'

> 'You shall not pervert justice; you shall not show partiality, nor take a bribe, for a bribe blinds the eyes of the wise and twists the words of the righteous.'

The Greek word 'hetaire', mostly translated as friend can also be translated as companion or comrade, the same word that Matthew used in two of Jesus' parables: that of the labourers who were hired at different times of the day in chapter 20:13, and that of the wedding guest who was found to be without the proper clothes in chapter 22:12. In these parables, the term referred to those who appeared as righteous but were in fact not in keeping with the will of God. Jesus was addressing Judas as someone who had just a short while ago sat at the same table for a meal together as an apparently righteous companion, loved by Jesus, but who was in fact prepared to betray Him, as we read in Psalm 3:1-2, Psalm 38:11-12, Job 19:13-14 and 19,

> 'Lord, how they have increased who trouble me! Many are they who rise up against me. Many are they who say of me, "There is no help for him in God".'

'My loved ones and my friends stand aloof from my plague, and my relatives stand afar off. Those also who seek my life lay snares for me; those who seek my hurt speak of destruction, and plan deception all the day long.'

'He has removed my brothers far from me, and my acquaintances are completely estranged from me. My relatives have failed, and my close friends have forgotten me.'

'All my close friends abhor me, and those whom I love have turned against me.'

The Church will, of course, always be vulnerable to traitors from within due the very nature of the Church - that of opening arms in unconditional love to all who seek Salvation, making the Church vulnerable to hypocrites and the self-seeking. The Law reminds the people of God not to stand false against another, nor take a bribe, but always to speak the truth, as we read in Leviticus 19:16, Exodus 20:16, Exodus 23:1, and Psalm 15:1-3 and 5,

'You shall not go about as a talebearer among your people; nor shall you take a stand against the life of your neighbour.'

'You shall not bear false witness against your neighbour.'

'You shall not circulate a false report. Do not put your hand with the wicked to be an unrighteous witness.'

'Lord, who may abide in Your tabernacle? Who may dwell in Your holy hill? He who walks uprightly, and works righteousness, and speaks truth in his heart; he who does not backbite with his tongue, nor does evil to his neighbour, nor does he take up a reproach against his friend [...] He who does not put his money at usury, nor does he take a bribe against the innocent. He who does these things shall never be moved.'

Matthew 26:52-54

In verses 52-54, after one of Jesus' disciples had drawn a sword and struck one of the high priest's servants, Jesus rebuked him, saying,

> "Put back the sword of thee into the place of it; for all the ones taking a sword by a sword will perish. Or thinkest thou that I cannot to ask the Father of me, and he will provide me now more than twelve legions of angels? How then may be fulfilled the scriptures that thus it must be?"

Murder was forbidden in the law, and of course those who fight in battle are highly likely to die, but there has been some debate about whether Jesus intended His followers to abstain entirely from using the sword. Before even the ten commandments were given to Moses, God spoke to Noah about the consequences of shedding another's blood as being the shedding of their own blood at the hand of man. If a man causes another's blood to be poured out, his own will be poured out at the hand of man. Violence inevitably leads to more violence. The Mosaic law is more explicit, stating that one who kills another is worthy of death, but it does not follow that Christ's followers are to be the arbiters of the consequences, as we read in Genesis 9:6, Exodus 21:12, and Psalm 55:23,

> 'Whoever sheds man's blood, by man his blood shall be shed; for in the image of God He made man.'

> 'He who strikes a man so that he dies shall surely be put to death.'

> 'But You, O God, shall bring them down to the pit of destruction; bloodthirsty and deceitful men shall not live out half their days; but I will trust in You.'

By commanding the disciple, according to John's Gospel it was Peter, to put back his sword, Jesus was not permitting him to use physical violence even for self-defence or defence of another. Resistance implies a lack of trust in the protection of God. The Kingdom of heaven was not to be advanced with any kind of physical force. Jesus had already made clear elsewhere that the Kingdom of God could only advance through love and that violence has no place in that kingdom, as we read in Isaiah 2:4,

> 'He shall judge between the nations and rebuke many people; they shall beat their swords into ploughshares, and their spears

into pruning hooks; nation shall not lift up sword against nation, neither shall they learn war anymore.'

Jesus reminded His disciples of His divine nature by which He could call on legions of angels for protection, but He did not call on these legions of angels because it was contrary to the Father's will. Nevertheless, Christians can be sure that God has angels that can serve as guardians when they are following the will of the Father, as for example when Elisha was under attack by the Syrians, as we read in 2 Kings, 6:17, Psalm 91:11-12 and 103:20-21,

> 'And Elisha prayed, and said, "Lord, I pray, open his eyes that he may see." Then the Lord opened the eyes of the young man, and he saw. And behold, the mountain was full of horses and chariots of fire all around Elisha.'

> 'For He shall give His angels charge over you, to keep you in all your ways. In their hands they shall bear you up, lest you dash your foot against a stone.'

> 'Bless the Lord, you His angels, who excel in strength, who do His word, heeding the voice of His word. Bless the Lord, all you His hosts, you ministers of His, who do His pleasure.'

In order to fulfil the prophecy of Isaiah, Jesus and His disciples had to offer no resistance, but yield to those who had come to arrest Him. Not just the prophecy of the arrest, but the trial and crucifixion, and of course His resurrection, as we read in Isaiah 53:3 and 7,

> 'He is despised and rejected by men, a man of sorrows and acquainted with grief. And we hid, as it were, our faces from Him; He was despised, and we did not esteem Him.'

> 'He was oppressed, and He was afflicted, yet He opened not His mouth; He was led as a lamb to the slaughter, and as a sheep before its shearers is silent, so He opened not His mouth.'

Matthew 26:55-56

In verses 55-56, Jesus spoke to the crowd that had come to arrest Him, saying,

> "As against a robber came ye forth with swords and clubs to take me? Daily in the temple I sat teaching, and not ye seized me. But this all has come to pass that may be fulfilled the scriptures of the prophets."

At that time in Judea, armed men were employed against robbers, highwaymen, or any other desperate villain who would need to be overpowered by force of arms. Jesus had been teaching in the temple in Jerusalem but also throughout the region over several years, but this was the moment that the High Priest decided to arrest Jesus, making himself the instrument by which God's purposes would be fulfilled, confirming that which He had already determined, as we read in Isaiah 44:24-26,

> 'Thus says the Lord, your Redeemer, and He who formed you from the womb: "I am the Lord, Who makes all things, Who stretches out the heavens all alone, Who spreads abroad the earth by Myself; Who frustrates the signs of the babblers, and drives diviners mad; Who turns wise men backward, and makes their knowledge foolishness; Who confirms the word of His servant, and performs the counsel of His messengers; who says to Jerusalem, 'You shall be inhabited,' to the cities of Judah, 'You shall be built,' and I will raise up her waste places."

The essential injustice of this night-time arrest, that was so unnecessary, is something that many people in succeeding generations can and have been able to identify with. Armed soldiers coming in force to hunt down and arrest innocent civilians in the early hours when the night is at its coldest and the body at its most vulnerable. Was it cowardice? Jesus was no threat to the Roman occupation, or the Jews; He was no criminal hiding from justice; His teaching had not been conducted in secrecy. The troops, referred to in John's Gospel, were sent by the High priest – it is unlikely that Pilate would have spared his sparse troops for such an apparently insignificant operation. The manner of Jesus' arrest was in fulfilment of the prophecies, as we read for example in Zechariah 13:7 and Lamentations 1:14,

"Awake, O sword, against My Shepherd, against the Man who is My Companion," says the Lord of hosts. "Strike the Shepherd, and the sheep will be scattered."

'The yoke of my transgressions was bound; they were woven together by His hands and thrust upon my neck. He made my strength fail; the Lord delivered me into the hands of those whom I am not able to withstand.'

The manner of Jesus' death also, found in the writings of the prophets foretold His sufferings and death, as we read for example in Isaiah 53:3, Psalm 34:20, Psalm 22:15-18, Psalm 69:21, and Zechariah 12:10,

'He was wounded for our transgressions, He was bruised for our iniquities; the chastisement for our peace was upon Him, and by His stripes we are healed.'

'He guards all his bones; not one of them is broken.'

'My strength is dried up like a potsherd, and My tongue clings to My jaws; You have brought Me to the dust of death. For dogs have surrounded Me; the congregation of the wicked has enclosed Me. They pierced My hands and My feet; I can count all My bones. They look and stare at Me. They divide My garments among them, and for My clothing they cast lots.'

'They also gave me gall for my food, and for my thirst they gave me vinegar to drink.'

'And I will pour on the house of David and on the inhabitants of Jerusalem the Spirit of grace and supplication; then they will look on Me whom they pierced. Yes, they will mourn for Him as one mourns for his only son and grieve for Him as one grieves for a firstborn.'

Matthew 26:64

In verse 64, after the high priest had asked Jesus to tell them if He is the Christ, the Son of God, He answered saying,

> "Thou said it; yet I tell you, from now ye will see the Son of man sitting on the right hand of the power and coming on the clouds of heaven."

At the court of enquiry, presided over by the high priest, to the question 'Are you the Christ the Son of God?', Jesus effectively said, 'yes', and qualified this by referring to Himself as the Son of man, sitting at the right hand of the power – the Almighty, and underlined this by quoting from Daniel, saying that He would come on the clouds of heaven. The right hand of God was the highest place of honour; the clouds were the 'vehicle of the divine glory', as we read in Psalm 110:1, Psalm 104:3, Isaiah 19:1, and Daniel 7:13-14,

> 'The Lord said to my Lord, "Sit at My right hand, till I make Your enemies Your footstool." The Lord shall send the rod of Your strength out of Zion. Rule in the midst of Your enemies!'

> 'He lays the beams of His upper chambers in the waters, who makes the clouds His chariot, who walks on the wings of the wind.'

> 'Behold, the Lord rides on a swift cloud.'

> 'I was watching in the night visions, and behold, One like the Son of Man, coming with the clouds of heaven! He came to the Ancient of Days, and they brought Him near before Him. Then to Him was given dominion and glory and a kingdom, that all peoples, nations, and languages should serve Him. His dominion is an everlasting dominion, which shall not pass away, and His kingdom the one which shall not be destroyed.'

Jesus affirmed that He is the Christ, stating that this truth would be revealed henceforth. Jesus would one day sit in judgement over them and the nations and then justice would be served. The suffering and death would soon be accomplished and then glory would be His at the right hand of the Father. In the future they would not see Him in this broken and humiliated form, but as the true Messiah and Judge. When Jesus used the term 'Son of man', those to whom He was speaking would have understood this as a claim to be the Messiah. He was not the Messiah that the people expected – a political or military ruler who would defeat the Romans, but a Messiah who would inaugurate a kingdom given to Him by the Ancient of Days. Jesus declared Himself to be the Son of God who would be highly exalted, as we read in Psalm 2:7-8, Psalm 89:24-27, and Isaiah 52:13,

"I will declare the decree: The Lord has said to Me, 'You are My Son, today I have begotten You. Ask of Me, and I will give You the nations for Your inheritance, and the ends of the earth for your possession.'

'But My faithfulness and My mercy shall be with him. And in My name his horn shall be exalted. Also I will set his hand over the sea, and his right hand over the rivers. He shall cry to Me, 'You are my Father, My God, and the rock of my salvation.' Also I will make him My firstborn, the highest of the kings of the earth.'

'Behold, My Servant shall deal prudently; He shall be exalted and extolled and be very high.'

It is apparent from Matthew's account that in their desire to put an end to Jesus, the members of the Sanhedrin broke their own rules as to time, location, evidence, and witnesses in the process of a criminal trial. They sought false witnesses with claims that Jesus had committed blasphemy so that they could condemn Him to death. Jesus could have walked away a free man if He had denied His claim to be the Messiah. Instead, His answer made the crucifixion inescapable. Again breaking their own rules, Jesus was blindfolded and abused, fulfilling the prophecies in Isaiah 50:6, Psalm 35:15, 27:12, and Micah 5:1.

'I gave My back to those who struck Me, and My cheeks to those who plucked out the beard; I did not hide My face from shame and spitting.'

'But in my adversity they rejoiced and gathered together; attackers gathered against me, and I did not know it; they tore at me and did not cease.'

'Do not deliver me to the will of my adversaries; for false witnesses have risen against me, and such as breathe out violence.'

'They will strike the judge of Israel with a rod on the cheek.'

MATTHEW CHAPTER TWENTY-SEVEN

Matthew 27:11

In verse 11, we read that Jesus had been brought to face the Roman Governor, Pontius Pilate, who evidently mistrusted the Jewish leaders. In response to the accusations of the Jews, Pilate asked Jesus if He was the King of the Jews, to which Jesus answered,

"Thou sayest."

Jesus' words are usually rendered, "It is as you say." In effect Jesus was answering 'yes' to Pilate's question. It is interesting to note that Pilate did not ask 'Are You the Messiah?', suggesting that the Jewish leaders had accused Jesus of claiming to be an earthly king that Pilate could misconstrue as meaning a claimant for the non-existent political throne of the Hebrews and thus a potential threat to Roman supremacy, and not accusing Him of claiming to be the divine Messiah for which Pilate would no doubt have had no interest other than possibly a superstitious wariness of Jesus. Jesus accepted the title of King of the Jews as His rightful title, knowing that in Him the prophesies were fulfilled as we read for example in Isaiah 9:6-7 and Zechariah 9:9,

> 'For unto us a Child is born, unto us a Son is given; and the government will be upon His shoulder. And His name will be called Wonderful, Counsellor, Mighty God, Everlasting Father, Prince of Peace. Of the increase of His government and peace there will be no end, upon the throne of David and over His kingdom, to order it and establish it with judgement and justice from that time forward, even forever. The zeal of the Lord of hosts will perform this.'

> "Rejoice greatly, O daughter of Zion! Shout, O daughter of Jerusalem! Behold, your King is coming to you; He is just and having salvation, lowly and riding on a donkey, a colt the foal of a donkey."

When Jesus stood before Pilate, He had already been beaten by the servants of the High Priest and accused of being a criminal, but evidently remained calm and silent. The chief priests and elders had already determined to have Jesus put to death. Under Roman occupation, they did not have the right of capital punishment, so they had to bring charges that would stand up in a Roman court – charges of insurrection against the Roman government. Having confirmed His Kingship, Jesus remained silent, as we read in Isaiah 42:1-4,

"Behold! My Servant whom I uphold, My Elect One in whom My soul delights! I have put My Spirit upon Him; He will bring forth justice to the Gentiles. He will not cry out, nor raise His voice, nor cause His voice to be heard in the street. A bruised reed He will not break, and smoking flax He will not quench; He will bring forth justice for truth. He will not fail nor be discouraged, till He has established justice in the earth; and the coastlands shall wait for His law."

The anticipated King of the Jews was also given the name Messiah which means 'Anointed One'. Jesus was recorded by Matthew as being from the royal line of David. Kings were anointed with holy oil and the kingdom of the Messiah, represented as a Sceptre, had long been foretold, as we read for example in Numbers 24:17, Psalm 45:6, Psalm 89:20-21, Psalm 22:27-28 and 2:6,

> 'I see Him, but not now; I behold Him, but not near; a Star shall come out of Jacob; a Sceptre shall rise out of Israel.'

> 'Your throne, O God is forever and ever; a sceptre of righteousness is the sceptre of Your kingdom.'

> "I have found My servant David; with My holy oil I have anointed him with whom My hand shall be established; also My arm shall strengthen him."

> 'All the ends of the world shall remember and turn to the Lord, and all the families of the nations shall worship before You. For the kingdom is the Lord's and He rules over the nations.'

> "Yet I have set My King on My holy hill of Zion."

Matthew 27:46

In verse 46, after Jesus had been on the Cross for six hours, He cried out in a loud voice, saying,

> "Eli Eli lema sabachthani? This is: God of me, God of me, why me didst thou forsake?"

There are times when it seems that God has forgotten His world, when the suffering is so great, that we ask, 'Where is God?'. At this point, Jesus Himself asked 'Why?' but seemingly received no reply; there was no deliverance from the Cross. Jesus was quoting from Psalm 22, likely from the Aramaic form, which may account for bystanders thinking that He was calling for Elias. The crowd surrounding Jesus had themselves quoted from Psalm 22:8 in derision, and then responded to Jesus' words by saying that He should be left alone to see if Elijah, or Elias, would come to save Him, thus further fulfilling the prophetic words as we read for example in Psalm 22:1, and 6-8, Psalm 71:10-11 and Job 16:10-11,

> 'My God, My God, why have You forsaken Me? Why are You so far from helping Me, and from the words of My groaning?'

> 'But I am a worm, and no man; a reproach of men, and despised by the people. All those who see Me ridicule Me; they shoot out the lip, they shake the head, saying, "He trusted in the Lord, let Him rescue Him; let Him deliver Him, since He delights in Him!"

> 'My enemies speak against me; and those who lie in wait for my life take counsel together, saying, "God has forsaken him; pursue and take him, for there is none to deliver him."

> 'They gape at me with their mouth, they strike me reproachfully on the cheek, they gather against me. God has delivered me to the ungodly and turned me over to the hands of the wicked.'

Jesus showed no resentment to those who caused His suffering, instead He offered His life as an atonement for their sins and the sins of the world; as a ransom for many. By His suffering He demonstrated the cost of wholehearted obedience to His Father. Jesus' prayer is not one of hopelessness, but a request for mercy and deliverance – for the task to be finished. Sin is incompatible with holiness, thus when Jesus bore the iniquities of humanity, in that moment He was separated from the presence of God and must have felt forsaken in a way that we cannot possibly imagine, as we read for example in Isaiah 53:8-11, and Habakkuk 1:13,

'He was taken from prison and from judgement, and who will declare His generation? For He was cut off from the land of the living; for the transgressions of My people, He was stricken. And they made His grave with the wicked – but with the rich at His death because He had done no violence, nor was any deceit in His mouth. Yet it pleased the Lord to bruise Him; He has put Him to grief. When You make His soul an offering for sin, He shall see His seed, He shall prolong His days, and the pleasure of the Lord shall prosper His hand. He shall see the labour of His soul and be satisfied. By His knowledge My righteous Servant shall justify many, for He shall bear their iniquities.'

'You are of purer eyes than to behold evil and cannot look on wickedness.'

Psalm 22 begins with a cry of desolation but goes on to express faith and thanksgiving for the help that does eventually come from God. Jesus knew the rest of the psalm that expressed faith in God. He was not delivered from dying, but having died, He was brought back to life and delivered from death. Psalm 22 is a picture of Jesus on the Cross that begins in the depths of despair but finishes with the accomplishment of Jesus' task of bringing the nations to worship the Lord. We also read in verses 21 and 24 that Jesus was heard by His Father and received an answer.

'You have answered Me.'

'For He has not despised nor abhorred the affliction of the afflicted; nor has He hidden His face from Him; but when He cried to Him, He heard.'

517

MATTHEW CHAPTER TWENTY-EIGHT

Matthew 28:9-10

In verses 9-10, the two women named Mary had found an angel in the empty tomb and were on their way to give the disciples the angel's message when they met Jesus, who spoke to them, saying,

> "Hail." "Fear ye not; go ye announce to the brothers of me that they may go away into Galilee, and there me they will see."

The Greek word 'chairete' translated variously as: hail, health be to you, be safe, greetings and rejoice, was a joyful term of salutation. Jesus evidently did not want the women to fear what they saw, but to rejoice in the resurrection of their Lord. Those who are called by God to righteousness are also called to rejoice, as we read in Isaiah 64:4-5,

> 'For since the beginning of the world Men have not heard nor perceived by the ear, nor has the eye seen any God besides You, who acts for the one who waits for Him. You meet him who rejoices and does righteousness, who remembers You in Your ways.'

Here Jesus called His disciples brothers. Perhaps this was to reassure them that their desertion of Him had been forgiven and dealt with forever. During His ministry, Jesus had told His listeners that all who do the will of His Father in heaven are His brother, sister, and mother (Matthew 12:50). Those who live according to the will of the Father are His family, in His kingdom, and have had their sins removed through His mercy, as we read for example in Psalm 103:11-13 and 15-19,

> 'For as the heavens are high above the earth, so great is His mercy toward those who fear Him; as far as the east is from the west, so far has He removed our transgressions from us.'

> 'As for man, his days are like grass; as a flower of the field, so he flourishes. For the wind passes over it, and it is gone, and its place remembers it no more. But the mercy of the Lord is from everlasting to everlasting on those who fear Him, and His righteousness to children's children, to such as keep His covenant, and to those who remember His commandments to do them. The Lord has established His throne in heaven, and His kingdom rules over all.'

In verse 7 we read that the angel that spoke to the women had already told them to remind the disciples that they had an appointment with Christ in Galilee. This appointment was recorded in Matthew's Gospel 26:32. When Jesus made that appointment it was in the context of gathering His scattered flock and this was now coming to pass; He would be going ahead of them to lead them as their Shepherd, and as light to guide their way. The passage in Isaiah chapter 9, that refers to Galilee, is often read during the Christmas season, yet we can see how it may also have been a foretelling of the risen Christ going ahead of His disciples to Galilee where He would be seen by them in His risen glory, as we read in Isaiah 9:1-2 and 60:1-3,

> 'Nevertheless the gloom will not be upon her who is distressed, as when at first He lightly esteemed the land of Zebulun and the land of Naphtali, and afterward more heavily oppressed her, by the way of the sea, beyond the Jordan, in Galilee of the Gentiles. The people who walked in darkness have seen a great light; those who dwelt in the land of the shadow of death, upon them a light has shined.'

> 'Arise, shine; for your light has come! And the glory of the Lord is risen upon you. For behold, the darkness shall cover the earth, and deep darkness the people; but the Lord will arise over you, and His glory will be seen upon you. The Gentiles shall come to your light, and kings to the brightness of your rising.'

Matthew 28:18-20

In verses 18-20, we read Jesus' final words from Matthew's Gospel, spoken to the remaining eleven disciples, saying,

> "Was given to me all authority in heaven and on the earth. Going therefore disciple ye all the nations, baptising them in the name of the Father and of the Son and of the Holy Spirit, teaching them to observe all things whatever I gave command to you; and behold I with you am all the days until the completion of the age."

Throughout Matthew's Gospel, Jesus the Son reveals the Father. Jesus claims a unique personal knowledge of God who has given Him authority. It is Jesus who imparts this knowledge and special relationship to others. By His Sonship, Jesus has been given all authority by the Father, as we read for example in Proverbs 8:15-17, Psalm 2:6-8, and Isaiah 9:6-7,

> 'By me kings reign, and rulers decree justice. By me princes rule, and nobles, all the judges of the earth. I love those who love me, and those who seek me diligently will find me.'

> "I have set My King on My holy hill of Zion. I will declare the decree: The Lord has said to Me, 'You are My Son, today I have begotten You. Ask of Me, and I will give You the nations for Your inheritance, and the ends of the earth for Your possession.'

> 'For unto us a Child is born, unto us a Son is given; and the government will be upon His shoulder. And His name will be called Wonderful, Counsellor, Mighty God, Everlasting Father, Prince of Peace. Of the increase of His government and peace there will be no end, upon the throne of David and over His kingdom, to order it and establish it with judgement and justice from that time forward, even forever.'

Having declared His authority in heaven and earth, Jesus told His disciples to go to all the nations, baptising them in the name of the Father, Son, and Holy Spirit. In the nations will be those who seek the truth, in the words of Psalm 42, 'As the deer pants for the water, so pants my soul for you.' The deer does not seek sermons and books or interesting conversations or academic debate about water but seeks water itself from which to drink, and all the nations will turn to the Lord, as we read for example in Psalm 22:27-28 and Psalm 98:2-3,

'All the ends of the world shall remember and turn to the Lord, and all the families of the nations shall worship before You. For the kingdom is the Lord's and He rules over the nations.'

'The Lord has made known His salvation; His righteousness He has revealed in the sight of the nations. He has remembered His mercy and His faithfulness to the house of Israel; all the ends of the earth have seen the salvation of our God.'

God's timing is always perfect. Jesus was born at a time when the Roman Empire, already well established, extended at its height to almost two million square miles, reaching from Britain, Spain, and Morocco in the west to the Caspian Sea, Arabian Gulf and deep into what is today Saudi Arabia in the East. The Romans arrived in Britain just a few years after the Resurrection, bringing Christianity with them. From there Christianity spread out to the German, Flemish, and Irish people. With the rise of the British Empire, the most extensive in history, Christianity spread to the United States and across the globe. In the assurance that Jesus, in the Holy Spirit, is with His people, having reached all the nations, His disciples are to teach all that God the Father has commanded His people to do, as we read in Deuteronomy 5:32, 12: 32, and Jeremiah 26:2,

'Therefore, you shall be careful to do as the Lord your God has commanded you; you shall not turn aside to the right hand or to the left.'

'Whatever I command you, be careful to observe it; you shall not add to it nor take away from it.'

'Thus says the Lord, "Stand in the court of the Lord's house, and speak to all the cities of Judah, which come to worship in the Lord's house, all the words that I command you to speak to them. Do not diminish a word.'

Amen.

K
up UK Ltd.
4
0001B/1